Neither Fugitive nor Free

America and the Long 19th Century

GENERAL EDITORS
David Kazanjian, Elizabeth McHenry, and Priscilla Wald

Black Frankenstein: The Making of an American Metaphor
Elizabeth Young

Neither Fugitive nor Free: Atlantic Slavery, Freedom Suits, and the Legal Culture of Travel
Edlie L. Wong

Neither Fugitive nor Free

Atlantic Slavery, Freedom Suits, and the Legal Culture of Travel

Edlie L. Wong

NEW YORK UNIVERSITY PRESS
New York and London

NEW YORK UNIVERSITY PRESS
New York and London
www.nyupress.org

© 2009 by New York University
All rights reserved

LIBRARY OF CONGRESS CATALOGING-IN-PUBLICATION DATA
Wong, Edlie L.
Neither fugitive nor free : Atlantic slavery, freedom suits, and the legal culture of travel / Edlie L. Wong.
p. cm.—(America and the long 19th century)
Includes bibliographical references and index.
ISBN-13: 978-0-8147-9455-5 (cl : alk. paper)
ISBN-10: 0-8147-9455-6 (cl : alk. paper)
ISBN-13: 978-0-8147-9456-2 (pb : alk. paper)
ISBN-10: 0-8147-9456-4 (pb : alk. paper)
1. American literature—19th century—History and criticism.
2. American literature—African American authors—History and criticism.   3. Slaves—Legal status, laws, etc.—United States—History—19th century.   4. Antislavery movements—United States—History—19th century.   5. Slavery—Law and legislation—United States—History—19th century.   6. Law and literature—United States—History—19th century.   7. Slavery in literature.   8. Travel in literature.   9. Law in literature.   I. Title.
PS217.S55W66   2009
810.9'3552—dc22   2009001473

New York University Press books are printed on acid-free paper, and their binding materials are chosen for strength and durability. We strive to use environmentally responsible suppliers and materials to the greatest extent possible in publishing our books.

Manufactured in the United States of America
c 10 9 8 7 6 5 4 3 2 1
p 10 9 8 7 6 5 4 3 2 1

A book in the American Literatures Initiative (ALI), a collaborative publishing project of NYU Press, Fordham University Press, Rutgers University Press, Temple University Press, and the University of Virginia Press. The Initiative is supported by The Andrew W. Mellon Foundation. For more information, please visit www.americanliteratures.org.

Contents

	Acknowledgments	vi
	Introduction: Traveling Slaves and the Geopolitics of Freedom	1
1	Emancipation after "the Laws of Englishmen"	19
2	Choosing Kin in Antislavery Literature and Law	77
3	The Gender of Freedom before *Dred Scott*	127
4	The Crime of Color in the Negro Seamen Acts	183
	Conclusion: Fictions of Free Travel	240
	Notes	263
	Index	325
	About the Author	339

Acknowledgments

I am indebted to the many individuals whose generosity and support helped make this book possible. At the University of California, Berkeley, I had the opportunity to work closely with Saidiya Hartman, who challenged me to produce meaningful work. She continues to inspire me. Caren Kaplan reprised her mentorship from my undergraduate to graduate studies with warmth and enthusiasm. In my final year, Bryan Wagner offered me much encouragement and constructive criticism.

The Slavery and the Constitution seminar at the Institute for Constitutional Studies, George Washington Law School (2005), organized by director Maeva Marcus and led by Paul Finkelman and Mark Tushnet, was invaluable in helping to shape the interdisciplinary contours of this book. In particular, I want to thank fellow participants Chris Curtis, Dan Mulcare, and Linda Tvrdy for answering all my pesky queries with patience and knowledge. The Rutgers Institute for Research on Women seminar on Diasporas and Migrations (2005–6) gave me the opportunity to share my work with a brilliant collective of feminist scholars, who helped me to further refine and hone my project. An Andrew W. Mellon Postdoctoral Fellowship in the Penn Humanities Forum at the University of Pennsylvania (2006–7) provided me with the resources to complete the majority of this book and with the camaraderie of Kinga Araya, John Ghazvinian, and in particular, Neil Safier, who was unstinting with his thoughtful suggestions and advice.

At Rutgers, I have had the company of some wonderful colleagues, past and present, to whom I am grateful for friendship, encouragement, and guidance: Wesley Brown, Abena Busia, Chris Chism, Brent Edwards, Brad Evans, Chris Iannini, Stacy Klein, Daphne Lamothe, Minkah Makalani, Meredith McGill, Sonali Perera, Jasbir Puar, Josie Saldaña, Shuang Shen, Mary P. Sheridan-Rabideau, Evie Shockley, and Cheryl Wall. I must also thank the participants of my Rutgers British Studies Project faculty workshop—Paul Clemens, Anne Coiro, Lynn Festa, Tom Fulton, Seth Koven,

John Kucich, and David Kurnick—for their helpful suggestions on a portion of the manuscript. I have been fortunate to find a supportive department chair in Richard Miller and a brilliant research assistant in Carrie Hyde. I must extend a special thanks to David Eng for his incredible generosity as both mentor and friend. Tom Glynn of the Rutgers Alexander Library entered into my project with zeal, and I am grateful for his friendship and invaluable research support. For careful reading and incisive suggestions, I thank my series editors, David Kazanjian, Elizabeth McHenry, and Priscilla Wald, as well as Amy Kaplan. My editor at New York University Press, Eric Zinner, and his assistant Ciara McLaughlin guided me through the publication process with enthusiasm, good humor, and frankness.

I shared these past years with many remarkable friends who generously lent me their wisdom, unflagging support, and reassurance as this book took shape. In graduate studies, I was fortunate to have the friendship of Mike Ferguson, Kathryn Koo, Robert Soza, and June Yoshii. Old friends from California, Brian Ginnever, Cathy Paiste, and Jae Suh, and friends in Philadelphia, Amze Emmons, Adalaine Holton, James Ker, Jena Osman, Josephine Park, and James Salazar, gave me both the intellectual and emotional sustenance to complete this book. Linda Chandler, Stafford Gregoire, and their children, Chandler, Mason, and Lennox opened their home to me in New York. Shinhee Han offered me her insights when I needed them most. I also extend my gratitude to two individuals, in particular, who selflessly devoted their time and energy to reading and commenting on countless drafts of the manuscript. Hsuan Hsu and Zack Lesser were challenging and perceptive critics who suffered through the manuscript piecemeal. I thank them for their patience, understanding, and intellectual generosity.

My family, King Tong, So Man, Edson, and Edlen Wong, and Lui, King Kui, King Luen, Linda, Edwin, and Eddie Wong, and my godmother, Violet Hoffer, were all present throughout the long process of research, writing, and editing. Finally, this book is dedicated to my beloved grandmother, Yue Sun Ng, who passed away while it was being completed. As I struggled to find the words to tell the stories of kinship and longing in these pages, I found myself sorting through my own muddled, imperfect memories in search of new meanings for our life together. This book would not have been written without her love, strength, and unfaltering convictions.

Introduction

Traveling Slaves and the Geopolitics of Freedom

It has just been decided by the Supreme Court of Massachusetts, that a Slave carried into that State by his owner, becomes *eo instanti* free! . . . If a southerner carries a servant or a nurse with him into the State of Massachusetts, the highest tribunal of that State is ready with its writs and processes to wrest that servant from him, and pronounce him a freeman before his face! . . . People of the South! Will you sleep forever over your dearest rights? Are you willing to sustain forever a confederation with States into which you dare not travel with your property, lest that property become by law actually confiscated?
—*Augusta Sentinel*, quoted in *Liberator*, 15 October 1836

The *Augusta (Georgia) Sentinel* demanded no less than the dissolution of the Union when word began to spread throughout the states south of Mason-Dixon of Massachusetts Chief Justice Lemuel Shaw's judgment freeing a young slave girl named Med.[1] Med had accompanied her mistress from New Orleans to Boston, and in *Commonwealth v. Aves* (1836), Shaw ruled that this journey into and extended residence in a free state had effectively emancipated her. Med numbered among the many slave attendants whom slaveholders brought with them on their long journeys north. As former Tennessee bondsman James Thomas recalled, "during the summer months the people from the south would invade the northern cities and pleasure resorts with their servants."[2] These early southern travelers presumed that their right to free mobility extended to the slaves who served as an extension of their power and prestige.[3] Colonel Andrew Jackson Polk, for example, told his manservant, "dress well. Don't let those fellows down you," when he registered at New York's Astor House hotel.[4] The display of mastery in the figure of a well-dressed valet or waiting maid was just as important to slaveholders as their legal title to the human property.[5]

In the decades before the Civil War, the North was a popular destination for southern travelers who converged on cities such as Saratoga, Newport, Cape May, Boston, New York City, and Philadelphia for recreation, health, and business. These slaveholders had long relied on "sojourner laws" to protect their property rights while traveling through free territory. As northern states legislated abolition and emancipation within their borders, they generally made an exception "in favor of the master voluntarily bringing his slave into the state temporarily as a traveler," in order to maintain interstate harmony and national unity.[6] The successful freedom suit that Boston abolitionists brought on Med's behalf initiated the rejection of this right to unrestricted travel, as the North began to make freedom coextensive with its territorial and jurisdictional boundaries. The *Augusta Sentinel*'s condemnation of the precedent set in Med's case proved prophetic, for the judicial and legislative struggles over the status of these "traveling slaves" helped to precipitate the dissolution of the federal compact in southern secession and the Civil War.

Neither Fugitive nor Free: Atlantic Slavery, Freedom Suits, and the Legal Culture of Travel draws on a largely unexplored archive—the freedom suit as recorded in the press and court documents—to offer a more critically and historically embedded understanding of the freedom celebrated in the literary and cultural histories of transatlantic abolitionism. While recent scholarship has begun to examine forms of slave resistance that did not necessarily result in escape—such as *marronage*, truancy, absenteeism, and lying out—scholars have paid less attention to these lawsuits involving the valets, nurses, and maids who accompanied slaveholders onto free soil. *Neither Fugitive nor Free* examines the largely forgotten stories of these traveling slaves to limn the legal construction of freedom, will, and consent in the antebellum United States. Literary and cultural historians have often turned their gaze on the fugitive's clandestine movements, but although that work has been of crucial importance, it has nonetheless led us to overlook the complex ways in which traveling slaves challenged, even more profoundly than did the fugitive, the cultural logic of slavery and freedom. Freedom suits number among those "untold stories" against which, as Priscilla Wald argues, the "official stories" of U.S. national culture and identity were constructed.[7] This book places the key figures of organized antislavery movements—such as Frederick Douglass, Olaudah Equiano, William Lloyd Garrison, Granville Sharpe, and Sojourner Truth—alongside those lesser-known slave plaintiffs, including Med, Lucy Ann Delaney, Grace, Catharine Linda, and Harriet Robinson Scott, whose freedom suits allow us to explore what abolition's liberal imagination occluded.

Slavery and the law were not merely intertwined in Anglo-American jurisprudence; the existence of slavery required the sanction of law.[8] Slaves seeking freedom had only three options: short- or long-term escape, manumission, and freedom suits.[9] The freedom suit took one of two forms. In free jurisdictions where slavery either had no legal sanction (Great Britain) or where that sanction had been repealed (the U.S. North), the lawsuit generally began as a habeas corpus action that charged the slaveholder with detaining a person against his or her will. In slave jurisdictions such as Missouri, Virginia, or Kentucky, statutes carefully outlined the legal process by which a slave could petition courts to sue, as a putatively free person, for wrongful enslavement against the offending slaveholder. In both forms of freedom suit, the legal claims to freedom of these black men and women were based occasionally on their free birth or willed emancipation but most commonly on extended travel or residence on free soil. Because slaveholders brought their slave attendants willingly into free jurisdictions, the U.S. Constitution's fugitive slave clause and its enforcement by the Fugitive Slave Acts of 1793 and 1850 did not apply, since they governed only escaped slaves. Once northern states repealed the sojourner laws that had allowed slaveholders to travel through or remain in the state with their slaves for a certain period of time without forfeiting their "property," no law remained to enforce or justify the slaves' bondage in these jurisdictions (see figure I.1). By default, upon setting foot on free soil, slaves were left informally free, even if they were taken back to a slave jurisdiction—at least according to abolitionists and the enslaved themselves. The slaveholders, of course, generally disagreed. In order to secure these slave attendants' formal, recognized freedom, therefore, either the slaves themselves or abolitionists on their behalf had to bring suit in a court of law. The contexts, forms, and stories of these freedom suits structured the legal culture of travel in the nineteenth century. In an Atlantic world divided into free and slave territories, travel across these legal and geopolitical boundaries enabled abolitionists opportunities and alliances, even while disclosing the powerful constraints on freedom that abolitionism had difficulty recognizing.

Freedom suits reveal the contradictions at the heart of an emerging American national culture that had begun to constitute itself around individualistic notions of consent and free will. The historical force of slavery's ambivalence—its peculiarity—animates the freedom suits examined in this

Fig. I.1. William C. Reynolds's *Political Map of the United States* (1856). (Courtesy of the Library of Congress, Geography and Maps Division [g3701e.ct000604])

book. Southern law generally held slaves in the character of "persons" in criminal cases and of "property" in all others, and legal history organizes criminal and civil law according to this dichotomy.[10] James Kent's *Commentaries on American Law* (1826–30) specifies that slaves continued to be regarded "as human beings under moral responsibility as to crimes," even though they were defined as chattel under slave law.[11] Saidiya Hartman reminds us that forms of domination not only subordinated but also constituted the partial humanity imputed to the enslaved: the slave's "double character" as property *and* person. The legal logic of freedom suits gave particular expression to this "double character." U.S. Chief Justice John Marshall once described traveling slaves as a unique kind of property that "resembles a passenger, and not a package of goods."[12] The paradoxical dimensions of the traveling slave's liminal position both inside and outside the category of the human confounded the geographical and ontological boundaries between freedom and slavery.

An incredible set of contradictions was built into the freedom suit's procedural form. Freedom suits were specifically designed to protect the rights of *free* persons and not slaves, yet legal process required legal fictions to make it accord with the property logic of slavery. Slave plaintiffs assumed the guise of free persons to bring petitions for freedom even as the outcome of the trial was to determine their status. Slaves were only presumed free until proven free; liberty was belated and contingent on a favorable verdict. The elliptical temporality inherent in these lawsuits gave rise to a host of other contradictions. In accordance with the legal procedure in slave states, the slave had to acknowledge the idea of *just* subjection under slave law in order to petition courts for emancipation based on *wrongful* enslavement. Even in the free jurisdictions of the U.S. North, the slave's freedom often depended on establishing that he or she was *not* a fugitive—not, that is, still legally the property of his or her master under the Constitution and the law.[13] Slave plaintiffs therefore affirmed the legitimacy of the institution that oppressed them in seeking legal recognition from the state, whether slave or free. In this sense, the legal freedom granted through freedom suits might have served only to intensify the slave's institutional subjection. The formal ambivalence of the freedom suit refracted the countervailing impulses of any appeal to the state for recognition of legal personhood. One of the major arguments of this book is that, in a multitude of ways, the freedom suit—an appeal to the law—reveals the incoherence of the law in a country divided into slave and free.

In addition to being racialized, the legal culture of travel was inherently transatlantic in scope. Landmark British and U.S. freedom suits including *Somerset v. Stewart* (1772), *The Slave, Grace* (1827), *Commonwealth v. Aves* (1836), and *Dred Scott v. Sandford* (1857) reveal how disputes over traveling slaves form a set of cultural forces that helped establish *and* unsettle what Amy Kaplan describes as "the geopolitical boundaries of nation-states and colonies and the conceptual borders between the domestic and the foreign."[14] These legal contests troublingly crossed the national boundaries separating the United States from Britain, even while they imbued that "arbitrary political line," in Frederick Law Olmstead's words, dividing "the north part from the south part" of the United States with legal meaning.[15] This book builds on and extends the now classic work of legal historian Paul Finkelman, who first catalogued these lawsuits in his efforts to chart the crisis in interstate comity or legal reciprocity when the laws of freedom and slavery came into conflict.[16] Such a crisis is only exacerbated when set in its full Atlantic context. Were slaves free by virtue of travel on free soil, or did slave law "follow" them into a free jurisdiction? They were neither fugitive nor free according to the law. By the early decades of the nineteenth century, the uncertain status of these traveling slaves had become, according to Don Fehrenbacher, "one of the classic issues in the legal history of slavery."[17] Geopolitical boundaries—whether the Mason-Dixon, the parallel 36° 30′, or the perimeters of Great Britain—cut across the lives of freeman and slave alike, reshaping them in profoundly complex ways.

Freedom suits in the United States were largely the consequence of the escalating legal, legislative, and political disputes over geopolitical boundaries in a partially free Atlantic world. The shift in northern legal culture from guarding slaveholders' property rights to enforcing the traveling slave's right to liberty provoked vehement responses from the slave states. It further antagonized growing interstate hostilities over the political future of slavery. In campaigning for the Fugitive Slave Bill before Congress, the popular Kentucky statesman Henry Clay cited the northern repeal of sojourner laws as a "just and serious cause" of southern complaint: "a man from a slave State cannot now, in any degree of safety, travel in a free State with his servant, although he has no purpose of stopping there any longer than a short time."[18] Of all forms of abolitionist activity, Clay found the liberation of enslaved servants in free states the most insulting and injurious to the individual rights of slaveholders. He voiced the growing resentment of slaveholders who found their property rights under attack once they set foot on free soil. These northern outrages against "our citizens when travelling among them for pleasure, health or business, by taking their servants and liberating the same" numbered prominently among the wrongs enumerated in Mississippi's secession resolutions.[19] The status of those "servants" brought into free jurisdictions continued to be bitterly disputed right up until the Civil War, as *Lemmon v. The People of the State of New York* (1860)—the appeal of a Virginia slaveholder who had been divested of eight slaves in New York City—made its way onto the U.S. Supreme Court docket. The trial of that case was prevented by the outbreak of war. Freedom suits thus offer one interpretative framework to understand the geopolitics of slavery and freedom that determined the distribution of rights, belonging, and citizenship in the Atlantic world.

Reconstructed from pamphlets, magazines, law journals, newspapers, and casebooks, these legal stories constitute a loose genre of antislavery literature, charting the struggles of jurists, slaveholders, free blacks, slaves, and abolitionists as they negotiated the predicament of territorialized freedom. The vast majority of these freedom suits did not make their way before higher courts or into court reports, and actual statistics are therefore difficult to determine. The few reports of freedom suits published in pamphlet form, however, circulated widely and were read by publics beyond judicial commentators. These oft-sensationalized legal controversies played a prominent role in the U.S. antislavery print campaign even as the emergence of a popular national movement created a market for antislavery texts that ranged from the legal to the literary. Some legal pamphlets and compendiums—such as Isaac Knapp's *Case of the Slave-Child, Med* (1836), William Goodell's *The American Slave Code* (1853), and Horace Greeley's *Narrative of Facts in the Case of Passmore Williamson* (1855), *Case of Dred Scott in the United States Supreme Court* (1860), and *Report on the Lemmon Slave Case* (1860, 1861)—were as popular, profitable, and influential as any fugitive slave narrative. Greeley even offered the *Dred Scott* pamphlet at discount prices for bulk quantities of five, twelve, or one hundred. Such keen public interest was not unusual given that antebellum judges, as legal scholar Mark Tushnet reminds us, often crafted court opinions with reading audiences in mind.[20]

These readings in law and literature illuminate the way the practice and ideology of early Atlantic travel helped shape the volatile relationships among race, gender, and the law. Feminist historians observe that the lives of women and children too often elude the written records of slavery, yet women frequently appear as plaintiffs in these freedom suits, as antislavery organizations such as the Boston Female Anti-Slavery Society were moved to assist those they deemed most vulnerable to the abuses of slavery. That fact alone is an important facet of the freedom suit, given the relative absence of enslaved women and children from the slave narrative genre. Women throughout the various regions of the South constituted but a small minority of those who escaped to the North. Louisiana had the largest percentage of female runaways, yet it was still less than one-third of all documented fugitives in the state.[21] Thus, the extant book-length antebellum slave narratives (outside of the WPA narratives) are almost all authored by men, and they often reflect the conservative gender politics and moralism of Garrisonian antislavery, which represented abolitionism as a means of rectifying the dangerous degendering of slaves and slaveholders.[22] Women's freedom suits therefore fit uncomfortably within an abolitionist tradition that embraced the male fugitive slave as its romantic archetype of the freedom seeker. Parts of this book, therefore, reread the slave narratives of Frederick Douglass, Olaudah Equiano, Harriet Jacobs, and Sojourner Truth by resituating them in the context of freedom suits, a context that was central to their original production and reception but that has fallen away in efforts to recover them as a coherent canon of literature. By interweaving fugitive slave narratives with legal cases, this book reconstructs the stories of these slave litigants who have largely disappeared from the historical record as figures in their own right.

Neither Fugitive nor Free joins a growing body of scholarship that resists telling the story of slavery as the abolitionist story of freedom.[23] Freedom suits unsettle the abolitionist imaginary of freedom as mapped onto a trajectory from south to north. Although northern abolitionists tended to imagine the story of freedom as a single and finished event once the slave reached the free states, these freedom suits show that for many black men and women, the line between slavery and freedom was far less clearly demarcated. Freedom suits thus reveal that the stark dichotomy of slavery and freedom was itself a regional fiction of abolitionism. Such received critical histories and cultural formations have excluded alternative forms of historical accounting. Writing the stories of those people from whom the technologies of self-representation were largely withheld requires, in the words of Hartman, "not only the interrogation of dominant narratives and the exposure of their contingent and partisan character but also the reclamation of archival material for contrary purposes."[24] This book offers a critical engagement with the nature of the literary and legal archives and the political imperatives that shaped them.

Reading slave narratives in the context of the freedom suit presents new epistemologies that ask us to reckon critically with the liberal narratives of freedom that have come to dominate the historical memory of slavery and its abolition. I draw on the work of Stephanie Camp, Ariela Gross, Walter Johnson, Jennifer Morgan, and Dylan Penningroth in the field of slavery studies, the work of feminist scholars of American literary and cultural studies such as Gillian Brown, Karen Sánchez-Eppler, Hortense Spillers, and Cindy Weinstein, and the scholarship of the "transnational turn" in American studies by Amy Kaplan, David Kazanjian, and others to explore the quandaries that the gendered discourses of "possessive individualism" created within the slavery controversy.[25] The revisionist work undertaken by the critical legal studies movement also guides my exploration of the complex ways in which historically disempowered individuals regard and use the law.²⁶ Legal scholarship in the form of critical race theory has begun to reflect more critically on law's narrative structures—its perspectives, tropes, and plots—to better understand the mechanisms of power at the site of the law.²⁷ *Neither Fugitive nor Free* interrogates those terms—will, agency, and consent—that were central to the lexicon of liberal jurisprudence to understand how slaves strove to "re-elaborate them in fashioning themselves as agents."²⁸

Much of this book is devoted to illuminating the way enslaved women and their children negotiated the unexpected predicaments that the laws of freedom and slavery created in their lives. The logic of kinship *as* property under slave law disfigured social reproduction into the reproduction of property. In a pronatalist slave society, enslaved mothers gave birth to property, not children. That is not to imply that kinship gripped enslaved men less powerfully than women; however, law and legal process mediated slave kinship in specifically gendered ways. The book's discussion of gender and kinship focuses on enslaved women because of the particular conundrums that the doctrine of *partus sequitur ventrem* (children follow the condition of the mother) created within the law and literature of abolitionism. Once freed, enslaved women often took up the instrumentalization of maternity under slave law to reconstruct the meaning of motherhood and individual self-proprietorship through litigation aimed at securing their children. These women negotiated the ongoing effacement of their desires within both proslavery and antislavery propaganda as they struggled with the conditions that freedom entailed and the contexts in which it was to be lived. In this way, *Neither Fugitive nor Free* interrogates the gender of freedom in the literature of slavery: gender fundamentally shifts our understanding of the meanings and forms of these legal stories of freedom.²⁹

As freedom became territorialized in the North, southern travelers began to take advantage of the political, economic, and social utility of the slave's "double character" to circumvent the law of freedom. It was not unusual for more circumspect slaveholders to select attendants with kinship ties in slavery as a guarantee of their continued compliance once in a free state. As Hartman has shown, slaveholders used the humanity and individuality denied under slave law to "tether, bind, and oppress."³⁰ They used those same affective social attachments that helped slaves to buffer themselves from brutalization in order to fetter them to slavery. A visit by the celebrated English stage actress Fanny Kemble to her husband's Sea Islands plantations convinced her of the "partializing standards of humanity" under slave law.³¹ "I once heard a conversation," she relates, "between ... the two overseers of the plantation on which I was living, upon the question of taking slaves, servants, necessary attendants, into the Northern states; Mr. O—— urged the danger of their being 'got hold of,' i.e., set free by the abolitionists, to which Mr. K[ing] very pertinently replied: 'Oh, stuff and nonsense; I take care, when my wife goes North with the children, to send Lucy with her; *her children are down here, and I defy all the abolitionists in creation to get her to stay North.*'"[32] Slaveholders such as Roswell King used the ties of kinship to counterbalance the slave's desire for freedom. The recognition of the slave's humanity thus intensified rather than ameliorated his or her sufferings. Absolute coercive necessity was an essential feature of social control in slave society, yet effective mastery was not achieved through force alone.[33]

Travel thus held out a very different set of conditions and meanings for those slaves chosen to accompany slaveholders into free territories than it did for their masters. One ironic commentator noted that slave property was prized precisely because it "possesses the power of locomotion, which gives it a surprising advantage over a hogshead of rum, or a box of sugar."[34] Slaveholders even included the slave's capacity for movement in the slave economy's calculus of value. Under these circumstances, travel was not a form of resistance or empowerment, and slaves understood it more generally, according to Douglass, "in the shape of a threat, and in punishment of crime."[35] "Going out in the world," he writes, "is like a living man going into the tomb, who, with open eyes, sees himself buried out of sight and hearing of wife, children and friends of kindred tie."[36] Movement or flight was not the antithesis of immobilization in the fugitive slave narrative but was the expression of a profound yearning for stasis. The terrible ease of displacement made the desire for kinship, home, and belonging all the more powerful and insistent, and slaveholders used these longings to secure power over those they enslaved. Rather than embracing freedom on free soil, some slave attendants took the risk of returning to slave jurisdictions in the hope of establishing their legal freedom before a southern court. Thus, mobility and stasis emerge as two powerfully intertwined forces in early African American life and cultural expression.

Neither Fugitive nor Free charts a circum-Atlantic course from London to Antigua, Jamaica, Boston, St. Louis, and Charleston, in which the fraught lines between freedom and slavery were repeatedly drawn and redrawn. Each of the following four chapters examines a landmark legal case as its central source material to explore the contradictions of slavery and abolitionism revealed by the freedom suit. The story of American slavery that this book tells begins on English soil. Chapter 1 introduces the long legal history of these contestations over liberal agency, consent, and the geopolitics of freedom that began with the celebrated case of *Somerset v. Stewart* (1772). My reading of *Somerset* establishes the procedural form of freedom suits and its territorialized logic in Anglo-American jurisprudence. The earliest legal contests over slavery in Britain were fought over the status of those slaves whom slaveholders had brought into the realm. *Somerset* was the culmination of a score of earlier freedom suits that abolitionists had initiated on behalf of these slave attendants, and it established a powerful antislavery precedent favoring freedom for slaves once on free soil. Decided a few years before the American Revolution, *Somerset v. Stewart* became part of the English common law that the new republic eventually adopted.[37] Lord Chief Justice Mansfield's decidedly terse ruling in *Somerset*, and its controversial corollary in the *Case of the Slave Grace* (1827), exerted a powerful influence over American thinking about slavery. Mansfield's configuration of slavery and the law became axiomatic to the development of a law of freedom and the campaigns against slavery on U.S. soil.[38]

Somerset and Grace numbered among the small population of slave attendants whom absentee planters, officials, and sailors brought into England before Parliament legislated emancipation in the West Indies. The ambiguous legal status of these slaves in England forced jurists, abolitionists, and political commentators to confront the problem of freedom as they sought, in various ways, to secure Britain's national boundaries. Unlike the West Indies, where the law enforced the slave's "obedience and subordination to the will of his owner," England had no positive laws for the control of slave populations.[39] Did the slave remain enslaved once on English soil? Time and again, this question worried English courts. Solicitors defending slaveholders' property rights often analogized enslavement in Britain to those contractual obligations subsisting between master and *servant* in their attempts to manage the master-slave relation under the conflicting laws of slavery and freedom. By reframing slavery as contractual service in England, jurists could argue, in the *Grace* case and afterward, that the attendant's return to a slave jurisdiction was a voluntary decision to reenslave him- or herself. Chapter 1 reads these landmark freedom suits alongside the autobiographical narratives of Ottobah Cugoano, Olaudah Equiano, Mary Prince, Ashton Warner, Robert Wedderburn, and James Williams to investigate these paradoxes of consent and will within this emergent law of freedom. The stories of lesser-known enslaved West Indians, including Kitty Hilton and Eleanor Mead, who appealed to the law for amelioration help to reveal the political tensions between an increasingly liberal metropole, invested (in the wake of *Somerset*) in nationalistic notions of British freedom, and its slave colonies across the Atlantic.

By the nineteenth century, British abolitionists had established a revisionist history of *Somerset* in their imagination of a perennially free Britain, just as freedom suits in the United States helped to establish a regional imaginary of a historically free New England. Abolitionists throughout the early Atlantic world seized on these freedom suits in their nation- and region-making projects. Some northern states later implemented the language of *Somerset* wholesale, aligning themselves as they did with this long tradition of Anglo-American liberal jurisprudence. The Pennsylvania Supreme Court ruling in *Kauffman v. Oliver* (1849) invokes the "principle sprung fresh, and beautiful, and perfect from the mind of Lord Mansfield, in the great case of the negro Somerset, that, by the common law, a slave, of whatever country or color, the moment he was on English ground, became free—endowed with the sanctity of reason."[40] Following *Somerset*, slavery required a foundation in positive law, and this distinction soon prevailed within the courtrooms of the U.S. North, as these states began to abolish and repeal the legal sanctions they had once extended to slavery.

Turning back to the other side of the Atlantic, chapter 2 charts the legal controversies over slaves brought into New England after Chief Justice Lemuel Shaw's landmark decision in the case of the slave girl Med, or *Commonwealth v. Aves*. The most forceful application of *Somerset v. Stewart* in U.S. courts, Shaw's ruling freed those enslaved servants whom slaveholders brought into Massachusetts; other free states soon followed Shaw's lead.[41] The U.S. context both reproduced and transformed the tensions, discourses, and legal procedures that are examined in the first chapter. In chapter 2, I reconstruct the records of several Massachusetts freedom suits from popular literature, newsprint, and legal pamphlets to explore material that has been largely left out of the American abolition story. Maria Weston Chapman, Harriet Jacobs, William Still, Sojourner Truth, and Passmore Williamson appear alongside a number of largely unknown slaves—including Anson, Betty, Jane Johnson, Catharine Linda, and Med—as I chart the complex ways in which legal discourses circulating in newsprint constituted the liberal agency and subjectivity of those who petitioned northern courts for freedom. Their cases reveal the contradictory logic by which abolitionists often disregarded the slave's express desire to remain with a master and in many cases argued for the very sorts of separations from kin that usually figured so large in abolitionist attacks on slavery. A number of the women and children who unexpectedly became the beneficiaries of such antislavery activism declined the northern freedom extended to them as they sought to return to those kin whom their masters had kept behind in slavery precisely to ensure this return.

These often-occulted stories of kinship and return find powerful but unexpected expression in Peter Still's dictated slave narrative, known popularly as Kate E.R. Pickard's *The Kidnapped and the Ransomed* (1856). Chapter 2 concludes with a striking account of the collaborations between the manumitted slave and his amanuensis in the preparation and sale of the biographical slave narrative. At Still's request, Pickard fictionalized his story. Although Still was born into slavery, Pickard narrated his kidnapping into slavery from New Jersey to protect the Still family, who were fugitive slaves liable to recapture and return to their masters. My reading of the narrative and of the correspondence between the two authors delineates a poetics of theft that emerges from the contradictions that the competing laws of slavery and freedom created in black culture and life. The remaining chapters trace over a range of texts this critical reinterpretation of legal slavery as the crime of abduction. The autobiographies and novels examined in chapters 3 and 4 offer a powerful critique of slave law in their insistence that this law violates natural right. By thus depicting the unlawful *theft* of freedom, these writers and orators could more effectively insist on the institutional processes that *made* free men into slaves. The "theft" fictionalized in these various narratives figures the separations entailed in slavery *and* in freedom as crimes that cry out for restitution.

Whereas chapter 2 reveals the nefarious ways that traveling slaveholders recognized kinship to tether enslaved servants to slavery, chapter 3 examines how those who returned to slave jurisdictions used the law to secure familial and collective autonomy from within slave society. It redirects the flow of migration and travel highlighted in the preceding chapter to focus on free and emancipated blacks in slave states. The movement of slaveholders into the western territories acquired by the Louisiana Purchase and the Mexican-American War precipitated the nation's first great constitutional crisis. Sectional strife over the expansion of slavery into the western territories began to shift the north-south axis of freedom and slavery.[42] Westward travel and migration brought slaves into jurisdictions where slavery was illegal and gave them "claim to sue for freedom in numbers not seen before, under the principle that they had become free while on free soil."[43] Moving deeper into the U.S. Southwest, the chapter interweaves the freedom suits catalogued in the St. Louis Circuit Court Historical Project with material from the autobiographical narratives of Cyprian Clamorgan, Lucy Ann Delaney, Elizabeth Keckley, Lunsford Lane, and John Berry Meachum, as well as Benjamin Drew's compilation of American fugitive slave narratives in Canada.

At the heart of the chapter lies the landmark case of *Dred Scott v. Sandford*. When *Dred Scott* first came to the notice of the editors of Garrison's *Liberator*, they saw that the case was centrally concerned with the slaveholder's "right to travel with slaves through free territory."[44] Simultaneously, the case brought before the highest tribunal in the nation the uncertain status of traveling slaves and their legal right to freedom once they returned to slave jurisdictions. The Supreme Court seized on *Dred Scott* as an opportunity to expand its power of judicial review when it judged that Congress had overstepped its bounds in legislating the Thomas Amendment of the Missouri Compromise, which prohibited slavery north of the parallel 36° 30′. The contested majority opinion thus secured the political future of slavery in the nation by opening the vast tracts of the unsettled western territories to slave labor.

But although Harriet and Dred Scott may have been the most famous plaintiffs in a freedom suit, they were only two among a number of slaves who brought petitions for freedom before St. Louis circuit court on the basis of extended travel and residence on the free soil of the Northwest Territory. By reading their story in the context of this full archive, chapter 3 shows that the circumstances surrounding their decision to seek legal freedom rather than risk fugitive flight gesture to the profound entanglements of kinship, property, and the geopolitics of travel that have generally been elided from *Dred Scott*'s legal histories. In their successful freedom suits, enslaved mothers such as Winny, Rachael, Julia, and Polly Crocket took up what was used against them in the doctrine of *partus sequitur ventrem* to free their children and force courts to acknowledge the authority of their motherhood. Like chapter 2, chapter 3 asks us to reconsider the meaning of liberal agency and the circumscribed forms of action available to slaves within the system of chattel slavery. Such appeals to legislated freedom—either in self-purchase or at law—lent further validation to the slave system oppressing them, for they yielded to slavery's "chattel principle." These legal stories offer a much more complex understanding of the countervailing forces that structured the agency and lives of those who sought from the state legal recognition of their personhood.

As free northern states repealed the sojourner laws they once offered to slaveholders, slave states enacted increasingly punitive regulations, including the Negro Seamen Acts, that prohibited free blacks from traveling into slave jurisdictions. These antiblack police laws, the breaking of which was punishable by imprisonment and enslavement, made it increasingly impossible for abolitionists to address the problem of slavery without, according to Jeannine DeLombard, "simultaneously taking into account the status of free persons of color in the American polity."[45] As the North began emancipating those slaves whom slaveholders brought into free jurisdictions, slave states strove to strengthen a slaveholding power structure thought to be under northern attack. They seized on their sovereign right—according to the federalist principle—to police people who entered and circulated within their borders to steadily undermine the rights accorded to the free black citizens of sister states and the free black subjects of foreign nations such as Britain and France.

Recuperating a fascinating if oft-ignored episode in the history of transatlantic abolitionism, chapter 4 examines the appeals to law made on behalf of black Atlantic mariners caught up in the workings of these Negro Seamen Acts in coastal slave states. The formal ambivalence of these appeals, like that of the freedom suits discussed in earlier chapters, raises critical questions about the meaning of freedom—specifically the "privileges and immunities" of black citizenship. Black maritime labor was essential to the capitalist world economy, as European nations began to reconsolidate their Atlantic empires in the wake of the Haitian Revolution and West Indian emancipation. British merchant vessels plying the waters of these lucrative Atlantic economies were often crewed by those colonial subjects whom they once held as commodities. In 1822, South Carolina enacted the first of these Negro Seamen Acts, which soon extended to North Carolina, Georgia, Florida, Alabama, Louisiana, and Texas. These statutes subjected all black mariners, regardless of national allegiances, to immediate imprisonment under threat of enslavement. British and American sailors instigated a number of legal actions, from *Elkison v. Deliesseline* (1823) to *Roberts v. Yates* (1853), to test the law's constitutionality and secure its repeal, yet none of these cases reached the U.S. Supreme Court. Denied the courtroom, uneasy and shifting transatlantic alliances in the 1850s began to appeal directly to the public to address the failure of the law.

Chapter 4 thus returns to the transatlantic context of the first chapter but reverses its trajectory by looking at the movement of free black British subjects into U.S. slave jurisdictions. I reconstruct a number of their cases, reading them alongside material from the *Anti-Slavery Recorder*, John Brown's slave narrative, David Walker's antislavery jeremiad, Samuel Ringgold Ward's British oratories, and the largely unexamined antislavery writings of F.C. Adams—specifically the novel *Manuel Pereira*—to examine these "literary" appeals to the law in light of the formal ambivalence of the freedom suit. *Manuel Pereira*'s cautionary tale of postemancipation freedom and its stress on the crimes against "free-born British subjects" brought international scrutiny to bear on the question of federal powers in relation to state sovereignty and institutional slavery in the United States.[46] The unresolved question of American slavery thus had become the problem of British freedom. These memorials, lectures, novels, and pamphlets stressed the Atlantic contours of an antislavery campaign that transcended national identifications and borders. The poetics of theft found in these appeals and narratives disclose a persistent belief in the law and justice even as it confronts the law's continuing failure. In the movement from the domestic sphere of kinship to the global regimes of abolitionism, slavery, and colonialism, chapter 4, like those that preceded it, reveals that freedom in a partially free world was far more constrained than the "official" story of abolition has led us to believe.

Black exclusion regulations such as the Negro Seamen Acts were framed within the same paradoxical logic that characterized the structure of the freedom suit. Such statutes did not deny outright the legal personhood of free blacks. Rather, they recognized it in order to punish it. It would be an oversimplification to assume that slave states produced—in a reactionary gesture—regulations unilaterally opposed to the northern law of freedom. Slave states such as North Carolina fashioned antiblack regulations that worked *in tandem* with the northern law of freedom to restrict and punish their black populations. Such measures served to intensify the institutional subjection of free black personhood through recognition rather than denial. The effect of such laws was to make free blacks "guilty of [the crime of] being free" in southern jurisdictions.[47] Acknowledgment thus functioned as pretext for punishment. Such measures sought further to ensure the territorialization of freedom in the Atlantic world as they outlawed free blacks from slave jurisdictions, part of the systematic containment of the physical, social, and political dimensions of black mobility that was fundamental to the logic of mastery and the consolidation of slave power.[48]

The movements of enslaved servants between and among jurisdictions not only changed their status; it also challenged the most basic legal definitions of citizens and foreigners, rights and property, sovereignty and jurisdiction. *Neither Fugitive nor Free* concludes with an examination of a number of black passport disputes that captured transatlantic headlines in the 1840s and 1850s and anticipated the shape that the struggles for black political inclusion would take after emancipation. Abolitionists and reformers were outraged when it came to light that the U.S. State Department had long adopted a "customary" practice of denying passports to free blacks seeking to travel abroad. Protests against the U.S. State Department's denial of free black citizenship eerily rehearsed the struggles over social and political rights that would find powerful expression in *Plessy v. Ferguson* (1896). Fought over Louisiana's Separate Car Act, *Plessy* sought to challenge those regulations on black mobility that had persisted well into the era of legislated freedom. Slavery's racialized power structures and social systems did not end with emancipation, and the "color line" constrained black freedom in ways that descended directly from the legal contests over traveling slaves in the first half of the century. This book resists narratives of temporal succession to trouble the traditional periodization of American and African American literary and cultural history, showing how the contradictions of "contract freedom" that emerged in the antebellum period continued to beleaguer the political ideologies of radical Reconstruction.[49]

Neither Fugitive nor Free articulates an unexplored set of links between the uneven historical experiences of travel and the law, as the combined pressures of a burgeoning domestic tourist economy, escalating sectional conflicts, and westward territorial expansion began to attenuate the existing boundaries of slavery. Disputes over traveling slaves were central to the legal culture of the antebellum United States as lawmakers, jurists, abolitionists, free blacks, and slaveholders sought to secure the geopolitical boundaries between freedom and slavery. The freedom suits that abolitionists brought on behalf of enslaved servants illuminate the way that liberty was contingent on the loss of kinship or exile in a foreign state in an Atlantic world where freedom had become coextensive with political borders. When read through these freedom suits, the quintessential American fugitive slave narrative discloses yet another kind of a journey—a retrospective flight into the past—to address the painful losses sustained in the passage to freedom. When Frederick Douglass first arrived on free soil, he captured this predicament of being caught in a present that resembled and unsettled the past of slavery: "I was not only free from slavery, but . . . free from home as well."[50] Slaves who sought legal freedom from northern courts faced the forfeiture of home and kinship in their difficult journeys to remake themselves into free individuals. Liberty was thus contingent on separation and loss, and these conditions govern the legal stories recounted in the following chapters. Challenging the cultural narratives of Anglo-American abolitionism, these freedom suits chart the strange and uneven continuities between freedom and slavery in the Atlantic world.

1

Emancipation after "the Laws of Englishmen"

> [I]t is the very end and scope of the Constitution, to hold inviolable, and to secure to every British subject;—so that *no Man can be a Slave in England.*
> —Charles Edward Herbert Orpen, "The Principles, Plans, and Objects, of 'The Hibernian Negro's Friend Society,'"
> 8 January 1831

Charles Orpen's words form the epigraph to this chapter not, as one might expect, for their philosophical originality but rather for so plainly expressing what had become a "universal admission" of popular British antislavery in the heady years preceding West Indian emancipation.[1] Orpen, one of the self-professed "Directors" of the Dublin-based Hibernian Negro's Friend Society, published the organization's political objectives in an open letter to Thomas Pringle, secretary of the London Anti-Slavery Society.[2] Frustrated with the ever-receding horizon of West Indian emancipation, Orpen sought to distinguish his recently established Irish men's organization from the metropolitan Anti-Slavery Society, insisting in the words of Elizabeth Heyrick's 1824 pamphlet on "Immediate Not Gradual Abolition." England may have transformed itself into a moral exemplar among nations in the crusade to suppress the slave trade after 1807, yet it continued to condone slavery in its colonial territories. Heyrick minced no words when she condemned the earlier campaign as a decided failure: "It is now seventeen years since the *Slave Trade* was abolished by the Government of this country—but *Slavery* is still perpetuated in our West India Colonies, and the horrors of the Slave Trade are aggravated rather than mitigated."[3] This notion of a failed political present was fundamental to the way British abolitionists reconstructed their pasts and anticipated a transformed future.⁴ They reenergized debates over black freedom as they questioned why the government had not yet proposed "a final date, however distant, to slavery in the British colonies."⁵

The Hibernian Negro's Friend Society differed with its London counterpart over what the project of freedom should entail, yet they both called on a humanitarian tradition that reached back to the previous century to illuminate their political present. Against the specter of lawlessness that colonialists promulgated as the inevitable consequence of West Indian freedom, these societies advocated for a "lawful liberty" that had become part of the very warp and weft of British national identity. The "natural love of liberty," as William Wilberforce proclaimed, "has been increased from . . . acquaintance with British laws."⁶ This rhetoric of a uniquely British humanitarian tradition upheld by the rule of law harked back, in Orpen's words, to the "line of procedure . . . so successfully pursued by the illustrious Granville Sharp, whereby he established the memorable legal position, that every man, who touches English ground, is *free.*"⁷ Statements of this kind mythologized Sharp's agency in the landmark civil case *Somerset v. Stewart*—or correctly, *England, The King v. James Somerset* (1772)—tried before Lord Chief Justice Mansfield of the Court of King's Bench, the highest common-law court in England.⁸ In 1808, Thomas Clarkson distinguished Sharp as "the first labourer . . . in the cause," and later writers attributed the emergence of a distinctively British "love" of freedom to his early humanitarianism.⁹ By 1831, the rallying cry of *"no Man can be a Slave in England,"* according to Orpen, had become "the very basis and elements of our fundamental laws," as it marked the wide acceptance of abolitionist sentiments that had once been the preserve of only a few men.¹⁰

Antislavery organizations with differing "principles, plans, and objects" hailed Sharp's victory in *Somerset v. Stewart* as evidence of freedom as a British cultural inheritance. Christopher Brown argues that Clarkson "was the first to characterize the campaign as the working out of impulses deeply embedded in the society from which it emerged, as the . . . expression of a distinctively British devotion to liberty and the rule of law."¹¹ Antislavery print culture shaped the narratives of nation and empire as metropolitan abolitionists actively remade the past according to their desires. Clarkson's invention of an antislavery tradition in his voluminous *History of the Rise, Progress, and Accomplishment of the Abolition of the African Slave-Trade by the British Parliament* (1808) was firmly established by the first meeting of the London Anti-Slavery Society in 1824, when the young Baptist Noel lauded the membership for "emulating the great examples which have been set us by men dear to our hearts; and who, having begun the mighty struggle before some of us were yet in being, have continued to this day to maintain it with undiminished energy and effect."[12] The fact that Mansfield's decidedly terse pronouncement in *Somerset* did not declare slavery unlawful within England did not hinder it from becoming mythologized as an "origins story" in the "history of Anti-slavery ideology."[13]

By the 1820s, it was not unusual for humanitarians to transform the purposively limited scope of Mansfield's ruling to broad effusions: "There is freedom in the respiration of its air, and in the very contact of its soil!"[14] The Anti-Slavery Society even promoted the salutary effects of English habitation on people with significant West India interests as it drew attention to the differences between the "many enlightened West Indians residing in England, and the great body of planters, agents, managers, and overseers, who form the White population of the Colonies."[15] Later figures such as Orpen, Pringle, and Joseph Sturge exported this territorialized discourse of freedom in countless legislative petitions, lectures, pamphlets, circulars, appeals, addresses, slave narratives, and polemics against West Indian slavery.

Mansfield's ruling in *Somerset* also exerted a powerful influence over antebellum American law and letters, giving rise to a poetics of freedom that was widely embraced by abolitionist campaigns on U.S. soil. Fugitive slaves including Henry Box Brown, John Brown, William Wells Brown, William and Ellen Craft, Frederick Douglass, Moses Roper, and others fleeing the 1850 Fugitive Slave Act found refuge and "true" freedom on British soil. Martin Delany effused in his famously unfinished novel *Blake; or, The Huts of America* (1859–61): "How sublime the spectacle of the colossal stature (compared with the puppet figure of the Judge of the American Supreme Court), of the Lord Chief Justice when standing up declaring to the effect: that by the force of British intelligence, the purity of their morals, the splendor of their magnanimity, and the aegis of the Magna Charta, the moment the foot of a slave touched British soil, he stood erect, disenthralled in the dignity of a freeman, by the irresistible genius of universal emancipation."[16] This "invented tradition" of British freedom was to become a central feature in the cultural imaginary of the transatlantic antislavery campaign.

A number of figures from the literary and legal histories of the early black Atlantic—including Quobna Ottobah Cugoano, Olaudah Equiano, Grace Jones, Joseph Knight, Mary Prince, and James Somerset—found this freedom to be far more elusive. The ambiguous legal status of these slaves, who arrived on England's shores as unwaged servants, forced jurists, antislavery humanitarians, and political commentators to confront the problem of freedom as they sought to secure England's national boundaries. Servants constituted one of the largest groups of African-descended slaves in England prior to 1807, as traveling or absentee planters and officials brought enslaved body servants, nurses, waiting maids, and barbers to the British Isles.[17] Once in the metropole, these slaveholders from England's far-flung colonies found it increasingly difficult to maintain control of their human property, given the dearth of slave laws. Some slaves petitioned for wages to certify their free status, while others simply ran away in the absence of a fugitive slave law.[18] Edward Long, an ardent advocate of colonial slaveholding interests, observed that "the owners of Negroes, brought hither upon motives of absolute necessity, for want of other attendants in the voyage, have frequently endeavored to send them back, and have as often been defeated, by the quirks of Negroe solicitors, and the extra-judicial opinions of some lawyers," who exploited a mere oversight in England's laws since a "Negroe running away from his master here is not by statute declared liable to imprisonment for any such offence."[19] Unlike the West Indies, where the law explicitly enforced the slave's obedience and subordination to the slaveholder's will, England had no positive laws for the control of slave populations.[20] Colonialist ideologues such as Long insisted that this legal deficiency did not make slaves into free subjects. Legal disputes over the status of these enslaved servants grew more numerous after 1770 as antislavery interests began to invest the geopolitical "line" dividing English from colonial jurisdictions with ideological meaning.[21] Did travel or residence on English soil remake colonial slaves into free British subjects? The anomalous status of slaves in England brought public pressure to bear on the meaning of British freedom well before abolition became a legislative issue.[22]

Mansfield's judgment in *Somerset* did not fully resolve the status of slaves in England, despite the popular imagination of the case in antislavery print culture. The question returned in different guises to worry the English courts. Indeed, the elaborate judgment of Justice Stowell of the English High Court of Admiralty in the *Case of the Slave Grace*, or *The King v. Allan* (1827), restricted further the narrow compass of Mansfield's ruling and powerfully reanimated public controversies over "slaves in England." Enslaved servants continued to challenge the logic of freedom in profound ways, as English courts began with *Grace* to curtail the protections once extended them in England. Abolitionists viewed the failure of English law to secure Grace's freedom some fifty years after *Somerset* as a decisive check on the moral and political progress toward emancipation that the previous generation of campaigners had supposedly secured in *Somerset v. Stewart*. The Hibernian Society, for example, sought to ascertain "what measures would make it impossible, to reduce again to Slavery, (as is the present illegal law and practice,) a Negro, who had become free, by visiting England, and afterwards had returned to the Colonies."[23]

Following *Grace*, Pringle and other abolitionists began to construct narratives of legal failure in the effort to reenergize the flagging campaign for West Indian emancipation, insisting that a better, more progressive future lay just beyond the horizon of the failed present. That refrain was not uncommon among the more radical abolitionists such as Heyrick who faulted the earlier campaign for failing to secure universal freedom. This chapter explores how the popular campaign both absorbed and responded to the contradictions produced in its endeavor to make law and legal process responsive to the contingencies and constraints of freedom. Stowell's judgment marked the failure of English law to secure freedom, and it began to unravel what had become one of the deeply held "origin stories" of popular antislavery ideology. In the wake of *Grace*, the antislavery print campaign emphasized the law's failure to do certain kinds of epistemological work, pressuring Parliament to legislate immediate emancipation by focusing on the West Indian slaves whom the law had failed. These personalized accounts emphasized the failure of English and colonial laws, in the words of the West Indian apprentice James Williams, to "do justice."[24]

Abolitionists seized on the legal struggles of West Indian slaves such as Grace Jones, Mary Prince, and Ashton Warner to dramatize the encroachment of colonial slavery on free English soil. The largely unsuccessful efforts of these enslaved men and women to claim and use their freedom in specific ways intensified the political tensions between an increasingly liberal metropole invested in notions of personal freedom and its slave colonies.[25] As the pages of the *Anti-Slavery Reporter* stressed the law's failure to secure justice for those most in want of it, abolitionists transformed the question of geopolitics into the threat of a degenerate colonial periphery encroaching on Britain's moral center.[26] The rest of the chapter explores the terms of black freedom and the unexpected predicaments that the law of freedom created in the lives of enslaved people in Britain. Legal discourses circulating in transatlantic antislavery print culture constituted their agency and subjectivity in complex ways, and *Somerset v. Stewart* and *Case of the Slave Grace* provide two particularly rich moments of discursive emergence and transformation within antislavery print culture.

An abolitionist counternarrative begins to emerge from the popular slave autobiographies—Mary Prince, Ashton Warner, Robert Wedderburn, and James Williams—that were produced primarily for the antislavery campaign. While examining the legal freedom that abolitionists hoped to bestow on these enslaved men and women and the freedoms that they sought to fashion for themselves, this chapter rereads the antislavery archive to explore what was made illegible by that campaign's interpretative frameworks and political imperatives.

That "Fantastic Idea of English Liberty" in Somerset v. Stewart

> I don't know what the consequences may be, if the masters were to lose their property by accidentally bringing their slaves to England. I hope it never will be finally discussed; for I would have all masters think them free, and all Negroes think they were not because then they would both behave better.
>
> —Lord Mansfield, quoted in Prince Hoar, *Memoirs of Granville Sharp*, 1828

Slaveholding on English soil became a matter of serious public controversy in the 1760s and 1770s as the growing number of enslaved servants in the metropolis became an issue of criminal concern. Sir John Fielding made a number of revealing observations on this "troublesome and dangerous" population of black slave attendants in Britain. He cautioned against the "dangerous" practice of importing West Indian slave attendants in his editorialized distillation of the voluminous English criminal code: these slaveholders "bring them to England as cheap Servants," but they "no sooner arrive here, than they put themselves on Footing with other Servants, become intoxicated with Liberty, grow refractory."[27] Such oft-reiterated expressions from the metropole cast black emancipatory desire as the artificial consequence of English habitation, in a twofold gesture that made freedom coextensive with Great Britain and naturalized the servile condition of enslaved blacks.

The freedom suit of John Lewis, brought on a writ of habeas corpus before Mansfield, was among the first of the cases from the 1770s to challenge the status of people enslaved on English soil. Mansfield professed a powerful reluctance to pass judgment when Lewis's case was brought to trial. Two hired watermen seized Lewis in Chelsea, carried him to Gravesend, and dragged him aboard the Jamaica-bound *Captain Seward* at the instruction of his slaveholder, Robert Stapylton. Stapylton had hatched this "wicked conspiracy," according to biographer Prince Hoare, for the sole purpose of selling Lewis "for a slave on his arrival in the island."[28] These "ruffians" made the further affront of falsely invoking the law as they "pretended to have a warrant from the Lord mayor for his apprehension" when men came to Lewis's aid.[29] Granville Sharp secured a writ of habeas corpus to free Lewis and brought an indictment against Stapylton and the two watermen.[30] Motions were made over four successive terms, but Mansfield resisted giving judgment in *Rex v. Stapylton*, refusing to permit sanctions against Stapylton even after the jury found him guilty (1771).[31]

The particulars of Lewis's story were less significant than what his "rescue" represented to the antislavery cause. It seems that he was not a particularly grateful subject of these legal efforts executed on his behalf. Sharp informed Lewis's benefactor, Sarah Banks, of "the poor ignorant lad's indiscretion," fearing that it "should... frustrate your generous intention of establishing his liberty."[32] Later abolitionists expressed similar ambivalence toward those in whose name they advocated when they too rejected the moral imperatives on which the campaign based its actions. The gift of freedom came with specific obligations and duties. Later redactions of Lewis's case, not surprisingly, made no reference to his recalcitrant behavior as they sought to make his case expressive of antislavery ideals and values. Such acts of cultural myth-making worked in tandem with certain forms of forgetting. Thomas Clarkson's romantic *History*, for example, based its account of Sharp's thrilling rescue of a "poor African" on circumstances similar to those entailed in Lewis's liberation:

> The vessel on board which a poor African had been dragged and confined had reached the Downs, and had actually got under weigh for the West Indies. In two or three hours she would have been out of sight; but just at this critical moment the writ of habeas corpus arrived on board. The officer, who served it on the captain, saw the miserable African chained to the mainmast, bathed in tears, and casting a last mournful look on the land of freedom, which was fast receding from his sight. The captain, on receiving the writ, became outrageous; but knowing the serious consequences of resisting the law of the land, he gave up his prisoner, whom the officer carried safe, but now crying for joy, to the shore.[33]

The outraged captain, in Clarkson's dramatic plotting, must acquiesce to the "law of the land" and surrender his prisoner just within sight of international waters. This retelling of the Lewis case again confirmed English law as the arbiter of justice and freedom and confirmed antislavery advocates such as Sharp as the true servants of the law. Clarkson may have also drawn on John Bicknell and Thomas Day's widely acclaimed "The Dying Negro" (1773), which he praised among those literate endeavors "plead[ing] the Negro's cause."[34] The poem dramatizes a similar account of illegal slave deportation in which the unnamed "Negro," "preferring death to another voyage to America . . . took an opportunity of shooting himself" while held aboard his master's West-Indiaman.[35] In the moments before death, the imagined sufferer utters aloud his thoughts with a final, wistful glance toward the English shoreline: "Thy dreadful mercy points at length the shore, / Where all is peace, and men are slaves no more."[36] As in Clarkson's *History*, Britain's "land of freedom" here becomes the horizon of black emancipatory longing. The injustice of the unnamed negro's forced deportation immediately after *Somerset* only heightened the poem's pathos, and such images further reaffirmed the moral and political imperatives of organized British antislavery. British freedom became a powerful trope in the antislavery literary productions from this period.

Antislavery print culture thus seized on the powerful contradiction of slaves in England to wage its early campaign against the African slave trade. Growing metropolitan concerns about the encroachment of colonial law helped propel these early struggles over slave attendants to the top of the public agenda, and jurists faced increased pressure to draw the line between English and colonial, free and slave jurisdictions. Less than a dozen law cases deliberating the status of slaves in England existed in the century before Sharp took up what Samuel Johnson wryly cast as "the cause of the sooty stranger" in reference to Joseph Knight's freedom suit shortly after *Somerset*.[37] Sharp oversaw many of these habeas corpus actions, including those of Lewis, Jonathan Strong, and John and Mary Hylas, before *Somerset* compelled the King's Bench to resolve the uncertain status of slaves in England.[38] Abolitionists enlisted these freedom suits in nation-making projects throughout the early Atlantic period. The specter of slavery in the West Indies and the United States continued to help secure these cultural narratives of British liberty well after the passage of the Slave Trade Act (1807).

The case of *Somerset v. Stewart* began in 1772 when Thomas Walkin, Elizabeth Cade, and John Marlow petitioned Mansfield for a writ of habeas corpus to release James Somerset (also spelled "Somersett" or

"Sommersett"), "a negro ... confined in irons on board a Ship called the *Ann and Mary*... lying in the Thames, and bound for Jamaica."[39] Massachusetts customs official Charles Stewart (also spelled "Steuart") had brought Somerset to England as his personal servant in 1769.[40] After two years' service, Somerset "quitted it without his consent," only to be recaptured and imprisoned aboard the *Ann and Mary*, a Jamaica-bound ship captained by John Knowles.[41] Scholarly debates abound over the exact scope and meaning of the precedent set in *Somerset* and its significance to the eventual abolition of slavery in England, since Mansfield neither wrote nor published an authoritative opinion in the case.[42] Early abolitionists reshaped the memory of *Somerset* to do certain kinds of cultural work in their print campaign against slavery. Colonialist rhetoric also underwent a shift as it strove to counteract the popularity of antislavery interpretations of Mansfield's purposively ambiguous ruling.[43] *Somerset* did not settle the status of slaves in England, although it nullified the longstanding, albeit informal, opinion of Attorney General Sir Phillip Yorke and Solicitor General Charles Talbot, which had protected slaveholders' property rights in England since 1729. Though not a binding precedent, the popularly known Yorke-Talbot opinion stipulated that "a Slave by coming from the West-Indies to Great Britain, doth not become free, and that his Master's Property or Right in him is not thereby determined or varied," which right included the power to "legally compel him [the slave] to return again to the Plantations."[44] Slaveholders had long wielded this right of forced return as a powerful tool of social control over the slaves they brought into England.[45] Mansfield's judgment in *Somerset* made slaves technically if not formally free by removing this right. What had once been a prerogative of mastery was now viewed as the crime of kidnap or abduction. Freedom in England was assumed unless subordinated to legal will in the form of positive law.[46] Abolitionists successfully imposed this interpretative framework on Mansfield's narrow ruling, which worked in concert with the narratives of moral and social progress they constructed around the organized movement.

Indeed, one of the solicitors in *Somerset* described the widely publicized lawsuit as one of a number of similar cases "where the laws were silent."[47] *Somerset v. Stewart* was decided shortly before American independence and, as part of the English common law, was incorporated into the jurisprudence of the new North American republic.[48] It established a precedent for freedom in later U.S. suits fought over the status of traveling slaves, including the landmark *Commonwealth v. Aves* (1836), which proceeded, like *Somerset*, as a civil action on a writ of habeas corpus. The language that

Mansfield used in crafting his oral opinion and its reportage in newsprint proved far more significant than the specific legal questions it addressed (or avoided). American abolitionists later cited Mansfield's decision in *Somerset* to argue that slavery was both "contrary to natural law and without legal status beyond the boundaries of the jurisdiction establishing it by positive law."[49] This "neo-Somerset" doctrine, according to legal scholar David Konig, "became an article of popular legal belief and spread across the Atlantic."[50]

The opposing counsels in *Somerset* pursued a number of arguments as they sought to redefine the master-slave relationship under the conflicting laws of freedom and slavery. Indeed, solicitors for the slaveholder Stewart insinuated the implied contract of slavery (as master and *servant*) to defend his virtual, if not legal, title to Somerset's labor in the absence of slave law, while Somerset's solicitors insisted on the virtual, if not expressed, law of freedom in England. Somerset's lawyers drew on the hyperbolic rhetoric of British freedom that shaped what became a moral maxim of the antislavery campaign. These metaphors became interwoven with the invented tradition of the freeborn Englishman, which antislavery print culture marshaled to do powerful epistemological work in its early campaign against the slave trade. The young lawyer Francis Hargrave embraced metaphor in the lacuna of positive law to claim that the eternal principle of freedom (or natural right) prevailed in England.[51] He self-published the expanded arguments in pamphlet form as *An Argument in the Case of James Sommersett, a Negro* (1782), in which he contended that slavery was unlawful and unrecognized by law in England, with the exception of villeinage, an ancient form of English slavery that had died out long ago. "Consequently," Hargrave reasoned, "there is now no slavery, which can be lawful in England, until the Legislature shall interpose its authority to make it so."[52] Among the legal cases cited in support of this argument, Hargrave began with one mentioned in "Mr. Rushworth's *Historical Collections*; and it is there said that in the eleventh of Elizabeth, one Cartwright brought a slave from Russia ... and it was resolved, that England was too pure an air for a slave to breathe in."[53]

While the legal minds disputed the meaning of the "free air of Britain," newsprint popularized the strange metaphor into a powerful testament to British freedom, and it became a leitmotif of the antislavery print campaign. Clarkson's *History*, for example, traces back to *Somerset* this metaphor further popularized in William Cowper's "The Task" (1784): "Slaves cannot breathe in England; if their lungs / Received our air, that moment

Emancipation after "the Laws of Englishmen"   29

they are free;/They touch our country, and their shackles fall." Clarkson's annotation reads, "Expression used in the great trial, when Mr. Sharp obtained the verdict in favour of Somerset."[54] North Carolina fugitive Moses Roper later reenergized this metaphor in the context of the antiapprenticeship campaign when he quoted Cowper's verse upon his 1835 arrival into Liverpool.

Hargrave's powerful metaphor—his insistence that "slaves could [not] breathe in England"—also influenced James Wallace and John Dunning's defense of Stewart, as Wallace cautioned the court to "consider the great detriment to proprietors . . . by setting them free."[55] Dunning, too, derided the "absurdity" of the expression and mocked Hargrave for substituting legal conceit for a positive law of freedom. Dunning's criticisms were justified, given how literary metaphors reveal new meanings in unexpected contexts through the introduction of a "logical absurdity" between a subject and its modifier. Hargrave's use of metaphor as legal argument introduced just this sort of "infinitely paraphraseable meanings of words" into the trial.[56] Dunning was caught in the rhetorical snares of this "absurd" conceit even as he argued against its applicability to African enslavement: "neither the air of England is too pure for a slave to breathe in, nor the laws of England have rejected servitude."[57] Long's *Candid Reflections upon the Judgement Lately Awarded by the Court of King's Bench*, likewise, drew on this "absurd" metaphor to argue against the "ridiculous . . . idea of such a local emancipation" advanced by the counsels for Somerset.[58] "Something more," Long dryly noted, "than the pretended magical touch of the *English air* seems requisite, to divest him [the slaveholder] of what has been so solemnly guaranteed by the consent of the nation in Parliament; for, when he made the purchase, he was not apprised of those mysterious and invisible emanations of *English liberty*, which were to make the bargain void."[59] The "strange efficacy of the *English air* . . . [to] redeem his Negroe from, bondage," he further observed, was called on to do legal work in the absence of positive law. Long even insisted on indemnification for slaveholders thus "compelled to sustain" the loss of "*renegado blacks*" or fugitive slaves upon arrival into England.[60] This poetics of freedom strangely seduced colonialist and antislavery polemicists alike, who found themselves drawing on this metaphor, if only, as with Dunning and Long, to contest its purported absurdity.

Somerset became a cause célèbre over the course of a long trial that dragged over three court terms, as curious spectators flocked to Westminster Hall "to hear the Negro cause."[61] After a lengthy and well-publicized series of eight hearings between December 1771 and June 1772, Mansfield finally ruled that Stewart had no right to transport Somerset back to the West Indies against his will. As in the earlier case of Lewis, Mansfield elected not to address the more expansive claims that Hargrave and others made regarding the general unlawfulness of slavery within England, choosing to narrow his ruling to the question of whether the *Ann and Mary*'s captain, Knowles, had sufficient cause to hold Somerset "to be sold abroad" upon his refusal to serve Stewart.[62] In "a written speech, as guarded, cautious, and concise, as it could possibly be drawn up," Mansfield reportedly declared, "No master ever was allowed here to take a slave by force to be sold abroad because he deserted from his service, or for any other reason whatever."[63] English law alone regulated the question of Somerset's freedom since "colonial laws did not hold sway in England," and Mansfield's pronouncement effectively curtailed the jurisdiction of colonial law within the territorial bounds of England, Ireland, and Wales.[64] Slaveholders had a right to the service of the people they enslaved, but they could not enforce this right on English soil with the threat of forced deportation.[65]

As Seymour Drescher notes, Mansfield "had clearly said that uncertainty had always been his aim concerning the status of blacks in Britain," in Lewis's case well before *Somerset* came to trial.[66] Mansfield allowed these public misinterpretations of *Somerset* to circulate even though he "saw to it that, in his court, no back wages were ever paid for unremunerated service," in a tacit acknowledgment of the legitimacy of enslaved labor.[67] During the *Somerset* trial, Mansfield expressed much concern over the loss of the capital that colonialists had invested in human property, and he calculated the economic impact of his ruling on slaveholders, who held an estimated fifteen thousand slaves in England, at "50£ per head."[68] Lord Stowell of the High Court of Admiralty later drew attention to the curious fact that "Lord Mansfield . . . never interposed in the slightest manner to correct the total misapprehension, if it is so to be considered, of the law which he himself had introduced.[69] Mansfield expressed his unwillingness to issue a judgment during the argumentation and even urged Stewart to "end the question, by discharging or giving freedom to the negro."[70] His purposive terseness frustrated colonial interests as well, and Long's *Candid Reflections* dismissed the judgment as confirming a "fantastic idea of *English liberty*" that was at variance with its laws of commerce.[71] Long insisted that Parliament held the sole power to pass legislation forbidding the entrance of slaves into England as he dismissed the idea of "a Negroe-slave . . . entitled to the rights of an Englishman, on the instant of his inhaling the air of *England*."[72]

However, the persuasive power of the "absurd" metaphor continued unabated in the face of criticism. The *London Chronicle* further popularized the metaphor when it drew attention to "Several [blacks who] were in Court to hear the event of the above cause so interesting to their tribe, and after the judgment of the court was known, bowed with profound respect to the Judges, and shaking each other by the hand, congratulated themselves upon the recovery of the rights of human nature, and their happy lot that permitted them to breathe the free air of England."[73] The "fantastic idea of *English liberty*" thus came to stand in the place of a positive law of freedom in the popular memory of Mansfield's ruling.

Mansfield stated not that freedom was henceforth the condition of all slaves in England but that slaves, according to Peter Fryer, "could not lawfully be shipped out of England against their will."[74] The ruling neither rendered slavery unlawful nor abolished it. Slaveholders in England, however, found it far more difficult to enforce their claims of possession once they lost the right to remove recalcitrant slaves to the colonies. Some commentators lauded the judgment, inaccurately, as the end of slavery in England, and they presumed English law, after *Somerset*, as the most certain assurance of liberty. While the majority of British newspapers including the *London Evening Post, London Chronicle, Daily Advertiser, General Evening Post*, and *Morning Chronicle* reported accurately on the particulars of the case, the *Middlesex Journal* and *Felix Farley's Bristol Journal*, according to Folarin Shyllon, misreported Mansfield's pronouncement in *Somerset* to mean the emancipation of all slaves in Great Britain.[75] These broad interpretations took on the powerful likeness of legal truth once they traveled across the Atlantic to the Americas.[76] The black American newspaper *Freedom's Journal* reviewed the legal doctrine of *Somerset* and concluded that "the ever memorable result of this trial established the following axiom, that, as soon as any slave sets his foot on English ground, he becomes free."[77]

Somerset made forced deportations from England illegal until the *Case of the Slave Grace* established the doctrine of reattachment of slave status upon voluntary return. The ruling in *Grace* extended the semblance of legal sanction to the forced deportations that continued illegally after Mansfield's landmark ruling.[78] Such crimes on English soil continually undercut the discourse of territorialized freedom that had become the subject of much nationalistic effusion in the wake of the *Somerset* victory.[79] Cugoano, Equiano, William Green, and a number of the self-described Sons of Africa were assiduous in bringing public attention to the continued violations of this supposed law of freedom.[80] They intervened with varying degrees of success in a number of cases to prevent the forced deportation and reenslavement of ex-slaves who had either escaped or had been brought onto English soil. Cugoano, for example, oversaw the successful application of *Somerset* in the attempted kidnap and deportation of Henry Demane to the West Indies in 1786. He and Green appealed to Granville Sharp to obtain a writ of habeas corpus on behalf of Demane, whose master had forced him onto a Barbados-bound vessel. As in the earlier case of John Lewis, Demane's dramatic release was secured two days later while the ship was under sail.[81]

In the autobiographical *Interesting Narrative*, Equiano also recollected, in vivid detail, his unsuccessful efforts to prevent, through writ of habeas corpus, the kidnapping and forced deportation of John Annis to the West Indies. Annis, according to Equiano, "had formerly lived many years with Mr. William Kirkpatrick, a gentleman of the island of St. Kitts, from whom he parted by consent, though he afterwards tried many schemes to inveigle the poor man."[82] Equiano also sought out Granville Sharp, in the first of a number of such consultations, and engaged the services of an attorney, who unfortunately "proved unfaithful" and "did not do the least good in the cause" (*IN*, 180–81). The *London Chronicle* carried the following account of Kirkpatrick's "vile act": "a Merchant, who had kept a Black Servant some years, having some words with him they parted by consent; and the Black had his Master's leave to go; he accordingly went, and entered himself as a Cook on board a West India ship; the Master hearing where he was, went with two Gentlemen and two Watermen and took the poor Fellow by violence, tying his hands and legs, and carried him on board a ship bound to St. Kitt's, on which he was put in chains to be carried into slavery."[83] Annis's forced deportation to the West Indies openly flouted the pronouncements that Mansfield had made in *Somerset* just two year earlier. These ongoing crimes of "disciplinary deportation" proved that the customs and norms of slavery continued to flourish in free England.[84] While enslaved to Quaker merchant Robert King, Equiano witnessed the repeated failure of legal doctrine to control the practice of slavery in the New World colonies, where "free men . . . [were] villainously trepanned and held in bondage." Once emancipated, Equiano suffered similar depredations firsthand, deploring that "there was no law for free men" in the West Indies (*IN*, 159). These scenes of colonial injustice convinced Equiano, whose faith in legal liberty remained relatively unshaken, to "make every exertion to obtain [his] freedom and return to Old England," but he found only greater disappointment in the "land of freedom" (*IN*, 122).

"[H]aving known the want of liberty," Equiano employed a curious "well-plotted stratagem" to serve the slaveholder Kirkpatrick with the writ of habeas corpus to free Annis. "I whitened my face," he writes, "that they might not know me, and this had the desired effect" (*IN*, 180). Equiano "whitened" himself in order to put the law into effect, even though this plot, like the others, failed to secure Annis's freedom. When brought before the judge, Kirkpatrick simply claimed that "he had not the body in custody, on which he was admitted to bail" (*IN*, 180). Equiano does not elaborate on this powerfully coded stratagem to deceive Kirkpatrick, which illustrates the potent working of racial particularization that necessarily undercut the abstract rights supposedly secured to blacks in England by law. Equiano is forced to witness, helplessly, as Annis's plaintive cries for justice, like those of Cugoano, remained unanswered. This "disagreeable business" disenchanted Equiano from the beloved country of his adoption. The violation of Annis's rights on English soil made such "a mockery of freedom" that Equiano "resolved at that time, never more to return to England" (*IN*, 181). Annis's kidnapping marks a significant emotional transformation in the autobiography, as an unnamable melancholy suffuses Equiano during "this disagreeable business," so that he "often wished for death" (*IN*, 181). The failure of law to protect Annis's rights on English soil initiates Equiano's spiritual crisis, as he "travel[ed] in much heaviness, and frequently murmured against the Almighty, particularly in his providential dealings" (*IN*, 181).

Equiano's psychic "heaviness" is striking given his emotionally restrained narrative, and it finds a parallel expression in Cugoano's radical antislavery jeremiad. Cugoano's "language of grief and woe" articulates their shared struggles to seek justice for "those injuries[,] which cannot be restored . . . but . . . admits of a possible restoration," as Cugoano sought to translate his experiences of captivity and enslavement into literary form (*TS*, 15). His *Thoughts and Sentiments on the Evil of Slavery* gestures toward the insufficiency of language to "give an adequate idea of the horror of their feelings, and the dreadful calamities they undergo," as it questions the law's ability to adjudicate a penalty commensurate to "involuntary slavery or compulsory service, [which] is an injury and robbery contrary to all law, civilization, reason, justice, equity, and humanity" (*TS*, 51).[85]

Alexander Campbell brought Cugoano from brutal enslavement in Grenada to England as his servant John Stewart just months after *Somerset*.[86] By the mid-1780s, Cugoano had left Campbell to find waged employment in the household of the fashionable painter Richard Cosway and his wife, Maria (see figure 1.1).[87] Cugoano numbered among those whom proplanter ideologue Long dismissed as fugitive "Negroe domestics," who constitute a "dissolute, idle, profligate crew, retained in families more for ostentation than any *laudable* use."[88] He first self-published *Thoughts and Sentiments* in 1787, the same year that Sharp and Clarkson oversaw the establishment of the Society for the Abolition of the Slave Trade, and again in 1791 in a substantially abridged form. In a time when many professed abolitionists supported gradual abolition, Cugoano passionately advocated for the "total abolition and an universal emancipation of slaves, and the enfranchisement of all the Black People employed in the culture of the Colonies ... without any hesitation, or delay for a moment" (*TS*, 83) Cugoano, like the antislavery class radical Robert Wedderburn, insisted on a more heterogeneous understanding of freedom as he challenged the nationalist and imperialist narratives proliferated by the antislavery campaigns in which he also participated. Wedderburn, for example, identifies his Jamaican slave mother, Rosanna, as the wellspring of his revolutionary fervor, and Cugoano insisted in a similar vein that "[t]hose people annually brought away from Guinea, are born as free, and are brought up with as great a predilection for their country, freedom and liberty, as the sons and daughters of fair Britain" (*TS*, 27, 28). Their writings firmly maintained that neither freedom nor emancipatory longing were the unique cultural properties of white Britons.

Cugoano's profound yearning for justice or "retribution" is powerfully tempered by what Saidiya Hartman and Stephen Best identify as his critique of the law's ability to administer justice for "the evil, criminal and wicked traffic of enslaving men" (*TS*, 10). This ambivalence energizes the text of *Thoughts and Sentiments*, an ambivalence expressed in the new preface to the later abridged edition. The preface acknowledges Sharp's humanitarian labors and the "most amiable disposition of the laws of Englishmen" even as it draws critical attention to the duplicitous nature of the law:

> For so it was considered as criminal, by the laws of Englishmen, when the tyrannical paw and the monster of slavery took the man by the neck, in the centre of the English freedom, and thought henceforth to compel him to his involuntary subjection of slavery and oppression; it was wisely determined by some of the most eminent and learned counsellors in the land. The whole of that affair rested solely upon that humane and indefatigable friend of mankind, Granville Sharp esq. whose name we should always mention with the greatest reverence and honor. The noble decision, thereby, before the Right Hon. Lord Chief Justice MANSFIELD, and the parts taken by the

Fig. 1.1. Richard Cosway, *The Artist and His Wife in a Garden, with a Black Servant* (1784). The black servant is presumed to be Quobna Ottobah Cugoano, who may have posed for this etching while serving the Cosways at the Schomburg House. (Courtesy of the Whitworth Art Gallery, The University of Manchester)

> learned Counsellor HARGRAVE, are the surest proofs of the most amiable disposition of the laws of Englishmen. (*TS*, 115–16)

These laudatory words draw attention to the contradictions within the laws of a society purportedly committed to freedom. The proof offered by the "noble decision . . . of the Right Hon. Lord Chief Justice MANSFIELD" of the law's "amiable disposition" toward black subjects was far from reliable. England may protect the man from "the monster of slavery . . . in the centre of the British freedom," yet these same laws sanctioned his continued enslavement in its West Indian colonies.

What made the black slave, in Cugoano's words, a "man" in England but property elsewhere? Cugoano impugned the absurd logic of extreme legal formalism, which invested geopolitical lines (and here the territorial bounds of Great Britain) with the arbitrary power to redefine person from property. Cugoano's approbation of Sharp, Mansfield, and Hargrave thus does not efface his skepticism of the law and its ability to offer justice, so forcefully expressed in the first volume. "[J]ustice and equality," writes Cugoano, "does not always reside among men, even where some considerable degree of civilization is maintained," and abolition was merely a "just commutation for what cannot be fully restored" (*TS*, 51, 102). Highlighting the contradictions in English law, Cugoano hyperbolically inverts the trajectory of British freedom as he reimagines the enslavement of free Britons on English soil: "if these unconstitutional laws, reaching from Great Britain to her colonies, be long continued in and supported," it will "mark out the whole of the British constitution with ruin and destruction; and that the most generous and tenacious people in the world for liberty, may also at last be reduced to slaves" (*TS*, 81, 70). How are Britons to rest secure with a government entrusted with protecting their rights and liberties on English soil that continues to ensure the enslavement of people in its colonies?

Equiano and Cugoano thus offer powerful literary counterpoints to the triumph of a uniquely British humanitarian tradition emerging from the popular myths of *Somerset v. Stewart*. Even as they insisted that the law of Englishmen "do justice," their narratives critically questioned the capacity of those "laws of Englishmen" to secure justice for blacks in Britain, let alone in its slave colonies. They positioned their accounts agonistically against what Marcus Wood delineates as "the sophistries of eighteenth-century pro-slavery discourse" and "the ultimately solipsistic constructions of abolition rhetoric."[89] Their writings mobilized notions of present failure to interrogate these popular histories of antislavery triumph in a nation that had begun to circumscribe freedom territorially in ways that anticipated the extreme legal formalism of the *Case of the Slave Grace*.

The Implied Contract of Slavery in the Case of the Slave Grace

Like Equiano and Cugoano, radical black American David Walker offered ambivalent praise for English "friendship" in the face of the country's ongoing histories of colonial expropriation and enslavement. Walker embeds the following remark in a supplementary "Addition" to Article III of his *Appeal to the Coloured Citizens of the World* (1829): "The English are the best friends the coloured people have upon earth. Though they have oppressed us a little and have colonies now in the West Indies, which oppress us *sorely*.—Yet notwithstanding they (the English) have done one hundred times more for the melioration of our condition, than all the other nations of the earth put together."[90] Walker's qualified approbation forces readers to pause in a text that otherwise unequivocally denounces slavery and the racial nation-state. Walker's *Appeal* betrays a similar skepticism toward these "laws of Englishmen" that energized the writings of Equiano and Cugoano. He published the *Appeal* in the decades after the British abolition of the slave trade but before West Indian emancipation. The stalled project of universal freedom forced American and British abolitionists to face a disturbing congruence: the emergence of "liberty as the most cherished political value" in the West *and* the rapid hemispheric expansion of "slavery as a global business, a labor regime, and a legal practice" in the South.[91] Mansfield's ruling in *Somerset* may have contributed to the "withering away" of slavery in England, but courts almost immediately began to curtail the qualified protection it proffered to the men and women enslaved in England. A number of legal cases began to limit severely *Somerset v. Stewart*, leading to its practical if not formal nullification in Lord Stowell's controversial judgment in *Case of the Slave Grace*, or *The Mongrel Woman, Grace*.

Enslaved West Indian servants, such as Mary Prince and Grace Jones, who were informally free in the British Isles, quickly discovered that their freedom expired once they left English soil. *Grace*, brought before the English High Court of Admiralty in 1827, established that unmanumitted slaves acquired a mere "temporary freedom" while resident in England. Stowell's ruling declared that slaveholders' property rights over their slaves revived immediately upon return to the West Indies, even after a prolonged residence in England. Such nominally free subjects again became slaves once they "voluntarily" returned to the West Indies, where slave law was enforced regardless of the ruses, ploys, and intimidation that slaveholders may have employed to coerce slaves' return. A "slave who returns to his country," insisted Stowell, "returns to a state of slavery" and, furthermore, does so "with a perfect knowledge of the state which they are to re-enter."[92] American jurists later adopted this doctrine of the reattachment of slave status upon return to jurisdictions where slave law held sway. The Missouri Supreme Court, for example, enforced the *Grace* doctrine against Harriet and Dred Scott in the judgment of their initial freedom suit, *Scott v. Emerson* (1852).

Decided in the years before the Slave Trade Act, *Williams v. Brown* (1802) began the legal process of restricting the Mansfield ruling in *Somerset*. *Williams v. Brown* established the peculiar "intermediate character" of black Britons who were no longer slaves yet not sovereign subjects. Williams had escaped enslavement in Grenada and made his way to London, where he found maritime employment. In 1797, Williams entered himself as an "ordinary seamen" aboard the Grenada-bound *Holderness*. Williams's former master claimed him as a runway slave upon his arrival into Grenada, and Captain Brown of the *Holderness* manumitted him with the stipulation that he continue as sailor, but for far lower wages than the other crewmen.[93] Williams brought suit against Brown for unpaid wages once they returned to London, claiming that English soil had emancipated him prior to his ill-fated voyage back to Grenada. Lord Chief Justice Alvanley of the Court of Common Pleas ruled against Williams, citing that "he was a slave in Grenada, though a freeman in England," and therefore "unable to fulfill his contract with the Defendant" on his return voyage and reclaim his wages. Williams was a free contractual agent while in England but a slave subject to the will of his master once back in the West Indies. Such an extreme legal formalism strained to resolve, even as it intensified, the contradiction of slaves as person *and* property under the law. Stowell relied on *Williams v. Brown* in his review of English law to justify the similar conclusion he rendered in *Grace*: "slaves never have been deemed and considered as free persons on their return to Antigua, or the other colonies."[94] Return became the consequence of the slave's "legal choice," and reenslavement the result of this "free act." Frederick Douglass once noted, "Freedom of choice is the essence of all accountability."[95] The ruling in *Grace* presupposed the slave petitioner as a free agent and saw no contradiction in deeming reenslavement as consistent with this freedom of choice. Antislavery advocates thus began to face rulings in which jurists declared slaves to have *voluntarily* chosen slavery over freedom.

Such a legal misnaming sought to manage the double character of slaves as it reanimated the implied contract of slavery that defense attorneys in *Somerset v. Stewart* marshaled out to preserve slaveholders' property rights in England. Stewart's lawyers offered their own "fantastic idea" as they attempted to transform the enslaved Somerset into a servant bound to contractual servitude. Solicitor Dunning, according to one account, "supposed a contract, as between master and servant," but "modified this contract . . . as far as two propositions directly militating against each other could possible be maintained."[96] This misrepresentation provoked Serjeant William Davy, Somerset's lead consul, to note rather wryly, "the air of England . . . has been gradually purifying ever since the reign of Elizabeth. Mr. Dunning seems to have discovered so much, as he finds it changes a slave into a servant."[97] Hargrave also dismissed Dunning's logic, invoking John

Locke's *Second Treatise of Civil Government* (1690) to assert that "freedom from arbitrary power is essential to the exercise of that right [of contract]; and . . . no man can by compact enslave himself."[98] Mansfield, too, dismissed the implied contract of slavery as inadmissible in the case, although this particular line of argumentation reappeared in those subsequent cases that began to limit the already narrow compass of *Somerset*.[99] Later jurists, such as Stowell, found themselves paradoxically imposing a model of contract on slaves, who became legal persons only as a matter of form. Contract, according to Thomas Holt, "presupposed individual autonomy and rights; its reciprocity presupposed formal equality," and it found its antithesis in enslavement.[100] But this "fantastic idea" of implied contract proved altogether too plausible in *Grace*, and it helped shape the formal construction of consent in those cases of "voluntary" return that began appearing periodically before English courts after *Somerset*.

Subjection to English law, according to Granville Sharp, was the obligation of all who enter the "kingdom of Great-Britain," regardless of circumstance or distinction.[101] Sharp's *Representation of the Injustice and Dangerous Tendency of Tolerating Slavery* (1769) argued that enslaved servants became British subjects upon arrival onto English soil and "ought not to be denied the benefit of the King's court" in cases of attempted kidnap and forced deportation. Slaveholders could *legally* deport only those slaves who made "*a contract in writing, by which it shall appear, that the said slave have voluntarily bound himself without compulsion or illegal duress.*"[102] For Sharp, the rights of mastery may be permitted only in those cases governed by a contract; otherwise, the slave on English soil, as any free British subject, may call on his right to habeas corpus to challenge his confinement. Voluntary engagement, following Sharp's logic, was the only exception to the rule of freedom in England.[103] Stowell later seized on this exception to affirm the lawfulness of reenslavement upon "voluntary return" to the West Indies. The notion of consent and contractual obligation that Sharp had outlined in *Representation* to protect the civil liberties of the enslaved men and women brought to England was thus reelaborated as legal sanction for what was tantamount to reenslavement by the time of *Grace*.

Eminent jurist William Blackstone incorporated the deceptive analogy between *slave* and *servant* in his hugely influential *Commentaries on the Laws of England* (1765) to further insinuate the contractual obligation of slavery under the English law of freedom. Indeed, James Kent's *Commentaries on American Law*, following Blackstone, placed slaves under the category of "servants" in the section explicating "the Law Concerning the

Rights of Persons" between master and servant.[104] Blackstone's *Commentaries* may have declared personal liberty coterminous with English territorial soil—"a slave or a negro, the moment he lands in England, falls under the protection of the laws, and with regard to all natural rights becomes *eo instanti* a freeman"—but the revised editions of his work offered a far more equivocal assessment of the status of slaves in England.[105] Folarin Shyllon notes that Blackstone immediately amended the second (1766) and third (1768) editions to read, "a slave or a negro, the moment he lands in England, falls under the protection of the laws, and so far becomes a freeman; though the master's right to his service may probably still continue."[106]

Such anxieties over the contradictory status of slaves in England are evident in Blackstone's section "of Master and Servant," which sought to disguise the slave under the heading of servant. "And now it is laid down, that a slave or negro, the instant he lands in England, becomes a freeman," explains Blackstone,

> that is, the law will protect him in the enjoyment of his person, his liberty, and his property. Yet, with regard to any right which the master may have acquired, by contract or the like, to the perpetual service of John or Thomas, this will remain exactly in the same state as before: for this is no more than the same state of subjection for life, which every apprentice submits to for the space of seven years, or sometimes for a longer term.[107]

Blackstone's elaborate rationalization seeks to represent slavery as a form of contractual labor akin to apprenticeship; it limns what Paul Gilroy and others describe as the complicity between Enlightenment "rationality and the practice of racial terror."[108] Blackstone does not define slavery *as* apprenticeship but insinuates their homologous legal relation through noticeably imprecise analogies. He likens the contractual servitude of an imagined apprentice to the "perpetual service of . . . [a] slave or negro," just as the trick of ambiguous statements such as "by contract or the like" rhetorically transforms "perpetual service" into "the space of seven years." (Parliament also embraced this language of apprenticeship when it finally legislated emancipation in the West Indies.) Blackstone insists that "pure and proper slavery does not, nay cannot subsist in England" even as he confirms that the master does indeed have a right to the "perpetual service" of his slave within the deceptive language of this implied contract. In other words, the slave becomes a free person on arrival to England, yet the master's claim on the slave's "perpetual service" remains constant. The slave is thus liberated in England only to be refashioned into an agent who contracts his or her perpetual unwaged servitude.

Edward Long found much to lampoon in such contradictory principles. "The import of this distinction, I must own, I cannot well comprehend," he remarked, "nor how the master can exercise a right of perpetual service, without restraining the Negroe of his personal liberty, his power of locomotion, or of removing his person wheresoever his inclination may direct."[109] Equivocation follows upon greater equivocation in Blackstone's attempt to refashion the slave into a free subject who contracts his or her own enslavement. Blackstone reasserts this idea of slavery as a form of contractual servitude when correcting the common misconception that baptism conferred liberty: the slave may be "entitled to the same liberty in England before, as after, baptism"; yet, "whatever service the heathen negro owed to his English master, the same is he bound to render when a christian," because English law will not "dissolve a civil contract, either express or implied, between master and servant on account of the alteration of faith in either of the contracting parties."[110] Blackstone again redefines the master and *slave* relation in England as analogous to the binding "civil contract" struck between "master and servant."

Blackstone's paradoxical argument thus presumes the slave to be a contractual agent and bearer of abstract rights, which the slave, by definition, was not. In so doing, he engages in a kind of legal tautology: he redefines the slave as a free servant irrevocably contracted to lifetime servitude, which is merely a slave by another name. Blackstone's tautological legal fiction tethered the slave to perpetual unwaged servitude in England while preserving the fiction of English "free soil." Sharp seized on the inconsistencies in the implied contract of slavery and doubted the lawfulness of a right to contract perpetual service.[111] His *Representation* cautioned that slaves who were subject to the will of the master were not competent to make civil contracts enforceable on English soil, where the law of freedom took precedence. But the misnaming of slave as contractual agent did exert some influence over the perceptions of the antislavery campaign. One British abolitionist criticized American fugitive Moses Roper for having "brought willfully" on himself his "cruel usage ... by repeatedly running away" as he applied the deceptive "contract of man to man" to the master and slave relation.[112] The implied contract of slavery and its logic of consent shaped representations of slaves in English law and antislavery literature over the following decade of campaigns for West Indian emancipation, reemerging in subtle yet injurious ways in public disputes over the slave Grace, as legal commentators invoked consent to suture the increasingly insupportable gulf between metropolitan liberalism and the practice of colonial slavery.

Grace had traveled as a domestic slave from Antigua to England with her mistress, Mrs. Allan, in 1822 and was compelled to return to the West Indies the following year. The *Anti-Slavery Monthly Reporter* reported that Grace had been "induced to return to Antigua . . . after a considerable residence in this country" under the misconception that she was now a free woman.[113] She departed England, according to the *Reporter*, "on an understanding which is asserted by Grace, but has not been proved, that she should henceforth enjoy, in Antigua, the liberty of which she was put into possession by her arrival in England."[114] In 1825, Grace applied to customs official George Wyke to challenge her mistress's claim on her as a slave "on the ground that her exportation to England and reimportation into Antigua contravened the slave laws."[115] Her case created "much prejudice in Antigua" when it came to trial before the colonial Vice-Admiralty Court, and the "acting governor of the island suspended the further progress of the cause till he had received instructions from this government."[116] The court finally ruled in 1826 that Grace was still legally a slave and that her sojourn in England did not confer permanent freedom on her. A year later, Lord Stowell upheld this colonial verdict upon its appeal to the English High Court of Admiralty, ruling that the slave "forfeited the freedom to which he had been entitled in England" once he "voluntarily returned to the place from which he had been brought as a slave."[117]

Unlike Mansfield's purposive terseness in *Somerset*, Stowell's decision occupied twenty-eight columns in the State Trials and over forty pages in pamphlet form. Stowell used *Grace* as an opportunity to reflect "upon the interpretation of the well-known case of Sommersett" and the popular "notion of a right to freedom, by virtue of a residence in England."[118] He observed that the prosecuting attorneys in *Somerset* did not contest the legality of slavery as an institution and looked "no further than to the peculiar nature, as it were, of our own soil; the air of our island is too pure for slavery to breathe in."[119] Stowell insisted on the necessary territorial limits of England's "gift of liberty entire and unencumbered" as he emphasized the "limited liberation conferred upon him in England."[120] Lord Mansfield, he noted, "confines the question . . . expressly to *this country*."[121] Stowell endlessly reiterated the contingency of the slave's "temporary freedom" and "limited liberation," as he redefined the circumstances of the case from forced deportation to "voluntary return," and articulated an extreme legal formalism that sought to erect more firmly the geopolitical boundaries between freedom in England and slavery in the West Indies.

Stowell not only further restricted the already narrow compass of Mansfield's ruling but also sought to disabuse the British public of what had become a powerful antislavery precedent and the stuff of popular legend: "This cry of 'Once free for an hour, free for ever!' it is to be observed, is mentioned as a peculiar cry of Englishmen," even though slavery, as he later remarked, "continued in our colonies, favoured and supported by our own Courts, which have liberally imparted to it their protection and encouragement."[122] Stowell thereby accused organized antislavery of hyperbole. Is it plausible to assume, he queried, that one purposively narrow judgment could effect the moral, social, political, and economic "conversion" of the nation and the "fall" of an institution that permeated all aspects of British life? The law of England, he asserted, "discourages slavery, and so it certainly does within the limits of these islands; but the law uses a very different language, and exerts a very different force, when it looks to her colonies; for to this trade, in those colonies, it gives an almost unbounded protection."[123] Stowell authored a striking critique of British liberalism and its contradictory impulses as he resecured the property rights of traveling slaveholders. He unexpectedly shared Cugoano's criticisms of the "laws of Englishmen," which tacitly supported colonial slavery yet allowed public misapprehensions of their "amiable disposition" to circulate.

Colonial newspapers in Antigua and Jamaica celebrated Stowell's ruling, while the unexpected failure of the "laws of Englishmen" to secure Grace's freedom sounded piercingly from the transatlantic platforms of the antislavery campaign.[124] American abolitionists asked, "If the air of England is not yet too pure to sustain a dormant slavery, probably an act of parliament might be procured which would impart to all its boasted purity."[125] The meaning of freedom came under attack in *Grace* in ways that marked all too painfully for some observers the decline rather than the social progress of Britain. "It had hitherto been the boast of Englishmen," commented the *Liverpool Mercury*,

> that the air of their country was incompatible with slavery, that its soil admitted no servile tread, but that, from the moment a slave set foot upon this land of liberty, he became then, and for ever, free. This boast, like many others which honest John is in the habit of making, proves to be most woefully unfounded, as appears from the recent decision of Lord Stowell, in the matter of the slave Grace.[126]

It appears that Solicitor Dunning and Lord Stowell were not alone in finding "a kind of absurdity" in what had become by 1828 a master trope of the antislavery print campaign. An anonymous antislavery pamphlet reviewing the Grace case faulted Stowell for misinterpreting the principles set out in *Somerset* and offered a revisionist hagiography of Granville Sharp:

> On the "Somersett" Case, Lord Stowell's information seems to be alike defective. It originated, in no degree, in deference to the "soil" or "air" of England neither in the nice sensibilities attendant on "refinement." An upright, honest, well-read Englishman, the late Granville Sharp, stung with the idea, that in a country, blessed with a Protestant Church and a free Constitution, where Christianity was held in its purest form, and where the laws were professedly founded upon, and in accordance with, that Christianity, there could exist such a thing as "a Slave;" betook himself to earnest research into the subject. . . . He took up the Case of Somersett, furnished counsel with their most powerful arguments, particularly Hargrave . . . wrote some convincing pamphlets on the subject . . . and at last . . . Lord Mansfield, beaten out of all his rooted prejudices, and ill founded arguments, bowed, and gracefully bowed, to the conviction of truth.[127]

This unnamed "Briton," who was undoubtedly well-versed in Clarkson's *History*, sought to reestablish on more stable historical ground what had become a widely accepted poetic fallacy: that "fantastic idea of *English liberty*." If Mansfield's ruling was not enough to secure the certainty of individual liberty and personal freedom, then surety might be found elsewhere, in Christianity and in the "Magna Charta and the Bill of Rights."[128] Like a number of abolitionists, this unnamed Briton saw Stowell's ruling as a retrograde path in a campaign that had begun its march forward with Sharp's victory in *Somerset*. Like Thomas Pringle in his extensive "Supplement" to Mary Prince's autobiography, he marshals the "phantom" of "SLAVERY IN ENGLAND" to dramatize this course of national retrogression: in Stowell's judgment in *Grace*, the jurist "endeavored to place in a questionable and equivocal light the liberties of a grieved and mourning Nation."[129]

The recognition of Grace's legal personhood in England incited what Stephen Best describes as "a crisis in (and a provisional resolution of) the tenets and practices of law" even as it introduced new forms of violence in its wake.[130] Stowell could make his arguments legally consistent only through the omission of a critical fact from the circumstances of the case. Solicitor Robinson argued on Grace's behalf that "he would not believe that the act was voluntary: and as a point in the history of the case, he was entitled to state that the woman had denied to the Governor that she had willingly returned."[131] Stowell suppressed the charge of kidnap from the trial, rewriting the circumstances of the case to introduce the fiction of Grace's "voluntary return" to Antigua, even as he then held her responsible for a "choice" she did not make.

On this point, British public sentiment in response to Stowell's verdict was in some venues outright hostile, with the *Sunday Times* and *New Times* leading the critical assault. The *New Times* was one of the few periodicals openly to denounce Grace's kidnap, over three consecutive days of reportage: "The female in question was not a voluntary agent in the re-imposition of her chains; *she was kidnapped*; and a criminal indictment may be as legally preferred against those who seduced her to quit England, as if she had been a white native of this island."[132] The *Sunday Times* likewise faulted Stowell for his "solecism, or a contradiction in terms," declaring, "This may be law ... but it certainly is opposed to common sense. It strikes us as manifestly absurd."[133] The "absurd" solecism of Stowell's reasoning—that Grace had freely chosen her own enslavement—was a kind of tautology roughly parallel to the "fantastic idea of English liberty" marshaled in defense of Somerset; juridical rationality yet again turned to rhetorical forms to resolve the contradiction of slaves in England.

Just as popular misconceptions transformed Mansfield's rather ambiguous ruling into a truism of British liberty, Haggard's official report reiterates Stowell's fiction as a factual circumstance of the case. Grace, according to Haggard, "resided with her mistress in this country until 1823, and accompanied her voluntarily on her return to Antigua."[134] Stowell's dogged attempt to demystify antislavery ideology created new legal fictions in its stead. The *London Times* offered this rather wry distillation of Stowell's controversial ruling:

> It was universally apprehended, and indeed proudly boasted, that a slave, however purchased or obtained, who had in any way reached the British island, who had once breathed British air, was thenceforth for ever free. Lord Stowell's judgment has taken from the friends of humanity this pleasing error.... So that a lady, the wife of a planter, bringing a black nursery maid to this country, places her in a state of freedom among us: from that state there are no legal means of removing her; but should the maid consent to return, or be entrapped on board a ship and carried back, she is, when in the island from whence she was conveyed, a slave again.[135]

Stowell's efforts to dispel the "pleasing error" of Mansfield's landmark ruling served to further obscure the difference between "consent" and "entrapment." He fashioned Grace as a willful agent to fit his particular legal narrative as he transformed the mistress's coercion into the slave's consent. The antislavery campaign, in response, seized on these misleading implications of "free will," "voluntary return," and "consent" in the *Grace* ruling to reanimate powerfully public concerns over the meaning of British freedom, rights, and legal personhood.

Abolitionists anxiously sought to recalibrate this calculus of coercion and consent in four subsequent cases of illegal slave importation, including those of William Otto, William Robday, Jack Martin, and John Smith and Rachel, brought on appeal before Lord Stowell.[136] Counsels for the various slave petitioners sought, vainly, to distinguish their cases from the circumstances of *Grace*. They struggled to convince Stowell that their petitioners had been kidnapped and deported to slave jurisdictions against their will. An antislavery organizer by the name of Chipehase seized John Smith and Rachel in 1825, alleging that the two had been "unlawfully conveyed from Gibraltar to Barbados, and illegally imported into Antigua."[137] The King's Advocate in the appeal before Stowell emphasized coercion as he argued that "the slaves, being free at Gibraltar, were induced to return to the colony by the idea that they were really manumitted, and that therefore their return was not voluntary."[138] Antislavery solicitor Stephen Lushington, reprising his role in *Grace*, further emphasized the distinction between the two cases and argued that "[t]he exportation of these slaves from Barbados to Antigua was compulsory; whereas the return of Grace had been free and spontaneous."[139] Antislavery solicitors such as Lushington were thus placed in the paradoxical position of conforming to the logic of voluntary return in the *Grace* case in order to argue for kidnap or compulsory deportation in subsequent cases—a process that only reinforced Stowell's original paradoxical fiction of voluntary slavery.

The same antislavery agent who seized John Smith and Rachel also brought Jack Martin's case before the Vice-Admiralty Court of Antigua in 1827.[140] The King's Advocate argued that Martin had "enjoyed his liberty, had been employed on board a King's ship, which was British territory," and had been taken from it by force.[141] Lushington, again, emphasized this distinction from the *Grace* case: "This was no case of voluntary return; the slave had been forced from o[n] board a King's ship, in which he served."[142] Stowell rather peremptorily dismissed these arguments and, again, affirmed the lower court's decision against the slave's freedom since he "could find no circumstances that distinguished them from that of 'Grace.'"[143] Lushington argued unsuccessfully for the particular circumstances of each of these later cases, while Stowell turned a blind eye to the charges of kidnap and forced deportation to enforce the abstract formalism he had decided in *Grace*. The acknowledgment of slave agency and will in these cases became a pretext for punishment. Stowell deemed the slaves willful free agents in legal form so that their cases conformed to the dichotomous logic he had established in the *Grace* case: free in England but slave upon voluntary return to the West Indies.

The controversial *Case of the Slave Grace* captivated not only British audiences; American abolitionists saw it as a dramatic rehearsal for their own impending sectional crisis as free northern states began repealing those sojourner laws that once protected the property rights of traveling slaveholders.[144] The Philadelphia-based *Friend* lamented Stowell's ruling even as it geographically extended the metaphor popularized in *Somerset* to observe, "the air of several of our states is nearly as pure as that of Great Britain; and had not this quality been impaired by an article of the constitution, would probably been wholly so."[145] The black American *Freedom's Journal*, in another vein, contested Stowell's reasoning, claiming that "the woman Grace, became to all intents a subject of the empire, as soon as she touched the soil of England by the express decision of Lord Mansfield, as delivered in the case of Somerset."[146] Facing present failure, transatlantic antislavery forces sought to return to a victorious past when "that fantastic idea of English liberty" still held sway. Battered in the press, Stowell turned to Associate Justice Joseph Story of the U.S. Supreme Court for support.[147] Story assured Stowell that his reasoning in *Grace* was "impregnable" and added that, even in the free state of Massachusetts, "if a slave should come hither, and afterwards return to his own home, we should certainly think that the local law would re-attach upon him, and that his servile character would be re-integrated."[148] Indeed, Massachusetts's Chief Justice Lemuel Shaw later upheld the principle of reattachment outlined in *Grace* when applying *Somerset* to his ruling in *Commonwealth v. Aves*.[149]

The controversies over the *Grace* case reenergized transatlantic debates over the status of slaves in England and anticipated the kinds of struggles that soon beset U.S. courtrooms. Was freedom immanent and inborn or contingent on geopolitics? Did slaves, following Sharp's argument, become free subjects once they set foot on free soil? *Grace* legalized the kidnapping and forced deportation of blacks that had occurred with tragic regularity in England since the time of Somerset, although it did so in the name of disabusing the British public of its "fantastic idea of *English liberty*." The outcome of *Grace* dealt a severe blow to the antislavery cause, and later abolitionists such as Thomas Pringle sought to understand a ruling that upheld the slave's right to freedom in England as long as it did not conflict with the slaveholder's property rights in the West Indies.[150] As the following section shows, the London Anti-Slavery Society, failing to challenge successfully the *Grace* precedent in the courtroom, turned with renewed energy toward mobilizing Britons through its print and petition campaigns, with "No Slavery in England" as its watchword.

Mary Prince, Ashton Warner, and the Idiom of Failure

> I am only a lodger—and hardly that.
> —Ignatius Sancho, Letters of the Late Ignatius Sancho, 1782

Thomas Pringle, then secretary of the London Anti-Slavery Society, offered no recorded response to Orpen's 1831 open letter, possibly because he was more immediately preoccupied with the case of a slave attendant named Mary Prince who sought return to Antigua as a free woman. Like Grace, Prince first arrived in London as a servant in the household of an Antiguan slaveholder, John A. Wood, in 1828. Her autobiography chronicles her enslavement to five sets of abusive slaveholders in the Bahamas, Turk's Island, and Antigua, a story that culminates in England with the dramatic scene of what literary critics almost unanimously depict as the act of resistance that secured her freedom: Prince walked out of slavery. She left her master's household in the face of escalating abuse, although she later chose to represent herself as "turned out of doors." As an unmanumitted slave in the wake of *Grace*, Prince could not return to Antigua without also submitting to reenslavement. Consequently, she was forced to remain in a foreign nation she could not leave, the oppressive terms of her "freedom" as dictated by the law. The circumstances of Prince's case presented the Anti-Slavery Society with an opportunity to challenge the *Grace* precedent when she first asked for assistance in November 1828. After discovering, with dismay, that English courts had no power to compel Wood to manumit her formally, the organization then brought before Parliament a private petition for freedom on Prince's behalf, which was, according to Clare Midgley, one of only two female antislavery petitions before 1830.[151] Antislavery solicitor Stephen Lushington introduced Prince's petition alongside a bill "to provide for the entire emancipation of all slaves brought to England with the owner's consent,"¹⁵²

Pringle intervened on Prince's behalf, as he had done in a number of women's cases in England and the West Indies, including those of Nancy Morgan and Kitty Hilton. He successfully negotiated the manumission of Morgan and her child, whom slaveholders had brought as servants from St. Vincent, and procured twenty pounds of the sixty-pound fee through the Female Society for Birmingham.¹⁵³ Attempts to procure Prince's manumission privately, however, found Wood to be "so full of animosity against the woman, and so firmly bent against any arrangement having her freedom for its object, that the negotiation was soon broken off as hopeless" (*HMP*, 97). Pringle eventually employed Prince as a waged servant in his household, and she urged him to publish an account of her life once they exhausted all legal avenues to return her to Antigua as a free woman. Even though Pringle was a celebrated poet in his own right (in his former country of South Africa), Prince orally dictated her autobiographical experiences to Susanna Strickland (later Susanna Moodie), who transcribed the narrative at Prince's behest into *The History of Mary Prince, a West Indian Slave*.¹⁵⁴ Pringle published the *History* simultaneously in London and Edinburgh, where it garnered immediate interest, going through three editions by the end of 1831, as news of slave uprisings in Jamaica began to reach England. Inspired by the collaboration with Prince, Strickland, who later became a successful novelist in Canada, published with Pringle a second slave narrative later that year entitled *Negro Slavery Described by a Negro: Being the Narrative of Ashton Warner, a Native of St. Vincent's*, which advocated for the "*early and total abolition*" of colonial slavery.¹⁵⁵

Prince's predicament became a powerful illustration of the way slaveholders manipulated the "laws of Englishmen" to control slaves from afar, dictating the limits of their mobility and social being.¹⁵⁶ The Woods readily used "psychological ploys" against Prince, who had left in Antigua her "dear husband," Daniel James, whom she had "joined in marriage, about Christmas 1826" and who was awaiting her return. The Woods had thought that her personal attachments in Antigua would guarantee her continued compliance once in free England. "I would rather go into my grave than go back a slave to Antigua," Prince later professed to the Anti-Slavery Society, "though I wish to go back to my husband very much—very much—very much!"¹⁵⁷ Enslaved attendants brought to England were forced to weigh their emancipatory desires against severance from those social ties that helped buffer them from the brutalities of slavery. Indeed, Prince describes her feelings in her own words: "[I] am as comfortable as I can be while separated from my dear husband, and away from my own country and all old friends and connections" (*HMP*, 92).¹⁵⁸ Her predicament offers yet another instance of the way the recognition of slave humanity (exemplified by ties of affection and kinship) produced new forms of violence in its wake. Proplanter ideologue Long remarked with understated menace that enslaved servants brought to England "who have left wives and children behind, return very willingly."¹⁵⁹ Prince's testimony was particularly valuable to the antislavery campaign for its stark illustration of the way vindictive slaveholders such as Wood were more than happy to exploit their slaves' humanity to intensify their suffering. The punitive dimension of Prince's freedom—its contingency on exile from Antigua—was the consequence of the precedent set in *Grace*.

Prince's dictated *History* provides one of the few documents from the campaign for West Indian emancipation written from the perspective of an enslaved woman. Pringle added a sixteen-page interpretive "Supplement" that emphasized the political imperative of the antislavery campaign and that doubled the length of her short first-person account. Pringle expressed concern in the "Supplement" over those "baneful influences" that held sway in England as he stressed the miscarriage of justice and named Prince a "slave" to mobilize his readers.¹⁶⁰ "I may observe," Pringle admitted, "that the history of Mary Prince furnishes a corollary to Lord Stowell's decision in the case of the slave Grace, and that it is most valuable on this account" (*HMP*, 124). The "Supplement" reads failure as the primary characteristic of the antislavery present and concludes with a call to action that, to abolitionists in 1831, no longer seemed axiomatic: "NO SLAVE CAN EXIST WITHIN THE SHORES OF GREAT BRITAIN" (*HMP*, 125). The alarming anachronism of slaves on English soil transcended internal divisions over the question of immediate or gradual emancipation that beleaguered the campaign. Abolitionists, Pringle insisted, needed to make England the land of freedom once more. The proslavery counsel in the subsequent libel suit that Wood brought against Pringle sought to "correct" this anachronism and emphasized Prince's freedom according to legal precedent: "a woman of colour named Mary Prince, who is falsely designated a '*West Indian Slave*,' but who is, in fact, a *free* woman residing in London" (*HMP*, 152). This strict construction of the "laws of Englishmen," however, refused to acknowledge the tragic conditions of Prince's status as a "free woman." Her residence "in London" was not a free choice but the legal condition, following *Grace*, of "choice" itself.

Baffled and outraged antislavery advocates such as Pringle questioned how slaves such as Grace and Prince could have chosen freely as liberal subjects when they had to do so from within a condition of profound dependency: "It is true that he has the option of returning, but it is a sad mockery to call it a voluntary choice, when upon his return depend his means of subsistence and his re-union with all that makes valuable" (*HMP*, 124). Enslaved attendants were thus caught in the inexorable grip of legal forms. "Abstracted from legal technicalities," insists Pringle, "there is no real difference between thus compelling the return of the enfranchised negro, and trepanning a free native of England by delusive hopes into perpetual slavery. The most ingenious casuist could not point out any essential distinction between the two cases" (*HMP*, 125). The slave in England "tasted 'the sweets of freedom,' to quote the words of the unfortunate Mary Prince; but if he desires to restore himself to his family, or to escape from suffering and destitution, . . . he must abandon the enjoyment of his late-acquired liberty, and again subject himself to the arbitrary power of a vindictive master" (*HMP*, 124). The cases of Grace and Prince illuminate the duplicity of slaveholders invoking the will and consent of enslaved persons to secure the fiction of "choice" in their reenslavement. "Representations of slave agency," as Saidiya Hartman argues, "intensified the effects of subjugation and dispossession in the guise of will," making it "difficult to imagine a way in which the interpellation of the slave as subject enables forms of agency that do not reinscribe the terms of subjugation."[161] Prince's *History* deconstructs the willfulness imputed to her as a free agent of contractual liberty in England, challenging her misnaming as a free subject with the power to choose freely.

The Woods had brought Prince as a nursemaid and laundrywoman when they relocated the household temporarily to London, where their two daughters attended school. Once in London, the Woods exploited Prince's isolation and dependency to keep her under their power. "I did not know well what to do," admits Prince. "I knew that I was free in England, but I did not know where to go, or how to get my living; and therefore, I did not like to leave the house" (*HMP*, 88).[162] Indeed, the Woods threatened Prince with expulsion whenever she voiced any dissent in England. "Mr. and Mrs. Wood," Prince narrates, "rose up in a passion against me. They opened the door and bade me get out. But I was a stranger, and did not know one door in the street from another, and was unwilling to go away. They made a dreadful uproar, and from that day they constantly kept cursing and abusing me" (*HMP*, 87). Prince refused to work altogether once her rheumatism, aggravated by the cold climate and the Woods' incessant demands, begins to impair her health. In an attempt to coerce her labor, Wood intimidates her with two equally undesirable alternatives: "if I again refused ... to do the whole of the washings," she recalls, "he would either send me down to the brig in the rover, to carry me back to Antigua, or he would turn me at once out of doors, and let me provide for myself" (*HMP,* 87–88).

In the disputes over the legislative petition and the narrative's publication, Wood insisted that Prince left Antigua with the intent to escape in England and fashions her captivity there as a continuing act of rebellion. Wood enlists a legal discourse of personhood, will, and choice to mask the power he continues to exert over her. "I have already told Molly [Mary]," testified Wood, "and now give it to her in writing, in order that there may be no misunderstanding on her part, that I brought her from Antigua at her own request and entreaty, and that she is consequently now free, she is of course at liberty to take her baggage and go where she please" (*HMP,* 96). He creates the illusion of consent in a situation in which there was an absolute impossibility of choice, misrepresenting Prince as a "free" woman given the "liberty" to choose between residence in England and Antigua. Wood perversely insists that she enact the by now ritualized display of choosing without the capacity to select freely from among the proffered options. As in the case of Grace, colonial advocates relied on this idiom of agency and choice to hold Prince accountable for the consequences of a choice she did not make.

Prince insists on her legal manumission when faced with either forced deportation or expulsion from the household. "I said I would willingly go back if he would let me purchase my own freedom," she reports. "But this enraged him more than all the rest: he cursed and swore at me dreadfully, and said he would never sell my freedom—if I wished to be free, I was free in England, and I might go and try what freedom would do for me, and be d——d" (*HMP,* 88). Wood perversely refused to manumit Prince *because* he identified it as her willful desire, her "wish" to be free. His derisive suggestion for Prince to "try what freedom would do for" her reveals the duplicitous meaning of liberty in an Atlantic world where freedom was subject to extreme territorialization. Prince, however, elected to accept his threat at face value: "go where I might, I was determined now to take them at their word" (*HMP,* 88). Her subversive response is part of a much longer pattern of resistance that began in Antigua; throughout the narrative, she draws on the logic of mastery to undermine Wood's proprietary will.[163] Wood repeatedly ordered her to look for another owner: "Not that he meant to sell me; but he did this to ... frighten me." Prince responded by tactically misunderstanding these threats as direct commands (*HMP,* 81). She returned on three occasions with offers to purchase her (from a free black cooper named Adam White, Mr. Burchell, and Captain Abbott), but Wood insisted "that he did not mean to sell" her, even though he sold five other slaves in this period (*HMP,* 81, 85).

Prince's *History* chronicles this performance of submission as a challenge to her master's authority, precisely because "choice" had become, after *Grace*, another means to secure her subjection. Prince recounts a telling exchange with Mrs. Pell, a friend of the Woods, in which Prince again uses the language of servile obedience to authorize her departure. This "is the fourth time," Prince insists, that "my master and mistress have driven me out, or threatened to drive me—and I will give them no more occasion to bid me go. I was not willing to leave them, for I am a stranger in this country, but now I must go—I can stay no longer to be used'" (*HMP,* 89). Thus, Prince's departure is not a voluntary act of "free will." Prince also asks the man who is removing her trunk to witness her obedience to command: "I am going out of this house, as I was ordered, but I have done no wrong at all to my owners, neither here nor in the West Indies.... I told my mistress I was very sick, and yet she has ordered me out of doors. This is the fourth time; and now I am going out" (*HMP,* 90). Prince publicly emphasizes, time and again, her unwillingness to leave the household, as she refashions submission into a challenge and protestation of her enslavement.

The *History* thus offers an understanding of submission that tethered Prince to subjection under the authority of "white people's law" *and* also exceeded it. She first articulates this tactic of compliant noncompliance in the narrative's account of her first mistress, Mrs. Williams: "My obedience to her commands was cheerfully given: it sprung solely from the affection I felt for her, and not from fear of the power which the white people's law had given her over me" (*HMP,* 58). She thereby distinguishes her "obedience" to Williams from that to the Woods, even though they derived their mastery from the same proprietary logic of ownership. This distinction, ever so slight, between "obedience ... from affection" and "obedience ... from fear of ... power" becomes a tactic in her efforts to undermine the authority that the "white people's law" invested in men such as Wood. Each time Prince recounts her performative submission, she calls into question how she, like Grace, continues to be misnamed a free liberal subject with the power to choose.

The antislavery print campaign successfully made the plight of West

Indian slaves such as Prince palpable to people in England, but it did so by emphasizing certain narrative frameworks.[164] Pringle's "Supplement," for example, fashioned Prince's *History* as a powerful illustration of the law's failure to secure British freedom. Such portrayals mobilized the frightening anachronism of slaves in modern England for persuasive effect in their appeals to the "progressive" spirit of Britons. This idiom of failure stressed a political present that was painfully "out of joint" with the glorious traditions of the past as the campaign rallied its membership to forge a future consistent with the past: "No Slaves Can Exist within the Shores of Great Britain."[165] Zachary Macaulay established the *Anti-Slavery Reporter* in 1825 as the official publication of the Anti-Slavery Society, and it sought, among other things, to "exhibit to the view of the British public" the failure of colonial law to arbitrate justice for enslaved people. The *Reporter* condemned colonial magistrates for their "passionate attachment to those vile laws, which shut out the oppressed from all protection against the power and cruelty of the oppressor."[166] Such accounts of ongoing legal failure called on Britons to live up to the national ideals that the campaign had forged in the time of *Somerset*.

Ashton Warner's dictated *Negro Slavery* offers one such critique of the miscarriage of justice as it charts the experiences of an emancipated man kidnapped and illegally reenslaved through the nefarious operation of "the iniquitous *Colonial Law*."[167] Warner's aunt and mother petitioned the chief justice and governor of St. Vincent to no avail: "It is of no use trusting to what the white people in the West Indies say, they always forget their promises to slaves" (*NS*, 22). "Clause after clause has been appended to the slave-code," observed British missionary J.M. Trew after eleven years residence in Jamaica, yet these amelioration acts are legislated "to please the people of England," and "the law, when framed . . . often become obsolete, or a mere dead letter" (*NS*, 97). Pushed to extremes, Warner escaped to England, where he hoped to establish his freedom claim. At the time of the narrative's production, Warner had spent three months in England, although "nothing," he reports, "has been done for me, except that Mr. Wilson's executors have consented to allow me something for subsistence while my case is under investigation. . . . If Mr. Wilson's executors mean to walk right, they will not withhold my freedom from me" (*NS*, 63). His master's representatives, as Strickland's concluding note relates, "cannot, it appears, guarantee Ashton's enfranchisement," which meant that he would be reenslaved upon return to St. Vincent (*NS*, 64). "While he remains in England," Strickland continues, "no doubt he is free; but here he is in danger of utter destitution—is anxiously longing to return to his colonial home and connections" (*NS*, 65).

Warner's fruitless legal struggles found amplification in countless other cases of failed justice in the administration of the "law for bettering the condition of the slaves," cases that filled the columns of the *Anti-Slavery Reporter*.[168] Appeals courts or councils of protection were instituted throughout the British West Indies in the 1820s to enforce the amelioration laws that sought to control, if not abolish, physical coercion of slaves, particularly the whipping of women. Based on the Spanish system of *coartación*, these amelioration acts encouraged planters to move toward emancipation. They established a minimum requirement for food, clothing, and holidays and instructed slaveholders to give slaves religious instruction and protect their marriages and families.[169] The *Anti-Slavery Reporter* drew its accounts from the reports of officers named "Protectors," who were appointed to oversee the complaints that slaves lodged against masters in Demerara, Berbice, Trinidad, St. Lucia, Cape of Good Hope, and Mauritius. These editorialized "Protectors' Reports" extensively catalogue the flagrant violation of the amelioration laws across the West Indies. Almost every case republished in the *Anti-Slavery Reporter* concludes with the "complaint dismissed" against the slave petitioner. The *Anti-Slavery Reporter* juxtaposed these official "catalogues" of injustice with more personalized individual cases, selected, undoubtedly, for their persuasive power, as if in acknowledgment of Elizabeth Heyrick's insight that "[u]nder the contemplation of *individual* suffering ... our compassion is prompt and quick in its movements,—our exertions, spontaneous and instinctive ... in effecting the relief of the sufferer."[170]

The *Anti-Slavery Reporter* thus seized on the St. Kitts case of Betto Douglas to illustrate the law's failure to ameliorate conditions under slavery when colonial courts refused to enforce Douglas's limited rights. Douglas's case, urged the *Anti-Slavery Reporter*, "affords some striking illustrations of the spirit and influence of slavery ... as it operates to subvert and vitiate the best sympathies of our nature, to such an extent as to render slaveholders, generally speaking, unfit to discharge the functions of legislature or of judicature towards enslaved populations."[171] The fifty-two-year-old slave woman entertained hopes of manumission from her absentee slaveholder, only to find her condition infinitely worsened once under the control of his brutal new agent, Mr. Cardin. Douglas brought her case before the colonial courts in 1827 when her petition to the governor failed "to procure her relief and justice."[172] The "unrighteous spirit of the Colonial judiciaries" threw out her charges and further reprimanded her for "wounding" the "feelings of an honourable, humane, and respectable man."[173] Cardin punished her severely for this "great insubordination" and confined the elderly woman to the stocks "for twenty hours in each day, during a period of six months and eleven days."[174] Douglas's predicament illustrated the failure of amelioration laws to secure justice for enslaved persons: "when an attempt is made, by course of law, to relieve this poor creature from such a merciless infliction, the grand jury (to say nothing of the magistracy) . . . [is] roused to 'indignation' by the attempt; stigmatize the prosecution as if it were a public nuisance; and reconsign the wretched Betto to the tender mercies and considerate care of Mr. Cardin."[175] When these legal remedies failed, the Female Society for Birmingham attempted to ransom Douglas, but the application "first to the Proprietor, and then to the Agent on the spot . . . [was] alike unsuccessful."[176] The failure of colonial law thus reconfirmed the moral authority of metropolitan law, even as the cases of Grace and Prince revealed the inequitable contradictions of metropolitan law and reenergized fears over the encroachment of colonial laws on English soil. Indeed, Wood's authority to dictate the terms of Prince's freedom was a terrifying example, as Pringle insisted, of the powerful sway that colonial influence exerted over English sovereignty.

Rosanna's "Rebellious Disposition"

Controversies over the publication of Mary Prince' *History* illuminate how the legal notions of consent and will that shaped the public debates about West Indian emancipation took on a particularly sexualized and gendered cast. Antislavery print culture portrayed enslaved women, such as Douglas and Prince, as the helpless victims of rapacious planters and their corrupt judiciary, while colonialist propaganda insisted on the enslaved women's willful license and immoral agency. Advocates on either side of the "West India Question" made competing claims on behalf of enslaved West Indian women who were cast as either utterly willful (and *not* in need of humanitarian aid and protection) or will-less (and *in* need of humanitarian aid and protection). The construction of enslaved women as innocent victims in the antislavery print campaign stressed their inability to act for themselves as moral justification for metropolitan intervention. Such rhetoric tended to feminize all slaves from the viewpoint of its rescue narrative; for example, in Pringle's "Narrative of Louis Asa-Asa, a Captured African," appended as a "convenient supplement" to all editions of Prince's *History*, Pringle urges readers to throw "the shield of British power over the victim of oppression," casting Asa-Asa as a helpless victim in need of masculine British intervention (*HMP*, 132–33).[177] In this section, I contextualize the public debates about Prince's narrative with accounts from the *Anti-Slavery Reporter* and Robert Wedderburn's autobiographical antislavery writings to explore how enslaved people sought to reelaborate the countervailing legal terms of public debate to fashion themselves as agents. Slave women such as Eleanor Mead, Kitty Hilton, Daphne Crosbie, and Rosanna resisted the moral imperatives of the antislavery campaign as they sought to secure measures of freedom from within colonial slavery.

Pringle drew specific attention in his "Supplement" to the *Reporter's* weekly accounts of a few roughly contemporaneous cases of enslaved West Indian women, with particular reference to Hilton and Mead, to broaden the scope of Prince's claims. These cases, like Prince's narrative, captivated British readers, who turned them into causes célèbres as they devoured the details of the legal disputes, eyewitness reports, and trial testimonies.[178] "These cases alone," Pringle writes, "might suffice to demonstrate the inevitable tendency of slavery as it exists in our colonies, to brutalize the master to a truly frightful degree—a degree which would often cast into the shade even the atrocities related in the narrative of Mary Prince; and which are sufficient to prove . . . that . . . similar deeds are at this very time of frequent occurrence in almost every one of our slave colonies" (*HMP*, 120). As Moira Ferguson observes, the reportage of these cases undoubtedly shaped the form of Prince's narrative.[179] A predominantly white, middle-class audience sympathetic to the antislavery campaign produced, disseminated, and consumed Prince's *History* along with the accounts featured in the *Anti-Slavery Reporter*. Conventional techniques of authentication, including extratextual prefaces, attestations, and appendices, mediated and "framed" the voice of the enslaved subject of the autobiographical narrative.[180] Pringle, for example, claimed to make only the most minimal of textual alterations, even as his self-appointed task of making "legible" Prince's oral testimony also meant making it "clearly intelligible." This dialectic of erasure and exposure shaped the gendered representations found in antislavery print culture, ranging from Prince's *History* and Warner's *Negro Slavery* to the columns of the *Anti-Slavery Reporter*.

The plight of "unprotected slave women" powerfully galvanized British public sentiment against colonial slavery even though the circumstances of their individual cases tended to resist the script of victimized womanhood that antislavery discourse imposed on them. The Female Society for Birmingham, in its sundry "Reports" and "Albums," repeatedly resolved to "awaken ... a deep and lasting compassion" for those "Negro women [who] have none in the land of their captivity to plead for them—that their sighs and groans reach us by no audible sounds." Such "mute and unseen wretchedness," one report concluded, "possessed an irresistible claim to [the] ... sympathies and assistance" of all Britons.[181] Antislavery organizations repeatedly cast slave women as the passive victims of slavery's violence in the effort to rouse public sentiment to action. Other organizations, such as the Ladies Association for Calne, specifically framed their canvassing activities "in behalf of those who are not allowed to speak their own wrongs, nor plead for the restoration of those imprescriptible rights and privileges of which a baneful oppression had deprived them."[182] The failure of colonial courts of law to arbitrate justice for enslaved women such as Grace, Douglas, Hilton, and countless others made legislated emancipation ever more urgent, even as the stories of these women unsettled the gendered narrative of rescue that abolitionists fashioned on their behalf. Readers of the *Anti-Slavery Reporter* were faced with undeniably "quarrelsome" and "provoking" slave women who refused to conform to the existing paradigms of injured and "weakly" womanhood.

The print disputes surrounding the libel suit that Pringle brought against the editor of *Blackwood's Edinburgh Magazine* and that Wood then brought against Pringle for the publication of Prince's *History* exemplify the tenor of the gendered representations at stake. In November 1831, James Macqueen published a letter in *Blackwood's* that purported to expose Prince's *History* as fraudulent. Strickland numbered *Blackwood's* among the "literary periodicals on the side of the planters," and Macqueen was a known agent for the Jamaica planter lobby.[183] Macqueen's inflammatory rhetoric sought to position West Indian slaveholders, beleaguered by recalcitrant slaves and misguided abolitionists, as the most deserving of British sympathy. Such a defense reappropriated the powerful rhetoric of humanitarians such as Pringle to insist on the rights and liberties of West Indian colonists as the "true subjects of the nation."[184] Macqueen's opposition to the Anti-Slavery Society long predated Prince's case, but he seized on the publication of her *History* to vilify further the antislavery campaign. Following Macqueen, Wood embellished the wrongs he suffered to insist that meddlesome abolitionists and slaves such as Prince had violated his natural rights as a "freeborn Briton."[185] He portrayed Prince as a powerfully duplicitous agent who actively sought her freedom in England, while he deserved empathy as the innocent victim of her machinations. In a letter addressed to the governor of Antigua, Wood relates, "In England she made her election and quitted my family.... She has taken her freedom; and all I wish is, that she would enjoy it without meddling with me" (*HMP*, 100–101). Wood endows Prince with a monstrous willfulness as he occupies the position of the powerless in his exaggerated claims that her newfound freedom had come to limit or "meddle" with his own. Indeed, Macqueen ends his purported exposé by inverting the master-slave relation: the West India planter has become, figuratively, the "slave" of Great Britain: "she [Britain] has no right to call on the colonist to become her slaves."[186]

Colonialist propaganda rooted the monstrous agency of enslaved women in their sexuality as it launched an attack on Prince's moral character in its efforts to discredit her allegations. Such depictions appear often in proslavery colonial newsprint in other accounts of enslaved West Indian women. The struggles over Prince's legal status and her petition to return to Antigua as a free woman were tied to the assessment of her character as a woman. She was thus forced into the "paradoxical position," in the words of Jenny Sharpe, of "one who existed outside the structures of domesticity but was expected to uphold its ideals."[187] The public battle that Wood conducted in the transatlantic press after Pringle's publication of the *History* specifically sexualized the implications of Prince's "freedom" in England. He claimed in letters and supporting testimonies published in the *Times*, *Blackwood's Magazine*, and the *Bermuda Royal Gazette* that he "induced her to take a husband" and "gave him the house to occupy during our absence; but it appears the attachment was too loose to bind her" (*HMP*, 100–101). Prince's domestic life in Antigua becomes a construct of Wood's will, for he "induced" her to take a husband, and his recognition of her marriage, disallowed under slave law, further enables him to present Prince as a sexually wayward woman whose immoral license cannot be held in place by the affective bonds of conventional "womanly" sentiment. Wood negatively reinterprets Prince's newfound freedom in terms of a domestic discourse of femininity: she is in essence a "loose" woman scandalously free from the moral constraints of respectable society.

Under cross-examination in *Wood v. Pringle* (1833), Prince acknowledged two sexual relationships that she had had, one with a Captain Abbot and one with a freeman by the name of Oyskman in Antigua. Prince testified that she had "told all this to Miss Strickland when that lady took down her narrative," yet these "statements were not in the narrative published by the defendant," who omitted them from the published text in an effort to cast her as a moral woman (*HMP,* 148).¹⁸⁸ Strickland's editorial tendencies to reframe and omit are also at work in *Negro Slavery*, in which she redirects attention away from the sexualized agency of Warner's aunt toward the young man's struggles to assert his lawful liberty. Warner's autobiographical account describes his aunt's powerful agency in securing the freedom of her kinfolk. Strickland's introduction to *Negro Slavery* draws attention to the "singularly interesting . . . character of his aunt, Daphne Crosbie," who devoted "all her little property to the emancipation of her former companions in bondage," but Strickland refuses to discuss how Crosbie came to acquire her "singular" economic autonomy (*NS,* 14). The narrative informs readers in especially discreet terms how Crosbie "had been a slave, but a favoured one . . . [who] had money left her by a coloured gentleman of the name of Crosbie, with whom she lived, and whose name she took" (*NS,* 17–18). Crosbie later applied the newfound wealth from this sexual liaison—a relationship that she openly avowed in her self-renaming—into the emancipation of her surviving kin from Cane Grove plantation. She purchased the manumission of her aged parents, Plassey and Archibald, her brother John Baptiste, her sister Margaret, and her nephew Ashton. Strickland's reticence was typical of antislavery print culture in response to colonialist attacks on the willful and immoral license of those whom the campaign professed to be most in want of metropolitan intervention.

While overseeing the publication of Prince's *History*, Pringle also involved himself on the behalf of Kitty Hilton, a Jamaican "quadroon slave girl" who had brought a charge of "cruelty and maltreatment" against her master, the Reverend G.W. Bridges. Appalled by what many observers considered a "flagrant violation of the law," Pringle appealed to George Murray, the colonial secretary of state, who in turn advised the attorney general of Jamaica to take up Hilton's case.¹⁸⁹ The *Reporter* chronicled developments in the case over three separate issues as evidence of "the deplorable state of law and manners in Jamaica."¹⁹⁰ Pringle's dogged efforts eventually led to another private petition, which was laid, in the same manner as Prince's, before the House of Commons in 1831. Hilton's case provoked much public outrage in Jamaica and abroad in England.¹⁹¹ Just as Antigua newspapers had represented Wood as the unwitting victim of Prince's monstrous willfulness, Jamaican newsprint held up Bridges "as a grievously persecuted man" and Hilton as the powerful agent of his persecution.¹⁹² The proslavery *Bermuda Royal Gazette* defended Bridges by claiming that "[t]he woman, Kitty Hilton, was proved both by her former, and present owners, to be of notorious bad character and evil propensities." Another account condemned her "constant habit" of running away and alleged that she was "suffering... under a virulent and disgraceful disease" at the time of the trial, in an effort to undermine her credibility, as Wood did in Prince's case, with insinuations of immoral willfulness and sexual license.[193] The *Anti-Slavery Reporter* insisted on Hilton's victimization and offered up her lacerated and battered body as evidence. In its efforts to make enslaved women legible as victims who demanded metropolitan intervention, however, the antislavery campaign was unable to acknowledge how these women themselves contested the terms of their enslavement by being "troublesome."

The *Anti-Slavery Reporter* sought to make these enslaved women fit the campaign's narratives of moral womanhood regardless of their contrary actions. This tendency is perhaps best illuminated in the sensationalized case of Eleanor Mead. Slaveholders recognized slave motherhood in the effort to intensify suffering as they compelled Mead's daughter to assist in the brutal "correction" of her mother. For a petty dispute, Mrs. Earnshaw ordered Mead's daughter Catharine not only to witness the brutal whipping of her mother but also to hold her down "while she was writhing under the lash."[194] Mead later escaped from her fetters and ran away with Catharine to Falmouth to lodge a formal complaint with the magistrate. Mead again ran away and sought the protection of another magistrate when Earnshaw sent her to the workhouse with an order for thirty-nine more lashes, the limit permitted by the current law of Jamaica. Mead's actions were not exceptional. West Indian slave women such as Mead and Hilton often registered their discontent by being "troublesome women." Hilton had also "contrived to be quite at large for several weeks" after she was remanded to the workhouse. These women risked the wrath of white slaveholders to contest the terms of their enslavement through a range of quotidian acts that included physical aggression, running away, and feigning illness.[195] These practices were, in Michel de Certeau's terms, tactics as opposed to strategies, and constituted a kind of politics that resisted the instrumentalizing logic of plantation slavery.[196] These women appealed to the colonial state to enforce their limited rights under the amelioration laws, challenging slaveholders' absolute authority even with the foreknowledge that magistrates rarely ruled in their favor.

The *Anti-Slavery Reporter* returned to Mead's case a few months later, when she was arraigned for assaulting the white overseer James M'Claren, a serious crime that carried penalties of "death, transportation, or confinement to hard labour for life" upon conviction.[197] Reassigned to field labor, Mead had repeatedly refused to "turn out" to the field in a timely manner, because, as the black slave driver Allick Graves testified, "she had several young children, and had to procure breakfast for them." Mead's subsequent actions, however, undercut this narrative of injured motherhood. After receiving a flogging of twenty lashes, Mead "went on in a most violent manner," chased M'Claren over a wall, and "took hold of him round the waist." On reviewing the case, the judge, who had also presided over the previous charge, concurred with the overseer's opinion that Mead was "a very quarrelsome woman" and again discharged her to Earnshaw for "strict justice." The court reporter described Mead as the "personification of the passion of Hate" when she received the unfavorable verdict; she "manifested her turbulent temper" and left the courtroom saying she would "not return to the estate."[198]

The antislavery response, tellingly, stressed the aggression of the overseer while describing Mead as "the most weakly brown woman on the estate."[199] The proslavery *Royal Gazette* originally published the trial account, and the *Anti-Slavery Reporter*'s editorialized reprinting of it sought to mitigate what it perceived as an "unfavorable" portrayal of Mead, which was "doubtless intended to operate unfavourably to the wretched sufferer in the mind of the English reader" but had "very probably, no foundation, except in prejudice, and in the desire to blacken her character, and thus to relieve her persecutors from some of the odium which cannot fail to attach to their conduct, and still more to a state of law and manners such as is here displayed."[200] The *Anti-Slavery Reporter* expressed concern over the impression that a wrathful Mead would make on the "mind of the English reader," fearing that her "blacken[ed] . . . character" would justify both her mistress's repugnant actions and the discredited colonial judicial system. According to this well-intentioned defense of Mead, slaves must be uniformly "victims," and slaveholders the vicious perpetrators of the moral, if not legal, crime of enslavement. Mead's open hostility before the court, even in the name of injured motherhood, destabilizes the master narratives of gendered victimhood that the *Anti-Slavery Reporter* customarily offered its readership. Antislavery print culture often employed the rhetoric of righteous indignation, yet Mead's rage—a passionate eruption of emotions emphasizing its mad or bestial features—set her well beyond the sphere of human sympathy. Her unmediated wrath was evidence of moral failure, and a hateful woman surely did not invite the empathetic identification of Christian readers. The *Anti-Slavery Reporter*, therefore, reframed this rage in the context of powerlessness as it redirected readers from the disturbing image of a combative Mead to the flogging and physical subjugation she suffered at the hand of the overseer. The "assault," it argued in a footnote, "was *his* not hers, as we shall see," even though Mead, by her own admission and witnesses' testimonies, unquestionably attacked M'Claren.

The *Anti-Slavery Reporter* sought to curtail further Mead's threatening, unfeminine agency with the editorialized reprinting of a second account (from the *Jamaica Watchman*) that rooted Mrs. Earnshaw's inexplicable hostility in Mead's sexual appropriation by her master. This claim was by no means improbable given the sexual subjugation of enslaved women within slave society. However, this accusation, with its concomitant trope of the jealous mistress, seems motivated more by a desire to make Mead's story conform to representations of enslaved women as victims than to "investigate" the case thoroughly.[201] This "unfortunate creature," the *Reporter* concludes, "still suffer[s] for a crime, the guilt of which is chargeable upon the man solely, who, taking advantage of her condition, drives her to the commission of a crime."[202] This hypothetical alternative contains Mead's fury within a narrative of sexual subjection to the will of her master: he "drives her" to commit the "crime" for which she now stands accused. Once thus purified of her troublesomeness, Mead offered a powerful indictment of the miscarriage of colonial law, for the 1816 amelioration act "exempted from all hard labour in the field or otherwise ... every female slave who shall have six children living." "This is one of the pretended ameliorating acts of Jamaica," condemned the *Anti-Slavery Reporter*. "We see how it works. It is a dead letter. It was made for England, not for Jamaica."[203] The *Reporter* asked readers to understand Mead's case as a sign of a failed colonial system, for it involved "not particular individuals only, but the whole frame and structure of Jamaica slave law and Jamaica society, in the heavy charge of cruelty and oppression."[204]

Mead's troublesomeness, like the "*rebellious* disposition" of Robert Wedderburn's Jamaican slave mother, Rosanna, largely rejected the moral imperatives of the antislavery campaign. Wedderburn's autobiographical writings offer an unexpected elaboration of Mead's wrathful female agency and will to freedom that refuses to "fit" the narrative of moral womanhood (see figure 1.2). His periodical *Axe Laid to the Root*—a combative collection of exposition, correspondence, verse, and appeal—begins with a forceful autobiographical proclamation that charts his right to freedom back to his enslaved mother.[205] "Be it known to the world," he announces, "that, I Robert Wedderburn, son of James Wedderburn, esq. of Inveresk, near Musselborough, by Rosannah his slave whom he sold to James Charles Shalto Douglas, esq. in the parish of St. Mary, in the island of Jamaica, while pregnant with the said Wedderburn, who was not held as a slave, (a provision made in the agreement, that the child when born should be free)."[206] Wedderburn's stilted legalistic language relates how his enslaved mother brokered his prenatal freedom from the master who fathered him. Rosanna renegotiated the oppressive entanglements of kinship and property under colonial slave law to insist on her unborn child's freedom as a condition of her transfer in ownership. Wedderburn's various writings often returned to this primal memory of his mother. Indeed, his short autobiographical narrative *The Horrors of Slavery*, first published in 1824 as a pamphlet, further enhanced Rosanna's powerful maternal agency and the legacy of freedom she bequeathed him: "At the time of sale, my mother was five months gone in pregnancy; and one of the stipulations of the bargain was, that the child which she bore should be FREE from the moment of its birth. I was that child" (*HS*, 48).

As several critics have noted, Wedderburn's autobiography marked a departure from the radical propaganda that characterized his earlier work, a formal shift often attributed to the momentous visit that abolitionist luminary William Wilberforce paid Wedderburn in 1822 while Wedderburn was imprisoned in Dorchester jail on a charge of blasphemous libel. Wilberforce suggested that he pen an autobiographical account of his life in West Indian slavery to assist the antislavery cause. Wedderburn recalled his pledge to Wilberforce in the narrative's dedication: "When in prison, for conscience-sake, at Dorchester, you visited me, and you gave me—your advice, for which I am still your debtor" (*HS*, 44). Wedderburn complied with the request but felt little need to uphold the moral imperatives of the campaign.[207] *Horrors of Slavery* gives expression to a powerful rage against slavery and its racial proscriptions that overspills the bounds of Wedderburn's debt to Wilberforce. The references to colonial slavery in Wedderburn's writings were far more than political allegories for English wage slavery and political repression, as some scholars have argued.[208]

Rosanna bestowed on Wedderburn her "rebellious disposition," and he embraced the ambivalent legacy of his mother's anger as a powerful rhetorical figure in his autobiographical writings. "My heart glows with revenge," Wedderburn professed in the first issue of *Axe*, "and cannot forgive" (*HS*, 86). Not only does anger tie him to his West Indian past, but it also held out a possible future in which revenge would be fulfilled. Freedom in later U.S. slave narratives also called on this imagined future moment of redress. "The thought of only being a creature of the *present* and the *past*," wrote Frederick Douglass, "troubled me, and I longed to have a *future*—a future

Fig. 1.2. Portrait of Robert Wedderburn in 1824. From *The Horrors of Slavery*. (Courtesy of the British Library Board. All Rights Reserved 8156.c.71.(4), frontispiece)

with hope in it."²⁰⁹ Wedderburn's open expressions of rage, like Cugoano's yearning for retribution, exhibit the messiness of fury along with the eloquence of righteous indignation.²¹⁰ This anger is the symbolic inheritance of his mother, from whom he was parted at the age of four months and "delivered over to the care of [his] grandmother," Talkee Amy, a well-known obeah woman in Kingston (*HS*, 48). His accounts of Rosanna, though marked by a species of gallantry, proffer an understanding of black female agency that was often erased from the petitions, pamphlets, and addresses published and circulated by organized British antislavery. Wedderburn's anger both responds to her loss and enables him to create an alternative genealogy of political radicalization.

Wedderburn's reimagination of his enslaved mother allows him to chart a different trajectory of emancipatory longing and idealism, one that does not emanate from the British metropole: "I have not the least doubt, but that from her rebellious and violent temper during that period, that I have inherited that same disposition—the same desire to see justice overtake the oppressors of my countrymen—and the same determination to lose no stone unturned, to accomplish so desirable an object" (*HS*, 48). This anger becomes a precondition for justice; wrath impels Wedderburn onward in his political radicalism. Like Rosanna, he renegotiates the instrumentalization of motherhood under slave law in the doctrine of *partus sequitur ventrem* (children follow the condition of the mother) to claim her "rebellious and violent temper" as his maternal birthright. With characteristic aplomb, Wedderburn recasts the uniquely nationalized tradition of *British* freedom as issuing from his Jamaican slave mother. Indeed, he ends his first issue of *Axe* with his dual identification as "a West-Indian" and "a lover of liberty" (*HS*, 83).

Wedderburn recounts a visit to Scotland, seven years after his arrival to England, to see his father, James Wedderburn, who held expansive West Indian estates adjoining those of notorious slaveholder Thomas Thistlewood.[211] Wedderburn, then an unemployed journeyman tailor expecting his first child with his wife, Elizabeth Ryan, appealed to his father, who, according to Wedderburn, "had the inhumanity to threaten to send me to gaol if I troubled him" (*HS*, 60).[212] The symbolism of this event was not lost on him, as his later writings chart the turn away from this British paternal legacy to embrace his West Indian maternal birthright. His public estrangement from his white half-brother, Andrew Colville, published in *Bell's Life in London*, again recasts this dynamic of paternal disaffiliation and maternal identification. In an effort to deny Wedderburn's claims of kinship, Colville vilified Rosanna as "a negro woman-*slave*, whom he employed as a cook; this woman had so violent a temper that she was continually quarrelling with the other servants, and occasioning a disturbance in the house" (*HS*, 52). Wedderburn responded with a defense of his "unfortunate mother, a woman virtuous in principle" that openly avowed her "*rebellious* disposition" (*HS*, 58). Unlike the slave women found in the pages of the antislavery print campaign, Rosanna is both virtuous *and* wrathful: "*My dear brother* states that my mother was of violent temper, which was the reason of my father selling her;—yes, and I glory in her *rebellious* disposition, and which I have inherited from her" (*HS*, 59). Wedderburn's maternal legacy of liberty, his angry inheritance, profoundly redraws the geopolitics of freedom that had become, since *Somerset*, coextensive with the borders of Great Britain. His appeals to "countrymen and relatives yet in bondage" reposition his wrathful West Indian slave mother, rather than his debt to abolitionist luminary Wilberforce, as the true wellspring of his political radicalization.

In the hands of a writer such as Wedderburn, wrath became a political legacy that exceeded the moral imperatives of the antislavery campaign and looked forward to a future shaped by the claims of slavery's past. Despite narratives of juridical failure, slave women repeatedly appealed to the law to (in the words of apprentice James Williams) "do justice," as they challenged slaveholders' authority regardless of the consequences. Jenny Sharpe observes that it was not unusual for West Indian slave women to bring charges against slaveholders who violated the amelioration laws; slaveholders generally ignored these laws, and Protectors only loosely enforced them, yet this did not prevent slave women from demanding justice even if they risked punishment by the court or an irritated slaveholder.[213] Wrath exceeds the bounds of moral womanhood and unsettles abolitionist narratives of rescue, issuing a profound challenge to "the laws of Englishmen," in the manner of Cugoano, to arbitrate justice and restitution for the crimes of slavery. The oft-repeated refrain "complaint dismissed" did not dissuade a wrathful Hilton, who risked the whip and workhouse to go before different magistrates until she found one willing to inquire into her charges. Like Prince's *History*, the *Anti-Slavery Reporter* transformed defeat in the courtroom into a powerful form of public advocacy: "If the laws are insufficient to protect the unfortunate slaves from the tyranny of such owners as Mrs. Earnshaw, the press is all-sufficient to expose their conduct, and to hold them up to the detestation of the world."[214] Abolitionists seized on these accounts to illustrate the failure of amelioration laws, but they were less able to acknowledge the furious agency of these women who challenged the conditions of their enslavement even with the foreknowledge that justice was rarely if ever served on "white people's law."[215]

"Do Justice"

> Beloved Countrywomen—Let Slavery disguise itself as it may, it is unutterably, inconceivably bitter. Yes, she may attire herself in the gay garb of a pretended freedom; or she may array herself in the mock garment of a legalised apprenticeship, nevertheless, her heart, true to its nature, whispers that she is Slavery still. The iron of bitterest bondage still enters onto the soul of her victim, and though he lives, it is but to drag out a hated existence.
> —Catharine Elizabeth Alma, "Second Appeal from the Dublin Ladies Association," 26 October 1837

When the Sheffield Female Anti-Slavery Society dissolved in 1833, following the passage of the Abolition Act, it did so with some regret: "England, in her legislative capacity ... has not dared to right. She has shrunk, not from the terrors of a servile insurrection, but before the influence of a handful of Planters. Let her come down from her lofty throne, and lay her triumphant laurels at their feet."[216] A number of transatlantic abolitionists saw emancipation as the continuation of slavery in the "garb of pretended freedom" rather than the crowning triumph of over fifty years of antislavery campaigning. These critiques of apprenticeship harked back to the ways slaveholders had sought, in Hargrave's word, to "disguise" their slaves as servants within English law. Apprenticeship was a political compromise between the immediate emancipation that abolitionists demanded and the indefinite perpetuation of slavery that West India planters desired. Emancipation provided for the immediate abolition of legal slavery, as Thomas Holt notes, to be followed by a period of apprenticeship during which ex-slaves were required to work for their former masters in return for their customary allowances of food, clothing, housing, and medical care.[217] Emancipation also marked the generational transfer of organized antislavery with the passing of "nearly all the leading advocates of emancipation."[218] Pringle, the *Liberator* respectfully noted, "lived only just long enough to hear of the passing of that Act which has proved, or rather will prove the consummation of his labors."[219] The victory was rather bittersweet for some abolitionists, as the horizon of freedom was yet again deferred. As the odd temporal slippage of the *Liberator*'s eulogy reveals, apprenticeship became yet another failed present with the passage of the Abolition Act, "which has proved, or rather will prove the consummation" of freedom throughout the British Empire.

A younger generation of radical humanitarians led by Birmingham Quaker Joseph Sturge continued the unfinished campaign for universal black freedom. Sturge founded the Agency Committee (1831) and the Central Negro Emancipation Committee (1837), which became the longstanding British and Foreign Anti-Slavery Society after the end of apprenticeship in the West Indies. Sturge reshaped the metropolitan crusade for West Indian emancipation into the antiapprenticeship campaign in ways that presaged the direction later taken by organized transatlantic campaigns against U.S. slavery. In 1836, he traveled to the West Indies with fellow abolitionists Thomas Harvey, William Lloyd, and John Scoble to investigate the system firsthand.[220] Sturge engineered the manumission of apprentice James Williams while in Jamaica and returned with him to England with the intent of publishing his autobiographical testimony for the antiapprenticeship campaign. A short pamphlet of twenty-four pages entitled *A Narrative of Events, Since the First of August, 1834, by James Williams, an Apprenticed Labourer in Jamaica* was published in London and Glasgow and sold for one penny in June 1837.[221]

Williams's *Narrative*, the only extant West Indian account of the apprenticeship system, played a key role in the successful British campaign to end apprenticeship in August 1838, two years earlier than had been envisaged by the Abolition Act.[222] The Agency Committee constellated itself around the publication of Williams's *Narrative*, which was one of its most powerful political tracts against the apprenticeship system. Impressed with what Seymour Drescher describes as the "vastness of unfreedom," the Central Negro Emancipation Committee advocated the kind of universal and, indeed, global freedom that transformed British abolitionism into a world human rights movement. Williams's *Narrative* thus marks the end of the earlier British campaign for abolition and the beginning of the transatlantic campaign to end slavery throughout the Americas. Political imperatives dictated the form of Williams's *Narrative*, yet his account, like those of Cugoano and Prince, issues a cry for justice that lies beyond the scope of legislated freedom. After Williams told Sturge all about his "bad living" as an apprentice, Williams recalls, "Mr. Sturge tell me, me mustn't discourage, that it only to last seventeen months out" (*NE*, 24). Angered by Sturge's initial attempt to conciliate him to apprenticeship, Williams offered a sharp and effective retort: "I tell him, I don't know if I can live to see the seventeen months out" (*NE*, 24). This exchange augured later tensions between the two. Uneasy over the growing public attention paid to the young ex-apprentice, Sturge returned Williams to Jamaica just four months after the publication of his *Narrative*.

Sturge arrived in Jamaica in January 1837, first meeting the eighteen-year-old apprentice on Penshurst Plantation, a moderate-sized pimento (allspice) plantation belonging to the siblings Gilbert William Senior and Sarah Jane Keith Senior. Sturge engineered Williams's manumission and, after they arrived in England, immediately set him to work with Archibald Palmer to produce the *Narrative*. To better demonstrate the "self-evident proof" of the *Narrative*'s "fidelity," Sturge and his colleagues "deemed it better to preserve his [Williams's] own peculiar style, rather than by any attempt at revision" (*NE*, 3). Williams's *Narrative*, unlike the dictated narratives of Prince and Warner, was written in an anglicized form of Jamaican Creole or patois. The densely printed *Narrative*, according to Diana Paton, sold well, and newspapers in England and Jamaica reprinted it; seven slightly different editions were in concurrent circulation by 1838.[223] Its wide dissemination, as the *Falmouth Post* observed from Jamaica, "created a considerable sensation in England" (*NE*, 121). William Lloyd Garrison's *Liberator* reported the stereotyping of Williams's *Narrative* along with J.A. Thome and J.H. Kimball's *Emancipation in the West Indies* for "universal circulation" with an initial publication run of "TEN THOUSAND COPIES of each work."[224] Abolitionists on both sides of the Atlantic used Williams's *Narrative* to campaign for "the extinction of the system" of apprenticeship in England's colonies in the West Indies, Cape Colony, and Mauritius. Thomas Price supplied the prefacing "Advertisement" and postscripts that reanimated tropes of black victimization from the earlier campaign into a call for the immediate end of apprenticeship: "will the people of England, permit the deeply injured, the helpless, the unoffending negro, still to remain the victim of such accumulated misery and brutal outrage?" Present failure demanded the reestablishment of those defunct antislavery organizations: "Let our anti-slavery Societies be immediately re-organized—let the country be aroused—let the people, with one voice, instruct their representatives peremptorily to demand the instant, the unconditional, and the everlasting annihilation of the accursed system" (*NE*, 26).

Williams's prompt return to Jamaica, possibly against his wishes, emphasizes the largely symbolic function that he served in the metropolitan campaign to end apprenticeship. It also illustrates the way the abolitionist imaginary constituted freed blacks as morally obligated and indebted persons. The proplanter *Jamaica Despatch* hinted at the underlying reasons that prompted Williams's sudden return to Jamaica: "Is it not, however, rather singular that Friend Sturge, with his boasted philanthropy, should have so soon become tired of his *protégé*" (*NE*, 123). Sturge stressed in private communications how exposure to British freedom had wrought a baneful effect on Williams's moral character: "all the attention that James Williams has attracted, has . . . produced an unfavourable effect upon him" (*NE*, 97). Williams was not using his freedom in the specific ways that Sturge had imagined; he was not yet morally fit for the unlimited freedom of England. "[A]lthough he perhaps behaves as well as I ought to expect," Sturge continued, "I find him going on so very far from satisfactory that I believe it will be the kindest thing to him or at least by far the best chance for him to escape complete ruin to send him back as soon as I can" (*NE*, 97). Sturge soon concluded that "the only means of bringing him to a proper sense of situation is for him to be compelled to labour for his bread" and that the "dread of falling into the hands of those from whom he suffered so much may be a good check upon him" (*NE*, 98).[225] His decision to return Williams to Jamaica confirmed the prevailing anxieties, to be articulated in Thomas Carlyle's satirical "Occasional Discourse on the Negro Question" (1849), that black West Indians were incapable of exercising their freedom properly, a stagist theory of history that deemed people of African descent "*not yet* civilized enough to rule themselves."[226]

Sturge's anxieties betray the unstated mechanisms of power that had long shaped the relations between British humanitarians and the slaves and apprentices fortunate enough to receive their assistance. Orators and writers preferred to invoke Williams as a figure for the appalling degradation perpetrated on apprentices throughout the British West Indies rather than to deal with the actual man.[227] The needs of the "cause" also powerfully shaped the form of Williams's autobiography, which was limited to the three years since apprenticeship had begun. Sturge fended off attempts to discredit the *Narrative*'s claims, as with Prince, through the vilification of Williams's moral character. Fearing that colonial interests would entice Williams to "contradict his story by some means or another," Sturge transferred him to Kingston with directions that "if he can be kept out of harms way the next 6 or 8 months even if he should turn out an indifferent character afterwards the *cause* might not suffer by it; with this view it may be well to bear with a little indiscretion or indolence in him for a time than cast him off at once" (*NE*, 98, 100). Williams's unruliness was tolerated only for the sake of the campaign. Sturge impatiently awaited the judgment of the colonial commission convened to investigate the *Narrative*'s charges to dispel the danger that Williams's immoral conduct now posed to the "cause."

The governor of Jamaica, Sir Lionel Smith, began an investigation of Williams's allegations after he received the copy of the *Narrative* that Sturge sent to the Colonial Office. Smith's Commission of Inquiry directed two magistrates to "ascertain the truth of the Allegations contained in the said Pamphlet of James Williams," and the commission opened its public proceedings on 20 September 1837 (*NE*, 47–48). Over the following three weeks, magistrates John Daughtrey and George Gordon heard evidence from over 120 apprentices as they investigated twenty-two other cases of abuse in addition to the charges alleged in Williams's *Narrative*. John Castello, a free man of color and the editor of the abolitionist-friendly *Falmouth Post*, published the only extant record of the evidence in a 119-page pamphlet, which was later appended to subsequent editions of the *Narrative*, creating, as Diana Paton observes, one of the most substantial collections of first-person testimonies by once-enslaved West Indians.[228] This re-formed heteroglossic text reveals, in rich detail, how the new apprenticeship laws affected the lives of ex-slaves and how they made use of these laws to challenge the authority of individual slaveholders.

Castello's record stylistically transformed the individual testimonies solicited under questioning into first-person monologues and removed traces of the apprentices' Jamaican Creole or patois. In the new sixpence edition of Williams's *Narrative*, the exculpatory results of the commission's investigation replaced Price's introductory "Advertisement," and Castello's record followed the narrative.[229] Castello's densely printed fifty-page evidentiary *Minutes of Proceedings at Brown's Town, St. Ann's* thus becomes a sequel to an autobiography that ends conventionally with the reanimated trope of freedom on English soil. Earlier editions of the narrative conclude, "Mr. Sturge take me with him on board the ship, and we go to New York, and then sail to Liverpool and so here I am in England" (*NE*, 25). The new edition exceeds this earlier metropolitan frame by returning readers, along with Williams, to Jamaica, and multiplying his individual account, in dizzying fashion, across a range of perspectives and voices. This edition also reformatted Williams's *Narrative* with a system of notational signs "for the purpose of giving the Reader an idea of the questions proposed to Mr. Senior and the other witnesses, by the Commissioners of Inquiry." The book thereby insists on a reading practice that oscillates between the *Narrative* and the trial testimonies. The supplementary materials, with their array of witness reports, challenge the representational function of Williams's narrative. Williams, too, eludes containment to his mediated *Narrative*, as he reappears—alternately kind, brave, and provoking—in Castello's trial testimonies. True to this extensively re-formed document, the multivocal evidence given before the inquiry did indeed vindicate Williams's claims; the two magistrates reported in late October that "the allegations of James Williams's narrative have received few and inconsiderable contradictions, whilst every material fact has been supported and corroborated by an almost unbroken chain of convincing testimony" (*NE*, 86).[230]

Williams's narrative testified to the fact that apprenticeship did not improve the lives of ex-slaves, and it was, in many ways, more punitive than the slavery that preceded it. These new laws shifted the mechanisms of social control from individual masters and overseers to the state in the effort to regularize and, therefore, humanize the "correction" of laborers. Apprenticeship conferred limited legal rights on formerly enslaved persons, yet it also produced new forms of violence in its wake. Overseers, masters, and the workhouse superintendent, for example, exploited the immediate freedom that the emancipation bill conferred on slave children to further oppress their apprenticed kinfolk. The corrupt workhouse superintendent refused women apprentices the liberty to nurse their hungry infants, citing the fact that "the children free, and the law don't allow no time to take care of them" (*NE*, 16–17). Janette Saunders from Orange Valley plantation was sent to the workhouse for "not delivering her free child to the overseer to let it work" (*NE*, 21). Enslaved children under the age of six (as of August) became free in 1834. These emancipated children could be apprenticed to work for planters with a mother's permission, although few in Jamaica gave their consent. "I hear," Williams continues, "that many people begin to talk that the free child no have no right to stop on the property, and that they will turn them off if the mothers don't consent to let them work" (*NE*, 21). Jane Shaw Pennock, an apprentice on Penshurst, reports that Senior removed the woman who minded the children while the apprentice mothers worked the pimento fields in the great gang. According to her testimony, "massa said that the children were born free, and he was not going to give them any nurse as they were born free and did not deserve any mercy" (*NE*, 66). The legal recognition of slave humanity and limited rights again ushered in new forms of violence.

The centralization of the mechanisms of punishment and discipline, as Williams's *Narrative* repeatedly demonstrates, worsened the living conditions of the ex-slave population. "I have been very ill treated by Mr. Senior and the magistrates since the new law come in," Williams reports:

"Apprentices get a great deal more punishment now than they did when they was slaves; the master take spite, and do all he can to hurt them before the free come" (*NE,* 5). The new system made it illegal for slaveholders to punish apprentices directly, as it transferred this power to the state in the form of stipendiary magistrates.[231] Apprenticeship law required all appointed magistrates to visit estates with forty or more apprentices every two weeks to hear complaints. These magistrates assumed the role of masters in the enforcement of work discipline, and their punishments ranged from fines in the form of extra labor, imprisonment in plantation dungeons or parish workhouses, and flogging (supposedly for men only).[232] Additionally, drivers and free blacks were recruited as constables and assigned to plantations to assist magistrates in maintaining order. Williams's *Narrative,* in consequence, recasts the struggles between master and slave into the complex conflicts between apprentice and various state representatives, including policemen who administered the floggings and corrupt magistrates who did not allow apprentices to defend themselves against false accusations. "When I was a slave I never flogged," Williams reports, "but since the new law begin, I have been flogged seven times, and put in house of correction four times" (*NE,* 5). Magistrates who were charged with ensuring that apprentices worked assumed in the minds of apprentices the punitive roles once occupied by masters and head drivers.[233]

The expanded editions of Williams's *Narrative* illuminate the way people who were once enslaved continued to use the law to challenge the terms of apprenticeship and its centralization of the master's power in the colonial state. Angered by Williams's public recitation of wrongs, Senior condemned the *Narrative* in letters addressed to various Jamaican newspapers; these letters emphasized how Williams regularly sought out legal means to challenge Senior's authority and the terms of his apprenticeship. On the first of August 1834, when the emancipation bill went into effect, Williams went before Special Magistrate Captain Connor, who "told him the law" (*NE,* 105). Senior described what happened next: "[Williams] told me he had been with Captain Connor, who ... had told him the law, and that he would not be imposed upon" (*NE,* 107). Other apprentices, such as Ann Campbell, also made use of the law's redistribution of power to challenge their master's authority. Senior had appointed Campbell—whom he described as "an old weakly woman, apparently about sixty years of age"—as driver of the "little gang" composed of children. When called on to testify, Campbell stated, "master told me when they behaved wrong, I must switch them; I said no! I could not do it. As the Law would not give me right if I switched any body; I told him that if he wanted the children to be switched, he must carry them to them mammies and let them switch them" (*NE*, 64). In the manner of Prince, Campbell refused to obey Senior's orders by deferring to higher authority of the "Law," but she also affirmed maternal authority, previously denied under the law of slavery, as the proper site for the children's correction. Senior rightly understood this deference to the "Law" as a pretence to challenge his authority and took the opportunity to punish Campbell with her own words: "I said to the driver, that I wanted to go aside for a particular purpose, but when master heard it he cried out, 'There was not law for that'" (*NE*, 64). Campbell again called on the law when her mistress ordered another apprentice to punish her: "No! he could not do so, as the law did not tell him to do any things like that."[234] The limited rights of the apprenticeship system created a number of contradictions in the lives of people who were once enslaved. Apprentices such as Campbell and Williams adapted the new laws into a tactic of everyday resistance as they purposively invoked laws fashioned to punish them, albeit in more regularized and thus "humane" ways, in order to contest the authority of masters and mistresses.

Williams resisted his construction as a helpless victim in antislavery print culture, even as he actively participated in the campaign's efforts to end West Indian apprenticeship. He resisted the conditions of his apprenticeship by running away, appealing to magistrates in the manner of Douglas, Hilton, and Mead, and challenging them to "do justice" by him.[235] Risking the whip and workhouse, Williams ran away from Penshurst plantation for a fifty-day period after repeated punishments doled out by an unjust magistrate: "he refuse to hear me or my witness; would not let me speak" (*NE*, 6).[236] Fearing another unwarranted punishment by the magistrate, Williams took matters into his own hands: "I go away to Spanish Town to see the governor. . . . I stop about seven weeks, and then go back to Spanish Town" (*NE*, 9). Williams again ran away when Senior swore "very vengeance against" him on a second occasion, and he made his way to "complain to the governor," only to be taken up and confined in the workhouse again. This unwarranted sentence was extended another week over Christmas when an indignant Williams openly challenged magistrate Rawlinson "to do justice 'twixt I and massa" (*NE*, 19). In another instance, Williams successfully invoked the apprenticeship laws as a deterrent to Senior's threat of physical violence: "I said, you can't lick me down, Sir, the law does not allow that, and I will go complain to magistrate if you strike me" (*NE*, 13). This confrontation, set as it is within the context of a larger, plantation-wide refusal to labor according to Senior's orders, attests to the various ways apprentices sought to invoke their newly conferred rights to dictate the terms of their labor. Like Equiano, Cugoano, Hilton, and Mead before him, Williams used the legal mechanisms available to him to secure his freedom even while well aware of the contradictions within the "laws of Englishmen" that continually deferred and qualified that freedom. Williams's repeated accusation "You don't do justice" offers a proleptic challenge that haunted later constellations of organized transatlantic abolitionism and their cultural narratives of "lawful liberty" well after the legislated end of slavery (*NE*, 18–19).

2

Choosing Kin in Antislavery Literature and Law

The slaves themselves are the original abolitionists; the story of their wrongs has simply made us their advocates at the bar of public opinion.

—William G. Hawkins, *Lunsford Lane; or, Another Helper from North Carolina*, 1863

Like many southern travelers, North Carolina Whig congressman Samuel Tredwell Sawyer, the equivocal "Mr. Sands" of Harriet Jacobs's *Incidents in the Life of a Slave Girl* (1861), brought his slave John S. Jacobs to attend him on his 1838 wedding journey from Washington City to Chicago. Sawyer, aware of the growing antislavery activism targeting slaves brought into free states, directed Jacobs as they crossed from slaveholding Baltimore into free Philadelphia, "Call me Mr. Sawyer; and if anybody asks you who you are, and where you are going, tell them that you are a free man, and hired by me."[1] Once in New York City, Jacobs slipped away from the popular Astor House Hotel and boarded a boat headed to New Bedford, Massachusetts.[2] The London *Leisure Hour* serialized his "True Tale of Slavery" in the same year that his sister Harriet self-published her autobiographical narrative (*IL*, 219).[3] John Jacobs's satirical version of the "escape" had long been a part of his rhetorical repertoire on the antislavery lecture circuit. One auditor was particularly entertained by his "witty allusions to the love he used to bear his old master, a North Carolina lawyer, and a member of Congress, and by his playful remarks upon the manner he escaped from bondage."[4] Sawyer was unable to accept Jacobs's agency in what was undoubtedly an act of self-emancipation, and he returned to Edenton stubbornly confident that meddlesome abolitionist "rascals" had "decoyed" away his slave, who would soon return (*IL*, 134, 220). The intricately intertwined journeys of Harriet and John S. Jacobs toward liberation and autonomy chart a far more complex story of freedom in and through travel than has yet been told.

Harriet Jacobs remained confined in their grandmother's suffocating crawlspace for another four years until certain of her children's safety before she too risked escape in 1842. She reunited with her kin on free soil but lived in constant fear of recapture as a fugitive slave. Her children and brother, however, did not share her dread, for they had been brought into the North, legally, with a master's consent. *Commonwealth [of Massachusetts] v. Aves* (1836), the most forceful application of *Somerset v. Stewart* (1772) in U.S. courts, determined in legal theory if not always in practice the emancipation of slaves such as John Jacobs who had not, like Harriet, "run from any Slaveholding State, being brought into the Free States by his master" (*IL*, 191). Dogged by fears of recapture on U.S. soil, Harriet Jacobs agreed to travel to England as the domestic servant of recently widowed Nathaniel Parker Lewis, a popular writer for the *New York Mirror*, *Graham's Magazine*, and *Godey's Lady Book* noted for his amusing travel sketches. Lewis's writings, however, make no mention of his young daughter Imogen's nursemaid, a North Carolina fugitive who accompanied them on many of their travels in the United States and abroad.[5]

In an unmistakable allusion to *Somerset v. Stewart*, Harriet Jacobs positions the "pure, unadulterated freedom" of the "Old World" against the "strange stagnation in our Southern towns," when she returned to Boston to discover "renewed invitations" from her self-professed "mistress and friend" Mrs. Daniel Messmore (née Mary Matilda Norcom) to "come home voluntarily" (*IL*, 187). These "invitations" disguised coercion in the language of solicitous concern: "Should you prefer to come home, we will do all that we can to make you happy" (*IL*, 172). Invitations generally imply a measure of choice (either to accept or to decline), but Jacobs's choice in this instance is a fiction, the rhetorical effect of a threat euphemistically rendered as a counterfactual suggestion: "If you come, you may, if you like" (*IL*, 187).[6] Jacobs knew quite well that return "home" also meant return to slavery, and the letter only confirmed that Messmore, facing beleaguered finances, had awaited Jacobs's return to U.S. soil to resume pursuit of her valuable human "property."[7] Such "invitations" vouchsafed no refusal after the 1850 Fugitive Slave Act enabled southerners such as Messmore to enter free jurisdictions and demand federal assistance in the recapture of their fugitive slaves (*IL*, 186–87). Jacobs suffered under this threat of recapture until her northern mistress, Cornelia Grinnell, brokered, explicitly against her wishes, her legal freedom through the American Colonization Society. Harriet and John S. Jacobs's compulsory routes of travel and flight illustrate the way the legal culture of travel both shaped and unsettled the geopolitics of slavery and freedom in the states north of Mason-Dixon.

Slaveholders had assumed the right to travel freely in the North without risking their slave property until the landmark case of *Commonwealth v. Aves*. By the 1830s, antislavery activists had begun to argue that the unrestricted travel of slaveholders allowed, in practice, the "introduction" of slavery into free states.[8] States such as New York and Pennsylvania, for example, offered traveling slaveholders the protection of sojourner laws until 1841 and 1847, respectively, and New Jersey granted them unlimited rights of travel and sojourn until 1865.[9] Massachusetts, through the powerful agency of the racially integrated Boston Female Anti-Slavery Society (BFASS), pioneered the rejection of this right to free travel as it instigated freedom suits on behalf of slaves brought into the state, beginning with *Aves*.[10] Sawyer's precautionary demand that John Jacobs masquerade as a "free man" indicates the increasing adoption of the *Aves* precedent—through court cases, legislation, and constitutional provisions—in other northern states. Statistics of freedom suits vary among the different free states and are difficult to determine given that many of these suits did not make their way before higher courts or into court reports. Those cases that we can trace, however, chart the struggles of jurists, slaveholders, freedmen, and abolitionists as they confronted the predicament of slaves in free states. Was the slave free by virtue of travel on northern soil, or did slave law "follow" the slave into a free jurisdiction?

This chapter reconstructs a number of these cases drawn from popular literature, pamphlets, magazines, law journals, newspapers, and casebooks to explore what abolition's liberal ideology was unable to assimilate. It places key historical figures known within the chronicles of U.S. antislavery—such as Maria Weston Chapman, Ellis Gray Loring, Lemuel Shaw, William Still, Sojourner Truth, and Passmore Williamson—alongside many lesser-known slave petitioners—including Anson, Betty, Catharine Linda, and Med—whose stories lived and quickly died in the ephemerality of newsprint. By examining the complex ways in which legal discourses circulating in antebellum newspapers constituted the agency and subjectivity of slave petitioners, this chapter offers a more critical and historically embedded understanding of the freedom so commonly celebrated in the fugitive slave narrative. The genre's paradigmatic *Narrative of the Life of Frederick Douglass* (1845), for example, charts the enduring physical and psychological struggles of a lone male slave to remake himself, at all costs, into an autonomous free black subject. William Andrews contends, in his influential *To Tell a Free Story*, that freedom is indeed the "theme and goal of life" in the slave narrative.[11] What kinds of critical lacunae have such hermeneutics created, what obstacles to identifying other texts of resistance and agency, especially given the "recovery" of slave voices in early African American literary studies? Although feminist literary scholars and historians have addressed, in various ways, the sexual ideologies created and sustained under slavery and slave women's fictions of self-fashioning, there is still a dearth of work that, in Jenny Sharpe's words, "tell[s] a gendered story of slavery."[12]

Traveling slaveholders responded to the perceived attacks of freedom suits on their slave property with a range of defensive tactics: from countersuits, as in the sensational charges that Col. John Hill Wheeler brought against Philadelphia abolitionists Passmore Williamson and William Still, to the selective acknowledgment of their slaves' humanity for use against them. The construction of black subjectivity within antebellum jurisprudence and cultural productions, as Saidiya Hartman reminds us, was premised on forms of domination that subordinated *and* constituted the partial humanity imputed to enslaved men and women.[13] Indeed, beleaguered slaveholders recognized slave kinship in informal and complex ways to ensure the return of their slave attendants, binding those slaves to slavery with those tenuous social attachments that helped buffer them from brutalization. The thought that "there was my sister and a friend . . . at home in slavery," recalls John Jacobs, was the *only* misgiving that seriously tested his resolve to leave Sawyer once in the North.[14] The journey to liberation and autonomy demanded such fundamental losses from the freedom seeker. While John Jacobs had to forgo these ties to remake himself into a free subject, a number of slave attendants, often women and children, refused to accept the terms of such a compromised freedom.[15] For these latter, reluctant beneficiaries of antislavery activism, northern travel threatened an unwanted severance from people and place—unexpectedly, in the guise of liberal benevolence. Antislavery organizations such as BFASS found themselves baffled by slave petitioners who stubbornly refused to relinquish kin for the "gift" of northern freedom. These freedom suits present a counternarrative both to the abolitionist plotting of freedom and to the conventionally masculine paradigms of resistance proffered by the criminal agency of fugitive flight. They challenge the masculine trajectory of fugitive individualism found in the slave narrative genre and illustrate the complex ways in which enslaved women and children negotiated the unexpected predicaments that the law of freedom created in their lives.

Slave Children before Massachusetts Courts

"Hot weather brings out snakes and slaveholders," remarked Harriet Jacobs in reference to the prosperous planters who "swarmed" on northern towns seeking escape from the sweltering miasma of summers south of Mason-Dixon (*IL,* 174). Like many slaveholders, Mary Slater made the long but increasingly affordable journey from New Orleans to Boston to visit her father, Thomas Aves, in 1836. Slater left her six-year-old slave girl, Med, in her father's custody when she left on a short trip to nearby Roxbury, "with the understanding, that when she returns to New Orleans, she will take the child with her."[16] The racially integrated Boston Female Anti-Slavery Society, during Slater's absence, instigated a lawsuit against Aves for restraining Med against her will. The figure of the slave child Med, like the sentimentalized figures of Harriet Beecher Stowe's Evangeline St. Clare or Louisa May Alcott's Beth March, stimulated a range of powerful emotions on the part of BFASS, which authorized its reform-based activism in the name of social mothering and republican motherhood.[17] *Commonwealth v. Aves* was initially brought before Judge Samuel Wilde, who, in acknowledgment of its significance, continued it one week later before the full court. Chief Justice Lemuel Shaw, known to many people as the father-in-law of writer Herman Melville, presided over the Massachusetts Supreme Court that heard the case.[18] Local newspapers carried detailed accounts of Med's case, and soon thereafter, Isaac Knapp, copublisher with William Lloyd Garrison of the *Liberator,* collected the complete arguments of the antislavery counsels, the writ of habeas corpus, and Shaw's opinion into the pamphlet *Report of the Arguments of Counsel, and of the Opinion of the Court, in the Case of Commonwealth v. Aves* (1836).[19]

Such legal pamphlets, predominantly written and published by people with abolitionist sympathies, performed certain forms of cultural work within the broader abolitionist project as they helped to constitute and shape the public knowledge of these rulings and the reception of slave petitioners as freedom seekers. They were central to the political work of literary abolitionism, as they educated "the American public about the specific points of law at issue in slavery's legal controversies," although political imperatives ensured that they told only certain kinds of stories.[20] Abolitionists Henry Ingersoll Bowditch, W.F. Channing, and Frederick S. Cabot, for example, published the triweekly *Latimer Journal and North Star* during the two-week trial of fugitive slave George Latimer in 1842, but they discontinued it once they brokered Latimer's legal manumission; the *Latimer Journal* had served its political purposes. It was not uncommon for abolitionists such as Bowditch, Channing, and Cabot to channel, as Jeannine DeLombard argues, "Americans' passion for legal spectatorship into support for their cause."[21]

The abolitionist print campaign was particularly fascinated with Med's case. The litigation in *Commonwealth v. Aves* precariously balanced the questions of choice and coercion, freedom and enslavement, kinship and alienation in unexpected ways that were profoundly different from the popular fugitive slave narratives of the day. Med's freedom rested on the key distinction between voluntary and involuntary mobility as it mapped ontology onto geography in a manner that, paradoxically, stripped the slave of social agency. Whereas the Constitution's fugitive slave clause, enforced through legislation passed in 1793 and 1850, fixed fugitive flight as a crime punishable by recapture and rendition, there existed no comparable regulations on those slaves who traveled to free jurisdictions with a master's consent. The slave became free, according to the legal reasoning in Med's case, because of the actions of the master or mistress rather than those of the slave. Although by definition the slave had no legal rights, freedom suits proceeded on the tacit assumption that the slave petitioner was a free individual, even though legal freedom depended on the successful outcome of the case at hand. Legal procedure in both free *and* slave states was thus forced to misname the slave petitioner as a free person in order to preserve the logic of liberal jurisprudence. Northern courts, as a matter of legal form, renamed Med as a willful free person once she was brought onto free soil, even as they enforced the chattel principle of slavery against fugitive slaves such as George Latimer and Harriet Jacobs.

Celebrated abolitionist lawyer Ellis Gray Loring strategically argued that Med was *not* a fugitive slave. Med had not traveled *to* Boston with the intent to escape. She was, however, detained *in* Boston against her will, an argument based on the popular antislavery interpretation of *Somerset v. Stewart* that travel on free soil had emancipated her. In other words, the antislavery counsel had first to prove that Med was will-less (as a traveling slave attendant) in order to assert her willfulness (as a free subject) in accordance with many free states' personal liberty laws. These statutes, effective in some form in most northern states in the period 1780–1861, were designed to protect freed blacks in free jurisdictions from kidnapping and forcible reenslavement. Med's petition was eventually successful precisely because, unlike the fugitive with a fixed criminal will, she had been subject to another's will to travel. Such contestations over traveling slaves largely redeployed the legal logic set in the infamous *State [of North Carolina] v. Mann* (1829), which defined the slave as "one who has no will of his own; who surrendered his will in implicit obedience to that of another."[22] The slave as an extension of the master's will was the sine qua non of antebellum slave law.[23] Loring's argument developed logically from this proslavery doctrine as he represented Med's mobility as an extension of her mistress's will to travel. Shaw based his judgment on this distinction and held Slater responsible for freeing Med.

Med's well-documented case illuminates the uncertain geopolitical limits of freedom. Traveling slaves such as Med and John S. Jacobs were caught between freedom and bondage, and their indeterminate status—neither fugitive nor free—reflects the countervailing tendencies within a legal culture that sought to reconcile slave law with the emergent "law of freedom" in the North. In its coverage of *Aves*, the black newspaper *Colored American* stressed Loring's rather peculiar clarification of "willfulness": "a slave brought into the state *voluntarily* by the master, is free—The master cannot take him back, *without his consent*."[24] However, Chief Justice Shaw's judgment extended freedom neither to fugitive slaves such as Latimer and Jacobs nor to slave attendants who *voluntarily* returned to slave states.[25] Med's status as a minor who was too young "to have any will or give any consent" by point of law further troubled such countervailing fictions of slave will. Antislavery organizations such as BFASS often cited the youthful naiveté of their child petitioners as justification to intercede on their behalf as they endorsed litigation that, as in Med's case, blurred the legal distinction between children and adults.[26]

Loring skillfully finessed this legal quandary by offering a compelling counterfactual claim that emphasized antislavery politics over a longstanding principle of interstate comity or legal reciprocity. Loring rhetorically inferred Med's *unwillingness* to return with her mistress: "If she were able to form an intelligent wish, we are bound to presume she would prefer freedom to slavery."[27] This counterfactual invocation of Med's "wish" also recalls Messmore's similarly structured "invitation" to Harriet Jacobs: "If you come, you may, if you like." Formed by negation, counterfactual statements are, by definition, contrary to the positivity of "fact," and they seek to transpose, according to Stephen Best, "the actual world into an imaginary and inverted equivalent."[28] Loring's counterfactual reasoning—an instance of what Pierre Bourdieu describes as the "law's elasticity"—conjured into being notions of "personal volition," "choice," and "voluntary exchange" central to the emerging contractual logic of U.S. liberalism as he represented Med as a willful agent capable of choice and free of coercive restraints.[29]

Loring saw no inconsistency in his uneven application of the logic of contractual will and free choice to Med's situation. Reciprocity and voluntary exchange based on self-ownership ideally define contract as a social relation antithetical to the coercive proprietary relations of enslaved labor. Contract was much more than a legal doctrine; it was a mode of social organization that held the promise of a world no longer bound by inherited status.[30] Contract later became the dominant metaphor for freedom in postbellum America as it idealized, according to Amy Dru Stanley, the "ownership of self and voluntary exchange between individuals who were formally equal and free."[31] Intimations of contract theory's contradictory liberalism, however, can be found in these earlier antebellum texts, as both masters and legal counsels sought to locate free will and volition squarely within the constraints of slave *and* minor status. Freedom of will was central to American law and its ideology of individualism, and the countervailing fiction of will found in Loring's argument was provoked by the incorporation, in legal form, of the "contradictions of a slave society in a bourgeois world."[32] Words such as "freedom" and "choice," as Patricia Williams reminds us, "function as the mediators by which we make all things equal, interchangeable. It is, therefore, not just what 'freedom' means, but the relation it signals between each individual and the world. It is a word that levels difference."[33] The all-too-common depiction of slave children such as Med as willful agents capable of choice and free of coercive restraints in legal and popular rhetoric illuminates the ideological paradoxes that underpinned the slavery controversy in northern courts.

Slater was represented by Benjamin Curtis, the jurist who later resigned from the Supreme Court after authoring one of the two dissenting opinions in *Dred Scott v. Sandford* (1857). Curtis defended the rights of traveling slaveholders to retain their slaves and urged that the slave law of Louisiana take precedence over the laws of Massachusetts, the state of visitation. Curtis also minimized the difference between fugitives and traveling slaves, the key distinction on which Loring based his arguments for Med's unconditional emancipation. In the pretrial hearing, Curtis further extemporized on the moral issue of familial separation: he "alleged . . . that a promise has been given to the mother that her child should be returned to her" and pleaded that keeping Med from her mother was an act of "inhumanity."[34] Curtis rather unexpectedly invokes the sentimental rhetoric of "slave maternity," better understood as the reproduction of property in the guise of social reproduction, to support a proslavery argument for the unconstrained freedom of traveling slaveholders.[35] The moral discourse of "mother love" in Slater's defense corresponds with a developmental narrative of white guardianship over a childlike black populace, which proslavery *and* antislavery advocates alike mobilized for often antagonistic political claims. Popular antislavery literature of the period, such as *Uncle Tom's Cabin* (1851), fashioned slaves as supplicants before white benefactors who would oversee their passage into proper rights-bearing subjects.[36] Loring admitted the "painful feature" of this case and even offered to compromise his petition in the event of Med's manumission; "placing her again in her mother's bosom" was worth the "peril" of returning her to "the midst of a slave city."[37] Slater's attorneys refused his offer even as they continued to stress the reunification of mother and child. One of the attorneys was so moved by Med's circumstances that, as Lydia Maria Child recorded, he "wiped his own eyes at the thought that the poor little slave might be separated from its mother by mistaken benevolence."[38] The final verdict in *Aves* freed Med, although it placed her in the chronically underfunded Boston Samaritan Asylum for Indigent Children that BFASS members had recently established.[39] In a renaming ritual depicted in many slave narratives, BFASS took the liberty of renaming her Maria Sommersett, in honor of the application of *Somerset* in the final verdict.[40]

Samuel Slater, Med's legal owner, publicly denounced Shaw's ruling for permitting the law to intercede in a domestic matter, proclaiming that a "mother bond or free should be the representative of her own child, and surely it ought to be so in this land of liberty."[41] He went on to condemn the abolitionists who in an "act of barbarity . . . robbed the mother of her child, and to cap all . . . call it freedom—is it not freedom with a vengeance?"[42] Slater's angry, indignant words offer a rather chilling critique of Med's necessarily conditional freedom. In the effort to regain his chattel property, he appropriates an abolitionist discourse of sentimentalized slave kinship to denounce the child's "theft" from her mother. Slater's critique of abolitionism was perhaps not so unusual for a New Orleans slaveholder, since Louisiana's black codes "expressly prohibited" the separation and sale of children under the age of ten from their mothers and heavily fined slaveholders who brought motherless slave children into the state.[43] Given Med's youth, Slater may very well have purchased her and her mother together in 1833, in compliance with the legislated "humanity" of these statutes, even as they emboldened him to marshal the pathos of severed maternal ties.[44] Slater demanded Med's return to New Orleans not out of crass pecuniary interests but for the sake of her anguished mother, whose "only anxiety and desire," Slater claimed, "was for the child to remain under my protection, and be returned to her in the fall."[45] Members of BFASS struggled against this competing claim of "mother love" as they were forced to negotiate publicly those deep cleavages in the "various inflections of patriarchilized female gender—'mother,' 'daughter,' 'sister,' 'wife'" that, as Hortense Spillers argues, were not historically available to slave women.[46]

Slater was not alone in his moral condemnation of BFASS, as a divided public continued to dispute the merits of Shaw's ruling well after the trial. Newspapers including the *Boston Transcript* and the *New York Courier and Enquirer* likened the abolitionist-instigated freedom suit to the criminal act of kidnap. The *Boston Transcript* further accused abolitionists of the *moral* crime of familial separation "in the name of *Freedom*": "Who will answer for the 'deep damnation' of the sin which separated—nay stole, a child, an infant in mind and in law, without the power of choosing between freedom and slavery under any circumstances, from its mother in the South, that she might be called free in the North? . . . Separate mother and child in the name of *Freedom*? What fanaticism is this!"[47] This proslavery account, like Loring's argument, inferred Med's preference for returning to her "mother in the South" even while emphasizing her status as a minor who was legally "without the power of choosing between freedom and slavery." The *New York Courier and Enquirer* denounced Med's "freedom" in even less ambiguous terms: "The wanton cruelty in the case of the little slave child, recently wrested from the protection of its mistress in Boston, is enough to curdle colder blood than ours towards those miserable—more than miserable—fanatics, the abolitionists. . . . They can never *fully* expiate their crimes, until offences such as theirs are punished by imprisonment at hard labor for life."[48] These partisan accounts sought to contest the legal implications of Shaw's ruling with a pathetic tale of familial disunion. Med, they argued, was a victim of abolitionists more interested in antislavery politics than in honoring the true wishes of the helpless young girl.

Such sentimentalized discourses of familial disunion were highly persuasive, and slaveholders, in the wake of *Aves*, quickly adopted the ideology of "mother love" to maintain control over the slave children they brought into Massachusetts. Just one year after *Aves*, for example, Alabama slaveholder Henry Bright brought a successful lawsuit against a prominent antislavery black Bostonian couple to regain custody of his five-year-old slave girl Elizabeth. The conviction of John and Sophia Robinson in *Commonwealth v. Robinson* (1837) "justly excited great interest throughout the New England States."[49] Bright brought a habeas corpus action against the couple for "kidnapping" Elizabeth "under the impression that she was a slave."[50] Bright eloquently pleaded that he was "only actuated by a desire for the good of the child," whom he treated as "a part of the family," even though the black abolitionists "thought differently" and argued that Bright "ill-used" Elizabeth.[51] The Robinsons refused to give up the child, even at the insistence of Ellis Gray Loring, whose confidence Bright had secured, and they countered that "there were marks of a bruise on its [sic] head, and that her hair had not, from appearance, been combed for a long time."[52] Sophia Robinson told Loring that "slaveholders, with their smooth tongues, could deceive Mr. Sewall and [Loring], but could not deceive the colored people."[53] The dispute over the child Elizabeth also revealed the divisions within organized antislavery, as black abolitionists such as the Robinsons remained unconvinced of Bright's professions of selfless parental concern.

On behalf of Henry Bright and his wife, Charles G. Loring convincingly dramatized, with sentimental flourish before a courtroom "thronged with spectators," the slave mother's dying wish for Mrs. Bright to raise her orphaned child "as her own."[54] The welfare of the motherless child, he argued, was the sole interest of the Brights, who saw the "nurture and education of this child" as "a high natural and moral obligation." Loring's appeal to sentiment persuaded the abolitionist press. Garrison's *Liberator*, for example, reported, "On her death bed, the mother delivered the infant to Mrs. Bright, and obtained her promise to take charge of, and bring it up."[55] However, Stephen Burt, a former slave of the Brights, offered a contrary account, in which the dying slave mother entrusted Elizabeth to a "colored fellow servant by the name of Eleanor."[56] Judge Thacker paid no heed to Burt's testimony; he sentenced the Robinsons to four months in jail, fined then two hundred dollars, and ordered them to return Elizabeth to the Brights, who he said had "acted with humanity."[57] Ellis Loring, who had cast a skeptical eye on Slater's similar claims, found himself supporting a slaveholder who had taken out guardianship letters to formalize his "parental" relation. As in Med's case, the slave woman's historical inability to claim her progeny was powerfully rearticulated to authorize the Brights' claim on Elizabeth in what judge, jury, and legal commentators all viewed as the compassionate fulfillment of a slave mother's dying wish.[58]

Such sentimentalized legal rhetoric responded to the ideologies of republican motherhood that BFASS took up with reformist zeal as the organization focused its energies on safeguarding the welfare of slave women and children in particular. Abolitionist Maria Weston Chapman reported in her controversial *Right and Wrong in Boston* how the women's organization had come across the slave woman Lucille, who had been "hunted from one part of the city to another" after her mistress posted a reward for her recapture. BFASS finally "resolved to disinter the law of Massachusetts" once it heard that the Lucille's searchers threatened to "seize and carry off any colored woman they could find."[59] BFASS anticipated the legal question that male members of the Massachusetts Anti-Slavery Society would later think to ask. Garrison, for example, expressed "surprise that the first article of the Mass. Constitution is not more frequently appealed to, in proof that no person can be seized or claimed upon the soil of the State as a slave."[60]

BFASS strategically engineered the habeas corpus action in Med's case to test the rights of slaveholders to reclaim slaves they had brought into a free state, reasoning, "It had always been our impression that the laws of Massachusetts would shelter the slave brought within their local limits by his master."[61] The group seized on the opportunity provided by "a family in the city, recently from the south, [that] had a child in their keeping, presumed to be a slave."[62] Med's situation, however, was not without its difficulties. When BFASS discovered that the child's mother "was alive, in New Orleans," the organization, composed of self-described "mothers," was at first hesitant to "interfere with the paramount claims of maternal love."[63] This maternal identity helped emphasize the female organization's guardianship role in those cases involving slave women and children, even though a number of its members were neither mothers nor wives.[64] BFASS rationalized that Med's mother, as a slave, had no legitimate parental claim on her child, and the writ of habeas corpus ultimately noted that Med was a child with no known relatives.[65] The tacit understanding was that slave women with little individual control over children were incapable of being good mothers, as BFASS assumed responsibility for Med's well-being in her mother's symbolic and physical absence. Such a conflicted sense of what constituted legitimate maternity was indicative of the way middle-class BFASS members began to reshape their social activism specifically within the terms of "mother love." The BFASS made use of a reform-minded sentimentalism that redefined the consanguineous ties of kinship, as Cindy Weinstein argues, "according to the logic of love."[66] Such allusions to imagined or adoptive kinship, however, erased asymmetries of power even as they facilitated other forms of exclusion and violence under the aegis of maternal affection. BFASS noted with strategic calculation, "If we should fail, the condition of the child would remain but where it was; while if we should succeed, a decision would be obtained of greater importance than any within the last half century."[67] Given the antislavery argument against familial separation under slavery, such justifications betrayed anxieties over the meaning and tactics of female antislavery activism even as the successful trial revealed the central role of this women's organization in the practices of antebellum lawmaking.

The child Med virtually disappeared from the public record after the trial, yet she continued to live on as legal precedent and as an opportunity for abolitionist literature to celebrate a new historiography of antislavery liberalism in Massachusetts.[68] The landmark antislavery victory in *Aves*, as David Delaney notes, participated in the development of a civic mythos of a "historically free New England."[69] The judgment, as some papers noted, was a signal victory for antislavery activists as it established "the principle that slavery cannot exist in Massachusetts, even for a temporary purpose, and that a slave, voluntarily brought here by his master, becomes free, although slavery is recognized by the laws of the State of which the master is a citizen."[70] Shaw subsequently expanded the *Aves* precedent, in *Commonwealth v. Potterfield* (1844) and *Commonwealth v. Fitzgerald* (1844), to cover slaves brought into Massachusetts through the agency of ship captains or naval service.[71]

Med's case charted new legal territory, since existing federal and state provisions applied only to fugitive slaves, and it helped shape a regional imaginary of the northern free states that sought to efface their recent and, some historians would argue, ongoing histories of slavery. After the successful trial, BFASS suggested in a letter to Loring that the twenty-sixth of August should henceforth be kept as a holiday, and the *Boston Daily Advertiser* cited Shaw's opinion as an instance of the exemplary liberalism of Massachusetts: "This is, we believe, the first decision in any of the free States, upon that precise point."[72] Loring congratulated the "female courage and energy" and "female agency" of the organization for bringing about "a decision not exceeded in interest or real moment by any decision made within the last hal[f] century."[73]

This victory came at a moment in BFASS's history when its members, now two hundred strong, powerfully channeled their energies toward a common goal, before controversies over competing ideologies of womanhood and reform work factionalized the group, leading to its collapse in 1840.[74] Lydia Maria Child, a founding member of BFASS, even reported that "[w]ork-bags were manufactured in commemoration of little Med's case, decided by Judge Shaw," and sold at the annual BFASS Anti-Slavery Fair.[75] These commemorative work-bags charmed Child, and she included an elaborate description of them in her report on the successful fair: "On one side, was the representation of a Slave kneeling before the figure of Justice; underneath these sentences were printed in golden letters: 'Slavery was abolished in Massachusetts by the adoption of the Bill of Rights as a part of the Constitution, A.D. 1780.' Slavery says of this law, 'Lo, 'tis cold and dead, and will not harm me.' Anti-Slavery replies, 'But with my breath I can revive it!' Then follows, 'The adjudication on the case of a slave brought into Massachusetts from another State, fifty-six years afterwards, Aug. 26, A.D. 1836.'"[76] This imagined dialogue between personified "Slavery" and "Anti-Slavery" uses Med's case as an occasion for enlivening the "dead" letter of the law with the revolutionary spirit of the past era. The familiar iconography of these work-bags offers a revisionist historiography of antislavery liberalism in Massachusetts. The successful adjudication of Med's case in 1836 pushed back the horizon of slavery's demise so that it could be claimed, without anachronism, that "Slavery was abolished in Massachusetts" in 1780. Despite the fact that Henry David Thoreau was compelled to remind fellow abolitionists that there was indeed "Slavery in Massachusetts" at the famous 1854 antislavery meeting held in Framingham, emancipation lay at the heart of racial thinking and the production of culture and social identity in New England.[77] Med's case was therefore used to suggest that slavery in Massachusetts had indeed ceased in the nation's founding period.

The antislavery campaign continuously mobilized Med to do symbolic work in the years following *Commonwealth v. Aves*, although she underwent a telling transformation that drew further attention to the predicament of consent, which had been finessed, but far from resolved, in her freedom suit. By 1852, Med had become a touchstone of the Commonwealth's liberal promise, which, as Wendell Phillips caustically protested before a crowded Faneuil Hall, was turned "upside down" as Boston was forced to "surrender" its first runaway under the new Fugitive Slave Act passed two years earlier.[78] Phillips cited the past heroism of Chief Justice Shaw, who had once declared, as Lord Mansfield had similarly done in the landmark *Somerset* case, "the slave Med a free woman the moment she set foot on the soil of Massachusetts."[79] Phillips's misnaming of Med as "a free *woman*" retrospectively transforms the child's uncertainty into the willful desire of an adult woman. In the same year, Massachusetts senator and jurist Samuel Sewall began a speech supporting the new personal-liberty bill with reference to *Aves* and the rights of free black citizens, who like (the child) Med were categorically not fugitive slaves.[80]

Med's case set a liberal norm in subsequent freedom suits brought before northern courts, but it raised a number of social and ethical questions concerning the meaning of free choice within the ideology of abolitionism. Sewall, for example, unsuccessfully pushed for the immediate application of *Aves* when abolitionists charged Asa D. Gove, another New Orleans slaveholder, on 15 October 1836 with "detaining a colored child, named Emma, for the purposes of taking her back to New Orleans, as a slave." This case, like Med's, proceeded on the counterfactual representation of the slave child's consent. According to the trial proceedings, Gove concealed Emma (sometimes called Amy) when he was served with the writ of habeas corpus; she was never found, but the trial proceeded without her.[81] The presiding Judge Merrill admitted to the possibility that "there had been a violation of the law" but dismissed the case because there was not sufficient proof that Emma was held against her will. Merrill focused on the question of consent raised, but not settled, in *Aves*: "The statute provides that her consent shall not be a defense, unless it is made satisfactorily to appear that the consent was not obtained by fraud, nor exhorted by duress, or by threats."[82] Witness accounts of Emma's apparent cheerfulness and contentment, in her physical absence, served as "proof" positive of her freely given consent. If Emma was not held *against* her will (as proven by her good humor), then, consistent with the juridical logic of these cases, she must be held *with* her consent.

Just months after Med's trial, northern states passed a number of personal-liberty acts that granted comprehensive procedural rights to individuals, including slave children, who otherwise had no standing within the law.[83] The Massachusetts legislature passed the first of these significant laws governing questions of personal freedom, which offered the right to a writ of personal replevin or trial by jury to any person unlawfully imprisoned, restrained of liberty, or held in duress. The 1839 trial involving another traveling slave girl, thirteen-year-old Anne, was one of the first cases brought under the provisions of this new statute. Olivia Eames brought Anne as a nurse on a visit to her mother, Betsey Sherman, after the death of her husband in New Orleans.[84] Eames alleged that four abolitionists forcibly kidnapped the unwilling Anne from her service. According to Eames, Anne had "*often expressed a wish to return to New Orleans*" and "*wanted* to go back."[85] The Holden Anti-Slavery Society published the *Report of the Holden Slave Case* in pamphlet form after the court acquitted the abolitionists. Their case had successfully tested the ability of the new law to protect the personal liberties of those individuals—including infants, married women, maniacs, and, as in Anne's case, "a child brought up in ignorance"—who had neither recognized legal will nor the ability to delegate authority.[86] Personal replevin was one method by which the state sought to resolve the countervailing notions of will and consent provoked by Med's case. Such cognitive dissonance, what Robert Cover refers to as the "moral-formal dilemma," found its way into the opinions of antislavery judges such as Lemuel Shaw, who adjudicated Med's freedom but later enforced the Fugitive Slave Act against runaways such as Anthony Burns, Shadrach Minkins, and Thomas Sims.[87] This ambivalence was deeply rooted in a liberal legal structure forced to accommodate the chattel logic of slavery.

Following *Aves*, lawyers and jurists constructed the slave's willfulness in binary absolutes: the slave was either a willful freedom seeker or will-less victim of slavery. This dichotomy shaped the representations of slave petitioners in the press. *Commonwealth v. Mary B. Taylor* (1841) freed the slave child Anson, brought from slaveholding Arkansas, on the principles laid out in Med's case—*in spite of* the boy's explicit wishes to the contrary. The *Liberator* reported that Anson was a "Negro boy about 9 or 10 years of age" who "was well and kindly treated; that he had father, mother, brothers and sisters in Arkansas, . . . that at first he was very unwilling to leave Mrs. Taylor."[88] Ellis Loring, reprising his role from *Aves*, joined Samuel Sewall to argue the case on behalf of their slave plaintiff. Perhaps learning from Med's case, when Taylor was brought before the Massachusetts Supreme Court, she did not claim Anson as a slave, which strategically prevented a charge of intended kidnapping.[89] Benjamin Franklin Hallett, on behalf of Taylor, argued that Anson wished to remain with his mistress. Taylor would not return Anson to Arkansas "unless with his consent," and she was quite confident that the child would fully "consent to go with her and her family."[90] Justice Shaw ruled against Taylor, citing that Anson—unlike Med, who was presumed to desire freedom—was "in the point of law . . . of such tender years" that he had "no will, no power of judging or electing." According to the *Law Reporter*, once Anson "understood that he was to be given up to his new guardian, to remain here, he broke out into most impassioned entreaties to be permitted to go back and see his father and mother and brothers and sisters, weeping bitterly."⁹¹ Relations between masters and slaves were not founded on sheer force alone. Traveling slaveholders often brought as attendants those slaves who would be less inclined to forgo kinship ties to remain in a free state. The court was forced to suspend business while Anson "was led away, shrieking and begging to be suffered to go back to his father and mother."⁹²

Despite the child's personal wish to return south, Shaw, perhaps defensively, offered a legal clarification: "The natural and strong feelings of a child, which induce him to cling instinctively to those whom he had been accustomed to regard as his natural protectors, cannot be regarded as the exercise of a legal will, or of an intelligent choice."⁹³ By adjudicating Anson's will, Shaw ensured his freedom at the expense of his desire. The concurrent legalization of adoption in Massachusetts courts offered an unusual corollary to these decisions, as judges such as Shaw and Wilde, according to Weinstein, began redefining familial relationships in terms of contractual obligations that tended to privilege children's wishes.⁹⁴ The separation of child from kin in northern freedom suits was not uncommon. Pennsylvania's commitment to antislavery legislation, for example, declared that a child born of a fugitive slave mother within the territorial boundaries of the state was legally free, whereas the mother, as a fugitive, was subject to "recaption and rendition."⁹⁵ The freedom proffered in such antislavery legal actions marked the necessary violence and loss attendant on certain forms of social inclusion, as Med and Anson were required to forgo their kin ties to be remade into free northern children.

Unruly Subjects of Antislavery Jurisprudence

Antislavery print culture was invested in the manufacture of acceptable forms of slave agency, and the epistemic violence of such literary and legal hermeneutics continue to mark our contemporary understanding of slavery and resistance to it. After *Aves*, activists began targeting female and minor slave attendants brought into the state of Massachusetts, even though deciding in those slaves' best interest meant, as it did in Anson's case, acting against their wishes. Children such as Med and Anson, unlike adult slave narrators such as William Wells Brown and Frederick Douglass, could be more easily positioned as the "spoken-for" recipients of antislavery activism, because the political demands of the campaign and the evangelical perspectives of black and white abolitionists imposed restrictions on what could be considered appropriate forms of resistance.[96] Slave petitioners were fitted to the literary archetype of the freedom seeker, whose actions reconfirmed the antislavery political mission and emphasized the North as the location of social change. The ventriloquism of the slave's will through legal hermeneutics—what Joan Dayan describes as "the cunning beneficence of white recognition"—was not unusual as other slave petitioners negotiated their continual effacement in pro- *and* antislavery arguments over what constituted their "true" desires.[97] Their lawsuits begin to illustrate that the liberal ideal of free will was not an abstract transcendent value but, more often than not, a rhetorical tool of ideological power. The law, as Ariela Gross argues, "created an image of blackness as an absence of will," but the stories discussed in this section illustrate the complex ways in which law and literature also *fashioned* the particular forms of will and moral agency attributed to slaves.[98]

Antebellum abolitionist writers, activists, and jurists found themselves at a hermeneutical impasse when faced with cases, like Anson's, in which the slave petitioner's desires challenged the unidirectional logic of freedom. Such contrary desires crystallized antebellum anxieties over the meaning of individual freedom in a liberal society. Although we may never know what slaves such as Med and Anson may have "truly" desired, we do have detailed records of what abolitionists believed those desires should have been. Their writings assimilated these unruly desires into the more acceptable yearning for freedom given narrative shape in the genre of the slave narrative. We can see these discursive practices at work in Olive Gilbert's dramatization of Sojourner Truth's courtroom battles to reclaim her son Peter, who insisted in the manner of the fictional Topsy, that he just "grow'd." Tried in 1828, Peter's case predates the Massachusetts freedom suits of Med and Anson, but it illustrates the discursive difficulties that abolitionist writers and reporters faced when they represented slave petitioners whose willful "choices" did not correspond seamlessly with the ideologies of antislavery. Abolitionist writers such as Olive Gilbert, the amanuensis of Truth's dictated *Narrative of Sojourner Truth: A Northern Slave* (1850), found themselves forced to rationalize or explain away those desires and "choices" at odds with their antislavery agendas.

Slavery legally denied Truth the right to "own" her progeny, yet she marshaled out the powerful trope of republican motherhood before northern courtrooms to lay claim to a "mother's right" to her child.[99] John Dumont, Peter's owner, anticipating the New York gradual emancipation law, sold him in violation of its prohibition against the sale of slaves into places where slavery continued to be legal.¹⁰⁰ The five-year-old Peter's new master, an Alabama planter named Fowler, was by all accounts a brutal master who viciously assaulted his slaves, irrespective of age or gender, and Truth later discovered ample signs of her child's physical abuse at his hands. The only means of retrieving Peter from Alabama, as Truth reasoned, was through New York courts. She immediately journeyed to the Ulster County Courthouse in Kingston, New York, and although illiterate, entered a formal complaint to compel the return of her child.¹⁰¹ Truth, as Gilbert writes, sought not only the return of her son but also his immediate freedom: "It had ever been . . . [her] prayer, not only that her son might be returned, but that he should be delivered from bondage, and into her own hands, lest he should be punished out of mere spite to her, who was so greatly annoying and irritating to her oppressors."¹⁰² When Peter, now nearly seven, was brought back to New York for the initial hearing in the spring of 1828, he refused to recognize his mother and, sobbing hysterically, stated that he preferred to remain with his master. Upon seeing Truth, "the boy cried aloud," according to Gilbert's biography, "and regarded her as some terrible being, who was about to take him away from a kind and loving friend. He knelt, even, and begged them, with tears, not to take him away from his dear master, who had brought him from the dreadful South, and been so kind to him" (*NST*, 35).

Peter's reaction to his mother, whom Gilbert represents in preceding chapters as selflessly acting in accordance with the feminine dictates of true mother love, is unexpected and shockingly at odds with the expectations of the antislavery audience to which Truth's narrative, published in a decade that saw a dramatic increase of public interest in nonmilitant and nonthreatening literature in the fashion of *Uncle Tom's Cabin*, was most likely directed.¹⁰³ In the attempt to resolve Peter's unruly attachment to his master and, it would appear, his preference for slavery over freedom, Gilbert subtly begins to interpret the courtroom scene for her readers. When Peter is questioned about marks and bruises on his body, he claims that they are the result of accidents and, according to Gilbert's narration, "looked imploringly at his master, as much as to say, 'If they are falsehoods, you bade me say them; may they be satisfactory to you, at least'" (*NST*, 38). Gilbert characteristically enters into Truth's narrative and "reads" Peter's unspoken words to denounce the master's manipulation. Her counterfactual assertion, "as much as to say, 'If they are falsehoods, you bade me say them,'" to a degree replicates the act of discursive violence—the ventriloquism of slave will—of which she accuses the master. Because Peter cannot voice his "true" desire (to remain with his mother in freedom), Gilbert's narrative must "speak for" him. Peter, however, continues "clinging to his master" even though the judge "bade him forget his master and attend only to him" (*NST*, 38). Gilbert's narration, therefore, must proceed counterfactually with the presumption that the boy would expose his master's perfidy and coercion if only he were given the opportunity to speak freely.[104]

Judge Charles H. Ruggles, like Shaw in Anson's trial, overruled Peter's choice and released him to his mother's guardianship only after discerning that Truth held no other interests than the maternal desire to reclaim her son. The judgment affirmed Truth's mother right to her child and "delivered" Peter "into the hands of the mother—having no other master," but the child continued "begging, most piteously, *not* to be taken from his dear master, saying she was not his mother" (*NST*, 39). It took the collective efforts of Truth, her legal counsel, and the clerks to calm "the child's fears, and ... convinc[e] him that ... [she] was not some terrible monster, as he had for the last months, probably, been trained to believe" (*NST*, 39). The narrative again attempts to resolve Peter's inexplicable behavior, with Gilbert speculating that the child had been "trained" to disavow what should have been the "natural" bonds of affection between mother and child. Indeed, Harriet Beecher Stowe's abbreviated version of the case, "Sojourner Truth: The Libyan Sibyl," published in the *Atlantic Monthly* in 1863, further rewrites Peter's contrary desire for master over mother. In an interview with Stowe, Truth reportedly professed that "they tried to frighten him, a' to make him say that I was n't his mammy, an' that he did n't know me; but they could n't make it out."[105] Peter's continued preference for master over mother marks him as an unruly subject of freedom even as it powerfully reveals how the property relation could supersede kinship in slavery.

The publicly understated conflicts between the desires of slave petitioners and the people who sought to be their antislavery "benefactors" and representatives are perhaps best illustrated in the sensationalized events surrounding the Massachusetts Supreme Court case of another traveling slave, *Catharine Linda v. Erastus D. Hudson* (1848).[106] Most likely under the influence of her infuriated master, W.B. Hodgson of Savannah, Linda brought suit against abolitionist Erasmus Hudson, who had attempted to emancipate her according to the methods adopted in *Aves*. The reportage of Hudson's arrest and imprisonment also rehearsed the kinds of public advocacy marshaled in defense of abolitionists—including Passmore Williamson, discussed later in this chapter—in connection with their role in the "rescue" of slave women. According to Hudson's prison letters, the case began as an informal conversation between Linda and "a friend from New-Bedford, a fugitive slave, in company with another family" lodged at the same Warriner's Hotel where the Hodgson household stayed briefly on a summer tour of the North. Such hotels, a staple of the burgeoning economy of antebellum travel, became as in the later case of Jane Johnson the unexpected sites of antislavery activism. When Linda was discovered to be "a slave travelling with her master" with an "expressed . . . desire to be free," her predicament was communicated to sympathetic free blacks in Springfield, who, in turn, notified Hudson and black antislavery activist David W. Ruggles.[107] Hudson, who was active in both the Connecticut and American Anti-Slavery societies, followed Linda to Northampton, where he brought a writ of habeas corpus on her behalf, claiming that she was, as in Med's case, "imprisoned and restrained of her liberty."[108]

Linda was brought before Judge Charles August Dewey, who "told her that she was free—that she would be protected in her freedom, if she chose to remain" in Massachusetts.[109] The slave woman, however, "chose to remain" with her master. Aware of the damaging implications of Linda's "choice," Garrison's *Liberator* announced, rather defensively, "If one chooses to be a slave, they would not hinder them."[110] This representation of Linda's willful "choice" of slavery over freedom became the focus of many local and regional newspapers covering the story. The *New-Hampshire Patriot*, for example, exulted in this "abolition failure" and sympathized with Hodgson, who "had with him a colored girl as servant, which some busy-bodies, led on by a fanatic named Hudson . . . wished to get away from him, because she was his slave at home."[111] According to the *New-Hampshire Patriot*, when the girl was "taken before Judge Dewey . . . she decided, of her own choice, to remain with her master and family."[112] The *Barre Patriot* offered a more elaborate account of what it represented as Linda's unambiguous exercise of free will: "She replied that she was not restrained of her liberty, and that she was fully aware of her rights, and that she did not wish any further proceedings on her behalf."[113] When Judge Dewey "told her that she was to act as she chose, freely and voluntarily," Linda "replied that she *chose to live with Mr. Hodgson*."[114]

These various news reports all chose to suppress a significant fact that shaped Linda's "choice" to return with her master and curtailed any emancipatory longings that she may have had. Hudson's prison letter carefully explains, "Her mistress told the officer that she had children, and she (the slave) said that she had father and mother, brothers and sisters—these were retained as hostages for her return."¹¹⁵ Linda's few spoken words are characteristically mediated through others. Only Hudson's prison letters consistently refer to the constraints on the slave woman's purported choice of slavery over freedom. Extant accounts of Linda's sensational case in both the pro- *and* antislavery presses neglect to mention her deep attachments to others still held in bondage and instead represent her in the liberal tradition as a social agent free of coercive restraints and capable of free choice. Caught within a closed discourse of utter willfulness or will-lessness, slaves traveling in the North who remained with masters or mistresses out of necessity could only be understood as social agents who voluntarily chose slavery over freedom.

Antislavery literature commonly constructed slaves as socioethical beings active in obtaining their freedom, but unruly adult figures such as Linda profoundly troubled such clear-cut archetypes. Her abolitionist advocates, perhaps with the exception of Hudson, were clearly unaccustomed to the different set of negotiations that Linda's situation entailed. Supposing "the matter ended" with Linda's decision to return with Hodgson, abolitionists were apoplectic when Linda charged Hudson for false arrest and for obtaining a writ of habeas corpus "without and against her consent."¹¹⁶ Damages were assessed at one thousand dollars, and Hudson, initially unable to meet the fifteen-hundred-dollar bail, was jailed in Springfield to await the early-October trial in Boston.¹¹⁷ The imprisonment of Hudson, according to one *Liberator* headline, was "the climax of slaveholding audacity on the soil of New-England."¹¹⁸ The outraged newspaper reported that Hudson, "long a most faithful laborer in the anti-slavery cause, has been thrust into prison, ostensibly by a slave woman whom he kindly endeavored to set at liberty by *habeas corpus*, but really, no doubt by her ruffian master."¹¹⁹ The irony of Hudson's imprisonment was not lost on the *Liberator*, and Hudson, writing to Garrison from his Springfield jail cell, took this opportunity to critique the leniency of Massachusetts's interstate politics (the comity issues that would be repeatedly raised throughout the next decade) as he depicted his loss of liberty as an instance of southern slaveholding aggression against the rights of northern citizens on their own soil.¹²⁰

There is no doubt that Hodgson decided to use Linda's travel in the North as "a test case, to have the matter decided, whether 'slave property' was secure to its pretended owner in Massachusetts or not."¹²¹ We will perhaps never know whether Linda's lawsuit masked other negotiations between the two. Did the promise of reward or indulgence help facilitate her compliance? Antislavery print culture, however, continued to struggle with Linda's litigious agency as it sought to assimilate her to their existing discourses and literary archetypes. Abolitionists countered proslavery accounts by stripping Linda of any willful intent in the legal events at hand. Newspapers such as the *Liberator*, usually invested in certain forms of black agency, represented her as a passive victim entirely subject to the will of her master; proslavery newspapers, by contrast, began to defend black civil rights, stressing Linda's entitlement to her legal rights as they attacked the misguided benevolence of Garrisonian abolitionism. Linda's lawsuit was, in practice, a legitimate exercise of her right in Massachusetts to engage in litigation, even though Georgia slave statutes would have prohibited her from the same action. Hudson denounced this "pretended regard for her rights" on the part of Hodgson and his proslavery supporters as "pretence" and "mere *ruse* for a malicious persecution. . . . What regard has Hodgson for the rights of Catharine Linda, when he claims her person and her services—her children, father, mother, brothers, and sisters as his property?"[122] Indeed, Hodgson and his associates recognized "the rights of this 'chattel personal'" only insofar as it served their interests in impeding the work of the abolitionist campaign.[123]

Few antislavery accounts could publicly acknowledge that Linda's case against Hudson was based on the successful application of Massachusetts law and was the logical conclusion drawn from the judgment in Med's case. The *Liberator* (and even Hudson's usually more considered letters) chose to overlook Linda's "restoration" to legal personhood in Massachusetts and depict her as a will-less "chattel personal." Later *Liberator* accounts further depicted Hudson's imprisonment, inaccurately and provocatively, as the imposition of Georgia laws unilaterally seeking the "subjection" of "the white men of the North."[124] Such omissions disclose the widely held assumption that freedom, once conferred, should be exercised in certain specific ways; the boon of northern freedom came with implied duties and obligations. The *Hartford Freeman* was perhaps one of the few commentators on the case that underscored the ironic legality of Hudson's "persecution," yet it also represented Linda as a will-less nonagent: "The seizure and imprisonment of Dr. Hudson is nothing less than *persecution*, and it seems the more flagrant because it is done under the cover of the law, at the dictation of a Southern man-thief."[125] Linda's contrary exercise of her rights in the North could only be resolved in antislavery accounts by her depiction as a tool of slaveholding power rather than as the unexpected consequence of the very freedom that they championed.

Such denunciations on the part of the white antislavery press indicate the inability of writers and editors to accept slave women such as Linda (or Anson and Peter, for that matter) as legal agents unless their willful desires corresponded with the antislavery agenda. While antislavery ideologies plotted freedom as the single goal of all slaves, it did not consider what northern freedom might mean for women such as Linda whose "choice" was not a matter of legal abstraction. Abolitionist accounts almost univocally disregarded the painful contingency of Linda's freedom on separation from kin as they depicted her as the unwitting instrument of her master's wrath and design. When *Linda v. Hudson* came up for a second trial, the *Liberator* praised Hudson for his "discretion, moderation and prudence" throughout the ongoing litigation and his refusal to jeopardize "the rights of the friendless girl, who now, in the hands of an enraged master, is made the innocent occasion of thus annoying and injuring him."[126] Although doubtless Hodgson coerced Linda into making the allegations, these reactions illustrate, more significantly, the complex discursive processes by which slave women became legible (or illegible) as social agents.[127] All antislavery accounts of the case were publicly convinced of Linda's "innocence" in the legal dispute, and they chose to deemphasize the adult woman's litigious agency by depicting her as an innocent "girl" or a will-less slave so that the moral condemnation of the act would be levied rightly at the willful slaveholder. Antislavery discourse transformed the unruly Linda into a "girl," even as the slave child Med, in reverse fashion, became an adult woman legally cognizant of her choice of freedom.

Unlike the comparable cases of traveling slaves, such as Med and Anson, and perhaps because Catharine Linda was an adult woman, antislavery activists found themselves at an impasse: the hermeneutic limit of an emergent liberal discourse of contract premised on universalized notions of will and free choice in a partially free world. The jury, it seems, was likewise at an impasse, for it was "unable to agree upon a verdict" when the case first came to trial in 1846.[128] At the second trial, Judge Wilde instructed the jury to deliberate only on the question of damages, and it returned a verdict for Linda in the nominal amount of $30.67 against Hudson.[129] When Hudson appealed the case to the Massachusetts Supreme Court, Chief Justice Shaw declared that "the question should have been left to the jury," set aside the verdict for the plaintiff, and granted a new trial, which most likely led to a settlement.[130] The *Liberator*'s coverage of Hudson's second trial again relied on a counterfactual suggestion as it further revealed the ideological fault lines within organized antislavery's insistence on choice and free will. "But suppose," the *Liberator* pondered, that Linda had "wished to remain a slave.

It appears to us that, under such circumstances, that would be a good kind of law which should decide that no human being has a *right* to be a slave. From whence does a person obtain authority to put himself or herself, body and soul, absolutely at the disposal of another?"[131] This rather pointed observation gestures toward the troubling limits of the formal logic of choice with little consideration of the terribly qualified life that abstract freedom offered to slaves such as Linda.

The hypothetical suggestion legally to foreclose the *"right* to be a slave" bespeaks the quandary of a juridical field unable to resolve the countervailing fictions of slave will. It also anticipated the 1857 case of the slave "girl" Betty, who, like Linda before her, "chose" to return to Tennessee after "several months traveling North" freed her. Lewis and Laura Sweet traveled with their twenty-five-year-old slave woman to Canada and several northern states before they arrived in Lawrence, Massachusetts, where the writ of habeas corpus was issued.[132] When brought before Shaw, the Sweets, like Anson's mistress, declared that "they would cheerfully abide by Betty's own choice in the matter."[133] Shaw dismissed the case after holding a private interview with Betty, secluded from the "restraint or intimidation" that her master might exert over her, in which she revealed that she was "strongly attached to Mr. and Mrs. Sweet, and wished to remain with them; and that she had a husband living in Tennessee, from whom she was not willing, upon any consideration, to be separated."[134] A crowd, thinking it was a fugitive slave case, gathered around the courthouse during the hearing. When Betty departed with "her master and mistress, apparently contented," reported the *Pittsfield Sun*, "several colored persons made strong but unavailing appeals to Betty to accept the freedom offered to her."[135] The *New York Journal of Commerce* chose to interpret Betty's case as a barbed commentary "on the assertions of that class of negrophilists who maintain that all slavery is inhuman, and that the slave would, if left to themselves, murder their masters and assume their freedom."[136] Betty, like the ungrateful slave of paternalist ideology, was an illustrative example of a "slave, [who] when offered freedom, has declined the gift and voluntarily chosen to return, with her master and mistress, to a state where she is held in slavery."[137] This newspaper, like the various accounts of Linda's case, elides the mitigating conditions on Betty's ability to choose and instead depicts her as a self-determining agent entirely free from duress of any kind.

Betty's story, however, ended neither with her return to Tennessee slavery nor with further antislavery litigation. The *Liberator* took much self-congratulatory pleasure in reprinting a notice a few months later reporting that "the slave woman, Betty, whose case caused some little excitement in this city some few months ago, and who refused to accept her liberty, after returning with Mrs. Sweet to New York, suddenly left her mistress whom she loved so much, took passage upon the under-ground railroad, and safely escaped to Cincinnati, where she was joined by her husband, who is a free man."[138] Betty eventually took advantage of northern law and geopolitics, in the manner of Harriet and John S. Jacobs, to emancipate herself on her own terms. Freedom for Betty was meaningful only upon reunion with the "kindred tie," to recall Douglass's words, from whom she was "not willing, upon any consideration, to be separated." This epilogue to Betty's case also reveals the tactical negotiations and "choices" made and unmade between slaves and masters once they left a familiar landscape. Her counterintuitive freedom story reveals one of the myriad ways that slave attendants negotiated the predicaments that the law of freedom created in their lives. Her story was not unusual, and these various freedom suits illustrate the complex ways that legal and literary hermeneutics were brought to bear on the geopolitics of kinship and mobility.[139] The seemingly contradictory legal reasoning found in all these cases emphasizes the extent to which these juridical texts, as Bourdieu argues, are struggles to "impose a universally recognized principle of knowledge of the social world."[140]

By 1860, all free states north of Mason-Dixon had adopted versions of the *Aves* precedent through court cases, legislation, or constitutional provisions, and all but Illinois, Indiana, and New Jersey had withdrawn all legal protections for slaveholders traveling with slaves.[141] The emerging culture of antislavery jurisprudence in the U.S. North was by no means uncontested, and some northerners condemned this denial of slaveholders' rights of transit and sojourn: "The Northern abolitionists, who steal the nurses, body servants, and coachmen from Southern families, are cheating our hotels and merchants of Southern custom, and our watering-place society of the beaux and belles who were want to grace it."[142] By 1848, slaveholders traveling in the company of enslaved servants had become such a common feature of the burgeoning northern economy that it inspired William and Ellen Craft's daring escape from Georgia slavery.[143] Slaveholders continued traveling to the North even though they risked losing their slave "property" whenever they crossed into a free jurisdiction. These travelers took precautions to circumvent northern law with varying degrees of success. Many found it more effective to curtail the loss of property through the selective recognition of slave humanity rather than physical force or intimidation. In 1848, Andrew Jackson Polk, a wealthy Tennessee planter related to President James Polk, for example, specifically requested an informally emancipated slave, James Thomas, to travel to New York as his personal valet.[144] Given the shape of northern antislavery activism in the wake of *Aves*, it is understandable why a southern slaveholder such as Polk would prefer to hire an informally free slave such as Thomas rather than risk his own valuable property in New York. Unlike Polk's chattel property, Thomas had little incentive to remain in the North once brought there because of his relatively liberated position within Nashville society and his affective and economic ties to the slaveholding city. Thomas later petitioned for formal emancipation in 1851. Thomas relates in his autobiographical manuscript, "[Polk] told me he was going to New York, and he wanted [me] to be ready and go with him."[145] When Thomas demurred—"I had just bought a business and I didn't think I would go"—Polk persuaded by coercion: "'Don't tell me about your business. I'll buy it and shut it up.' He offered to pay me liberally and told me to be ready Tuesday. I got ready" (*FTS*, 121). Thomas's travels as Polk's valet took him through Albany, Buffalo, Cincinnati, and New York City, where several individuals gave him advice: "[They] advised me to leave Mr. Polk, showing that they didn't believe What I had said as to being free" (*FTS*, 122).

Polk again traveled to the North with Thomas as his valet over the summer of 1851, but his growing household required him to risk the addition of a waiting maid to attend to the wants of his wife, Rebecca, and their two young children.[146] The Polks brought their slave woman, "Aunt Kitty," to nurse their two young children as they summered in Saratoga, Boston, Newport, and New York City. Polk was unusually anxious about Kitty once they arrived in New England; he directed Thomas to take guardianship of Kitty and offered her specific directions regarding deportment once they arrived in Boston over the July Fourth holiday. Thomas recollects, "I was told not to take Kitty out on the street after night to see the fire works or any sights ... because of the roughs on the street wouldn't let her pass unmolested"(*FTS*, 128). One suspects, as does Thomas in his observations, that Polk's prohibitions stemmed less from a concern for Kitty's well-being than from self-interested fear of losing his property in the famously antislavery city on the eve of commemorating the revolutionary birth of the nation.

Polk's subsequent directions to Kitty, like Samuel Sawyer's to John S. Jacobs, confirmed these apprehensions. "Mr. Polk addressed Kitty in a manner that she little expected," Thomas recalls. "He said, Kitty, 'you are not to call me Master While we are in Boston.' . . . 'Call me Mr Polk' you are just as free here as I am.... if those people knew you belong to me they would come and carry you off and you would never see Isaac again. When Kitty had recovered her breath, he told her to tell all inquirers that she was free" (*FTS*, 128–29). Polk persuades his slave woman to acquiesce to his "lie" of freedom with the threat that she "would never see Isaac again" if she fell into the hands of abolitionists. Thomas explained to the still uncomprehending Kitty that she was indeed free by the local law of Massachusetts, "as Mr. Polk said," although Kitty "thought after taking a look over the matter that she had rather get along in Boston without trouble. Besides she had a lot of presents to take home and she was anxious to get back when the trip was over to relate what she had seen and show her presents" (*FTS*, 129). Kitty expressed no desire for a freedom that would have meant the forfeiture of kin and community in Tennessee. Slave attendants were thus compelled to weigh their emancipatory desires against separation from all personal ties. Freedom was yet another form of trauma under these circumstances. Travel threatened slave attendants such as Med, Anson, Catharine Linda, Betty, and Kitty with unwonted severance from already tenuous connections to people and place, in the guise of northern freedom, even as it raised a host of ethical questions that jurists and abolitionists were largely unable to answer. Their stories of freedom illuminate the deep tensions within abolitionism as it struggled with the paradoxes and ironies of freedom in a partially free world.[147]

Jane Johnson, Peter Still, and the Slave Mother's Terrible "Choice"

By midcentury, antislavery organizations in other northern states had copied the *Aves* example in Massachusetts to establish similar strategies, but not without significant challenges. The bitter legal contests issuing from the "rescue" of the slave Jane Johnson and her two children, Daniel and Isaiah, aged about ten and eight, in Philadelphia offered one of the most widely publicized of these challenges to the extension of *Aves*. A legal sensation in its time, the Johnsons' escape has been largely forgotten, although speculation that Johnson may be the "Hannah Crafts" of Henry Louis Gates, Jr.'s recently recovered *The Bondswoman's Narrative* has reignited literary interest in the case.[148] The stories of slave women such as Johnson are too often subsumed into the public disputes between black and white men.[149] Headlines in 1855 referred to these events variously as "the Wheeler slave case" or the "case of Passmore Williamson," as abolitionists and proslavery ideologues vied over what constituted the "real" story of the "poor slave mother" in courtrooms and newspapers. This section examines the events surrounding Johnson's "rescue," a cause célèbre within organized antislavery, to illuminate the complex ways that these ongoing struggles over the geopolitics of freedom and slavery—the questions raised, but far from resolved, in Med's case—further unraveled the meaning of kinship, agency, and free will secured in the law. Johnson's case, in particular, illustrates the way slaveholders began to redeploy the writ of habeas corpus, "established as the defence of constitutional liberty," in the *Liberator*'s words, as a tool of proslavery jurisprudence.[150]

John Hill Wheeler, having recently been appointed U.S. minister to Nicaragua, returned to the states to deliver a package of treaties with directions from his wife, Ellen, to return with Johnson to serve the household in Nicaragua.[151] Wheeler had bought Johnson in 1853 from the Richmond merchant Cornelius Crew to serve as Ellen's maid.[152] Wheeler's route from Washington City to New York City—the port of embarkation for Nicaragua—"lay through the heart of the City of Philadelphia," where he paused at Bloodgood's Hotel before boarding the New York–bound steamship.[153] Warned of the risks to his human property, Wheeler commanded Johnson to masquerade as a free woman once they arrived in Philadelphia. "My master," Johnson reports, "told me not to speak to colored people, and that if any of them spoke to me to say that I was free" (*URR*, 94). Wheeler quickly regretted his boast that "Jane would not leave him" when his father-in-law, the celebrated portraitist Thomas Sully, informed him that he "could not have done a worse thing" than bring slaves into the city (*URR*, 90).[154] A waged black servant from the hotel brought word to the Anti-Slavery Society's offices of Johnson's desire to secure her freedom before Wheeler left Philadelphia.

Too short of time to procure a writ of habeas corpus, William Still and Passmore Williamson of the Philadelphia Vigilance Committee intercepted Wheeler just as the *Washington* tolled its five o'clock departure for New York (see figure 2.1).[155] The two men approached "the anxious-looking slave-mother with her two boys" to inform them of their rights as free subjects in Pennsylvania. In *Underground Rail Road* (1872), Still recalled that "when hearing of slaves brought into the State by their owners," the Philadelphia Vigilance Committee made sure to "inform such persons that as they were not fugitives, but were brought into the State by their masters, they were entitled to their freedom without another moment's service" (*URR*, 86–87).[156] "Many slave-holders," Still continued, "fully understood the law in

Fig. 2.1. "Rescue of Jane Johnson and Her Children." From third edition of William Still's *Underground Rail Road* (1883). (Courtesy of the Rare Book and Manuscript Library, University of Pennsylvania)

this particular, and were also equally posted with regard to the vigilance of abolitionists. Consequently they avoided bringing slaves beyond Mason and Dixon's Line in traveling North" (*URR*, 87). However, not all slaveholders were "thus mindful of the laws ... as may be seen in the case of Colonel John H. Wheeler, of North Carolina, the United States Minister to Nicaragua," who became, like Mary Slater, the "involuntary philanthropist" of his slaves (*URR*, 87).[157]

A series of suits and countersuits followed, as Wheeler's resentment toward the abolitionists who assisted in the "rescue" kept the case before the public.[158] Wheeler secured a writ of habeas corpus in Johnson's name and charged Williamson with her forced abduction. Judge John Kintzing Kane of the U.S. District Court in the Eastern District of Pennsylvania committed Williamson to Moyamensing Prison for contempt of court when he denied any knowledge of the Johnsons' whereabouts. The incongruity of "making the writ of Habeas Corpus—that glorious old bulwark of personal liberty—an instrument for getting possession of the mother and her children" was not lost on the Philadelphia Anti-Slavery Society.[159] The "opportunity," Still recalled sardonically, "seemed favorable for teaching abolitionists and negroes, that they had no right to interfere with a 'chivalrous gentleman,' while passing through Philadelphia with his slaves" (*URR*, 92). Wheeler's case "elicited no inconsiderable degree of public attention and interest," according to one jurist, partly because it came on the heels of Virginian slaveholder Jonathan Lemmon's appeal to the U.S. Supreme Court.[160] Lemmon had been stripped of his slave property as his household passed through New York, where they were to catch a Texas-bound steamer. Like Pennsylvania, New York had long before repealed its nine-months sojourner law. Louis Napoleon, a "vigilant colored man of New York," had secured a writ of habeas corpus for Lemmon's eight slaves, and the New York courts later ruled that they were free according to the state's personal-liberty laws. Was the suspension of property rights upon crossing from slave to free jurisdictions tantamount to a denial of the slaveholder's freedom to travel? That was the question in the slaveholder's appeal of *Lemmon v. The People of the State of New York* (1860) to the Supreme Court, even as the country tottered on the precipice of the Civil War. Only the war itself prevented the trial of the case, although the decision in *Dred Scott v. Sandford* (1857) would seem to have virtually guaranteed Lemmon a successful outcome.[161]

There had yet to be a definitive court ruling on the 1847 repeal of Pennsylvania's "sojourning law of 1780" when Williamson came before Judge Kane, and Kane's long opinion, an instance of what *Frederick Douglass'*

Paper deemed "arbitrary *dictum*," implicitly sought to address the questions raised in the ongoing Lemmon suit.[162] Kane's affirmation of the slaveholder's right "to transport his slaves through the free states, without violating his right of property in them," flew in the face of the longstanding precedent set in *Aves* and adopted by almost all free states in some form by the 1850s.[163] He sought, with particular vehemence, to mitigate the anomalous status of traveling slaves and argued that northern courts should treat slave attendants such as the Johnsons as a species of property like any other: "How can it be that a State may single out this one kind of property from among all the rest, and deny to it the right of passing over its soil—passing with its owner, parcel of his traveling equipment, as much so as the horse he rides on, his great coat, or his carpet bag."[164] Pennsylvania's statutory law, Kane argued, did not "rescind the rights of slave owners *passing through* our territory" but rather "left the right of transit for property and person, over which it had no jurisdiction, just as it was before, and as it stood under the Constitution of the United States and the Law of Nations." Kane did not so much invent a new constitutional right—"transit for property and person"—as enhance the existing "privileges and immunities" of citizenship through a tacit return to the Articles of Confederation, which provided, in its "original comprehensiveness" that "the people of each State shall [have] free ingress and regress to and from any other State."[165]

Alarmed abolitionists disputed Kane's interpretation of the Constitution and stressed its far-reaching consequences—the reestablishment of "Slavery in all the States of the Union"—if the U.S. Supreme Court elected to confirm his judgment.[166] The Pennsylvania Anti-Slavery Society demanded in its *Narrative of the Facts in the Case of Passmore Williamson* that state citizens take action to refuse slaveholders this purported "right of transit," seeing Kane's attack on Pennsylvania's law of freedom as an attempt to nationalize slavery.[167] The *National Era* likewise supposed that "if a Southern slaveholder may hold his slaves in the free States an hour, why not a year, or for life? Pretexts will never be wanting to protract the temporary stay of the visitor from the South with his 'family,' on pretence of transient business, or sickness, or pleasure."[168] Outspoken abolitionist newspapers in the years leading up to the Civil War cited the Wheeler slave case as a "glaring instance of the abandonment of State Rights by the sham Democracy" to further rouse northerners against the encroachments of "Federal slavery and despotism."[169] *Frederick Douglass' Paper*, possibly in response to the pro-South *Daily Pennsylvanian*'s claim that Wheeler "would have been safe from molestation, together with his servants ... [i]n any foreign country on the globe," argued that Kane's "monstrous doctrine" flew in the face of Anglo-American common law dating from *Somerset v. Stewart*. The principle of Mansfield's decision, it reasoned, "has been incorporated in the Constitution of the various Free States," including Pennsylvania. "She touched the free soil of Pennsylvania," it argued, in an unmistakable allusion to the deeply mythologized story of the slave Somerset, and "her shackles fell."[170]

Nearly five hundred visitors, including Frederick Douglass, William C. Nell, and Harriet Tubman, flocked to Pennsylvania's Moyamensing Prison to see the Quaker abolitionist Williamson, "the Philadelphia martyr."[171] James Pennington, speaking on behalf of the Shiloh Presbyterian Church of Rochester, New York, offered Williamson "the sincere prayers of Jane Johnson, her two sons," in a public letter of sympathy he addressed to *Frederick Douglass' Paper* (see figure 2.2).[172] Williamson appealed to the state supreme court with no success as his jail term dragged over the humid summer months.[173] Williamson's "martyrdom," like Hudson's, enraged abolitionists and confirmed their fears of a judiciary enthralled to slave power. Outspoken abolitionists harshly critiqued Kane, one of abolitionist writer Richard Hildreth's titular *Atrocious Judges* (1856), for "prostituting the writ of habeas corpus to the uses of slavery" and saw him as "a willing instrument of a pro-slavery government."[174] Williamson spent three months in jail before mounting public pressure finally forced Kane to release him.[175] "Thus has the voice of the People and the thunders of the Press," cheered abolitionist newspapers, "opened the prison-doors, and vindicated the cause of Freedom and Justice against the strong arm of Federal Tyranny."[176]

Conflicting reports flooded the nation over these summer months as Wheeler insisted on representing the Johnsons' rescue as a kidnapping. The *New York Evening Mirror* amplified Wheeler's charge in condemning the "sneaking Abolitionists, who seduces niggers from their masters."[177] Such charges against abolitionists were not unusual, and even Peter Still, the self-emancipated brother of William Still, had first "dreaded the Abolitionists of the North, of whose decoying people away and selling them at the far South he had so often heard."[178] The irony of Wheeler's charge was not lost on *Frederick Douglass' Paper*, and it questioned whether the Johnsons "were *forcibly* abducted from the state of Slavery in which he held them, and consigned to freedom greatly against their own will."[179] According to Wheeler's sensationalized account, "some dozen or twenty Negroes . . . by muscular strength carried the slaves" against their wishes to the adjoining pier while two other men threatened to "cut his throat if he made any resistance."[180] Of this so-called Negro mob, only Williamson was prosecuted

PASSMORE WILLIAMSON.

JANE JOHNSON.

Fig. 2.2. Portraits of Jane Johnson and Passmore Williamson. From the third edition of William Still's *Underground Rail Road* (1883). (Courtesy of the Rare Book and Manuscript Library, University of Pennsylvania)

in federal court, because he, in Kane's words, "was the only white man, the only citizen, the only individual having recognized political rights."[181]

Wheeler's claim of kidnapping set the terms of the public discourse in Johnson's case and forced abolitionists to marshal a legal rhetoric of "choice" in their own defense. Unlike the tactic taken in Med's case, they constructed Johnson as a willful agent in her self-emancipation. "The very fact that she chooses to remain free," the *National Era* reasoned, "proves that she wished to become so."[182] This language of choice pervades almost all abolitionist accounts of Johnson's case. William Still, aware of the legal import of Wheeler's charges, couched his eyewitness account carefully in the conditional language of free choice (*URR*, 87). "If you prefer freedom to slavery," he claimed to have said to Johnson at the time, "you have the chance to accept it now. . . . you will be protected by the law. . . . Of course, if you want to remain a slave with your master, we cannot force you to leave" (*URR*, 88–89). This verbal exchange positions Johnson as a free agent with the power to choose or reject freedom as she saw fit. However, Still's rhetoric also implied that slavery (or return to it) was equally a matter of choice. This is the way the *Liberator* portrayed the Johnsons' situation as well: "They are their own masters—they come and go at their pleasure, and when they get ready, they will doubtless go back to Mr. Republican Slave-driver Wheeler without a pass from Passmore Williamson or any body else."[183]

Partisan newspapers seized on Johnson's identity as a "poor slave mother" to advance their contrary political agendas. Wheeler trotted out the well-worn specter of familial disunion to dissuade abolitionists intent on her rescue. He insisted that Johnson "did not want to leave—that she was on a visit to New York to see her friends—afterwards *wished to return to her three children whom she left in Virginia, from whom it would be* HARD *to separate her*" (*URR*, 89). Indeed, Williamson recalled a panicked Wheeler admonishing Johnson as she escaped: "you know you have children and friends at Washington."[184] Wheeler continued to petition Pennsylvania courts in the hope of recovering Johnson and her children even after they settled into the black community of Boston's Beacon Hill, where they remained until Johnson's death in 1872.[185] Wheeler's 1860 memorial to the Pennsylvania legislature, for example, demanded indemnification for "the forcible taking away of my negroes . . . by a mob."[186] Unable to admit his slave's agency, Wheeler doggedly insisted that his "servants [had been] seized and stolen by a band of Abolitionists," even after Civil War and emancipation radically transformed the landscape of slavery and freedom.[187]

Johnson's efforts to tell her own story and claim her maternal agency helped vindicate abolitionist efforts even as they illuminated the limits of their legal rhetoric. Her dramatic appearance on the witness stand in a separate criminal case that Wheeler brought against Still, Williamson, and others—for inciting to riot and assault and battery—convinced the court to acquit five of the seven men involved.[188] Her widely reprinted affidavit and trial testimony countered Wheeler's charges of abduction: "I went away of my own free will" (*URR*, 95). Johnson's youngest son—like Truth's son Peter, "too young to know what these things meant—cried 'Massa John! Massa John!'" in alarm when the abolitionists seized him; however, the boy's reluctance mattered little to the court in the face of Johnson's authority as a mother (*URR*, 89).[189] Johnson felt compelled to testify after Kane dismissed her signed affidavit on behalf of Williamson and her request "that the *habeas corpus* issued to Passmore Williamson to bring herself and children into Court be quashed" since it was issued without her knowledge and consent.[190] "Jane Johnson," Kane insisted, had no standing in his court since Wheeler's habeas petition named "Jane" rather than "*Jane Johnson*" as party to the case; Kane exploited a legal technicality as he refused to recognize Johnson's self-renaming—her patronym, which slave law had banished along with her father. Johnson was not so easily dissuaded, and she risked recapture to face Wheeler in court. "[F]our of the most respectable ladies" in Philadelphia, including Sarah McKim, wife of James Miller McKim of the Pennsylvania Anti-Slavery Society and editor of the *Pennsylvania Freeman*, accompanied Johnson to and from the courthouse, where she spoke, in the words of one correspondent, "what was evidently the truth, tearing to tatters all the ingeniously devised lies of the prosecution as to her forcible 'abduction.'"[191]

The slave mother's choice of freedom over slavery offered abolitionists a powerful counterweight to the narratives of return raised with such frequency in the earlier cases of Anson, Catharine Linda, and Betty, yet the freedom Johnson embraced was contingent on another "choice" that abolitionists were far less inclined to avow. Johnson admitted, "I did not want to go without my two children" even as she acknowledged leaving "one other child ... in Richmond" whom she "never expected to see ... again."[192] Johnson's accounts, rendered in the terse language of legal documents, illuminate her ambivalent identification as a "slave mother" forced to leave one child in bondage in the hope of freeing the remaining two. She had insisted to Wheeler that her sons accompany them to Nicaragua and had already made plans to escape in New York when the abolitionists "rescued" her in Philadelphia: "I had made preparations before leaving Washington to get my freedom in New York; I made a suit to disguise myself in—they had never seen me wear it—to escape in when I got to New York."[193] In claiming this agency, Johnson was also forced to avow the other, implied "choice." "[T]he love of freedom," reads another report, "was stronger in the female slave than the attachment to her child."[194]

Antislavery print culture sought to transform Johnson into the paradigmatic "slave mother" of sentimental fiction, even as her personal accounts proffered a far more ambivalent understanding of maternal agency. Nearly a year after Williamson's release, Johnson made a surprising appearance in Abington, Massachusetts, at the August 1 celebration commemorating the British abolition of West Indian slavery. Hearty cheers greeted Johnson and her children when they took the stage. "It was a touching scene," reported the *Liberator*, "the mother and her boys—rescued slaves afraid to tell their abiding place, lest the minions of slavery should drag them back to perpetual servitude—standing on the stage, and mothers, tears standing in their eyes, looking on, while they gave what they could, with hearty blessings for their aid."[195] Such reports of the "rescued slaves" surround Johnson with the trappings of sentimentalism that do not appear in her own affidavits or testimony. Even Still deemphasized the agency of the slave mother in his depiction of the Johnsons being "providentially delivered from the house of bondage."[196] Tellingly, these abolitionist accounts also withhold mention of the unnamed child she left behind in bondage and the terrible *implied* "choice" she made to secure her freedom. As in popular histories of the case, they dwell on Johnson's sentimentalized rescue in ways that obscure the forfeiture that she was forced to make to secure freedom.

Although past BFASS leaders such as Maria Weston Chapman applauded the "slave mother" for taking "advantage of the decision we procured on the 'Med case,'" they remained far less able to acknowledge the conditions of her newfound freedom. Chapman's report on the successful twenty-second Anti-Slavery Fair described, in detail, the stir that Johnson's arrival in the exhibition hall created. Harriet Beecher Stowe was among the "friends present" who thronged around the slave mother. "We met her," Chapman continues, "not as one we were to condescend to and patronize" but rather "as our co-laborer in the cause, one whom neither threat or cajolery could overcome, but who swore, in the face of the world, for the truth, for her children, and for the man in prison on her account, that the miserably contemptible United States Minister to Nicaragua *lied* when he said she loved slavery, and was happy to return to it."[197] Although these women do not sentimentalize her as a passive "rescued slave," they could only meet Johnson as an equal—a "co-laborer in the cause"—through the suppression of the far-more-difficult "choice" she had made. Only through this strategic repression could the *National Era* and Chapman honor Johnson for acting "like a true woman . . . for her children."[198]

But the repressed, as Sigmund Freud cautions, inevitably returns. The difficult choice of the "poor slave mother" reemerged as the subject of Kate E.R. Pickard's literary reflection in *The Kidnapped and the Ransomed: Being the Recollections of Peter Still and His Wife Vina after Forty Years of Slavery* (1856). "It is in the nature of contingencies to haunt," Priscilla Wald argues, "if by *haunting* we understand the felt pressure of what has been refused or repressed."[199] Published the year after the Johnsons' well-publicized escape, Pickard's narrative explored, with imaginative flourish, the experiences of bondage from the perspective of the slave child who had been left behind; in it, we can see the haunting contingencies of freedom that more conventional abolitionist narratives tended to erase.[200] *The Kidnapped and the Ransomed* was among a number of hugely successful dictated slave narratives published and reprinted in the United States and Britain at mid-century, including, most notably, *Life of Josiah Henson, Formerly a Slave, Now an Inhabitant of Canada* (1849), *Narrative of Henry Box Brown* (1849), and *Narrative of Sojourner Truth: A Northern Slave* (1850). According to Pickard, the printed volume "contains 409 pages, and is to sell at $1.25."[201] She chose to narrate *The Kidnapped and the Ransomed* in the third person, and a biographical sketch by William Henry Furness of Seth Concklin, the white abolitionist who lost his life attempting to rescue Still's family, serves as the book's appendix.

The Kidnapped and the Ransomed offers one of the few detailed accounts of Jewish men—mercantile brothers Joseph, Isaac, and Levi Friedman—involved in antislavery activities. The Friedmans, who expressed "sympathy with the suffering, and . . . hatred of injustice and oppression," helped Peter Still secure his legal freedom after half a century of bondage (*KR*, 212, 214).[202] According to a letter from the Alabama slaveholder who continued to hold Still's family in bondage, Joseph Friedman "removed to cincinnati ohio & Tuck peter with him of course peter became free by the voluntary act of the master" (*URR*, 35). Like Missouri and South Carolina (examined in chapters 3 and 4), Alabama enacted statutory black codes that banished all free and emancipated blacks from within its borders. Still was well into his fifties when he secured his manumission and began his search for lost kin in 1850. With "carpet-bag in his hand, and his heart throbbing for his old home and people," Still headed toward Philadelphia to fulfill his one "great wish—that of seeking his parents, and his childhood's home" (*KR*, 234). Still's dictated narrative gestures toward those haunting contingencies that slave mothers faced when they sought freedom in a partially free world.

Still asked Pickard to shape his dictated recollections of slave life into a volume for publication shortly after he had secured the "ransom" of his wife, Vina, and their three children from the Alabama cotton plantation he had escaped. Vina also contributed her recollections to the narrative, although Still remains its principal subject. Abolitionist publisher Samuel J. May deemed Pickard "singularly qualified for the ... task" of transferring Still's life experiences into print, given their former acquaintance at the Seminary at Tuscumbia, where Pickard had taught and Still had labored as a hired slave (*KR*, 316).[203] Both May and Pickard professed an intimacy with Still, whom they addressed as "Dear Uncle Peter."

In 1811, Still's mother, Sidney, unable to escape with four children in tow, had fled Maryland with her two daughters, consigning Peter and Levin, aged six and eight, to the southern slave market.[204] Well after the end of slavery, William Still, Peter's younger brother who had been born after Sidney's escape, chronicled the story of his mother's perilous flight, but Peter and Levin were spared the knowledge of Sidney's painful decision until Peter's miraculous reunion with her forty years later (see figure 2.3). Private communications indicate that, *at Peter Still's request*, Pickard fictionalized his abandonment as an abduction to protect Sidney and his siblings from recapture under the Fugitive Slave Act. One letter that Pickard wrote in response to Still's insistence on secrecy is particularly revealing: "Uncle Peter, I had no intention of publishing anything that could in any way injure your mother's family.... I am sorry your friends have so little confidence in me as to suppose that I would by any means risk their safety or happiness" (see figure 2.4).[205] Still, however, took no chances with the safety of his northern-born kin, given the inherited status of slavery. Judges and commissioners remanded over three hundred individuals to slavery in the decade between 1850 and 1860.[206] Sidney, who had taken the precaution of renaming herself Charity, "was aware that the safety of herself and her rescued children depended on keeping the whole transaction a strict family secret" (*URR*, 38). These necessary repressions generate curious ambivalences in a narrative that also tells us much about the anxieties that the maternal agency of slave mothers such as Johnson and Sidney provoked in the imaginary of organized antislavery. The Still "family secret"—the repression of Sidney's

PETER STILL,
THE KIDNAPPED AND RANSOMED.

CHARITY STILL,
TWICE ESCAPED FROM SLAVERY.   See p. 37

Fig. 2.3. Portraits of Peter Still and Charity Still. From the third edition of William Still's *Underground Rail Road* (1883). (Courtesy of the Rare Book and Manuscript Library, University of Pennsylvania)

Choosing Kin in Antislavery Literature and Law 117

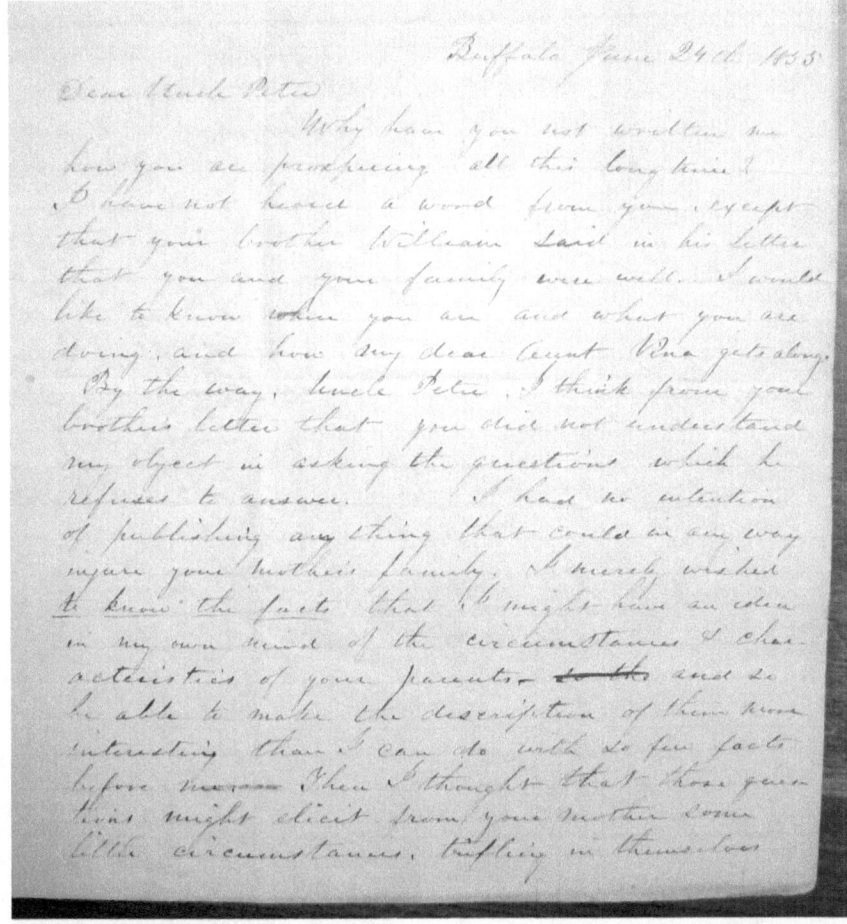

Fig. 2.4. Letter from Kate E.R. Pickard to Peter Still, Buffalo, New York, 24 June 1855. (Courtesy of the Special Collections and University Archives, Rutgers University Libraries)

painful "choice"—haunts, literally and figuratively, *The Kidnapped and the Ransomed.*

Pickard's version of Still's life begins in New Jersey with Sidney as a pious, *free* black mother. It opens with an idyllic scene of "two little boys ... playing before the door of their mother's cottage," awaiting her return from prayer-meeting at the "church ... in the woods, about a mile

Fig. 2.5. Portrait of an unidentified woman possibly based on a daguerreotype of Sidney (later Charity) Still. From Kate E.R. Pickard's *The Kidnapped and the Ransomed*. (Courtesy of the Manuscripts, Archives and Rare Books Division, Schomburg Center for Research in Black Culture, The New York Public Library, Astor, Lenox and Tilden Foundations)

off."²⁰⁷ The first few chapters read like a children's cautionary tale, as the wayward Peter and Levin, weary of waiting, accept an offer from a stranger, "a tall dark man, with black glossy hair," to help them "find their mother" (*KR*, 25, 28). Thus begins their wretched journey into southern bondage. Peter and Levin rejoice "in their childish hearts to think how their mother would wonder when she should see them coming," as "[c]akes of marvelous sweetness" lull them into obedience until they reach Kentucky, where they are sold for three hundred dollars (*KR*, 27). Their new master then points to "Aunt Betty, the cook" and tells the boys, "there is your mother—we've found her at last," as if to emphasize the fungibility of black motherhood in slavery (*KR*, 28). The boys shriek, "No! no! . . . that's not our mother!" with a dawning sense of the irreparable loss that their false friend has inflicted on them (*KR*, 28). This mother-loss is the constitutive rupture—the primal wounding—that initiates Peter and Levin's life in slavery. Indeed, the book's half-title page displays a woodblock engraving of an unidentified black woman dressed in a calico tignon, or head wrap, and shawl encircled by the words "the kidnapped and the redeemed," even though it is *Still*'s story that lends the book its title (see figure 2.5). This unidentified black woman, outfitted in the engraver's imagined garb of a southern slave, seems to gesture toward the slave mother who haunts Still's narrative of kidnap and redemption.²⁰⁸ The slave mother's necessarily unknowable past thus prefaces and frames the story of legal freedom that follows.

This motif of abandonment as abduction structures the remainder of Pickard's narrative.²⁰⁹ Told in this manner, the tale most closely resembles Solomon Northrup's best-selling dictated narrative *Twelve Years a Slave* (1853), which chronicles the abduction and sale of "a citizen of New York" into plantation slavery in Louisiana. *Twelve Years a Slave* was, in fact, among the titles that publishers Miller, Orton & Mulligan advertised in the back pages of Pickard's narrative. The unique power of Northrup's narrative, like *The Kidnapped and the Ransomed*, lay in its account of slavery dictated from the viewpoint of the free and unjustly enslaved. Black autobiographer Lucy Ann Delaney (examined in chapter 3) and white novelists such as John Jolliffe and F.C. Adams also seized on this trope of abduction to fashion compelling antislavery fictions. Responding to the identification of slavery with the law, such plots of kidnap retell institutional slavery as a form of criminal abduction. Pickard, by repressing the Still "family secret," asks her white northern readers to identify with the plight of a *free* black mother who is made the victim of a *legal* crime: the theft of her children. Gone is any intimation of what white northerners might have perceived as a kind of wayward, possibly monstrous *slave* motherhood associated with Sidney's desperate actions. Slavery thus becomes universalized under the sign of mother-loss, and true freedom in the narrative can be found only in the restoration of this severed kinship.[210]

Pickard's sentimental narrative was not so different from those abolitionist tracts that stressed the destruction of the slave family, often through ex-slave spokesmen, to attack the peculiar institution as "barbaric" and "primitive." In fact, abolitionist lawyer-turned-novelist Jolliffe's didactic antislavery novel *Belle Scott; or, Liberty Overthrown!* (1856) analogized slavery to cannibalism, asking rhetorically, in the words of its printer-hero Edgar Reed, "Where is the essential difference between the man who eats human flesh, and the one who buys and sells it?"[211] Fanny Kemble, too, declared southern slaveholders to be "a remnant of barbarism and feudalism."[212] Slavery, they argued, was essentially antagonistic to the development of the United States as a modern nation, and moralized appeals to the "slave family" became one of the most effective cornerstones of antislavery protest.

The slave's kinlessness, as Hortense Spillers argues, was essential to the maintenance of her status as inheritable property; the child cannot "belong" to a mother and a father when she belongs to the master as property.[213] In *The Kidnapped and the Ransomed*, Peter and Levin's new master decrees "those sweet memories of home and mother" to be a "forbidden subject" and forbids them to discuss their past lives as free children (*KR*, 30, 32). Northrup, likewise, recounts how he was "beaten until he had learned the necessity and the policy of silence" on his free past with his mother.[214] Enslavement, these narratives suggest, entails a violent ban on memory that denies the slave the power of social reproduction in kinship. The captive is a thing without history. Still's desire for freedom, consequently, finds expression in a deep yearning for his lost mother, and the ban against recalling her only makes this yearning more powerful. "[T]he memory of his mother," Pickard informs us, "haunted him" through the vagaries of slave life: unwarranted scourging, separations, and sales (*KR*, 70). Her insistent memory, fixed in his mind since childhood, prevents him from forging any lasting attachments to people or place in slavery: "But the thought of his mother far away, who could never hear from him, and whom now he might not hope to see, isolated him, in some sense, from his companions in bonds" (*KR*, 80).

Mother-loss also exerts a curious hold over young Vina, who was abruptly sold away from her mother, Sally, in Tennessee. On the McKiernan plantation outside South Florence, Alabama, "poor Vina's heart pined for her mother" (*KR*, 101). "To lose her mother thus," explains Pickard, "without receiving so much as a parting message, was harder far than all her previous trials" (*KR*, 140). Vina, too, seems haunted by ghostly figures of kin. "When she fell asleep," the narrative reads, "her heart was wandering still through strange, lonely places, in search of those whose forms, alas! she might never more behold" (*KR*, 101). Vina's "look of melancholy... [that] never left her face" first drew Still to her, and their shared mother-loss cements their mutual affection. Pickard gives her imagination free rein to reconstruct, with elaborate detail, the primal scenes of familial separation, and her rhetorical flourishes lend further romance to this extraordinary tale of family reunion, transforming autobiographical testimony into sentimental fiction. Advertisements insisted that *The Kidnapped and the Ransomed* was "the romance of real life," even though it read like a novel.[215] Pickard delighted in melodramatic excess, and the text's novelistic imperative can be seen most explicitly in her efforts to transform the motherless Vina into a romantic slave heroine.

Pickard's effort to preserve Vina's eyewitness accounts of slavery's sexualized violence conflicts with her equally powerful desire to make the slave mother suit the tastes and expectations of white abolitionist audiences. The narrative is perhaps most conflicted in its portrayal of Vina once it relegates Sidney, the other slave mother, to the story's margins. *The Kidnapped and the Ransomed* seeks to shape Vina according to the prevailing archetypes of proper womanhood, yet the wayward slave mother escapes such romantic typologies just as Johnson and Sidney unsettled the gender norms of antislavery print culture. The narrative charts Vina's development from a "timid shrinking maiden" into an exemplary slave mother. Indeed, motherhood allows her to rise above the degrading and miserable conditions of plantation slavery that surround her (*KR*, 108, 112). Her young countenance begins to wear, in Pickard's words, "a careful mother-look" after the birth of her first child, Peter (*KR*, 141). Vina, however, resists such idealized archetypes of slave womanhood as she professes resistance through a vengeful passion that eschews the feminine virtue found in a comparable narrative such as Harriet Jacobs's *Incidents in the Life of a Slave Girl*.

Pickard's moral critique of slavery, centered as it is on the destruction of slave families, produces the ambivalences that the narrative consequently seeks to contain. She must name the sexual violence of slavery—licentious master, jealous mistress, brutal overseer, and bastard children—as evidence of the immorality of the "peculiar institution" and its far-reaching effects on masters and slaves alike, yet she is unwilling to do so in her own, objective narrative voice. Instead, in keeping with her moderate abolitionism, Pickard reserves for Vina the enumeration of these "facts" of slavery, reproducing Vina's testimony "in her own words" in a coarse southern dialect and preserving it as direct quoted speech in the narrative (*KR*, 125). Unlike Still's largely unobtrusive narrative presence, Vina's pungent reportage cuts sharply through Pickard's overwrought prose: "when Bill Simms was oversee' he give me one mons's hard beatin', bekase I wouldn't s'mit to him 'bout everything he wanted" (*KR*, 125). Vina refuses to participate in the genteel trappings of moral womanhood as she takes vengeful delight in recollecting the well-deserved death of this cruel overseer: "When I heard he's dead, I's so glad! My heart couldn't help from shoutin' though it oughten't" (*KR*, 128, 188). Like Harriet Tubman, Vina prefers being a field hand to filling the more favored role of housemaid, and, by her own admission, she takes pleasure in challenging, and indeed thrashing, her master both physically and psychically. "I liked to fight him a little, anyhow, he's so mean," reports Vina, who rebuffed McKiernan's sexual demands repeatedly (*KR*, 171). Pickard applauds Vina's efforts to shield herself "from further insults" but expresses measured distaste for her candid enjoyment in recounting the wrathful methods she uses to do so (*KR*, 353).

Unlike the equally wondrous reunions depicted in contemporaneous fictions such as *Uncle Tom's Cabin*, *Clotel*, and the recently recovered *Bondswoman's Narrative*, Pickard—bound, however loosely, by Still's life experiences—presents a far more complex and, indeed, ambivalent familial reunion in the free North. The long-awaited chapter "The Kidnapped Boy Restored to His Mother"—two-thirds of the way into a narrative that charts Still's circuitous route into and out of bondage—finally fulfills such expectations, but not in the usual way. Still finds his way to the Anti-Slavery Society's offices in Philadelphia, where, unbeknownst to him, he is reunited with a brother he never knew, William Still: "When the two were left alone, the clerk questioned him further respecting his early memories of home and mother; and then, looking him in the face, he said, 'Suppose I should tell you that I am your brother?'" (*KR*, 249). Still's response, however, is fraught with ambivalence, as he doggedly resists William's identification: "your mother is not my mother, for my mother must be dead.... Yes, my mother must be dead. I don't expect to find her alive, but I thought I mought find her grave" (*KR*, 250). Still's yearning for kinship, by his own admission, was a search for knowledge that would permit closure in the face of separation and loss. William Wells Brown recorded similar sentiments: "The love of a dear mother, a dear sister, and three dear brothers, yet living, caused me to shed many tears. If I could only have been assured of their being dead, I should have felt satisfied."[216] Still had sought resolution in the confirmation of his mother's death only to be stunned to find a mother who continued to live. "In vain," the narrative continues, William "strove to convince him that they might both be sons of the same mother" (*KR*, 250). Still continues to deny this kinship even as his newfound northern siblings are eager to claim kinship with this self-described "stranger from Alabama" (*KR*, 254, 260).

Still's denial bespeaks the ongoing difficulty of claiming kin for those whom slavery had dispossessed of kinship. "[A]ll the family," Pickard describes, "pressed eagerly forward to greet him who had come as it were from the dead" (*KR*, 257). Reunion with lost kin figuratively reanimates Still and releases him from what Orlando Patterson describes as the social death of slavery.[217] The slave who once had been cleft, roughly, from kinship's synchronic and diachronic lines of filiation and descent suddenly finds himself in possession of a past and a possible future. Still's thoughts immediately turn to the past as he "gazed earnestly upon her [Sidney's] aged face," when the Stills bring him to his mother's New Jersey home: "His thoughts were busy with the past.... a sad procession, passed before him as he sat apparently a calm spectator of the joyous greetings of his kindred" (*KR*, 258). Pickard's omniscient narration delves, with loving detail, into Still's psychological responses—the ambivalence of claiming kinship even in freedom—but offers only a handful of unconvincing lines to Sidney in their momentous reunion. The "family secret" of Sidney's abandonment of Peter and Levin—the painful condition of the family's freedom—must remain untold and unexplored. The aged mother exclaims in one of her few lines of dialogue, "them two boys have been more trouble to me than all the rest of my children. I've grieved about them a great many years" (*KR*, 259). Pickard, however, interrupts this momentous encounter between mother and son to introduce instead another of Still's newfound siblings. The narrative restores to Still his long-lost mother, but it cannot restore to Sidney the meaning and power of her terrible agency. This is, indeed, the story of "mother's lost children" (*KR*, 259).

Pickard draws attention the institutional mechanisms of slavery—the literal and symbolic theft of bodies in the Atlantic slave trade and the ongoing theft of black kinship in domestic slavery—even as she smoothes over the contradictions and fissures in the ideals of republican motherhood and mother love revealed by slave women such as Vina, Sidney, and Johnson. The remainder of Pickard's narrative shifts away from Sidney's alternative story of freedom in its effort to reinstate the kind of romantic closure that an autobiographer such as Harriet Jacobs resisted. Still's determination to ransom his wife and children from the Alabama plantation he escaped propels the final third of the story. Like Josiah Henson, the figure on whom Stowe based Uncle Tom, Still "could not live in freedom, surrounded by his friends, and supplied with every comfort, and yet make no effort to redeem those he loved far better than life, or even liberty, from the cruel bondage which they endured" (*KR*, 316). William initially views his brother's efforts to raise the exorbitant "ransom" as a violation of antislavery principles, which offer cold comfort to Peter, who finds freedom meaningless without the presence of those he had been forced to leave behind. The remaining chapters chronicle Still's heroic labors to raise the five-thousand-dollar ransom. Even Ellis Gray Loring and J. Ingersoll Bowditch, the past champions of Med and George Latimer, make an appearance in this narrative as they pool their efforts to help Still raise the exorbitant sum that McKiernan demanded for his family.[218]

The narrative seeks to undo the antinomy of freedom and family, yet its movement toward a reconstituted family romance ends with a repetition crisis. Still had not made provisions to ransom his grandchild, who had been born while he was away, and so leaves this child behind on the McKiernan plantation when the rest of the reunited family journeys toward freedom. Still's own son, Pickard writes, "turned sadly from the joyful greetings of his new-found kindred, for the sound of a little voice rang in his ears. 'I am not there, my father!' was the wailing cry—and the last parting gift of his dying wife seemed stretching forth its little hands to claim a place among the free" (*KR*, 375). Pickard had given birth to her second child while preparing the manuscript for the press, and she repeatedly returned to this lost grandchild in letters to Still. "I am sorry to think of that poor little baby left behind," she expressed in one letter. "Do you think of trying to get it?"[219] There was no recorded reply. Still's son, like his grandmother before him, must live free but haunted by the memory of abandoned kin.

Pickard's story of freedom, like all freedom stories, was founded on necessary fictions. The Still "family secret" eludes containment in a narrative fraught with ambivalence. It bespeaks the insistent force with which the stories of slave women such as Sidney and Jane Johnson, repressed but not forgotten, demanded a hearing. William Still waited until 1872 to reclaim Sidney's terrible but powerful maternal agency in an extensive volume of until then unwritten narratives of slaves whom the Philadelphia Vigilance Committee assisted to freedom. Subscriptions from within the black community underwrote the publication of the first edition, which made public those stories that had once "called for still tongues." Inspired by the wondrous restoration of "his own brother . . . after forty years' cruel separation," Still published the *Underground Rail Road* with the hope that it would facilitate the reunions of those "thousands of mothers and children, separated by Slavery . . . living without the slightest knowledge of each other's whereabouts" (*URR*, 4). Even as radical Reconstruction began to grind to a halting stop, it "seemed reasonable to hope that by carefully gathering the narratives of the Underground Railroad passengers, in some way or other some of the bleeding and severed hearts might be united and comforted" (*URR*, 4). Jane Johnson's "rescue" numbered among the more than two hundred accounts, and Still implicitly dedicated her story to the unnamed son who had remained behind in bondage.

The issue that faced the slave petitioners studied in this chapter was not—as it was often framed—whether they saw freedom as liberating or oppressive but, rather, the conditions that freedom entailed and the contexts in which it was to be lived. In 1841, Judge Wilde of the Massachusetts Supreme Court reviewed the habeas action of George and Jack, two enslaved North Carolina seamen who yearned for freedom but "had wives and families" still in slavery: "they would like to go back, and be free, but they would rather go back as slaves, than not go back to their families at all."[220] Isaac Foreman, who left his wife enslaved in Virginia when he escaped in 1853, later regretted his actions in a letter to William Still: "If I had known as much before I left, as I do know, I would never have left until I could have found means to have brought her with me . . . because what is freedom to me, when I know that my wife is in slavery?" (*URR*, 65). William S. Edwards recalls that his mother was also offered the difficult "choice" of taking her child "with her into slavery, or [allowing him to] remain there and be free. . . . [She] chose to let me remain."[221] The unexpected responses of petitioners such as Anson, Catharine Linda, and Betty—bewildering to abolitionists—forcefully critiqued the terms of "free choice" in a world where the project of universal freedom was far from complete. The circumstances of their freedom reveal the contradictions inherent within an emergent U.S. culture of contract and its valuation of free and voluntary choices, as slaveholders and abolitionists vied over the conditions of its possibility.[222] Their necessarily partial and fragmented accounts draw attention to the mechanisms of power at work within the antislavery imaginary and challenge what they made legible as freedom. The destruction of the "slave family" was a cornerstone of antislavery protest, yet antislavery print culture often found it difficult to recognize the claims of kinship that endured the violence of slavery, as it advocated, relentlessly, for a freedom that entailed further separation and loss.

Taken as a loose genre of antislavery literature, these freedom suits—with their complex and often contradictory textures of desire, will, and choice—also insist that we critically revisit the fugitive slave narrative's mythopoetics of self-determination and the individualistic freedom it is primarily understood to champion. It was the slave's knowledge of an imminent sale and separation from kin, as Walter Johnson reminds us, that prompted many decisions to run away.[223] "The slave auction block," recalled William Still in 1872, "indirectly proved to be in some respects a very active agent in promoting travel on the U.G.R.R. [Underground Railroad]" (*URR*, 2). In these instances, flight preempted the inevitable destruction of kinship ties and what many slaves saw as the more debilitating uncertainty of interstate auction. David West, who left "a wife and four children" enslaved when he fled Virginia, reports that he "never should have come away but for being *forced*" by the threat of sale.[224] The slave narrator's journey to "freedom," in this context, may be reread in ways that subtly undercut, with serious implications, the masculine self-fashioning so commonly espoused on antislavery platforms and in print. These earlier cases of traveling slaves reveal how the fugitive individualism found, for example, in John S. Jacobs's narrative that began this chapter was necessarily enmeshed with gender and kinship in ways that were largely illegible to antislavery print culture. For the many slave attendants who became involved in these freedom suits, freedom necessarily prompted the question that haunted James Pennington's autobiographical *Fugitive Blacksmith* (1850), published decades after his escape from Maryland slavery in 1827: "What will you do with freedom without father, mother, sisters, and brothers?"[225]

3

The Gender of Freedom before *Dred Scott*

Former bondswoman and White House intimate Elizabeth Keckley authored one of the few extant postemancipation U.S. slave narratives, *Behind the Scenes; or, Thirty Years a Slave, and Four Years in the White House* (1868), as a defense of her patron, Mary Todd Lincoln, after the so-called old clothes scandal.[1] Critics often note in passing that Irene Sanford Emerson retained Keckley's former master, Hugh A. Garland, as her counsel against Dred Scott in the initial trial that was to become infamous in the annals of U.S. constitutional history, yet few have explored Scott's freedom suit as a broader context for understanding Keckley's controversial slave narrative and her autobiography as an index to the largely unexplored affective dimensions of Scott's case. Anne Burwell Garland brought the young slave mother (who also happened to be her unacknowledged half sister) to St. Louis, where her husband established a law practice after suffering financial failure in Virginia.[2] Garland became known for his appeals-court work and proslavery politics, and John Sanford hired him and his law partner, Lyman D. Norris, in 1849 to defend his sister's property rights in *Scott v. Emerson*, pending trial before the Missouri Supreme Court.[3] It is likely that Garland's most prominent client, Pierre (Cadet) Chouteau, Jr., whose father had recently faced a number of freedom suits including *Marguerite v. Chouteau* (examined later in this chapter), recommended the lawyer's services to his son-in-law Sanford.

Keckley began to press Garland for manumission once they settled in the border city. Her work as a dressmaker required her to travel regularly between St. Louis and Illinois. Garland's consent to this travel granted Keckley, as with the Scotts, the right to sue for freedom based on transit on free soil, although southern courtrooms by the 1850s had grown less inclined to rule in favor of freedom after the northern repeal of sojourner laws protecting traveling slaveholders' property rights. On one occasion,

Garland offered Keckley a "bright silver quarter of a dollar" with the suggestion, "If you really wish to leave me, take this: it will pay the passage of yourself and boy on this ferry-boat, and when you are on the other side of the river you will be free. It is by far the cheapest way to accomplish that which you desire."[4] Slaveholding St. Louis lay just across the Mississippi River from Illinois, a free jurisdiction since the passage of the Northwest Ordinance (1787), but Garland knew quite well that the boundary between slavery and freedom in the newly settled western territories was far more legal fiction than reality. As lead defense in *Scott v. Emerson*, Garland declared the Missouri Compromise "obnoxious" and professed no sympathy for laws prohibiting slavery "beyond a certain line."[5] Keckley was not deceived. "I do not wish to be free in such a manner," she countered. "I can cross the river any day, as you well know, and have frequently done so, but will never leave you in such a manner. By the laws of the land I am your slave—you are my master, and I will only be free by such means as the laws of the country provide" (*BS*, 35). Illinois held only an empty promise of freedom for a slave mother who faced the prospect of recapture under the Fugitive Slave Act and the subsequent displeasure of a master with the authority to sell her away from her child. Keckley's careful reply mollified Garland even as it illuminated the ways that kinship and geopolitics shaped her efforts to secure legal freedom. "He expected this answer," she noted, "and I knew that he was pleased" (*BS*, 35).

Keckley desired not a fugitive's freedom but the autonomy to become a free mother *and* to remain in urban St. Louis. Her commitment to self-purchase may be better understood as a calculated response to these deeper legal currents as western annexation began to reshape the geopolitics of slavery and freedom. She persisted in her appeals for manumission even though Garland "commanded [her] never to broach the subject again" (*BS*, 31). "I would not be put off thus," she recalls, "for hope pointed to a freer, brighter life in the future" (*BS*, 31). Motherly concern over the fate that awaited her son and the desire for freedom impelled her onward, risking Garland's displeasure. Her perpetually debt-ridden master eventually relented and set a manumission price of twelve hundred dollars for mother and son, in what he viewed as benevolent consideration of her fidelity to the family (*BS*, 35).[6] A number of Keckley's influential "lady patrons of St. Louis" loaned her the requisite amount, and the deeds of manumission for the slave woman known as "Garland's Lizzie" and her son, George, were finally entered into St. Louis circuit court on 15 November 1855 (*BS*, 39, 47, 40). Keckley joined a number of slaves, most famously Harriet and Dred

Scott, who secured legal freedom through manumission or the courts and obtained the requisite licenses to live as free blacks in Missouri.[7] "Lizzie Keckley"—aged thirty-nine years, height five foot two inches, occupation mantua maker—appears on a "List of Free Negroes, Licensed [in] ... St. Louis County," along with Dred Scott, steward (1858), and Harriet Scott, washer (1858), among the more than seven hundred black freemen and women who applied for residency licenses in St. Louis County between 1841 and 1859.[8] Keckley remained in St. Louis with George to ply her trade, leaving for Washington City only after she "repaid every cent that was so kindly advanced" (*BS*, 47).[9]

Keckley penned her recollections in the years immediately after the Civil War, as millions of former slaves first began to define freedom for themselves. For many of them, this process entailed long and possibly fruitless journeys to reconstitute those kinship ties sundered by slavery. Keckley may not have espoused a recognizable rhetoric of abolitionism, yet she numbers among a host of figures examined in this chapter—including Harriet and Dred Scott, Winny, Rachael, Julia, Lunsford Lane, John Berry Meachum, and Lucy Ann Delaney—who fashioned stories of freedom, but stories that unfolded in unusual ways. Missouri did not join the Confederacy, but "old St. Louis, which was closely associated with the south through family relations and business," recalls former bondsman James Thomas, "had a secession feeling."[10] Many of these legal stories are set in "old St. Louis," and the geopolitics of a western slave state bordered by free states influenced, in part, the kinds of freedom stories they told. Such stories unsettle the regional imaginary of freedom and slavery mapped onto a north-south divide. Unlike fugitive slaves, these men and women sought forms of legal freedom in the slaveholding Southwest—forms that often lent further validation to the very slave system that oppressed them. Such pathways to freedom flew in the face of the immediate abolitionism espoused by more radical figures such as William Lloyd Garrison and Frederick Douglass. Instead, their struggles toward legal freedom in the Southwest accommodated the law of slavery by succumbing to what William Wells Brown, Harriet Jacobs, and others condemned as the "chattel principle" or property logic of the slave system.

This chapter turns its gaze westward to reconsider the circumscribed forms of slave resistance available from within the system of chattel slavery. The accounts of freedom found in these narratives and legal suits reveal the "degrees of freedom," to borrow Rebecca Scott's words, that structured the agency and lives of those who sought legal recognition of their personhood from the slave state.[11] Their claims on kinship helped reshape the geopolitics of the antebellum United States as they undermined the legitimacy of a social system founded on the false dichotomy between slave and freeman. Their acts of bringing suit forced slaveholders and jurists to recognize slave petitioners in powerfully contrary ways. Southern courts (specifically, in this chapter, St. Louis circuit court) transformed slave petitioners, through the stroke of the clerk's pen, into free persons with limited rights and privileges, even though the outcome of the freedom suit at trial—often delayed for years—was supposed to determine the petitioner's legal status. Courtrooms embraced awkward legal fictions, like the paradoxes of will and choice found in comparable northern freedom suits, to preserve the chattel logic of slavery in frontier St. Louis, where the lives of slaveholders, free blacks, and slaves intersected.

Partus Sequitur Ventrem in St. Louis Freedom Suits

The unstated circumstances surrounding Elizabeth Keckley's decision to seek legal freedom in St. Louis gesture toward the messy yet dynamic entanglements of kinship, property, and the geopolitics of travel too often elided from *Dred Scott*'s legal histories. The *Dred Scott* opinion stands in infamy for its open avowal of sectional politics and failure to deliver justice to an elderly slave who embraced law and legal process in an eleven-year struggle to contest his enslavement and secure his freedom. Nearly all studies of the case view "Dred's story" as, in the words of one legal scholar, "the story of a slave ... struggling hard to gain his freedom through the courts."[12] This section reads "Dred's story" through the freedom suit and slave narrative, building on the feminist legal scholarship of Lea Vander-Velde and Sandhya Subramanian to shed new light on *Dred Scott* as a history of litigation profoundly shaped by gender and kinship. Harriet and Dred Scott *together* dedicated over a decade of their lives to the struggle for a legal freedom that would extend to their two daughters.

The tendency to imagine the infamous case as the freedom struggle of an individual man obscures the more complex story of familial or collective agency that motivated the Scotts' lawsuit. Indeed, commentaries on the case continue to ponder why Scott risked reenslavement to return to St. Louis to sue for freedom rather than take advantage of territorial geopolitics to escape in the manner of John S. Jacobs. Such questions betray an uncompromising view of freedom as both individual and absolute that overlooks the complex entanglements of kinship and property under slave law—oversights that are woven into the very fabric of those abolitionist narratives that have become, in Priscilla Wald's words, "the official story" of American freedom. As chapter 2 argues, northern abolitionists who were invested in individualistic notions of freedom found it exceedingly difficult to fathom the motivations behind what they deemed the slave's "voluntary return" to slave territories. They often viewed this "choice" as a rejection of the freedom that had come to define their regional identities, without fully understanding how slaves such as Anson, Catharine Linda, and Betty may have yearned to return to those kinship ties that also bound them to slavery. Harriet and Dred Scott met in free territory and moved in and out of slave and free jurisdictions with their daughters over roughly ten years. Litigation may have offered a far more desirable kind of freedom than the risks involved in fugitive flight or escape in free territories, especially with young children in tow. Focusing on the critically neglected figure of Harriet Robinson Scott, as VanderVelde and Subramanian do, provokes us to examine the significance of kinship in freedom suits to understand how the Scotts, like Keckley, may have sought to define the meaning of freedom for themselves.[13] The Scotts' desire to "keep the family intact and to protect the daughters" who would soon become valuable property on the southern slave market may have driven the lawsuit in ways that remain unnoticed in scholarship that insists on Dred's individual quest for independence.[14]

As Don Fehrenbacher notes, Dred Scott "remains a very indistinct figure," given the few "contemporary traces of the man."[15] The biographies of eminent jurists and the analyses of the formal questions raised by Dred's suit generally overshadow the story of kinship at the heart of the Scotts' struggle for freedom. That story began in the spring of 1836 when assistant surgeon John Emerson traveled with his enslaved manservant up the Mississippi River to Fort Snelling in Wisconsin Territory, where the Missouri Compromise had forbidden slavery.[16] Emerson had purchased Dred from Peter Blow, in whose household he had served since early youth. Dred maintained a close association with the Blows despite his transfer in ownership, and Taylor Blow, Peter's third son, continued to be Dred's benefactor until Dred's death. Harriet remains a far more "indistinct figure," especially because scholars have approached her story, such as the couple's dual freedom suits against Emerson, as "a repetition of Dred's."[17] Despite the feminist recovery work of VanderVelde and Subramanian, much contemporary scholarship, following Don Fehrenbacher's encyclopedic case study, has continued to find it "sufficient to describe the proceedings in

Scott v. Emerson, with the understanding that everything said applies also to *Harriet v. Emerson*."[18]

There are few records detailing Dred's relationship with Emerson, a sickly medical officer whose oft-repeated complaints and requests for transfer most likely led to his honorable dismissal from service in 1842, just one year before his death.[19] Emerson owned only one slave during his lifetime; he had purchased Dred in anticipation of his travels.[20] Dred met the seventeen-year-old Harriet Robinson at Fort Snelling, where she was enslaved to the resident Indian agent, Major Lawrence Taliaferro, who may have intended to free her by officiating her marriage shortly thereafter.[21] In April 1838, the Scotts joined Emerson in Fort Jesup for his marriage to Irene Sanford, daughter of a Virginia manufacturer then in St. Louis.[22] The Scotts then returned to Fort Snelling, remaining there until 1840, when Emerson brought them back to St. Louis. (During this period of itinerancy, Harriet gave birth to Eliza and Lizzie, who later became parties in the lawsuit.)[23] The Scotts remained in Irene's custody after Emerson's death. She loaned Dred to her brother-in-law in Louisiana and Texas and then hired out the couple again in 1846.[24] Once reunited in St. Louis, the Scotts attempted to buy their freedom from the widow Emerson, but she refused.

Scott v. Sandford began in 1846 as two separate freedom suits, *Dred Scott v. Emerson* and *Harriet (of Color) v. Emerson*, on the basis of the couple's extended sojourns and residence histories in Illinois and the Wisconsin Territories, where the Northwest Ordinance had forbidden slavery. Francis B. Murdoch, the former Alton district attorney who had prosecuted the murder of abolitionist newspaperman Elijah Lovejoy, filed their lawsuits in St. Louis circuit court (see figure 3.1). The Scotts sought to secure the family's freedom *and* the right to remain in St. Louis. Harriet was twenty-eight years old and Dred fifty-one; Eliza and Lizzie were eight and seven, not much older than Med and Anson had been at the time of their cases, although they were saleable as adult women by the time *Scott v. Sandford* ended. Judge Alexander Hamilton presided over the initial trial and directed that the two suits be collapsed into one, with the stipulation that the final judgment delivered in the one would apply to the other since the law was "identical" in both suits. The attorneys chose to advance Dred's suit, which partly explains why historical scholarship has largely forgotten Harriet's story, presuming it to be identical with, if not entirely subordinate to, Dred's.[25] Harriet's specific claims to freedom were elided from the litigation once it was subsumed into Dred's lawsuit.

The critical recovery of Harriet Robinson's story helps reveal "patterns

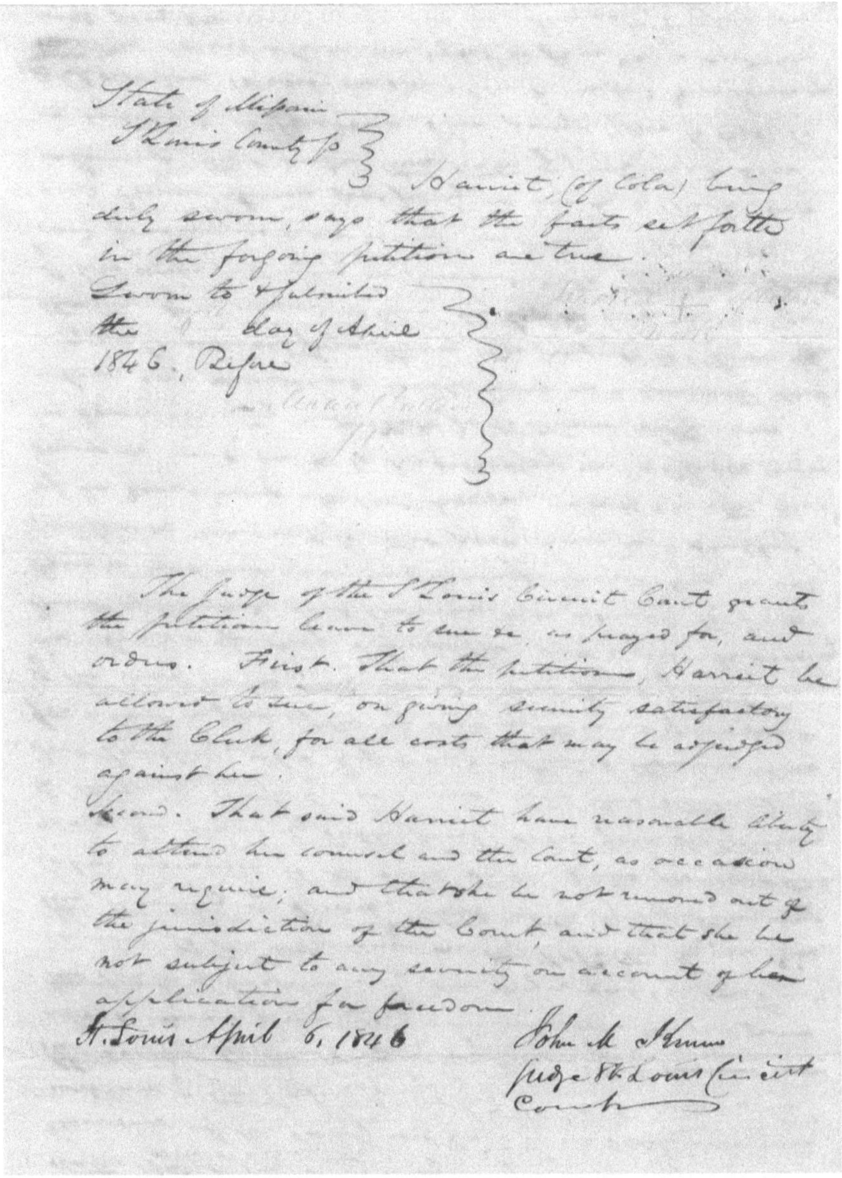

State of Missouri
St Louis County ss

Harriet, (of Color) being duly sworn, says that the facts set forth in the foregoing petition are true.

Sworn to & subscribed the day of April 1846. Before

The Judge of the St Louis Circuit Court grants the petitioner leave to sue &c. as prayed for, and orders. First. That the petitioner, Harriet be allowed to sue, on giving security satisfactory to the Clerk, for all costs that may be adjudged against her.

Second. That said Harriet have reasonable liberty to attend her counsel and the Court, as occasion may require; and that she be not removed out of the jurisdiction of the Court, and that she be not subject to any severity on account of her application for freedom.

St. Louis April 6, 1846

John M Krum
Judge St. Louis Circuit Court

Fig. 3.1. Petition of "Harriet, a woman of color." *Scott, Dred, a man of color v. Emerson, Irene* (Nov. 1846), Case No. 1, Circuit Court Case Files, Office of the Circuit Clerk, City of St. Louis, Missouri. (Courtesy of Missouri State Archives) of silences, or arguments unmade and lines of precedent ignored" in those studies dedicated to plotting out the long legal journey of *Dred Scott v. Sandford* from St. Louis to the U.S. Supreme Court.[26] Harriet was among a number of enslaved women who petitioned St. Louis circuit court for freedom, and she may have had the stronger freedom claim, given what James Kent's *Commentaries on American Law* (1826–30) referred to as the "doctrine of emancipation" set in these cases. Judgments favoring freedom were not unusual for a western state with long histories of Native American and African enslavement, where geopolitics and the desire to avoid interstate hostilities often mitigated the supposedly hereditary status of slavery. In these earlier freedom suits, enslaved mothers redeployed the doctrine of *partus sequitur ventrem* to secure the freedom of their children following their own emancipation. The establishment of Harriet's residence history on free soil was therefore of crucial significance in the Scotts' case: a decision in her favor would also free her daughters. This section broadens the legal story of *Dred Scott* by setting it in the context of the comparable cases of Winny, Polly Crocket, Julia, and Rachael, in which judgments for the mothers' freedom also established the freedom claims of their enslaved children in subsequent suits. Such an approach fundamentally shifts our epistemologies of freedom and slavery by framing *Dred Scott* not simply in the context of conflicts over race, rights, and citizenship in U.S. higher law (as it has traditionally been viewed) but also in the context of the contradictions of gender, kinship, and property in a United States divided into free and slave jurisdictions.

Winny's 1822 petition to St. Louis circuit court was the first freedom suit appealed to the newly established Supreme Court of Missouri.[27] *Winny v. Whitesides* (1824) set a precedent in favor of freedom based on residence on free soil, and the case may have shaped the freedom claims that emancipated mothers later made on behalf of their enslaved children.[28] In 1795, the Whitesideses had migrated from the Carolinas to Illinois, where they held Winny as their slave over a three- to four-year residence before they relocated to Missouri. The Missouri Supreme Court freed Winny in a unanimous decision (which, however, made no mention of her motherhood), upholding the Northwest Ordinance prohibiting slavery northwest of the Ohio River after finding that the Whitesideses' "intention to reside" in Illinois had obligated them to abide by its law of freedom.[29] The opinion also confirmed (contrary to the reattachment established in *Case of the Slave Grace*) that the right to property did not "revive" upon return to a slave territory, in what became known as the doctrine of "once free, forever free."[30]

When the Missouri Supreme Court judged that Winny's residence in Illinois freed her, it established the basis for the freedom claims of Winny's nine children and first grandchild.[31] Missouri law allowed emancipated mothers to file petitions for freedom on behalf of their slave children in the capacity of "next friend." Acting as "next friend" in her children's freedom suits, Winny successfully asserted that "by reason of having been held in Illinois she and her children born since are free."[32] *Partus sequitur ventrem*: a free mother, even retroactively determined, bears free children.

Julia v. McKinney (1833) and *Rachael v. Walker* (1836) also involved enslaved women who were mothers.[33] The Missouri Supreme Court verdicts for the mothers' freedom in these suits also affected the inherited status of slavery for their children. The legal records omit the maternal dimensions of these cases so that they appear, like the cases of Winny and Harriet Scott, as suits involving only the claims of an individual seeking freedom. Kinship was largely incidental to the immediate legal questions at stake in these cases, yet it motivated and influenced the shape of litigation for these women plaintiffs. Such omissions may also have been strategic: Lucy Ann Delaney's autobiography suggests that her mother's lawyers counseled her not to include her daughter in her initial freedom suit for fear of weakening her case before a southwestern jury that may have been disinclined to return a verdict that removed too much property from a single slaveholder.[34] Slave mothers such as Winny, Julia, and Rachael had to sue again and again as "next friend" to obtain freedom for their children.

The Missouri Supreme Court established its tendency to enforce the laws of its neighboring free states when it overturned the lower-court verdicts against freedom in *Julia v. McKinney* and *Rachael v. Walker*. Julia based her initial claim to freedom on residence in Illinois with her mistress, Lucinda Carrington, and Carrington's son. The Carringtons migrated from Kentucky to Illinois with the intention to hire Julia out in Missouri: they were aware that the Illinois constitution made the introduction of slavery into the state a crime punishable by the forfeiture and emancipation of the slave. The Carringtons did not intend Julia's emancipation and took particular precautions to circumvent the law of freedom in Illinois: they held Julia for a month in Pike County, Illinois, where they hired her out illegally, before sending her to Missouri, where she was sold to Samuel T. McKenney.[35] The lower court found for Carrington, but Justice Matthias McGirk overturned the judgment. The U.S. Constitution, he reasoned, extended "the undoubted right of every citizen of the United States to pass freely through every other State with his property of every description, including negro slaves without being in any way subject to forfeit his property for having done so," but the Carringtons, to his mind, had exceeded the "common modes of traveling ... through the State."[36] A number of influential jurists vehemently endorsed traveling slaveholders' constitutional right to property, yet this proslavery interpretation of the privileges and immunities of citizenship did not prevent McGirk from emancipating Julia. He held the Carringtons accountable for introducing slavery into a free state, regardless of their intentions to the contrary. Two years later, Julia again sued McKenney (along with slave traders William Walker and Thomas D. James), for her daughter's freedom, in the capacity of "next friend," and she succeeded in establishing her daughter's freedom on the basis of her own free motherhood, as Winny before her had done.[37]

Rachael's successful petition for freedom, as many legal scholars note, provided the most immediate precedent for the claims at stake in the Scotts' case. Rachael instigated her suit, in part, to forestall separation from her son James (John) Henry since, according to court documents, the two were soon to be carried by the slave trader William Walker "down the Mississippi River probably to New Orleans for sale."[38] Rachael had served army lieutenant Thomas Stockton at Fort Snelling, and her son had been born at Fort Crawford, Michigan; in 1834, Stockton brought the two to St. Louis, where they were sold and resold until they found themselves in the hands of the slave trader Walker.[39] Rachael may thus have known Harriet Robinson, as they would have numbered among the small community of slaves held by officers or Indian agents attached to federal forts in free territory.[40] Indeed, as VanderVelde and Subramanian note, the army paid officers an additional allowance (equivalent to the wages of a private) for the maintenance of one servant because many of these officers, graduates of West Point and younger sons of respected Virginia families, expected to uphold a certain social standard even while stationed on the frontier.[41] These officers, like Stockton, often availed themselves of these allowances to buy or hire out slaves when they married and established households on the frontier. Small groups of slaves, in this way, were introduced into the Northwest Territory against the provisions of the Thomas Amendment to the Missouri Compromise.[42]

Stockton had held Rachael and James Henry as slaves within the free territories of the Northwest Ordinance before he sold the two to Walker. Stockton's lawyer sought an exception to the Northwest Ordinance since "a soldier of the American army" was subject to military authority and could not be said to have "voluntarily" introduced slavery into a free territory.

The opinion, authored again by Justice McGirk, expressed open frustration with such individuals "disposed to deal in slave property" and their elaborate methods to circumvent the law. Although exemptions were to be based on "the nature of necessity," McGirk asserted that "no authority of law or the government compelled him to keep the plaintiff there as a slave. . . . this was his voluntary act."[43] Stockton's orders did not exempt him from the "consequence of introducing slavery both in Missouri territory and Michigan, contrary to law."[44] He had willfully procured a slave and held her, unlawfully, in free territories, an act punishable by forfeiture of the slave, as decreed by territorial law. Twenty years later, in a changed political climate, however, Hugh Garland successfully revived Stockton's rationale of necessity from *Rachael v. Walker* to defend Emerson's property rights in the Scotts before the Missouri Supreme Court.

Word of Rachael's successful suit for freedom, according to Vander-Velde and Subramanian, most likely reached Fort Snelling by the time of Harriet's arrival, since the outcome of Rachael's case affected the property claims of many of the officers.[45] When the Missouri Supreme Court again reversed the lower court's judgment and freed Rachael, it also established the grounds for her later successful suit against Walker for the freedom of her son.[46] Harriet may have drawn inspiration from Rachael's example to press a similar legal suit for her family's freedom in St. Louis after Emerson's death.[47] Faced with the awful fate that awaited Eliza and Lizzie on the southern slave market, Harriet, like Rachael, may have elected to embrace litigation in St. Louis as the best means to secure her family's freedom and prevent their separation by sale.

Decades after the legislated end of slavery, Lucy Ann Delaney published an autobiographical account of the freedom suits that her mother, Polly Crocket, instigated in St. Louis circuit court to secure their freedom (see figure 3.2). *From the Darkness Cometh the Light; or, Struggles for Freedom* (1891) offers its own form of legal storytelling as it transforms the material of the freedom suits, including the trial records, depositions, and judicial opinions, into a narrative that reveals how plaintiffs such as Winny, Julia, and Rachael negotiated the paradox of motherhood under slave law. Indeed, Delaney situates the "'scene of writing' so peculiar to African American autobiography" in the unexpected site of the U.S. courtroom, where black legal disabilities would seem to negate rather than support this form of narrative self-fashioning.[48] Reading Delaney's narrative with and against these freedom suits allows us both to interrogate the mechanisms that made litigation possible and to understand better how enslaved women renegotiated the law into a pathway to freedom. Delaney's mother, Polly Crocket ("Polly Wash" in court documents, presumably after former master Robert Wash), filed a petition for freedom in the St. Louis court in 1839 and a second freedom suit on behalf of her daughter in 1842.[49]

Like Peter Still, Delaney organizes her narrative around the powerful theme of theft, figured in the abduction and unjust enslavement of her mother, Polly. This theft opens Delaney's narrative and also establishes Polly and Delaney's right to freedom in St. Louis court. According to Delaney's narrative, the young Polly was kidnapped from Illinois and carried across the Mississippi River to St. Louis and then up the Missouri River, where she, along with four other black captives, was sold at auction. Polly's deposition in *Wash v. Magehan* (1839), by contrast, explained that she had formerly resided "in Wayne Country, Kentucky . . . as the slave of one Joseph Crockett," who held the fourteen-year-old in Edwardsville, Illinois, where his household remained "for several weeks over the winter and spring months."[50] Crockett hired Polly out "to different persons to spin and perform the usual labors and duties incumbent upon a house servant at the rate of two dollars a week."[51] One witness for the prosecution recalled hearing her husband speak with "old man Crockett and his son . . . about the consequences of keeping" Polly in Illinois.[52] Like Lucinda Carrington, Crockett was quite aware of the "consequences" of Illinois's law of freedom, despite his professed "intention," according to another witness, to set Polly free upon his death.[53] In 1818, Polly was unexpectedly "taken away" up the Missouri River, where she spent the next five years, and was eventually purchased by Taylor Berry and installed in his household until his death.

In rewriting Polly's history, Delaney subtly transforms her mother's enslavement, which was a legal right under slave law, into a *crime* in order to ask whether there was any justice to be had for this theft of black personhood. This question of justice also animated the bitter legal struggles over black civic inclusion that gripped the post-Reconstruction nation in which she penned her recollections. Delaney begins her autobiography with the crime of stolen birthright rather than with the usual profession—"I was born" a slave—that initiates the slave narrative's plot of bondage and freedom.[54] She reelaborates "the letter of the law" as part of her self-fashioning in an autobiographical narrative that takes up and completes the story that her mother began many years earlier in her legal deposition.[55] Lucy and her sister, Nancy, were born shortly after Polly's "marriage" to Berry's enslaved manservant, who remains unnamed in the narrative. After Robert Wash married the widow Berry, he became the legal owner of the family; Wash

Fig. 3.2. Portrait of Lucy Ann Delaney. From *From the Darkness Cometh the Light; or, Struggles for Freedom*. (Used with the permission of Documenting the American South, The University of North Carolina at Chapel Hill Libraries)

was "an eminent lawyer, who afterwards became Judge of the Supreme Court."[56] Wash sat in judgment before a number of appealed freedom suits, including *Julia v. McKinney*, *Milly v. Smith* (1829), *Hay v. Dunky* (1834), and *Marguerite v. Chouteau* (1834), and he consistently dissented from decisions in favor of freedom to uphold the property rights of slaveholders. Summoned as a witness for the defense in Delaney's freedom suit, Wash had claimed the slave family as his property upon his wife's death, acting, in Delaney's words, "in direct opposition to the will of Major Berry": Wash "tore my father from his wife and children and sold him 'way down South!'" (*FD*, 11, 14). Berry's surviving daughter, Mary Berry Coxe, later reclaimed the three women; she placed Delaney in another household and later sold Polly to a St. Louis lumberman.[57]

Polly resolved to seek freedom only in response to this threat of separation, even though she had been, according to Delaney's narrative, robbed of her rightful freedom since a young girl. Her mother made "a solemn vow that her children should not continue in slavery all their lives" (*FD*, 15–16). Delaney's narrative also registers the profound cleavages between Polly's desire for kinship—the yearning for familial integrity—and freedom. Indeed, Polly's subsequent actions are painfully constructed around these two antinomies under slave law. When Mary Berry Coxe took Nancy as a waiting-maid on her wedding tour of the North, Polly instructed Nancy "not to return with Mr. and Mrs. Cox, but to run away, as soon as the chance offered, to Canada," even though that meant Polly's permanent separation from her daughter (*FD*, 16). Thus advised, Nancy took advantage of northern geopolitics in the manner of John S. Jacobs to escape when the household arrived at Niagara Falls. "A servant in the hotel," Nancy reports, "gave me all the necessary information and even assisted me in getting away" (*FD*, 17). The increasingly recalcitrant Polly fled northward as a fugitive three weeks later, once she discovered that the Coxes resolved to sell her, leaving Delaney behind in slavery. Polly made it to Chicago before she "finally gave herself up to her captors, and returned to St. Louis . . . fearing that Mr. Cox would wreak his vengeance upon" Delaney (*FD*, 23). The "ties to life," in Harriet Jacobs's words, that bound Polly to Delaney also bound her in slavery.[58] Only after Polly had exhausted these more direct means of escape did she turn to the courts. She filed her suit in St. Louis circuit court on 3 October 1839, with the assistance of attorney Harris Sprout, although she was forced to wait another four years before it came to trial, on 6 June 1843.[59] The court emancipated Polly once the witness depositions confirmed beyond a doubt that she "was claimed by Mr. Crockett as his slave" on free soil, contrary to Illinois law.[60] "She had ample testimony to prove that she was kidnapped," Delaney recalls of her mother's trial, "and it was so fully verified that the jury decided that she was a free woman, and papers made out accordingly" (*FD*, 24).

Polly petitioned for Delaney's freedom in the capacity of "next friend" while awaiting her pending trial.[61] During this period, Delaney had been transferred to Coxe's younger sister Martha, upon Martha's marriage to David Mitchell, the regional superintendent for Indian Affairs.[62] Polly again instigated the legal proceedings as a last resort, when she discovered the Mitchells' decision to sell Delaney "down the river" for her disobedience (*FD*, 29). Delaney "with fleet foot" immediately sought refuge with her mother on the morning she was to be sold. Over forty years later, Delaney recalled in vivid detail the day that commenced her two-year legal struggle to secure her freedom: "On the morning of the 8th of September, 1842, my mother," Delaney writes, "sued Mr. D.D. Mitchell for the possession of her child, Lucy Ann Berry. My mother, accompanied by the sheriff, took me from my hiding-place and conveyed me to the jail ... and there met Mr. Mitchell, with Mr. H.S. Cox, his brother-in-law" (*FD*, 33–34). Attorneys Francis B. Murdoch and Edward Bates (later Lincoln's attorney general) represented Delaney's petition for freedom. Murdoch filed close to one-third of all freedom suits entered in St. Louis court from 1840 to 1847, and he later filed the Scotts' tandem suits for freedom and posted personal bond for Harriet in 1846.[63] Delaney recalled minutely how Murdoch defended her claims before an irate David Mitchell: "You need not think Mr. Mitchell," Murdoch reportedly replied, "because my client is colored that she has no rights, and can be cheated out of her freedom. She is just as free as you, and the Court will so decide it, as you will see" (*FD*, 34).

Delaney's narrative makes clear what can only be inferred from the documents in the cases of Winny, Julia, and Rachael, as it subtly retells the freedom suit as an autobiographical narrative. After Polly sues for the maternal right to take "possession" of her child, Delaney spends the next seventeen months in "long confinement, burdened with harrowing anxiety" to await her trial, imprisoned for the "crime" of seeking her freedom (*FD*, 47). The twelve-year-old suffers acutely in jail, and her attorney brings an additional petition "setting forth among other things that ... she is suffering from a severe Cold occasioned ... from a deficiency of clothing and the dampness of the room in which she is Confined."[64] "[H]ad it not been for the careful attention of her mother," the petition notes, "her sufferings would have been incalculable, and she believes that death would have been the Consequence of such Cruelty."[65] Polly cared for her daughter in jail and took pains to secure influential representation for her; Delaney recalls how "mother went to Judge Edward Bates and begged him to plead the case" (*FD*, 36).

Polly had withheld mention of her children from her earlier freedom suit, and Mitchell's defense attempted to disprove this relation to undermine Delaney's hereditary claims on freedom. "At the time my mother entered suit for her freedom," Delaney recalls, "she was not instructed to mention her two children, Nancy and Lucy" (*FD*, 35). Mitchell's attorneys subsequently "took advantage of this flaw, and showed a determination to use every means in their power to prove that I was not her child" (*FD*, 35). Bates first had to substantiate Polly's kinship to Delaney in order to establish her claim to freedom by maternal descent. Moreover, "Judge Bates," Delaney writes, "chained his hearers with the graphic history of my mother's life, from the time she played on Illinois banks, through her trials in slavery, her separation from her husband, her efforts to become free, her voluntary return to slavery for the sake of her child, Lucy, and her subsequent efforts in securing her own freedom" (*FD*, 41–42). Bates concluded his oral arguments with a stirring personal appeal that championed free motherhood while upholding the moral legitimacy of slavery, charging jurors to rectify the wrong of unjust enslavement:

> Gentlemen of the jury, I am a slave-holder myself, but, thanks to the Almighty God. I am above the base principles of holding any slave that has as good right to her freedom as this girl has been proven to have; she was free before she was born; her mother was free, but kidnapped in her youth, and sacrificed to the greed of negro traders, and no free woman can give birth to a slave child, as it is in direct violation of the laws of God and man! (*FD*, 41–42).

Bates constructs another narrative of theft around Polly to stress the difference between *just* and *unjust* enslavement. He does not denounce slavery but rather legitimates the practice in the hands of principled slaveholders such as himself.[66] Delaney's freedom issues from this rather ambivalent recognition of Polly's right to mother and therefore to "own" her child. Her mother, Delaney writes, "had at last been awarded the right to own her own child" (*FD*, 52).[67] Delaney, with noticeable wryness, restates her freedom as a form of parental ownership, drawing attention again to the entangled logic of kinship, gender, and property under slave law. The tautology of owning the child who is already "her own" undermines the logic of chattel slavery, and the ambiguous connotations of "own"—which can also signify "acknowledge"—point to the difficulties of recognizing kinship under slavery. Delaney's narrative, in this way, subtly suggests the paradoxical structure of Polly's appeal to the slave state for recognition of her legal motherhood.

Delaney's autobiography, like Harriet Wilson's *Our Nig*, was virtually forgotten until its republication in the late twentieth century. No contemporary critical reviews or advertisements for the book have yet been found. Perhaps the key to its scholarly neglect lies less in any "anachronistic" qualities that have been seen in the text than in the terribly qualified kind of freedom story that it attempts to tell.[68] As Bates's closing argument makes clear, claims on legal freedom, like the ones Polly made, required the slave petitioner to acknowledge slavery as a just institution in order to sue for *wrongful* enslavement. Her freedom suit, one of the many that passed through St. Louis circuit court, helps illuminate the ways in which slave law worked both to secure and to undermine black personhood. The complex entanglements of gender, property, and kinship that energize Delaney's autobiographical narrative and the legal petitions of Winny, Julia, and Rachael also shaped the story of Harriet and Dred Scott, who filed their joint petitions for freedom just two years after Polly Crocket "had at last been awarded the right to own her own child" (*FD*, 52).

Missouri had begun further to restrict the status of free blacks residing within the state just a year before Harriet and Dred Scott first brought their petitions to St. Louis circuit court in 1846. In response to the slow yet steady growth of a free black populace within its territorial boundaries, Missouri began to legislate more forcefully the conditions by which freed blacks could remain within the state. Revised 1845 statutes required all "free negroes and mulattoes" to obtain a license in order to "reside within the state," although licenses were granted only to a certain "class of persons," including those born free or emancipated *within* the state. Free blacks were barred from entering the state, and unlicensed freemen who were found within the state were to be arrested and committed as runaway slaves. These statutes were in keeping with the kinds of antiblack police laws effective in all slave states, including the Negro Seamen Acts examined in chapter 4. Missouri statutes even punished slaveholders with a five-hundred-dollar fine or six months imprisonment if they entered Missouri from a free state with slaves who may have been "entitled to freedom at a future period."[69] The broad temporal construction of this statute sought to curtail the reintroduction of slaves such as Winny, Julia, Rachael, and Harriet and Dred Scott, whose residences or extended sojourns on free soil enabled them to petition for freedom in Missouri courts. By the time the Scotts began their lawsuit, they found it necessary to seek formal emancipation *within* the state if they wanted to secure freedom *and* remain in urban St. Louis. In this way, the changing legal definitions of belonging and citizenship, state and national altered the meaning of freedom, particularly for men and women such as Elizabeth Keckley, Polly Crocket, Lucy Ann Delaney, and the Scotts who wished to continue their lives in the Southwest.

"Times now are not as they were when the former decisions on this subject were made," reads Justice William Scott's 1852 majority opinion in *Scott v. Emerson*, which overturned the St. Louis circuit court decision in favor of freedom.[70] Harriet, Eliza, Lizzie, and Dred Scott were again Emerson's legal property. "It is a humiliating spectacle," Justice Scott continued, "to see the courts of a State confiscating the property of her own citizen by the command of a foreign law."[71] The Fugitive Slave Act intensified interstate hostilities, and the Missouri Supreme Court had begun publicly to avow the state's proslavery principles by the time the Scotts' appeal came before it. The court judged that the Scotts had given up their right to sue for freedom once they voluntarily returned to St. Louis. This forceful application of the "reattachment" doctrine outlined in *Case of the Slave Grace* overturned decades of precedent, including those set in *Julia v. McKinney* and *Rachael v. Walker*. Justice Scott's opinion, the *National Era* noted with chagrin, "wholly repudiates the claims for freedom set up by the slave," and *Sylvia v. Kirby* (1853), on appeal from St. Louis circuit court, confirmed the immediate operation of this new precedent.[72] The Missouri Supreme Court quickly rejected Sylvia's claim, citing the opinion in *Scott v. Emerson* as "decisive of this" and all future freedom suits brought before it based on residence and extended sojourn on free soil. The Scotts brought a new freedom suit to the federal circuit court in Missouri and, when that failed, appealed to the U.S. Supreme Court, naming Emerson's brother John Sanford, who was then residing in New York, as the defendant.[73] It was Keckley's master, Hugh Garland, who first introduced, in circuit court, the counterargument that the Scotts as slaves of African descent were not U.S. citizens and therefore could not sue in federal courts.[74] Chief Justice Roger B. Taney's written opinion in *Scott v. Sandford* developed this line of reasoning, which fundamentally undermined the paradoxical but enabling legal fiction at the heart of freedom suits.

Antislavery print culture represented Dred Scott as a lone male litigant struggling for his freedom, in conformity with the archetype of the freedom seeker found in the fugitive slave narrative.⁷⁵ Those accounts that did mention the dependent claims of Harriet, Eliza, and Lizzie often sentimentalized Scott, as in Kate Pickard's depiction of Peter Still, as a tragic hero struggling to reconstitute the patriarchal family in the face of slavery's proscriptions. Although Harriet was illiterate, she did leave her imprint, however mediated, on an account published in *Frank Leslie's Illustrated Newspaper*, which came about as a matter of happy accident.⁷⁶ Because of either Dred's death shortly after the trial or Harriet's truculence, few interviews with the Scotts exist in the historical record. The lucky newspaperman stumbled on the chance for an exclusive interview with the then-famous Dred Scott in St. Louis shortly after his bid for legal freedom ended in Chief Justice Taney's vitriolic renunciation of black citizenship. A "prominent citizen of that enterprising city," reported the newspaperman, "suddenly asked us if we would not like to be introduced to Dred Scott."⁷⁷ The reporter thought he had succeeded where so many other correspondents had failed, but his good fortune was soon to end. In the quest to secure "Dred's story," the newspaperman, accidentally, found Harriet's.

His published account, entitled "Visit to Dred Scott—His Family—Incidents of His Life—Decision of the Supreme Court," found its way to *Frank Leslie's* front page just months after the Taney Court had passed its controversial judgment in March 1857. A number of events had occurred in the interim. Sanford died in a New York insane asylum two months after the Scotts' case was decided in his favor, but even before his death their ownership had passed to Irene Emerson's new husband, Massachusetts statesman Calvin C. Chaffee, a publicly acknowledged abolitionist.⁷⁸ The irony that Dred, Harriet, Eliza, and Lizzie were legally "held in bondage by a citizen of Massachusetts" was not lost on the many newspapers that reported on the case. One caustically observed that "Dred Scott is [now] the slave of one of the Massachusetts M.C.'s, Dr. Chaffee, through his wife."⁷⁹ A discomfited Chaffee responded with a public statement "protesting his innocence of any agency in keeping Dred Scott and family in bondage" and negotiated the immediate transfer of the Scotts to Taylor Blow, who appeared on Chaffee's behalf before St. Louis circuit court to enter their freedom.⁸⁰ Only Missouri citizens were permitted to emancipate slaves within the state, and only slaves emancipated within Missouri, such as the Scotts and Keckley, were authorized to apply for licenses to remain in the state. After the eleven-year struggle, Dred died on 17 September 1858, just sixteen months after his emancipation, although Harriet, many years his junior, lived to see the end of slavery in the postemancipation Southwest.[81]

When the *Frank Leslie's* reporter visited the Scotts in 1857, he said, "[Dred] made a rude obeisance to our recognition, and seemed to enjoy the notice we expended upon him," but Harriet was decidedly less enthusiastic. The newspaperman described Harriet as a "smart, tidy-looking negress, perhaps thirty years of age, who, with two female assistants was busy ironing." These two assistants were most likely Eliza and Lizzie. Harriet, busy with work, welcomed neither the reporter nor his inquiries for Dred. "What white man arter dad nigger for?" snapped an irate Harriet in an idiomatic regional dialect resembling that of Pickard's Vina; "why don't white men 'tend to his own business, and let dat nigger 'lone? Some of dese days day'll steal dat nigger—dat are a fact" ("VDS," 49). Indeed, Harriet's incivility exhibits a powerful desire to remove her household from further public intrusion. Her acerbic commentary on meddling "white men . . . steal[ing] dat nigger" marshals out the trope of "theft" found in the narratives of Still and Delaney to denounce the ongoing crimes against freed blacks in slave society. Stories of unscrupulous individuals who made a living kidnapping and reenslaving freed blacks undoubtedly shaped her resentment and fear toward these enticements for Dred, ill with the tuberculosis that would claim his life, to travel "thro' de North." "[S]outhern Illinois," according to William Hawkins's biography of Lunsford Lane, "had been the hunting-ground of the men-stealers, and it is stated that within the past ten years, scores perhaps hundreds, of freemen have been kidnapped. The law is powerless to punish the villains, or to bring back the captives."[82] Kidnappers in one notorious 1860 case ambushed three men from Clifton, Illinois, and carried them to St. Louis, where they were sold south. "Poor, friendless, and black, adjudged to have no rights that white men are bound to respect," writes Hawkins in an unmistakable allusion to *Dred Scott*, "what could they do?" (*LL*, 187).

Harriet's bitter reference to "theft" and the chattel logic of slavery did not go unnoticed. "These remarks," according to the amused reporter, "were uttered with a tone that assured us they were from the legitimate owner of Dred, *his wife*" ("VDS," 50). The reporter's reference to Harriet's marital proprietorship playfully inverts the gender coordinates of the doctrine of coverture, while it transforms the chattel principle into grist for traditional masculinist humor for the predominantly white readership of *Frank Leslie's*. Harriet further insisted that "she knew de white men did want Dred, and was trying to get him away; dat some gentlemen had promised to give Dred one thousand dollars a month if he would trabel thro' de North; dat de people wanted to see him; but . . . she'd always been able to yarn her own livin, thank God, and yarn an honest one, and she didn't want money got in day way" ("VDS," 50). Harriet insists on portraying herself as a self-determining agent—a wage laborer—in the manner of Keckley. She resists the archetype of helpless slave motherhood so popular in the antislavery literature of the day, with its sentimentalized narrative of rescue. She was also quite suspicious of those white abolitionists who, in her words, "want[ed] Dred" and sought to "get him away" now that the court case had made him into a household name. Harriet's forceful wish that these "white men . . . [would] let dat nigger 'lone" and her open resistance to Dred traveling "thro' de North" disclose some of the interpersonal dynamics that, as VanderVelde and Subramanian speculate, may have led to their return to a slave state and their joint petitions for freedom. To Harriet, the "trabel" promised by abolitionists was far from the idealization of freedom. Rather, it was yet another threat to the collective autonomy, albeit limited, that they had struggled so long to achieve together in St. Louis. The North held out no enticements for Harriet, and she was clearly suspicious of the uncertain promises of northern freedom.

Indeed, Eliza and Lizzie, now young women and valuable property on the slave market, had been placed in hiding while the Scotts awaited the outcome of their appeal before the U.S. Supreme Court. Harriet most likely devised the plan to hide the two while "Dred's position was in doubt" ("VDS," 50). The "disappearance" of the two young slave women remained a "mystery" until they "most unexpectedly made their appearance after the final proceedings" ("VDS," 50). Harriet and Dred Scott thus consistently acted out of concern for their children. The *St. Louis Daily Evening News* also reported on Eliza and Lizzie, whose "whereabouts have been kept a secret, though no effort has been, and none probably would have been, made to recover them. Their father knew where they were, and could bring them back at any moment. He will doubtless recall them now."[83] This report insists on Dred's protective custodianship of his daughters, but *Frank Leslie's* reveals that Harriet was the more forceful of the two when it came to making decisions for the household. Indeed, *Frank Leslie's* portrays Dred as largely acquiescing to Harriet's preferences for the family. The suspicious Harriet flatly refused, in her words, "to be made a Tom fool of" and gave her grudging permission for Dred to sit for a portrait, but not without specific conditions ("VDS," 50). She insisted that the Scott family be

Fig. 3.3. "Visit to Dred Scott--His Family--Incidents of His Life--Decision of the Supreme Court," *Frank Leslie's Illustrated Newspaper*, 27 June 1857. (Courtesy of the General Research Division, The New York Public Library, Astor, Lenox and Tilden Foundations)

photographed together and that Dred be provided with "some of the pictures" ("VDS," 50). Dred, as the reporter concluded, was "a real hero," and whereas he "was evidently hugely tickled at the idea of finding himself a personage of such vast importance," Harriet, on the other hand, "would evidently be satisfied with obscurity and repose" ("VDS," 50). The reporter's exclusive interview with the famous Dred becomes, through Harriet's will, the story of "His Family," boldly illustrated with the large engraved portraits not only of Dred but also of Harriet and their two daughters (see figure 3.3). In this way, Harriet insists on "Dred's story" being told as a story of kinship. Later reproductions of this "family portrait" preserved, in some fashion, the significance of their familial or collective autonomy, yet they often continued to occlude Harriet's story and her influence on their legal struggle for freedom: the reproduction found in William Alexander's voluminous *History of the Colored Race in America* (1887) misnames Harriet as "*Hannah*, Wife of Dred Scott."

Slaveholding Liberalism and Legal Form

The Scotts' case, and others like it, attest to the deep contradictions within the legal theories and principles governing freedom and slavery in the antebellum United States. The ban on slave testimony in southern courtrooms, which decreed that no person of color could appear as a witness in any case "except for and against each other," was tantamount, as many legal historians argue, to the erasure of black agency from the legal historical record.[84] Indeed, abolitionist George Stroud's treatise on American slave law identified the legal inadmissibility of black testimony as "the cause of the greatest evils of slavery."[85] Burdened with legal disabilities, enslaved people had little access to the law as plaintiffs, yet a number of slave states such as Missouri legislated laws, following Virginia and Kentucky, that carefully laid out the process by which slaves could petition courts to sue for wrongful enslavement.[86] Indeed, pre-Revolutionary codes in South Carolina (1749) and Georgia (1755) allowed persons wrongfully enslaved to bring suit to test the legality of their enslavement. Such provisions seem to undermine the prevailing perception of black legal outsidership in slave society, but it would be a mistake to consider them as "securing the rights of slaves."[87] These laws accorded with the logic of slavery because they protected the rights of *free* persons (not slaves) who were unjustly enslaved. The procedures for freedom petitions in Missouri were set out in statutory form as early as 1807, listed in the 1818 alphabetical digest of territorial laws under the heading "Freedom" and codified into state law in 1824.[88] Sixteen slaves petitioned the courts for freedom in the year that Missouri was admitted to the Union as a slave state.[89] The growing number of slave plaintiffs, many of whom were enslaved mothers with children, provoked one critic to opine that the liberty of suing for freedom "has become abused, at least in St. Louis, by the ruthless encouragement of those who left-handedly profit from such suits."[90] As sectional antagonisms flared, legislators revised these statutes to make it more difficult to sue for freedom.[91] Nevertheless, a number of slaves who based their claims on residence, domicile, and extended sojourn on free soil entered the courtroom to sue, often successfully, for freedom in the years between the constitutional ratification of the state (1820) and the Missouri Supreme Court opinion in *Scott v. Emerson* (1852).

The Scotts' case was by no means unusual. Nearly three hundred legal petitions for freedom were filed in St. Louis circuit court by or on behalf of persons of color held in slavery between the years 1814 and 1860; nearly sixty-five of these suits were either filed in or appealed to the Missouri Supreme Court.[92] This nearly complete docket of cases may be of little statistical importance, as legal scholar David Konig notes, "for a Missouri slave population approaching 115,000 by the time the Scotts lost their final appeal," yet these freedom suits reveal much about the complex meanings of agency, kinship, and freedom for enslaved people who petitioned southern courts for emancipation. Roughly three-eighths of these recorded St. Louis freedom suits were won by slave plaintiffs.[93] The exact number of cases prosecuted in trial courts throughout the antebellum slave states remains unknown, but nearly 670 were appealed to and tried before state supreme courts. Over half the recorded 575 appellate court decisions favored freedom for the black petitioner.[94]

A few freedom suits involved manumission by will or deed, but the vast majority, including *Scott v. Emerson*, tested the status of slaves who claimed freedom based on extended sojourn or residence on free soil. The Articles of Confederation (1787), which governed the Northwest Territory, declared slavery illegal within its territorial borders, and the Thomas Amendment of the Missouri Compromise further limited the westward expansion of slavery at an imagined line north of parallel 36° 30' within the remainder of the Louisiana Purchase.[95] The migration and travels of slaveholders into and out of these western territories increased the number of freedom suits in St. Louis courts. Case law on the status of slaves traveling across free soil, as Konig points out, "was new to the West" and remained unsettled in

St. Louis courts and throughout much of the nation.[96] Western judiciaries found it extremely difficult to establish a rule of law governing the difference between residence and temporary sojourn, even though judgments in freedom suits were largely based on this distinction. Changing itineraries and intentions often made such categorical definitions difficult if not impossible to maintain.[97] What constituted the "character" of a traveler as opposed to an immigrant, given the contingencies of antebellum travel in the West? One can only imagine the conditions of these western routes when one considers Fanny Kemble's observation "that half the routes that are traveled in America are either temporary or unfinished" as she made her way from Philadelphia to South Carolina.[98] It was also not unusual for migrating slaveholders to be unsure about their final destinations; and travel might be interrupted by unforeseen illnesses or inclement weather.[99] Did such interruptions lapse into "residence," or were they the unavoidable consequence of being "in transit" in the West?

In later cases, counsels and judges began to advance the principle of reattachment of slave status established in *Case of the Slave Grace*, deeming freedom to be a geopolitically bound property that was lost once the slave "voluntarily" returned to a slave jurisdiction.[100] The Missouri Supreme Court departed from past precedents when, in *Scott v. Emerson*, it ruled against the long-held doctrine of "once free, forever free." According to that ruling, freedom was not immanent in a slave, unless the slave legally claimed that freedom while on free soil. The ruling, later reaffirmed in the U.S. Supreme Court, established the doctrine that "if a slave be taken by his master to a free State, and does not *there* claim his liberty, but consents to return with his master to a slave State, he may be held as a slave there, if the higher court of that State considers him still to be a slave."[101] Slaves with legitimate claims on freedom who did not act on them while on free soil forfeited their right to freedom once they returned to a slave state. The Missouri Supreme Court, after *Scott v. Emerson*, virtually ceased hearing freedom suits originating in residence or extended sojourn in the free territories.[102] Indeed, Taney's *Dred Scott* opinion observed, "whatever doubts or opinions may, at one time, have been entertained upon this subject . . . it is *now* firmly settled by the decisions of the highest court in the State, that Scott and his family upon their return were not free, but were, by the laws of Missouri, the property of the defendant."[103]

Slavery was based on the idea of total power, and southern statutes carefully sought to preserve this ideology despite the seeming aberration of permitting slaves to sue for freedom. "Statutory law," according to Lindon

Barrett, "represents the convergence and 'distillation' of a plurality of discourses, a formalizing of values, practices, and customs."[104] The statutory law governing freedom suits expressed, in part, the contradiction at the heart of U.S. liberalism: Missouri, like other slave states, was dedicated equally to the idea of individual liberty and the system of chattel slavery. Freedom suits further eroded the distinction between person and property that many people held as essential to the maintenance of slavery as a legal institution.[105] Under southern laws, slaves held the character of persons in criminal cases and that of property in all others.[106] Kent's *Commentaries on American Law* also specifies that "slaves are considered in some respects, though not in criminal prosecutions, as things or property, rather than persons, and are vendible as personal estate."[107] Modifications to Missouri territorial statutes sought explicitly to delineate the plaintiff as a "free person" "before and at the time" of the lawsuit in order to avoid the potential paradox of a slave's suing a master for freedom. Such careful recalibrations of legal procedure tacitly responded to the formal incoherence of a law that in practice permitted slaves, who had no legal standing, the right to petition for freedom. Indeed, the statute also conferred legal protections, including habeas corpus, on slave petitioners while in this guise of free persons. Of course, these rights vanished once the verdict proved the petitioner to be a slave.[108]

The courtroom may have thus dramatized, as Barrett argues, a "complex political technology" of African American individuation and self-representation, yet it was by no means an unambiguous one.[109] Trials proceeded on the assumption that the slave plaintiff was free until proven otherwise. Procedural logic accommodated the definition of the slave as an extension of the master's will under slave law, as slave plaintiffs (who had no legal standing) sued in the guise of free persons to preserve the "chattel principle" of slave law. Such misnaming illuminates the degree to which legal fictions were called on to circumvent the paradoxes of "the chattel principle" that haunted the legal culture of the antebellum United States. For this reason, too, status designations (colored or free) were shifted into racial designations. Documentation in these cases, including depositions, trial records, and judicial opinions, do not identify plaintiffs as "slaves" but variously as "Jeffrie, a mulatto boy," "Susan, a black woman," "Aspasia, a woman of color," "Joe, a black man," "Margaret, a girl of color," "Edwards, Michael, a colored lad," "Delph (also known as Delphy), a mulatress," "Pierre, a mulatto," "Rebecca, a negro woman," or "Sarah, a colored woman." Some records even appended the description "free" to the plaintiff's racial designation, as in

"Malinda, a free girl of color," as if to call further attention to the tragic (legal) irony of these freedom suits.

Racial coordinates such as "mulatto," "black," "colored," "of color," and "negro" stood in place of the term *slave*, which southern courts could not acknowledge without also impugning the chattel logic of slavery. Such legal misnaming further facilitated the conflation of racial identity with political status in ways that anticipated the strategic conflation of free blacks with slaves in *Dred Scott*'s infamous declaration that "blacks have no rights that a white man need respect." Chief Justice Taney's fiercely contested majority opinion, in Fehrenbacher's words, "took advantage of the peculiar circularity that had characterized the case from the moment that it entered the federal court."[110] "[T]o bring suit," he explains, "Dred Scott had to affirm that he was a citizen of Missouri, which meant assuming that he was a free man. But if it should be determined from the facts that he remained a slave, this would mean that he was never a citizen and had no right to bring suit in the first place."[111] The tautological structure of the freedom suit forced proslavery jurists to embrace a number of legal fictions in their efforts to uphold the formal coherence of law and preserve the logic of slave property.[112]

Missouri's liberal statutes perplexed even the generally critical abolitionist William Goodell, whose revealing compendium of slave statutes sought to chart the "legal relation" between master and slave in the effort to "test the moral character of American slaveholding."[113] Goodell proffered uncharacteristic approbation for Missouri, which "mercifully allows the slave, on permission of Court, to 'sue as a poor person.'"[114] "So far," he continued, "the law appears praiseworthy," even though the conditions of enslavement generally prevented "thousands of free colored persons kidnapped into slavery, or otherwise held, contrary to even the Southern laws . . . to institute a suit at law for their freedom."[115] Such liberal provisions in a slaveholding state, though puzzling to Goodell, were by no means incompatible with the logic of slavery. Such forms of manumission functioned as "an exercise of the property-holder's inherent right to renounce ownership of his property" and served to strengthen the power of slaveholders.[116] The slave's desire for freedom, as Orlando Patterson reminds us, was often used by masters who promised manumission as an incentive for the slave to remain obedient and work harder.[117] In seeking legal recognition from the slave state, slave plaintiffs thus risked affirming the legitimacy of the institution that oppressed them. They had first to acquiesce to the idea of *just* subjection under slave law before petitioning courts for emancipation based on *wrongful* enslavement, as courts directed juries to distinguish *just* from *unjust* slavery. Many slaves secured freedom and the recognition of their legal personhood through these freedom suits, yet it would be an overstatement to regard these suits, as Konig does, as one "mechanism of antislavery."[118] Disgruntled slaveholders often avoided litigation simply by transporting litigious slaves out of the court's jurisdiction, and other plaintiffs awaited judgments in trials that extended over several years.[119] The Scotts did indeed seize on the freedom suit as a powerful means to assert themselves in the face of slavery's "legal death," yet such liberal measures were *not* inconsistent with the property logic of slave law.[120]

Perhaps because of these ambiguities, the antislavery print campaign largely ignored these Missouri cases, and Fehrenbacher notes the puzzling "failure of anti-slavery radicals to take an earlier interest" in the *Dred Scott* case. *Dred Scott v. Sandford* attracted little attention locally or nationally until the reargument of the case before the U.S. Supreme Court in 1856.[121] The *St. Louis Herald* couched its brief 1854 account of Scott's freedom suit in the form of a sentimental appeal to benevolence: "Dred is, of course, poor and without any powerful friends. But no doubt he will find at the bar of the Supreme Court some able and generous advocate, who will do all he can to establish his right to go free."[122] In erasing the litigious agency of the slave who brought suit, the *Herald*'s appeal to "some able and generous advocate" resembles the rescue narratives examined in chapter 1.

In the general absence of abolitionist print surrounding the case, Dred Scott's own printed narrative of the trial takes on even greater significance. With assistance, Scott published a rare twelve-page pamphlet entitled "The Case of Dred Scott in the Supreme Court of the United States, December Term, 1854" in the hope of raising funds for the appeal pending before the U.S. Supreme Court.[123] He signed his mark to the pamphlet's first-person narrative introduction, dated, with no undue irony, 4 July 1854, although its authorship and transcription remains unverified. The pamphlet retells the trial history from the perspective of the slave plaintiff. It opens with a short autobiographical appeal:

> To my fellow-men: I lay before you the record of a suit which I have brought to get the freedom of myself, my wife and children. I was born in the State of Virginia and was held as a slave there, and in the State of Missouri, up to 1834.
>
> The defendant says that I am a negro of African descent and that my

ancestors were of pure African blood and were brought into this country and sold as negro slaves. All this is true. There is not one drop of the white man's blood in my veins. My ancestors were free people of Africa.[124]

Scott bases his statements largely on the "agreed statement of facts" but departs from its legalistic form. Garland had filed a plea seeking to dismiss the case before the U.S. circuit court on the grounds that Scott was "not a citizen of the State of Missouri, as alleged in his declaration, because he is a negro of African descent; his ancestors were of pure African blood and were brought into this country and sold as negro slaves."[125] Scott's preface affirms this attestation of facts but adds an additional qualification: "My ancestors were free people of Africa." This invocation of a prior freedom draws on the genealogical metaphor of free birth and the natural rights of man found in the legal rhetoric of other freedom suits—including those of Winny, Julia, and Rachael—in which the child's freedom was founded on maternal descent. It resists the racialization of slave status in its introduction of another elided historical context for the case. The theft of Africans in the transatlantic slave trade lay beyond the qualified justice to be had in the freedom suit immediately at hand, even as that crime continued to demand redress. Indeed, the pamphlet embraced the theme of theft that powerfully organized the narratives of Peter Still and Lucy Ann Delaney. Scott's ancestors, "free people of Africa," like the abducted mother and child found in Delaney's and Still's narratives, were forcibly *remade* (rather than born) into American slaves.

A short narrative account of Scott's travels with Emerson follows in the pamphlet. The narrative transforms litigation history into autobiography as it offers Scott's subjective experiences of the trial—a hopefulness that quickly dissolved into disappointment—when he received the judgment against freedom:

> But after a little while the judge said that as soon as my master got me back this side of the line of Missouri, my right to be free was gone; and that I and my wife and children became nothing but so many pieces of property. I thought it hard that white men should draw a line of their own on the face of the earth and on one side of which a black man was to become no man at all. And never say a word to the black man about it until they had got him on that side of the line. So I appealed to the Supreme Court of the United States.[126]

Scott's words offer a powerful sense of what the geopolitics of slavery and freedom looked like from the perspective of the slave plaintiff. He exposes the legal fiction of those arbitrary "lines" that reinforced a false dichotomy between slavery and freedom. Those lines, for the unknowing traveling slave who crossed them, divided (white) personhood and rights on one side from the social death of (black) chattel slavery on the other. Legal personhood and social recognition depended on this strict geopolitical territorialization, for once Scott was "got . . . back [to] this side of the line of Missouri," he again lost his right to freedom and became, along with his family, "so many pieces of property." Personhood and rights did not inhere in black subjects but were entirely contingent on which side of the imaginary line they happened to find themselves. That was the same extreme legal formalism embraced by Lord Stowell in *Case of the Slave Grace*. Scott's account places pressure on the legal fictions involved in the geopolitics of slavery and freedom as it draws attention to the frightening power to determine the meaning of social life or death that legal culture attributed to such "lines."

The preface ends with Scott's heartfelt appeal for assistance while he awaits the trial before the U.S. Supreme Court. "My fellow-men, can any of you help me in my day of trial?" Scott asks. "Will nobody speak for me at Washington, even without hope of other reward than the blessings of a poor black man and his family?"[127] This pamphlet was most likely directed toward a white audience that was amenable to the idea of amelioration if not outright abolition of slavery. Its conservative tone with its stress on representation by proxy ("Will nobody speak for me") did not challenge the racial hierarchies that existed to some degree even within the ranks of the most radical of Anglo-American antislavery organizations. Indeed, Scott's text has much in common with those plaintive appeals found in the popular slave narratives of the day. "I can only pray," continues his appeal, "that some good heart will be moved by pity to do that for me which I cannot do for myself." The sentimental rhetoric of a "good heart," popularized by *Uncle Tom's Cabin*, expressed the profound belief that moral right would triumph over economic interests.[128] And yet, however mediated it may have been, Scott's appeal gestures toward the complex issues of kinship that had dictated the direction of the freedom suit since 1846. Scott did not make an individual appeal but issued it on the behalf of "a poor black man *and* his family." His appeal may have mobilized the well-worn sentimental trope of the imperiled slave family, yet its emphasis on familial or collective autonomy also undermined the telos of possessive individualism generally found in legal commentaries on the case.

These Missouri freedom suits held up an egalitarian ideal of the law even as they strengthened the racial ideologies of slavery. Indeed, in their efforts to stave off northern critique, proslavery legislators cited the statutory laws governing freedom suits as evidence that the slave system was an "enlightened" institution. Proslavery Missouri statesman Thomas Hart Benton took great pride in asserting that slaves seeking release from unlawful bondage preferred to be tried in Missouri and Kentucky than in the free states north of Ohio. Another senator admitted that "the courts of the slave States had been much more liberal in their adjudications upon the question of slavery than the free States," as he commended the "courts of Kentucky and Missouri" for "favor[ing] ... the right of freedom."[129] Proslavery ideologue William MacCreary Burwell, who later became editor of *DeBow's Review*, even penned a plantation satire of northern abolitionism that took the form of a freedom suit entitled *White Acre vs. Black Acre* (1856).[130] Another Illinois man reported on "several suits instituted by the negroes to recover their liberty" and praised the liberalism of the Missouri legal system in a letter reprinted widely in antislavery print culture.[131] The unnamed slave plaintiff who based his claim to freedom on residence in free Illinois "took his case to the Supreme Court, where although two out of the three judges were advocates of slavery, the decision was reversed and it was *unanimously* decided that he was a freeman."[132] The editorial celebrated the judgment as evidence of the "progress of correct principles" and, with unintended irony, held up Missouri jurisprudence as a shining example for its sister free states.[133]

The "Strange Benevolence" of John Berry Meachum

Slave law shaped the kinds of agency and freedom afforded to slaves and free blacks in slave society even as it allowed officials to defend the peculiar institution with a liberal egalitarian theory of justice. The remainder of this chapter examines the largely understudied writings of John Berry Meachum, Lunsford Lane, and Cyprian Clamorgan, which offer three different responses to the chattel principle of slavery and the conundrums of freedom in a slave state. This section reconsiders the "antislavery" activism and writings of self-emancipated Baptist leader Meachum (also spelled

"Meechum" and "Metchum") to explore how men and women who were enslaved used and challenged the logic of legal freedom. Meachum presented *An Address to All the Colored Citizens of the United States* (1846) before the National Negro Convention in Philadelphia the same year that the Scotts filed their freedom suits in St. Louis. He lived out his life as a freedman in St. Louis, where, according to one newspaper report, he "fell dead in the pulpit" of the First African Baptist Church that he helped establish in 1827 when the slaveholding city deemed it expedient to have separate black and white houses of worship.[134] Meachum remained a relatively local figure, despite the national circulation of his *Address*, and never attained the prominence of other social-minded religious leaders such as Henry Highland Garnet or Alexander Crummell. The *Address* remains his only known published oration. Its call "to all the colored citizens of the United States" immediately calls to mind David Walker's antislavery jeremiad, although it falls far short of Walker's powerful political critique. Meachum penned the *Address* out of "great . . . [concern] for the welfare of this people," yet his inability to name slavery, let alone denounce the theft of black personhood under slave law, produces powerful ambivalences within the text. The studied silences in the *Address* issue from Meachum's ties to St. Louis and his investment in "lawful liberty." The textual repression of slavery, in particular, unsettles the internal logic and rhetorical structure of this equivocal antislavery document.

According to the first-person preface of the *Address*, Meachum was born the slave of a liberal-minded slaveholder, Paul Meachum, "in Goochland county, Virginia, May 3d, 1789."[135] He worked the North Carolina saltpeter caves for nine years before he earned enough to purchase his freedom and return to Virginia, where he worked off the redemption price of his father, Thomas Granger (*AA*, 3). The two emancipated men then walked seven hundred miles to Kentucky to reunite with Meachum's mother and siblings. In 1815, Meachum followed his enslaved wife from Kentucky to St. Louis, where his industry as a carpenter and cooper soon enabled him to purchase his wife and children. "However this did not stop here," reads his preface: "I have purchased about twenty slaves, most of whom paid back the greatest part of the money, and some paid all. They are all free at this time, and doing well, excepting one" (*AA*, 3). Meachum's strategy of purchasing slaves and formally emancipating them once they worked off their cost was not the first time that he had used the logic of Missouri slave law to subvert its racial proscriptions. Local histories celebrate him as an early black activist who established the "Floating Freedom School" on the Mississippi River in 1847, when the education of "negroes or mulattoes" was a criminally punishable offense in Missouri.[136] Transforming a riverboat into a school for black children that operated successfully well into the 1850s, he successfully circumvented the "law of the land," since the Mississippi River was under federal, not state, jurisdiction.

Meachum's activities made him a figure of public interest, and Garrison's *Liberator* first used the former slave turned minister and local reformer to exemplify the "Capacity of Negroes to Take Care of Themselves" in an essay reprinted widely in antislavery newsprint.[137] The *Liberator* speculated that Meachum was "worth about $25,000" as it took pains to commend his experiment in "enterprising" emancipation: "he has purchased, including adults and children, about twenty slaves. He never sells again. His method is to place them at service, encourage them to form habits of industry and economy, and when they have paid for themselves, he sets them free."[138] That was indeed strong praise from the *Liberator*, given Garrison's rejection of self-purchase as, in Douglass's words, "a violation of anti-slavery principles—conceding a right of property in man."[139] Meachum's preface embraces manumission as a mode of antislavery activism even as other black abolitionists, such as St. Louis fugitive William Wells Brown, publicly rejected such "lawful liberty" as reaffirming the chattel principle of slavery. Meachum offers a practical critique of slavery's unfree labor in his successful experiment with waged black labor: "One of the twenty colored friends that I bought is worthy to be taken notice of to show what industry will do. I paid for him one thousand dollars. He worked and paid back the thousand dollars. He has also bought a lot of ground for which he paid a thousand dollars. He married a slave and bought her, and paid seven hundred dollars for her. He had built a house that cost him six hundred dollars" (*AA*, 47).[140] This mathematical calculus of hundreds of dollars emphasizes the moral and economic virtue of his gospel of industry. At the same time, his enumerative rhetoric acknowledges something of which slaveholders were well aware: the value of laboring black bodies.

Nevertheless Meachum's inability to name slavery makes for an oddly elliptical text that continually circles around the "disease," in his medical analogy, to which he seeks to find a "cure." Black Americans, Meachum observes, are a "people . . . away from home" searching for "a place somewhere" (*AA*, 6). "They are scattered in almost every part of the world," he continues; "few have houses or lands that are now in the United States and places around; take them in general, they have no home, though born in America. No home!" (*AA*, 27–28). He identifies this "scattered condition" as the "disease" of the "free colored citizens of America" but is unwilling to delve deeper into its etiology in institutional slavery and the national polity. Although Meachum embraces liberal narratives of economic progress and individualism, he also attends to their limitations. Farming becomes "the greatest office in the United States of America ... for the colored citizens of America" when other spheres of national participation are closed off "according to the laws of the different states" (*AA*, 26–27). Regardless of Meachum's qualifications, this abolitionist doctrine of "individual economic strivings and Christian self-help," as historian Steven Mintz notes, later "contributed to the abandonment of former slaves following Reconstruction."[141] The *Address* invites its auditors to "come together and search out the cursed thing that keeps us so far back in the world," yet its inability to point clearly to that "cursed thing" undermines those few critiques of systemic black underdevelopment that appear in the text (*AA*, 32).

Meachum's commitments to life in the slaveholding Southwest may, in part, have produced this studied refusal to attend to slavery's ongoing histories. He circumvents any direct mention of slavery; the slave is one who is "differently situated" from the free rather than one who is systematically divested of the positive rights of personhood (*AA*, 11). Meachum's calculated repression of slavery creates an odd developmental schema: we are divided; therefore, we need unity; industry will lead us to unity. "Come along, my dear friend, we have no desire to leave one behind," he insists in a telling moment. "But, sir, if you will not come and join this honorable society ... we must leave you" (*AA*, 54–55). The movement of the *Address*, as with this invitation, is relentlessly forward toward some kind of "general union" of "fellow beings of the same color," a union that is immediately belied by the impossibility of the men and women who are enslaved choosing to "come and join." Such "unity," as Meachum later reveals, "must begin among the free, then extend to all," as "it is more in the power of the free to promote it than those who are differently situated" (*AA*, 10–11). He proffers a doctrine of "unity" as the "Cure-all" to the ills of dispersal and homelessness without attending to the social, economic, and political dimensions of what the domestic expansion of the Atlantic slave trade had wrought on the United States (*AA*, 47–48).

Meachum's relentless insistence on "unity" and "union" makes little sense outside the historical context of sectional strife over the slavery question and its westward extension into the territories. Interstate antagonisms soon led to the bloody skirmishes between "Free Staters" and proslavery

"Border Ruffians" over the popular control of Kansas, culminating in the attack on Lawrence and in John Brown's retaliatory violence near Pottawatomie Creek.[142] Meachum makes no mention of this historical context, even as he uses tropes from the sectional contest over the slavery question. "Disunion," he says in the *Address*, "is the worst thing that ever happened to any nation of people" (*AA*, 23, 60). "We must have union," he insists; "we can and must have it," and "Union should be our constant watchword—it should be the standard to which all of us rally" (*AA*, 10). His insistence on a "general union of those free people of color that are now scattered in different directions of the United States of America," transcending "all party spirit and sectarian feelings," cannot but make reference to the larger public debates over the future of slavery in the nation. Garrison's American Anti-Slavery Society saw the Constitution as a proslavery compact and embraced "No Union with Slaveholders" as the catchphrase of its political ideology in 1844, just as proslavery radicals began to agitate more powerfully for disunion and the nullification of the Constitution.[143]

Meachum could not entirely elude the question of slavery, as he found it necessary to enumerate the events that first brought Africans to the New World. Rather than naming the Atlantic slave trade, Meachum tells a rather curious story of how "we came to America." African arrival is retold variously as the historical consequence of "strange benevolence," "Providence," and even "old African principles." "PROVIDENCE," Meachum says in the *Address*, "has placed us all on the shores of America," although he later concludes that "old African principle . . . was the means of throwing the first colored man on the American soil" (*AA*, 17). Such narratives remove Western agency from the African slave trade, placing it instead in the hands of abstract "providence" or barbaric customs removed from the enlightened rationality of the modern West. Indeed, Meachum proposes his most intriguing explanation in the story of Las Casas's "strange benevolence":

> Las Casas, who was a great friend to the Indians, who were then forced to work the mines by the Spaniards, interposed, and had these Africans forced to do that which the Indians had been compelled to do. The Indians therefore were released from bondage entirely, and the Africans made to substitute them. . . . Strange benevolence this, that he should employ so much of his time and influence in securing the liberty to the Indians, while at the same time he made every possible effort to reduce the African to the same

> state of servitude! He went so far as to go to Spain and procure a grant for the transportation of four thousand negroes in order to secure to the Indians their personal rights and freedom.
>
> About 1620 a Dutch vessel brought African slaves to the colony of Jamestown, Virginia.
>
> Our people had war among themselves in Africa. They brought with them the same principle here,—envy, hatred, malice, jealousy. (*AA*, 8–9)

Meachum presents an oddly truncated history of African arrival in the New World, as he jumps temporally and geographically from Hispaniola to Jamestown to Africa. He does not name Anglo-American participation either in the Atlantic slave trade or in its ongoing domestic expansion in the United States. He suspends this ongoing history of American slavery to represent it, implicitly, as a crude remnant of either a waning European (Spanish and Dutch) or African past.

Meachum's narrative is a far cry from the powerfully reimagined scene of two "tempest-tost and weather beaten" ships symbolically disgorging themselves on the shores of the New World in William Wells Brown's novel *Clotel*. "Behold the May-flower anchored at Plymouth Rock, the slave-ship in James River," writes Brown. "Each a parent, one of the prosperous, labour-honouring, law-sustaining institutions of the North; the other the mother of slavery, idleness, lynch-law, ignorance, unpaid labour. These ships are representative of good and evil in the New World, even to our day. When shall one of those parallel lines come to an end?"[144] Classical liberal ideology and slavery—the cornerstones of the new republic—issue simultaneously from the cargo holds of these two "parent" vessels. Brown thus allegorizes the organizing paradox of U.S. liberalism: a nation devoted to individual liberty but founded on slavery.[145] The sheer force of this internal contradiction should have burst apart the young nation, but the erasure of African slavery as "a plain historical fact" of its founding has held together, albeit tenuously, these two "parallel lines."[146] The story of Las Casas's "strange benevolence" outlines a similar paradox. Enslavement is profoundly articulated with "lawful liberty" and the conferral of entitlements and rights. Las Casas worked tirelessly to secure the "personal rights and freedom" of the Amerindians, just as he advocated the enslavement of Africans in their place. Meachum's story of "strange benevolence" contains a striking but relatively unspoken critique of the mechanisms of legal freedom in the face of his own advocacy of "enterprising" emancipation.

Meachum's project of social uplift through industry and moral education provokes questions about the legibility of certain kinds of antislavery agency and resistance. Julia ("Judy") Logan was among the first of Meachum's "colored friends" who sued him for freedom. Like Winny, Rachael, and Julia before her, Logan petitioned for freedom on the basis of her residence on free soil, in *Judy (also known as Julia Logan) v. Meachum, John Berry* (1835).[147] It is not without some irony that Meachum found himself promoting black westward migration to these free territories in his *Appeal*: "There is the state of Illinois, it is a fine country and a free state. And there is the state of Michigan, the finest country likely in America, and many others that I could mention, such as Iowa and Wisconsin" (*AA*, 26). Extended sojourn and residence in these western territories formed the basis for those freedom petitions brought against Meachum. Benjamin Duncan had held Logan as a slave in Indiana before returning to Kentucky, where he sold her to James Newton, who, in turn, sold her to Meachum.[148] Julia paid Meachum a twelve-dollar monthly fee to hire her own time, in accordance with his project of entrepreneurial emancipation. When Julia petitioned for freedom, she also claimed five hundred dollars in damages, the amount she earned while held as a slave. Meachum's attorney argued for a dismissal since "Logan, at the time of the commencement of [t]his action aforesaid was and still is a slave."[149] He laid stress on the legal misnaming involved in such proceedings in his efforts to redefine Julia as a slave "in fact," if not in legal "form," with no legal power to sue for freedom. The white jury of St. Louis circuit court remained unconvinced, granted Julia her freedom, and assessed court costs against Meachum.[150]

It appears that Meachum, too, was a practitioner of "strange benevolence." He professed to be "aggrieved by the judgment," sought an appeal, and brought *Meechum v. Judy* (1836) before the Missouri Supreme Court. His lawyer argued that Logan was still under warranty to Newton, a white man and the "real defendant," against whom the testimony of the primary witness, "Lewis, a negro," was invalid. In this way, Meachum's lawyer attempted to apply Missouri statutes stipulating the inadmissibility of black testimony against white defendants to close off Julia's right to freedom, but Judge Matthias McGirk affirmed the lower-court decision to grant Julia freedom. Meachum's appeal of the case may seem at odds with his antislavery activism, but it was entirely consistent with his practice of "enterprising" emancipation, given his desire, no doubt, to recover the costs of Julia—and of her five-year-old son, whom he had purchased with Julia and who was later freed by the doctrine of *partus sequitur ventrem*, with Julia acting as "next friend."[151] Julia again called on Lewis to testify on her child's behalf as, in a very different way than Meachum, she renegotiated the dictates of slave law to establish her child's freedom.

Meachum defended himself against a number of freedom suits instigated by those whom he held as slaves. Another slave woman named Judy also based her right to freedom on residence on free soil when she sued Meachum in 1837. Attorney F.W. Risque—who some condemned as a "nigger lawyer"—reprised his role from Logan's lawsuit to stand as counsel for the plaintiff.[152] According to a witness's deposition, Robert Burton had held Judy as a slave in free territories in violation of the Northwest Ordinance. Burton "owned...little Judy...until the year 1806 when the owners of slaves becoming alarmed at the prospect of loosing [sic] their slaves, a great number were sold off, and among others little Judy."[153] This same witness "saw and recognized" little Judy in St. Louis, where she, along with her children and grandchildren, had been resold to a series of men until she found herself in Meachum's custody. The white jury again sided with the slave plaintiff and awarded her freedom. White Missourians seemed inclined to favor freedom in petitions against a *black* slaveholder such as Meachum, but they were was far more divided when it came to the trials of her children and grandchildren, who were held by various *white* masters and hirers. Her daughters, Aspasia and Celeste, and grandchildren, Celestine, Lewis, and Andrew, eventually won their own freedom suits as a result of Judy's successful petition.[154]

Siblings Archibald and Brunetta Barnes also successfully sued Meachum for freedom in November 1840. The Barneses filed identical petitions, basing their right to freedom on their mother Leah's successful freedom suit in Ohio courts. Their tandem lawsuits asserted that they were children "of parents who were free at the time of her birth and still are, free," and the witness deposition affirmed that the Brown County Court of Common Pleas confirmed Leah's right to freedom in either 1826 or 1827, on the basis of her residence in Ohio, where Arthur Mitchel had held her as a slave.[155] "Mitchel," according to the witness, "afterwards moved to the state of Missouri and took Leah and her children with him."[156] Archibald even professed fear that Meachum might take steps to "remove [them]...unjustly and unlawfully beyond the limit of the State of Missouri (as he has often made threats of doing) in consequence of this application."[157] Allegations of abuse, ill treatment, and confinement were a convention of freedom suits based on "trespass and false imprisonment," yet the Barneses' fears cannot be entirely disregarded.

Brunetta's counsel mobilized a gendered discourse of rescue on her behalf, even as the purposes of such legal documents, steeped as they were in the misnaming required by formal procedure, made it difficult to recount the actual events that may have transpired. Meachum, according to Brunetta's carefully crafted statement, was "in the habit of sending her to sell and deliver milk on board the several steamboats lying at St. Louis wharf. . . . That she is exposed on these occasions to insults of the grossest character from various members of the crew of different vessels."[158] Despite her appeals, the intransigent Meachum "continued to send her as before to said steamboats," even though his *Address*, written six years later, awkwardly admitted, "boatmen are very apt to be rude" (*AA*, 31). [159] Unlike her brother's petition, Brunetta's plea took a more conciliatory form: it was "not made in a spirit of contention or through the least wish to give annoyance, or occasion inconvenience to said Meachum."[160] Her attorney appealed to the courts to protect her virtuous young womanhood from "wanton insult" as he sought to transfer her moral custodianship from the wayward black master to the white court. Such a feminized discourse of rescue offered the court the opportunity to play the gallant. The court readily granted the "prayer of petitioner," even though the gendered appeal of Brunetta's petition also forced it to recognize openly the sanctity of black femininity in ways that profoundly unsettled the instrumentalization of black womanhood under slave law.

In this way, the law shaped the kinds of freedom and autonomy to be had within a slave state. Some free blacks embraced, out of necessity, an informal freedom that did not outwardly challenge the chattel logic of slavery, especially since those who secured legal emancipation by means other than the ones stipulated by the slave state were forced by law to leave the territory, so as to prevent the rise of a free black society in these slave states. Others, like Meachum, turned to strategies that seem even more strongly to rely on the chattel principle. For instance, Lunsford Lane, as detailed in the next section, began to buy his family—one member at a time—once he returned to North Carolina as a freeman. Unable to manumit his kin in a slave state, Lane sought to hold them as property and thus prevent their separation by sale. William Johnson, a successful entrepreneur who remained in the South, also bought and sold a number of slaves.[161] By 1830, according to historian Loren Schweninger, approximately 1,556 free black masters from South Carolina, Georgia, Florida, Alabama, Mississippi, Arkansas, Louisiana, and Texas owned an aggregate 7,188 slaves.[162] The majority of black slaveholders held as slaves the kinfolk whom they were unable to free by law, although this "philanthropic" rationale, as Carter G. Woodson points out, led to other forms of gendered oppression.[163] Some black freedmen preferred to keep their wives in bondage so that they could sell them if they were not satisfactory, such as the black shoemaker in Charleston who purchased his wife for $700 and resold her a few months later for $750 after "finding her hard to please."[164]

Meachum sought, in this manner, to use slave law for both personal and collective benefit, but he found himself ensnared in its logic of "strange benevolence." Slaves such as Julia Logan, Judy, and Archibald and Brunetta Barnes clearly sought freedom on terms other than the ones dictated by his gospel of industry. They used the St. Louis courts to do so even as their legal appeals also reaffirmed the authority of the slave state. The same jurists who awarded their freedom also enforced those punitive exclusion laws that banished free blacks from the state. Reading Meachum's *Address* with and against the freedom suits of Logan, Judy, and the Barneses offers us a broader understanding of the shifting and, at times, clashing perspectives on freedom in a slave society. Their stories cast a more critical eye on those accounts, including the *Liberator*'s endorsement of "enterprising" emancipation, that locate figures such as Meachum within narratives of exemplary black "triumph" in the face of slavery's repressive limitations. Meachum's experiments in lawful liberty, like the freedom suit, freed a number of slaves within the state, but the slave law that he sought to circumvent also powerfully shaped the form of his antislavery agency and activism.

Return to Our Southern Home

> By common right, the South is the negro's home.
> —William Wells Brown, *My Southern Home; or, The South and Its People*, 1880

Regardless of the controversies the Taney Court provoked, it did resolve the uncertain status of traveling slaves in *Dred Scott v. Sandford* after decades of growing hostilities between free and slave states over the question of interstate comity. "[N]either Dred Scott himself, nor any of his family," reasoned Taney, "were made free by being carried into this territory, even if they had been carried there by the owner, with the intention of becoming a permanent resident."[165] Some traveling slaveholders took immediate advantage of the *Dred Scott* judgment and its nullification of the Thomas Amendment to the Missouri Compromise. "Every year," wrote the *Missouri Liberty Weekly*

Tribune, "men who come from the South bring their slaves as body servants to the hotels, and take them away again. . . . a Southerner is now holding his slaves at Stillwater [Minnesota], and declares that, under the Dred Scott decision, he defies the authorities to interfere."[166] Traveling slaveholders who were once cautious about risking their slaves in "free territories" were content to view the judgment as lending federal sanction to their property rights. In many ways, the Taney Court merely confirmed the divestment of black civil rights that was well under way in states south of Mason-Dixon. By the 1850s, Missouri had distinguished itself, according to the *Provincial Freeman*, "in recent acts of despotism" against free blacks, and former St. Louis bondsman William Wells Brown cautioned that "no part of our slave-holding country is more noted for the barbarity of its inhabitants than St. Louis."[167]

Slave states such as Missouri and South Carolina, in order to curtail the growth of free black populations within their borders, had begun to fashion antiblack regulations that worked *in tandem* with the northern law of freedom. The recognition of black freedom thus became the grounds for banishment and exclusion from the slave states. These antiblack regulations, which criminally prohibited the ingress, emigration, or settlement of free blacks, became fodder for antislavery literature. John Jolliffe's *Belle Scott* made ironic reference to these southern statutes "by which all free persons of color, are driven from the state, as a punishment for their impudence in being free; and under which, so many free persons of color, from the free states, have been imprisoned, and sold into slavery, for the gross crime of breathing the air, or treading the soil of those states."[168] Jolliffe (the lawyer who defended Margaret Garner) was not the only writer to draw on these black exclusion laws as evidence of slavery's despotism: F.C. Adams devoted a chapter of his antislavery novel *Manuel Pereira* (discussed in chapter 4) to expose how black exclusion laws in slave states such as South Carolina specifically sought to undermine the efficacy if not legitimacy of the northern law of freedom.

Slave states began to legislate punitive measures against free blacks and slaves who chose to take advantage of the law in the free North. Free blacks emigrating from Texas to Massachusetts became state citizens after a period of residence, but "should they return to Texas," warned the *National Era*, "they would be liable to imprisonment; and, for a second offence, to slavery."[169] Such regulations against free blacks were not limited to slave states. Even free border states such as Ohio and Illinois enforced punitive statutes to restrict the growth of free black populations at midcentury. Many of the black American "refugees" interviewed in Boston abolitionist

Benjamin Drew's collection of fugitive slave narratives, *The Refugee; or, The Narratives of Fugitive Slaves in Canada* (1856), had immigrated to Canada to escape "oppressive laws demanding security for good behavior" in these free border states.[170] Manumitted slave J.C. Brown records that Ohio legislators revived an 1804 "black law" that required "every colored man ... to give bonds in $500 not to become a town charge, and to find bonds also for his heirs. No one could employ a colored man or woman to do any kind of labor, under penalty of $100. There were then about 3,000 colored people there—by this law they were thrown out of employment" (*TR*, 244). The enforcement of such statutes forced free blacks to follow the fugitive's path to Canada. David Grier left his enslaved kinfolk in neighboring Kentucky after he was unable to give the security for good behavior in Ohio, and Henry Blue admitted that he "would rather have remained in Indiana ... [e]xcepting for the oppressive laws" (*TR*, 374, 372, 273). Elizabeth Keckley was also "very troubled" by similar antiblack laws upon her arrival in Washington City. "I was notified that I could only remain in the city ten days without obtaining a license to do so," she recalls of the journey in 1860, "such being the law.... I had to have someone vouch to the authorities that I was a free woman" (*BS*, 48).[171] Such legislation constituted a punitive recognition of free black personhood even in purportedly "free territories." Legally emancipated blacks such as J.C. Brown, David Grier, Henry Blue, and Lunsford Lane left their native homes rather than face the dire consequences of remaining in slave states against the law.

Lane's autobiographical slave narrative powerfully illustrates how slave states strategically acknowledged the law of freedom to oppress and control their black populations further. *Narrative of Lunsford Lane, Formerly of Raleigh, N.C. Embracing an Account of His Early Life, the Redemption by Purchase of Himself and Family from Slavery, and His Banishment from the Place of His Birth for the Crime of Wearing a Colored Skin* (1842) recounts his legal struggles to remain in North Carolina with his enslaved kinfolk after he secured his legal freedom in New York. The enthusiastic reception of the *Narrative* warranted three additional reprintings the following year, and William G. Hawkins published an expanded biographical version of it entitled *Lunsford Lane; or, Another Helper from North Carolina* (1863) shortly after the enactment of Lincoln's Emancipation Proclamation. Lane organized his *Narrative* around the theme of exile, and the lengthy title stresses the unexpected forms of loss entailed in his legal freedom. Indeed, in his text, banishment from home constitutes yet another kind of theft analogous to the kidnapping or human theft that structured the personal narratives of Peter Still, Lucy Ann Delaney, and Dred Scott.

Lane's autobiography critically reframes his journey toward legal freedom as a narrative of racial exclusion. Once the "body-servant and waiter" to Raleigh planter Sherwood Haywood, Lane had hired his time and husbanded his savings until he raised the one thousand dollars to buy his legal freedom in 1835 (*LL*, 31). He arranged with Benjamin B. Smith, the Raleigh merchant who owned his wife, Martha Curtis (identified as "Patsy" in legal documents), to purchase his freedom from his mistress, since slaves "could not legally purchase it, and as the laws forbid emancipation except for 'meritorious services.'"[172] Lane's self-purchase by proxy did not secure his legal freedom since it was merely a "bill of sale" that transferred his ownership from Haywood to Smith (*NLL*, 10). Lane later sought formal emancipation in the state but was unsuccessful: "Mr. Smith endeavored to emancipate me formally, and to get my manumission recorded; I tried also; but the court judged that I had done nothing 'meritorious,' and so I remained, nominally only, the slave of Mr. Smith for a year" (*NLL*, 10). Lane then tried another strategy, journeying as Smith's valet to New York, where he secured his formal deed of manumission. He had felt, in his words, "unsafe in that relation" until his legal emancipation in New York, where he was "regularly and formally made a freeman, and . . . [his] manumission recorded" (*NLL*, 10; *LL*, 51). Lane returned to his "family in Raleigh and endeavored to do by them as a freeman should" (*NLL*, 10).

Lane began the process of buying his wife and seven children from Smith on a twenty-five-hundred-dollar installment plan, and they soon found themselves in more independent circumstances: "living in our own house—a house which I previously purchased—in January, 1839" (*NLL*, 14). The household's domestic security was short-lived. People who tolerated Lane as a slave did not tolerate him as a freedman. One concerned individual even encouraged him to emigrate to Liberia, claiming that "if he would leave immediately for Liberia, many of the people of Raleigh would assist in paying expenses," although this plan did not include Lane's enslaved kinfolk. When that plan failed, another ploy was attempted for his "personal removal." Lane was soon served with an official notice charging him with violating a North Carolina statute regulating the migration of free blacks into the state. The law gave him twenty days "to remove out of this state" (*NLL*, 15). This action was a strategic application of the law in order to banish Lane, as North Carolina, like the Alabama from which Peter Still fled, insisted on its sovereign power to dictate entry into and circulation within its bounds. North Carolina law considered Lane a "foreign negro" since he had entered his emancipation in a northern state. "It will be remembered that my emancipation," Lane explains, "had been legally secured only by going to the State of New York, and having the evidence of my right to freedom placed on record there. My secret enemies in Raleigh reasoned that I must hereafter be looked upon as a free negro, from another State" (*LL*, 87). Forced to recognize the legitimacy of Lane's emancipation under New York law, his "secret enemies" invoked against him the exclusion statute, passed in the wake of Nat Turner's 1831 revolt, manipulating legal formalism to effect his removal from the state (*LL*, 285–86).[173] As Hawkins notes in the expanded *Lunsford Lane*, Lane "had not even violated the letter of the law, for the statute was one concerning the 'migration of free negroes and mulattoes into this State.' This was his native State; here he was born, and lived, and here he hoped to spend the remainder of his days; but the law did not even permit him to purchase his freedom" (*LL*, 101).[174]

Hawkins's expanded narrative attempts to show law and legal process as mechanisms for racial injustice in slave states. The letter of the law was rarely enforced against slaveholders, but it was applied with formal rigor against free blacks, who were viewed as "threats" to slave society. Slaveholders, for example, regularly hired out their slaves, even though, as Lane points out, this practice was "in violation of the laws of the State,—a slave having no legal right to make a contract of this kind which would be binding" (*LL*, 47). North Carolina did not deny the law of freedom. It acknowledged the legitimacy of Lane's emancipation in New York only to charge him with "migrat[ing] into this state contrary to the provisions of the act of assembly concerning free negros and mulattoes," with the penalty of banishment from the state (*NLL*, 14–15). Punishments for violating the twenty-day directive, a verbatim text of which Lane replicates in the narrative, included "a penalty of five hundred dollars" under threat of reenslavement for a ten-year term if he remained in the state beyond the allotted twenty days (*NLL*, 15). The authorities did not interfere with Martha and the children, however, since they remained slaves within the state. The state's action, Lane relates, "was a terrible blow to me; for it prostrated at once all my hopes in my cherished object of obtaining the freedom of my family, and led me to expect nothing but a separation from them forever" (*NLL*, 15). Lane managed to remain in Raleigh beyond twenty days through the interposition of his employer and patron, who was "then private secretary to Governor Dudley," but this respite did not halt the workings of the law set in motion against him. Lane was served a warrant to appear before the court "to answer," in his words, "for the sin of having remained in the place of my birth for the space of twenty days and more after being warned to leave," and he just narrowly escaped imprisonment (*LL,* 92).

A number of officials familiar with Lane from hiring his services as a valet and tobacconist were inclined to assist him in his petition to the state legislature to make an exception in his case. "[N]ot having paid in full" the purchase price for his family, reads Lane's petition, he "is not yet able to leave the State, without parting with his family" and requests to "remain only sufficient time in the State to secure their freedom" (*NLL,* 18; *LL,* 93). Lane was not alone in these costly and ultimately fruitless endeavors. Two other freedmen, named Issac Hunter and Waller Freeman, hoping to redeem their families from bondage also brought petitions before the state legislature, but these "nigger bills," as one statesman styled them, were all struck down in the Commons (*NLL,* 19–20).[175] "Nothing now remained," recalled Lane years later, "but that I must leave the State, and leave my wife and children, never more to see them" (*LL,* 98). "Is it strange that I asked myself why I was thus banished?" queried the desperate man as he faced permanent separation from his still-enslaved kinfolk (*LL,* 98).

Lane set out with his redeemed daughter Laura for New York, where, like Peter Still, he commenced the work of raising the balance to ransom the remaining members of his family (*NLL,* 21). Once Lane secured the requisite funds, he sought to ensure "as legal a transfer of their freedom into his hands, as the law would permit," not trusting this important task to anyone else (*LL,* 164). When Lane returned to Raleigh, he understood the nature of the visit: "[the] visit I was making to the South was to be a farewell one" (*NLL,* 23). Although Lane had written to the governor in advance for permission to return, constables seized him upon his arrival, and an attempt was made to convict him of the crime "of *delivering abolition lectures in the State of Massachusetts*" (*NLL,* 38). An angry mob collected outside the ad hoc court by the time he was grudgingly released, and he narrowly escaped death after the rabble tarred and feathered him. Lane finally bid an emotional farewell to his "old cradle," holding in his hand the bills of sale for "one dark mulatto woman, named Patsy" and his children Edward, William, Lunsford, Maria, Ellick, and Lucy (*NLL,* 33; *LL,* 199–200). The ban against the slave's birth into a "family"—his enforced kinlessness under slave law—served to heighten his attachment to place. "The emotions experienced at the moment of parting from my friends almost unmanned me," recalled Lane, "and I cried like a child" (*LL,* 158). The trauma of this separation continued to haunt Lane throughout his later life. Indeed, Sigmund Freud later identified this loss of native country as one of the most powerful preconditions of melancholia. Lane's mistress, moved to tearful benevolence, offered to release his aged mother for a nominal two hundred dollars, payable at a future date, while retaining his father, "Uncle Ned," as a household slave (*LL*, 195–96).

Lane reports how he felt when he first "pressed the pavements of Philadelphia" with his kinfolk in tow: "as though ... I could now draw a long breath and inhale without let or hindrance, the pure atmosphere of freedom." But he continued to identify himself as an "unwilling exile from home" some twenty years after his banishment from Raleigh (*LL*, 161). "Lunsford and his family" were indeed, in the words of Hawkins, "strangers in a strange land" when the "rescued household" found itself "on the soil of freedom" (*LL*, 175). Lane had deep ties to the slaveholding capital city of Raleigh. His ancestors and the land on which the capital city was built had been the property of planter Joel Lane, who had settled there in the 1760s. Indeed, Lunsford Lane, like Cyprian Clamorgan of St. Louis, had been named after Raleigh's "founding father." Lane never forgot his southern home, even though he spent the greater part of his life enslaved there. In 1856, he even sought to recapture, unsuccessfully, his lost Raleigh in Oberlin, Ohio, where "many of his acquaintances from North Carolina had settled," since it "remind[ed] them of home" (*LL*, 178). Place was far "more deeply a matter of belonging than of possession," and Lane returned to Massachusetts after only a handful of years.[176]

Hawkins first met Lane at one of Lane's Civil War speaking engagements in Massachusetts, where he gave powerful expression to his longstanding desire to return to his "old home in the South" (*LL*, 145). Speaking on behalf of the "four million slaves" and displaced "contrabands" of war, Lane insisted, "We have no desire to remain in the Northern States, except as a temporary refuge from slavery.... The South is our home; and we feel that there we can be happy, and contribute by our industry to the prosperity of our race.... We only desire a secure freedom in the South" (*LL*, 204–5). Lane undoubtedly sought to defuse, in part, mounting fears over black migration northward after the Civil War, but his speech also betrays the forms of loss that conditioned his experience of northern freedom. The sentence of banishment, with its taboo on return, only intensified Lane's yearning for his southern home. Many free blacks shared Lane's sense of estrangement in the North. Laying claim on the slave South was an emotionally complex act that betrayed the desperate need to repossess personal history and reoccupy place. Nearly every black American refugee interviewed in Benjamin Drew's collection ardently professed this same desire to return to "live in the South," in the words of one St. Louis fugitive, named Alexander Hamilton, "if slavery was done away with, and the laws were right" (*TR*, 178–79). "If slavery were abolished," professed fugitive Isaac Williams, "I would rather live in a southern State" (*TR*, 67).

The plaintive desire to return south filled the pages of Drew's volume of Canadian slave narratives. Many of these fugitives, like Lane, were forced to leave kinfolk in the South when they resettled in Canada. Fugitive Henry Crawhion admitted that he did not "feel reconciled" to freedom "on account of [his] wife and family," whom he had left in Louisville, and he confessed, "I would prefer Louisville, if I could be free there" (*TR*, 257). Thoughts of the children whom Mary Young had left behind haunted her in freedom: "I have children now who have got the yoke on them. It almost kills me to think that they are there, and that I can do them no good" (*TR*, 259–60). The celebrated Harriet Tubman best expressed the yearnings of these black American exiles when she asserted, "We would rather stay in our native land, if we could be as free there as we are here" (*TR*, 30). Indeed, Lucy Ann Delaney recounts in her narrative's final posttrial chapter her mother's long-sought-after reunion with her daughter Nancy, who had become one of Drew's American "refugees" in Canada. "After the trial was over," their thoughts "reverted to sister Nancy, who had been gone so long," and they longed to "visit Canada and seek the long-lost girl" (*FD*, 52). Polly eventually made the two-week journey from St. Louis to Toronto, where "after a long visit, [she] returned home, although strongly urged to remain the rest of her life with Nancy; but old people are like old trees, uproot them, and transplant to other scenes, they droop and die, no matter how bright the sunshine; or how balmy the breezes" (*FD*, 54). Polly bade farewell to her daughter and returned to the slaveholding city that she and the Scotts called home. The recognition of legal personhood for Lane and the many black refugees in Canada became a pretext for exclusion from the states where they had passed most of their enslaved lives. For those who secured freedom only to suffer banishment from their southern homes, return was not permitted until well after the Civil War.

Cyprian Clamorgan's Fictions of Law and Custom

When read alongside the selected freedom suits recounted in the previous sections, the autobiographical narratives of Elizabeth Keckley, Lucy Ann Delaney, and Lunsford Lane and the lesser-known writings of John Berry Meachum and, as discussed in this section, Cyprian Clamorgan offer us a glimpse into the complex social world of slaves and black freemen and women southwest of Mason-Dixon in the years leading to *Dred Scott v. Sandford*.[177] Chief Justice Roger B. Taney's infamous ruling asserted that free black Americans, the unexpected historical residue of the African slave trade, were not citizens of the United States and therefore not entitled to the rights secured in the Constitution—including, in Scott's case, the right to bring a lawsuit before federal courts. "It does not by any means follow, because he has all the rights and privileges of a citizen of a State," Taney reasoned, "that he must be a citizen of the United States."[178] Taney's exclusion of all blacks from the rights guaranteed in the Constitution went far beyond the question, putatively under review in the case, of Scott's claim on state citizenship. Taney dedicated twenty-four of the fifty-five pages of his opinion (as printed in Howard's *Reports*) to an inspection of those precedents, historical and legal, that allegedly confirmed the denial of black U.S. citizenship.[179] "Can a negro," he asks, "whose ancestors were imported into this country, and sold as slaves, become a member of the political community formed and brought into existence by the Constitution of the United States, and as such become entitled to all the rights and privileges, and immunities, guaranteed by that instrument to the citizen?"[180] The answer was decidedly no. The judgment in *Dred Scott* constituted free black Americans as subject to laws, but without the protections and political power that the nation-state extended to its white citizens. In other words, free blacks continued to be citizens of their individual states and subject "to strict police regulations," without the privileges and immunities of federal citizenship.[181]

Cyprian Clamorgan, a member of the free black elite in antebellum St. Louis, published *The Colored Aristocracy of St. Louis* (1858) in this charged political climate. *The Colored Aristocracy* was an ephemeral work "loosely bound and printed fairly cheaply" that offered an unexpected and powerful revisionist history of black Americans in the territorial frontier just as the Taney Court sanctioned the twofold nationalization and expansion of slavery westward.[182] Clamorgan's sardonic humor and relentless antisentimentalism (he refers to the characters in *Uncle Tom's Cabin* as the "monstrous creations" of a "morbid and diseased brain") proffered an unlikely southwestern challenge to the homogenization of racial difference and the conflation, as dictated in Taney's sweeping pronouncement, of racial identity with social status (*CA*, 45). All free blacks, after *Dred Scott*, were transformed into what the radical southern ideologue George Fitzhugh described as "slaves without masters."[183] Descended from one of the territory's earliest settlers, Clamorgan professed deep ties to the Southwest and was the coproprietor of a popular St. Louis barbershop and bathhouse when he penned his volume. The ostentatious "Depot of Elegant French and English Perfumeries, Toilet and Fancy Articles, Combs, Brushes, Razors, &c." stood near Hugh Garland's law office on Chestnut Street and was only eight blocks from Garland's Olive Street home, where he held Keckley as a slave.[184]

Dred Scott was as much a struggle over the meaning of national history as it was over the Supreme Court's power of judicial review. Taney's opinion, as Fehrenbacher's exhaustive case study argues, "depended primarily upon the interpretation of American history that he proposed to write into constitutional law."[185] Taney continually invoked history to authorize his pronouncements, even as he rewrote the histories of slavery and abolition in the process, and his legal conclusions were derived from *and* based on specific historical claims.[186] "We refer to these historical facts," reads his opinion, "for the purpose of showing the fixed opinions concerning that race."[187] Taney insisted that blacks "formed no part of the people who framed and adopted . . . the Declaration of Independence." Therefore, blacks were not U.S. citizens, according to his causal logic, since they had not numbered among the sovereign people included within the constitutional compact "at that time" of 1776.[188]

Clamorgan fashioned a wry literary response to the Taney Court's historical revisionism. "According to the decision of Chief Justice Taney," writes Clamorgan,

> a colored man is not a citizen of the United States, and consequently has no political rights under the Constitution. His life is all that he is entitled to, and in some States he holds that merely because he is useful to his master. We shall not, in this place, call in question the judgment of the learned Chief Justice . . . but we may be permitted to show in what manner the political influence of the colored man is felt. (*CA*, 47)

Clamorgan's historical counternarrative begins well before the emergence of the United States as a sovereign republic in order to contest the strategic occlusion of black Americans that Taney's *Dred Scott* judgment sought to turn into a "fact" of national identity. *The Colored Aristocracy* "traces back" the genealogical history of the western territories to Africa and the forced migrations of the transatlantic slave trade.

Clamorgan's revisionist black historiography of the West appeared at the precise moment that the young state began to legislate its official and public histories. Missouri's General Assembly incorporated the Missouri Historical and Philosophical Society in 1845, although it dissolved just four years later without having accomplished its charter mission "to collect, embody, arrange and preserve in an authentic form, the materials for the history of the State."[189] Regional publications such as the *Western Journal and Civilian* had begun to lament the fact that Missouri was still "without a historian" after "nearly a century, since the first settlements by a civilized race."[190] The "history of a people," it observed, was "necessary to make a people homogenous," and it deplored the want of chronicles charting the "progress of settlement" from the first pioneers, "Laclede, Piernas, Cruzat, Libya, St. Ange, Delassus, Trudeau, Soulard, Mackay, Chouteau, Cerre, Pratte, Lisa, LaBeaume, Musick, Delaurier, Tayon, Blanchard, Clamorgan."[191] In the vacuum of official state narratives, the *Western Journal and Civilian* suggested that its readers "gather up the fragments of history which lie scattered throughout the land." Some of these historical "fragments" lay within the St. Louis circuit court's docket, where the black descendants and heirs of these illustrious "first families" filed their freedom suits. They too found their way into *The Colored Aristocracy*. The *Western Journal* perhaps had intended neither these "fragments" nor the unlikely Clamorgan in its call for territorial histories to be preserved "in a durable form . . . to go down to a remote posterity."[192]

Clamorgan offers readers a glimpse of the "society as it exists amongst the free colored people of St. Louis," in the midst of the public contests over black citizenship and assimilability after *Dred Scott* (*CA*, 45). "Thousands," Clamorgan observes,

> have wept over the fictitious sorrows of "Uncle Tom". . . . The romantic autobiographies of Solomon Northrup, Box Brown, and other colored gentlemen, have been read in every quarter of the globe. The long-contested suit of Dred Scott excited the attention of the wisest heads in the land, and volumes have been written on both sides of the question. . . . When respectable white men and women can sit and listen to the oratorical displays of Fred.

Douglass and his able compatriots; when the question of Emancipation is taking hold of the minds of the people in our own State and is fast growing to be the leading topic of the day . . . the author deems it not inappropriate to take a cursory glance at society as it exists amongst the free colored people of St. Louis. (*CA*, 45)

Many members of the free black population of St. Louis, Clamorgan notes, were "separated from the white race by a line of division so faint that it can be traced only by the keen eye of prejudice" (*CA*, 45). This "line of division" was as arbitrary as the geopolitical "line" that demarcated freedom from slavery for the Scotts. The color line, like the imagined line at parallel 36° 30′, was yet another kind of legal fiction created to maintain the racial ideologies from which slavery drew its justifications. A "perpetual and impassable barrier," reads Taney's published opinion, "was intended to be erected between the white race and the one which they had reduced to slavery."[193] Taney sought to etch more deeply into the national culture this "line of *distinction*" between black and white that was otherwise, in Clamorgan's words, so "faint" as to be undetectable except to "the keen eye of prejudice" (*CA*, 45).[194] It is no accident that it was a Missourian, Mark Twain, who created the character Chambers, who, like his enslaved mother, Roxy, was "as white as anybody . . . [but] by a fiction of law and custom, a negro."[195]

The redefinition of national citizenship and belonging in *Dred Scott* sought to fix the meaning of this "fiction of law and custom" into a fact of U.S. history.[196] Blackness, regardless of status, became a legal index of improper (and impossible) assimilation to the United States. Black racial difference now came under the uniform sign of slavery and the "natally alienated," which marked the boundaries between inclusion and exclusion within the imagined community of the nation.[197] Clamorgan's "colored aristocracy," however, consistently resisted such categorical designations. Pierre Labadie, Louis Charleville, and Norton Reynolds, Jr., three of Clamorgan's black elites, not to mention the writer himself, were consistent racial enigmas to census takers. Their racial designations fluctuated among "mulatto," "white," and "colored" over a few decades' worth of schedules.[198] These census records, like the "white slave" or "tragic mulatto" found in sentimental fictions such as *The Quadroons*, *Clotel*, and *The Octoroons* and in Louisa Picquet's slave narrative, betray the construction of race as a social category. Antoine Labadie was "one of the wealthiest colored men in the city" and, as Clamorgan observes, was "nearly white, and look[ed] more like a Mexican than anything else" (*CA*, 56n.65). Labadie and his brother

Pierre, both descended from the prominent Labbadie, or Labadie, clan of St. Louis, repeatedly left census takers confused as to their racial identity (*CA*, 56n.65). An 1850 census taker listed Labadie, his wife, and their three children as "white," and another listed the household as "mulatto" a decade later (*CA*, 56n. 65). Census takers found Charleville, who was "once very wealthy, but his estate has now dwindled down to about sixty thousand dollars," like his neighbor Labadie, racially indeterminate (*CA*, 56). Charleville, his wife, Louisa, and sons, Louis and Joseph, were listed as white in the 1830 census, whereas the 1860 census listed the entire family as mulatto (*CA*, 90).[199] Reynolds, whom Clamorgan describes simply as, "an intelligent, well-informed young man," like Labadie and Charleville, underwent the transformation from "mulatto" to "white" and back to "colored" over the course of four decades from 1860 to 1900 (*CA*, 62).[200] These official misreadings of Clamorgan's colored aristocrats illuminate the way racial designations were inextricably tied to perceptions of social caste in ways that undermined the racial hierarchies of slaveholding society.[201]

The intersecting black and white lines of descent and affiliation that constitute the political, economic, and social histories of the slaveholding city are further illuminated when Clamorgan transitions into the fictional conceit of his book. The self-fashioned picaresque narrator takes the imagined reader on a guided "walking tour" of various establishments to visit, in pithy biographical sketches, the black elite of St. Louis. This leisurely walk through the city's commercial and residential districts is in studied contrast to another, didactic excursion published in the pages of the abolitionist Elijah Lovejoy's *St. Louis Observer*. The "abhorrent" evidence of southern racial "amalgamation" had rudely arrested Lovejoy in his perambulatory tour of St. Louis: "unless my eyes deceive me as I walk the streets of our city, there are some among us who venture to put it into practice."[202] Clamorgan's volume publicly exposes the history of miscegenation in a city that had long informally condoned the practice. Taney, as Fehrenbacher notes, relied primarily on antimiscegenation laws as evidence of the "subject condition" of black Americans.[203] Indeed, Taney draws on antimiscegenation statutes from Maryland (1717), Massachusetts (1705, 1786, 1836), and Rhode Island (1822) as "a faithful index to the state of feeling towards the class of persons of whom they speak, and of the position they occupied throughout the thirteen colonies."[204] In this way, Taney sought to evade the argument, valid in most northern states, that marriage and slavery were incompatible. Whereas slaveholding states denied the institution of marriage as a binding civil contract among slaves, most northern states held that marriage between slave and freeperson emancipated both.[205] Justice Benjamin Curtis's dissent endorsed this line of reasoning to argue for the Scotts' legitimate claim on freedom, since the two had married (in an official ceremony) in free territory with a master's consent.[206] Taney's rebuttal strategically shifted the political question of freedom raised in civil unions between freepersons and slaves into the far more polarizing predicament of racial amalgamation.

Clamorgan revels in gossipy anecdotes exposing for public amusement the social foibles and moral peccadilloes of his illustrious "hosts," yet his sketches, while playful, hint at the much more complex *genealogical* history of the city in the manner of William Wells Brown's *Clotel*. Brown used the metaphors of slave kinship to organize a narrative that imaginatively charts two generations of slave women descended from Thomas Jefferson. Clamorgan even hints that Chief Justice Taney, like *Clotel*'s Jefferson and *Pudd'nhead Wilson*'s FFVs (first families of Virginia), may have "in this State kindred of a darker hue than himself" (*CA*, 47). "We, who know the history of all the old families of St. Louis," confesses Clamorgan, "might readily point to the scions of some of our 'first families,' and trace their genealogy back to the swarthy tribes of Congo or Guinea" (*CA*, 45–46). In such moments, *The Colored Aristocracy* betrays a historiographic consciousness that expresses itself genealogically through slave kinship and its necessarily discontinuous lines of affiliation and descent. Such repressed family histories provide Clamorgan with a model for national history. Kinship and its logic of descent, in part, shaped Taney's opinion as he pondered the citizenship of "the *descendants* of such slaves, when they shall be emancipated, or who are born of parents who had become free before their birth."[207] It also shaped Clamorgan's alternative history. Given the codifications against slave marriage and kinship (the doctrine of *partus sequitur ventrem* in particular) and the ban against miscegenation, Clamorgan's genealogical history of Missouri traces a continuously discontinuous past that yearns to "fill in" the spatiotemporal ruptures of the African diaspora and the forced dispersals occasioned by the transatlantic slave trade.[208] The unknown, forgotten, unnamed, and unnamable marks his revisionist history of blacks in frontier America.

The early settlement of Louisiana Territory began with the violence of (forced) miscegenation, as the "French and Spaniards . . . found companions for their solitude and mothers for their children" in "the colored race" (*CA*, 46). These early settlers first "sought wives among the sylvan maids of the forest" before "the blood of Africa . . . crossed the Atlantic, and the colored race . . . found a foothold in the West Indies. It was there that many of the voyageurs up the Mississippi obtained wives . . . and from this union have sprung up many of those whom we designate the 'colored aristocracy'" (*CA*, 46). This practice of *placage* was widespread throughout the frontier settlements in the Americas because of the shortage of white women.[209] If "the blood of Pocahontus has ennobled many of the best families of Virginia," reasons Clamorgan, might "not the descendants of many of the early settlers of Missouri boast of a similar genealogy?" (*CA*, 46).

The successful freedom suit that Marguerite first brought against (Jean) Pierre Chouteau, Sr., a descendant of another "founding family," in 1825 undoubtedly influenced Clamorgan's reconstructed genealogical history of early settlement.[210] Marguerite, daughter of Afro-Indian Marie Jean Scypion, based her right to freedom on her maternal grandmother, whom she claimed to be an "Indian woman" of the Natchez nation. "To show descent from this race," Marguerite's counsel contended, "is to show right to freedom" since "Indians were around and among the settlements of white men, in the full enjoyment of their personal liberty," unlike "Negroes," whose "ancestors . . . [were] imported to the continent as slaves."[211] Like Las Casas's "strange benevolence," the suspension of Indian slavery under Spanish rule in 1769, once sanctioned during the French regime in the Mississippi Valley, provoked a number of legal uncertainties over the status of slaves, particularly Afro-Indian slaves such as Marguerite, when the United States annexed Louisiana Territory.[212] Indeed, James Thomas recalls that among the "free people" of St. Louis, "there were many who were Indians, Spaniards, French, whose chocolate brown mothers had lived under the three flags."[213]

In the Missouri Supreme Court's review of *Marguerite v. Chouteau* (1834), it established its tendency toward freedom in those lawsuits in which slave plaintiffs, such as Marguerite, asserted a right to freedom based on maternal descent. Unconvinced of Chouteau's property claims, Justices Tompkins and McGirk, with Wash dissenting, ordered a retrial of her freedom suit. The unanimous verdict by the Jefferson County jury in 1836 freed Marguerite and her surviving kinsmen, whose separate freedom suits had been joined to her trial.[214] Like so many other slave women examined in this chapter, Marguerite may have helped secure her children's freedom once she established her own right to freedom.[215] The long genealogical histories of kinship shaped the litigation of Marguerite and her children in powerful ways.[216] Indeed, Justice Tompkins's majority opinion admitted, "nearly one hundred years before the commencement of this suit the supposed maternal grandmother of the appellant was brought to Fort Chartres, in Louisiana, and was there held as a slave till her death."[217] The stories of kinship detailed in these freedom suits commenced long before the founding of the nation, and such stories provided Clamorgan with an alternative model of historiography to contest the purposively exclusive one that Taney had crafted in *Dred Scott*.

Indeed, Clamorgan's own personal history, with its own entangled genealogies of kinship and property, is deeply rooted in this early territorial history. Clamorgan was obsessed with litigation over vast and highly lucrative land claims (amounting to nearly half a million acres of the former Louisiana Purchase) that the Spanish crown had granted in 1796 to his maternal grandfather, the notorious frontiersman and voyageur Jacques Clamorgan (c. 1734–1814).[218] Jacques Clamorgan fathered a number of slave children with mistresses whom he manumitted and informally recognized. Upon his death in 1814, he divided his property evenly among his four surviving children, St. Eutrope, Cyprian Martial, Maximin, and Apoline, who was his only recorded daughter.[219] Cyprian Clamorgan later sought to establish his property claims through his mother, Apoline, filing "no less than a score of big claims in the name of Jacques Clamorgan," which would have amounted to "many millions of dollars" if the federal government ever recognized them.[220] Clamorgan's decades-long legal disputes rivaled that of Harriet and Dred Scott. Congressional representatives from Missouri had "more than once made the effort to get into that Court [of Claims] the famous Clamorgan land claim, which has been a subject for Congressional controversy for about a century."[221] The Missouri Supreme Court reviewed at least one lawsuit based on a Clamorgan deed or land claim in almost every decade of the nineteenth century, and the U.S. Supreme Court eventually dismissed the validity of the Clamorgan petition in 1879.[222] In 1906, Clamorgan died in St. Louis without federal recognition of the territory that he claimed as his legal inheritance from his white forefather.[223]

Clamorgan ends *The Colored Aristocracy* abruptly with the tantalizing but unfulfilled promise of a second volume: "Our next attempt will be to give a true account of the *second class* of colored people," of which the "number is large, and the developments we shall make will startle many of our white friends. The romantic incidents connected with this subject surpass the wildest dreams of fiction" (*CA*, 63). Lucy Ann Delaney, along with Keckley, Meachum, the Scotts, and the many others who found emancipation and residency through the St. Louis circuit court, undoubtedly numbered among this "*second class* of colored people." However, Clamorgan's literary pledge remained incomplete, and we are left to gather the fragments of that story without his guidance.

Harriet Robinson Scott and Lucy Ann Delaney both "lived to see the joyful time when [their] race was made free, their chains struck off, and their right to their own flesh and blood lawfully acknowledged" (*FD*, 59). Harriet lived on the corner of Seventh and Locust streets in what is now downtown St. Louis until her death on 17 June 1876. She was interred in Greenwood Cemetery in Hillsdale, and she was largely forgotten until volunteers fighting to save the derelict and overgrown cemetery stumbled on her grave site in 2002.[224] Delaney also outlived her husband and remained in St. Louis until her death on 31 August 1910. She lived to see the dawn of a new century but remained haunted by the loss of her father. "I frequently thought of father," she confesses, "and wondered if he were alive or dead," well after the Civil War had reshaped the geopolitics of freedom and slavery (*FD*, 59). The "line" that was once the subject of so much interstate strife and litigation, especially for the Scotts, faded into the realm of legal history. "[A]t the time of the great exodus of negroes from the South," Delaney finally located her father, who was reunited with his daughters after forty-five years of separation (*FD*, 60). "My sister," Delaney recalls fondly, "came down from Canada, and we had a most joyful reunion, and only the absence of our mother left a vacuum, which we deeply and sorrowfully felt" (*FD*, 61). Her father, however, could not be persuaded to remain in St. Louis, where he now "felt like a stranger in a strange land," and returned to Mississippi, where he had passed the greater part of his enslaved life (*FD*, 61). In this way, Delaney ends her narrative by pondering what the law cannot redress in its distribution of justice. Delaney cannot quite reclaim the father she lost in slavery, though they may both live in the world of freedom.

4

The Crime of Color in the Negro Seamen Acts

> If any of you wish to know how FREE you are, let one of you start and go through the southern and western States of this country, and unless you travel as a slave to a white man (a servant is a *slave* to the man whom he serves) or have your free papers, (which if you are not careful they will get from you) if they do not take you up and put you in jail, and if you cannot give good evidence of your freedom, sell you into eternal slavery.
>
> —David Walker, *An Appeal to the Coloured Citizens of the World*, 1829

Radical black abolitionist David Walker proposes this counterfactual journey into the slave states early on in his *Appeal to the Coloured Citizens of the World*.[1] In an Atlantic world where freedom had become increasingly territorialized, Walker seizes on travel as an ironic test of the individual freedoms purportedly secured in the federal compact. His series of conditional "ifs" reveal personal liberty to be both racially particularized and geographically bounded. Free blacks—citizens of northern states—either traveled as slaves or risked becoming enslaved upon entry into a slave state. Black movement was permissible only when it was subordinated to white authority. The misnaming of traveling slaves as "servants" or contractual agents with the freedom of choice was a fiction particular to the legal culture of travel and exemplified in the freedom suit. Punitive statutes directed specifically toward curtailing black mobility were common among the states south and west of Mason-Dixon, and they belie the discourse and reality of free travel and free will in a partially free Atlantic world. Free black mariners, whose lives perhaps best typified the cosmopolitanism of Walker's "coloured citizens of the world," discovered the dreadful accuracy of his words as they sailed into southern ports. Fearing slave insurrection from within and national interference with slavery from without, South Carolina was the first of the coastal slave states to enact a police law "for the better regulation of Free Negroes and persons of color," a law that targeted free blacks engaged in the seafaring trade; North Carolina, Georgia, Florida, Alabama, Louisiana, and Texas soon followed.[2] Officials and harbormasters in these states began seizing and imprisoning, under threat of enslavement, all black sailors once their vessels docked in southern ports.

The Negro Seamen Act (1822) was among a number of "quarantine laws" that guarded the waterways and thoroughfares into South Carolina, as lawmakers sought to delimit the power and potential of black revolutionary consciousness after the unsettling discovery of the 1822 Denmark Vesey plot in Charleston.[3] Vesey, who had supposedly "slaved in St. Domingo, studied with the Moravians, and learned several languages" before his master, a sea captain, resettled him in Charleston, embodied the radical promise of the Black Atlantic.[4] An early instance of what Robert Westley describes as "Black exceptionalism within the law," the Negro Seamen Act was twice amended by South Carolina to increase its severity.[5] The 1835 amendment subjected black mariners who "ever again enter into the limits of the State" to sale at public auction "*as a slave*," with the proceeds divided between the state and informer.[6] Southern states such as South Carolina seized on their sovereign power to decide on the value and nonvalue of life as they effectively deemed certain individuals outside the political community and, therefore, alienable as property.[7] Only two legal identities existed for black sailors under the specific provisions of such police laws: they were either prisoners or slaves. And the prisoner quickly became a slave if jail fees went unpaid. These Negro Seamen Acts made black citizens and foreign nationals, according to Connecticut's *New Englander*, "guilty of [the crime of] being free" in southern states.[8] Stripped of any legal means for redress or amelioration, these "mariners, renegades and castaways" of the black Atlantic became slaves of the state in an uncanny continuum between what Orlando Patterson theorizes as the slave's social death and what Joan Dayan reelaborates as civil death or "dead in law"; these men may possess natural life, but they had lost all civil rights.[9]

Black Atlantic scholarship has often looked to the chronotope of the seafaring ship in its efforts to limn the cosmopolitan contours of the nineteenth century. Black sailors, according to Jeffrey Bolster, "established a visible presence in every North Atlantic seaport and plantation roadstead between 1740 and 1865" (see figure 4.1).[10] Indeed, Peter Linebaugh and Marcus Rediker regard black maritime circulation as one aspect of the "many-headed hydra" that unsettled political sovereignty along these North Atlantic currents.[11] The "Atlanticist radicalism" of black seafaring life threatened slaveholding localisms in a world where freedom seemed to inch westward, and southern U.S. lawmakers used these fears to further expand state power in relation to the federal government.[12]

This chapter examines the appeals to law made on behalf of black Atlantic mariners caught up in the workings of these antiblack statutes in coastal slave states. Outraged transatlantic reformers such as F.C. Adams drew public attention to the work of "the *State* [in] trying to reduce human beings from a state of freedom into that of slavery."[13] British and American sailors, with the support of their national or state governments, instigated a number of legal actions to challenge the law's constitutionality and secure its repeal. As the *Liberator* reported, any of these lawsuits would have tested "before the Supreme Court of the United States the legality of imprisoning such, when color and not crime was the only indictment to be found," but South Carolina officials blocked all these cases from going before the federal high court.[14] Antislavery activists and opponents of this police regulation increasingly turned to the "bar of public opinion" once they realized that a federal hearing would not be forthcoming and that Congress, controlled by "slavocratic power," would not act on the issue. Black and white abolitionists and merchants, southern reformers, and free blacks within the Atlantic world forged unexpected alliances as they endeavored to push this issue to the top of the political agenda. In the failure of law, they turned to newsprint, pamphleteering, and literature as they sought to enlist the "public mind" to do the work that legislators and jurists refused to do. These writers and orators, such as Walker, drew forth a revolutionary black consciousness from the law's negativity and limits, creating an oppositional agenda over these many decades of intermittent transatlantic protest.

The controversial Vesey conspiracy unleashed a public discourse of black revolutionary agency that South Carolina officials and proslavery advocates sought to control for their own political ends, as they drew distinctions between their domestic and foreign black populations.[15] The specter of incendiary blacks foreign to local slaveholding customs justified, in various ways, the necessity of this controversial regulation, as southern ideologues insisted on the "paternal benevolence" of slavery as an institution. Throughout the many decades of public contestation, South Carolina lawmakers periodically reinvigorated this amorphous threat of black foreignness to resolve this rather conspicuous contradiction within slaveholding society: purportedly

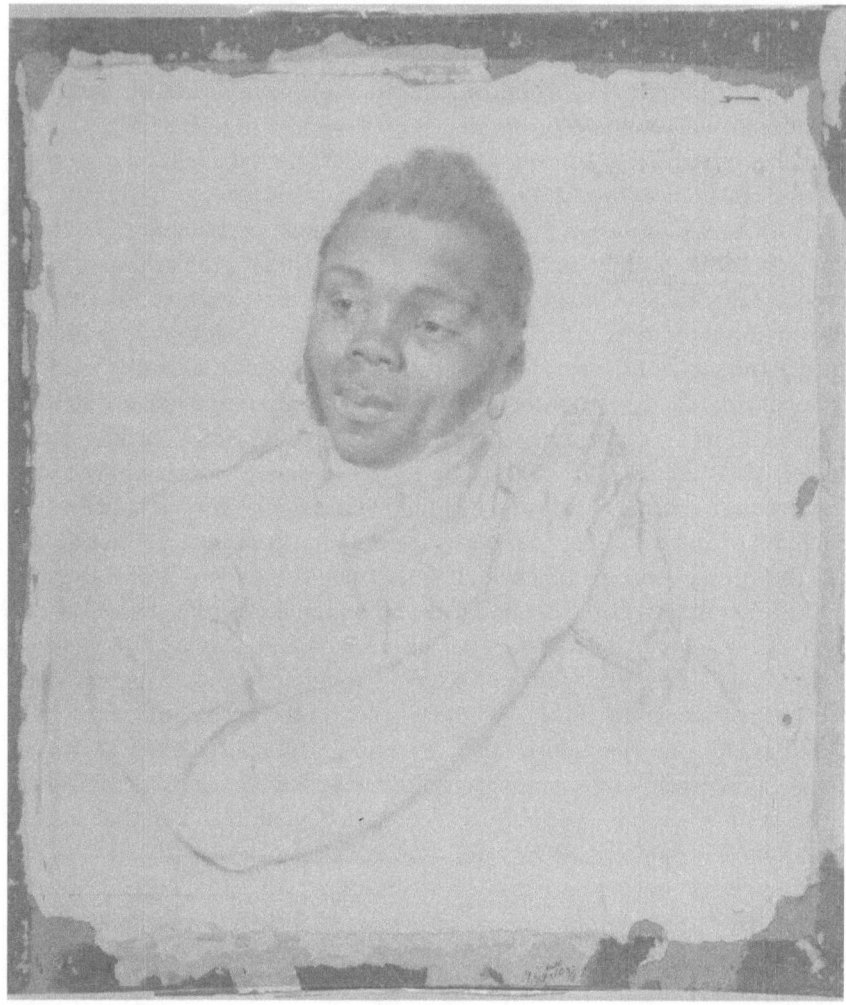

Fig. 4.1. Popular British portraitist John Downman (1750–1824) began this black chalk sketch, *Thomas Williams, a Sailor* (1815), in Liverpool. Williams's raised hands suggest the supplicating slave posture common in antislavery depictions. (Courtesy of the Tate Britain)

docile slaves capable of violent insurrection. Officials sought to relocate the threatening revolutionary potential of "domestic" slave populations onto the phantasm of free "foreign negroes."[16] This racialized regulation of transborder movement also indicates the degree to which U.S. borders were far from open; it offers an early history of the racial exclusions that continued to characterize U.S. geopolitics and the right to free travel well into the twentieth century.[17] Not only did local law thus define the borders of state and nation, but it also, according to Mary Dudziak and Leti Volpp, "delineate[d] the consequence of borders for the peoples within them."[18]

South Carolina officials sought to transform state aggression against its free black populace into a narrative of white victimization, as the police law activated a powerful sectional doctrine of self-preservation against a "racial" threat constructed as "foreign" to local customs. Public safety, insisted southern lawmakers, necessitated this statute, since "free negroes and persons of color, coming from the North . . . [had] attempted to corrupt our colored population by instilling into their minds false ideas of their duties and their station, till, by their insidious and exaggerated statements, they succeeded in exciting in the midst of this community a formidable insurrection."[19] South Carolina advocates insisted on this higher "law of self-preservation" as they marshaled out the language of public health to represent free black sailors as an "infectious disease" capable of overwhelming their domestic slave populations.[20] This history offers one of the starker illustrations of the racial moorings of police power, as lawmakers redefined these free blacks, regardless of national allegiances, into "foreigners" subject to punishment. They became stateless persons as officials stripped them of their legal personhood as either free citizens of northern states or subjects of Western nations. This geopolitical discourse of "foreignness" levied against free black American sailors, in particular, involved a troubling discourse of ontological dislocation and political alienation that was congruent with the slave's social death.[21] The sailors' claims on inalienable "native rights" went unheeded.[22] How was black life to be inscribed in the social order given that life or birth in the nation did not necessarily establish black persons as citizens or sovereign subjects? These conflicts over the extension of rights and entitlements to the free black citizens of "sister states," let alone the subjects of sovereign nations such as Britain or France, further pry apart the modern fiction of the equivalence of nativity and nationality.[23]

Black northerners, concerned about the ongoing violation of their constitutional rights, organized to take action against the Negro Seamen Acts. In 1842, notable black activists including William C. Nell, Benjamin Weeden, and Charles A. Battiste (who also financed a boarding home for black sailors) called a public hearing in Boston to "consider the imprisonment of colored seamen in foreign ports, and to take measures for petitioning Congress and the State Legislature on their behalf."[24] Such petitions sought to circumvent the Gag Rule that officially suppressed discussion of slavery in Congress from 1836 to 1844. "Several colored seamen," the *Liberator* reported of one well-attended meeting, "came forward to testify to the sufferings and cruelties they had experienced in southern prisons."[25] John Hatfield, a Pennsylvania native and barber aboard a "steamboat plying from New Orleans to Cincinnati," reported, "[I was] arrested, ironed in the street to degrade me, and put in the jail."[26] There he found "men from Boston, New York, Baltimore, and other places" who had also been jailed under the Negro Seamen Act, even though they, like Hatfield, "had committed no crime."[27] Black reformers periodically organized meetings to give "public expression . . . especially from those the most likely to become victims to the slave code," and boarding homes for black seamen, such as the one run by black abolitionist William P. Powell, founder of the Manhattan Anti-Slavery Society, became sites for antislavery organizing.[28]

Warned of the dangers of sailing into southern ports, some sailors took matters into their own hands and resisted through desertion or mutiny. Northern senators, for example, reported that "voyages had sometimes been broken up or delayed and embarrassed in consequence of the desertion of colored seamen who had left their vessels on discovering that they were to visit southern ports."[29] Eighteen black crewmen mutinied aboard the *S.L. Bogart* in 1857 when they discovered that their vessel was bound for Mobile, Alabama, rather than New York as they had been led to believe. "The alleged cause of the mutiny," noted the *Zion's Herald*, was "the unwillingness of the colored seamen to go where they feared to be reduced to slavery."[30] Some white captains also joined the fray to defend the rights of their black shipmen. Charles McLean, the British sailing master of the St. Lucia merchant vessel *Susan King* protested "the cruelty and injustice of such an act" and forcefully repelled the Wilmington harbor officials intent on arresting his black crewmen in 1845.[31]

Stories of free black seamen thus imprisoned and sold into slavery through the cupidity of unscrupulous captains and southern police officers became a common feature of the antislavery platform and print culture.[32] In 1834, the Committee on the Domestic Slave Trade of the United States emphatically reported, "There is a continual stream of free colored persons from Boston, New-York, Philadelphia, and other seaports of the United States, passing through the CALABOOSE into slavery in the country."[33] This report described in detail a number of cases of kidnapping, in which avaricious captains took advantage of the Negro Seamen Acts to profit from the enslavement of their free black crewmen. The experience of Boston seaman Robert Roberts—who was "kidnapped at New Orleans, and committed to the *calaboose*, preparatory to being sold and sent into the interior"—illustrates the utter precariousness of black freedom across the border separating free from slave state.³⁴ Roberts suspected "that his captain, a Scotchman named *Bulkley*, was privy to the outrage," and he narrowly escaped enslavement, in a telling instance of the cosmopolitanism of black seafaring life, for if he had not "been able to speak French" to the "creole French soldier who was on guard"—whom he convinced to deliver a message "to two friends in the city, who obtained his release"—he would have been sold.³⁵ Roberts shared his New Orleans prison quarters with "*nine* colored men, whom he knew to be free, having known several of them as stewards on board northern vessels. Two of them belonged to Boston, one to Portland, and three to New-York. After twenty days, they were to be sold."³⁶ Other shipmasters exploited their crewmembers' fears of enslavement to coerce them into signing disadvantageous contracts, until sailors successfully challenged this practice before Massachusetts court in *Stratton et al. v. Babbage* (1855).³⁷

Few statistics exist for the number of sailors incarcerated and sold as slaves in southern states, yet a keeper of a "Seaman's Home" in New York estimated that twelve hundred black sailors were seized annually in New Orleans, five hundred in Charleston and three hundred in Savannah.³⁸ London's *Anti-Slavery Reporter* likewise reported, "upon the very best authority, that in 1851, thirty-seven British subjects were seized and incarcerated, and forty-two in the course of last year; and that there is no doubt of many free coloured British subjects having been sold into slavery under the operation of this law, all traces of whom have been lost."³⁹ When the South Carolina Assembly finally deliberated the modification of its law in 1856, "[i]t was shewn," according to the *Anti-Slavery Reporter*, "that no less than seven hundred and thirty coloured seamen, for no crime whatever, were incarcerated in the Charleston prison during the short span of *ten months*."⁴⁰

American abolitionists opposed to the South Carolina law stressed unrestricted interstate travel as an essential right of citizenship to counter these proliferating regulations against black American seamen in southern ports. Indeed, Congress had long recognized the exceptional status of mariners in 1796 when it passed "An Act for the relief and protection of American Seamen" authorizing seamen protection certificates to black *and* white merchant seamen certifying their status as national citizens to protect them from impressment.[41] The popular conception of the constitutional right to "free travel" (discussed further in the conclusion) forced the government to reckon with the place of free blacks within the nation. What did legal freedom mean if police laws such as South Carolina's Negro Seamen Act disregarded the rights accorded to the free? Both American and British antislavery activists pondered this question. The various accounts of "kidnapped" free black sailors offered a powerful cautionary tale of postemancipation freedom. Memorials, lectures, novels, and pamphlets protesting these police laws repeatedly stressed the Atlantic contours of an antislavery campaign that transcended both national identifications and geopolitical boundaries. The uneasy and shifting alliances of abolitionists, sailors, reformers, and commercially affected merchants brought international attention to bear on the far-reaching effects of slavery in the United States. The British government insisted that the South Carolina statute violated the 1815 treaty providing for the "reciprocal liberty of commerce" between the two nations, and concerned Americans protested it for violating citizenship rights and interstate comity. Critics couched their protests within the legal paradigm most legible to the federal government: the constitutional privileges and immunities pledged to citizens as "agents of contractual liberty."[42] These overlapping protests challenged the United States to define itself as either a nation among a community of nations or a confederation of sovereign states.[43]

Outcries against the Negro Seamen Act ignited congressional debates over whether the individual states or the federal government possessed the authority to regulate travel or "free ingress and regress" across state lines. Massachusetts senator Robert Charles Winthrop, who also led the northern opposition to the proposed Fugitive Slave Bill, cited the Negro Seamen Acts as instances of southern noncompliance with interstate comity and the privileges and immunities of state citizenship secured in the Constitution.[44] Well in advance of the denationalization of black citizenship in *Dred Scott v. Sandford*, South Carolina's "extraordinary law" deemed free blacks *not* citizens of the United States within the meaning of the Constitution, instituting racial classifications instead as the basis for political entitlement.[45] Antislavery newspapers noted the complex political relays between the plight of fugitive slaves in the North and black sailors in the South, caustically attacking lawmakers "in favor of aiding in the capture of Fugitive Slaves" but "dumb in regard to the arrest and imprisonment of free colored seamen at the South."[46] A public discourse defining this constitutional right to free interstate travel emerged out of these protests against the Negro Seamen Act. The "right of free entrance into any of the states of the Union," urged northern advocates, "is the very first among the privileges of citizens."[47] Connecticut's *New Englander*, for example, insisted over three lengthy treatises in 1845 and 1846 that these black citizens of northern states simply exercised their right to "free ingress and regress," concluding that South Carolina's regulation violated this constitutional guarantee of reciprocal travel privileges.[48]

As sectional passions intensified, the South Carolina Assembly enacted additional measures that suspended habeas corpus, generally acknowledged as fundamental to citizenship, for all free blacks entering the state. The amended Negro Seamen Act of 1844 stipulated that "no negro or free person of color, who shall enter this State on board any vessel ... and who shall be apprehended and confined by any sheriff in pursuance of the provisions of said act shall be entitled to the WRIT OF HABEAS CORPUS."[49] This measure was significant given the longstanding role of habeas corpus in Anglo-American jurisprudence and political philosophy as "an instrument of individual freedom against arbitrary imprisonment" by the state and especially given the writ's centrality to the history of Anglo-American antislavery activism since *Somerset*.[50] "The doors of the courts of justice," observed a Massachusetts statesman, "are effectually closed, and apparently closed forever" to such sailors.[51] Black sailors were thus made "dead in law," possessing natural life but stripped of civil rights.[52] These legislative enactments appalled Douglass's *North Star*, which deemed them a "revolting injustice" in a "country and under a Government boasting of its Freedom, its Civilization and its Justice!"[53]

An individual who invoked habeas corpus asserted the right to be subject to the law rather than to arbitrary power; the revised Negro Seamen Act specifically prevented incarcerated black sailors from seeking reprieve through legal channels.[54] The "law is his enemy," announced the *New Englander*, "[i]f crossing the line of his native state, he is detained, by whatever necessity, beyond the short period of absence which the law may allow."[55] These excessive measures outraged newspapers such as the *New York Daily-Times*, which condemned the power invested in local sheriffs "to seize the unfortunate black freeman, convey him as a felon through the public streets, incarcerate him in the common jail, and release him only at the period, no matter how remote, of the sailing of the vessel to which he had been attached."[56] Few full accounts of the seizure, imprisonment, and auction of free black seamen exist within the historical record, precisely because these seamen were barred from appealing to courts for arbitration. The following sections critically reconstruct a number of these cases to read them alongside material from the *Anti-Slavery Recorder*, John Brown's slave narrative, David Walker's antislavery jeremiad, Samuel Ringgold Ward's British oratories, and the largely unexamined antislavery writings of F.C. Adams, specifically the novel *Manuel Pereira*. As these cases starkly exposed the limits of the law in a partially free Atlantic world, black and white abolitionists turned to literary and rhetorical appeals in their decades-long transatlantic struggle to reshape South Carolina's racial jurisprudence.

Preserving State Sovereignty

> The Negro finds himself an unprotected foreigner in his own home.
> —Sutton E. Griggs, *Imperium in Imperio*, 1899

Conspiracies such as Denmark Vesey's Charleston plot were undoubtedly flashpoints in the complex history of black resistance to slavery and its racial ideologies, yet the slave state also enlisted the potential of black revolt in the centralization of its power.[57] The trope of black revolt, notes Maggie Sale, was often "a site of contestation among unequally empowered groups."[58] Southern lawmakers marshaled the threat of black revolt as the groundwork for the exercise of police power.[59] The imagined dangers of "free foreign negroes" thus became the basis of a powerful racial jurisprudence that restricted individual rights in the name of "self-preservation." Indeed, Kent's *Commentaries on American Law* observed that the "great principle of self-preservation doubtless demands, on the part of the white population dwelling in the midst of such combustible materials, unceasing vigilance and firmness."[60] These ubiquitous Negro Seamen Acts sought, in Eric Sundquist's terms, the "countersubversive containment of revolutionary energy," yet southern lawmakers found themselves reinvigorating the revolutionary potential forestalled in Vesey's conspiracy in order to secure popular consensus for periodic expansions to the law.[61] South Carolina statesman and jurist Benjamin Faneuil Hunt, for example, defended the South Carolina act in *Ex parte Henry Elkison v. Francis G. Deliesseline* (1823), one of the earliest cases to challenge the police regulation, with an alarmist vision of the state convulsed in the throes of a mass slave uprising:

"If South-Carolina has to dread the moral pestilence which a free intercourse with foreign negroes will produce, she has, by the primary law of nature, a right within her own limits to use every means to interdict it—she is not bound to wait until her citizens behold their habitations in flames."[62] Lawmakers uncoupled black revolt from actual historical events and transformed it into a free-floating phantasm to authorize the continual expansion of police power against their black *and* white populations.

Black mariners sailing under the protection of Western nations such as Great Britain and France were also subject to this police law as coastal slave states acknowledged, in a negative fashion, the revolutionary possibilities of a black Atlantic reshaped by the Haitian Revolution and West Indian Emancipation. The *Richmond Enquirer*, for example, angrily justified South Carolina lawmakers: "Are they bound to receive *aliens*, who may carry the very seeds of insurrection into their bosom? Suppose our slaves returning from Hayti,—suppose suspected tools from that island should arrive in Charleston in a British vessel,—is there no right to guard against the danger?"[63] Proslavery lawmakers often invoked the specter of San Domingo's successful slave revolt to defend regulations against black sailors as necessary policing measures. In the beleaguered 1845 congressional debate over the admission of Iowa and Florida, Mississippi senator Robert Walker defended a similar prohibition in the Florida constitution as the only guarantee against the entry of "[f]ree colored seamen [who] were dangerous to a slaveholding community," including "runaway slaves from St. Domingo, who had been concerned in all the atrocities perpetrated there, and whose hands had been imbrued in the blood of their masters."[64] This slave revolution found localized intensifications in Nat Turner's uprising and the averted conspiracies of Gabriel Prosser and Denmark Vesey. Indeed, these compounded memories of black revolution persisted with vivid and unabated force within the political discourses of southern jurisprudence at midcentury. These historic slave conspiracies undoubtedly contributed to the fear of revolt, but southern lawmakers also actively reshaped the public memory of these events to serve their political interests.

South Carolina governor William Aiken, Jr., for example, offered a revisionist legislative history that cast the state's domestic tranquility as dangerously undermined by the combined corrosive forces of "foreign free persons of color" and abolitionist "fanaticism." South Carolina's native slave population, Aiken suggested, was vulnerable to the "seduction" of "foreign free persons of color"; the Negro Seamen Act was a "humane" measure to "protect" both the "slave and master." The historic events of Vesey's plot had become, in Aiken's words, "the most irrefragable evidence" for the continued necessity of South Carolina's policy against these dangerous foreigners:

> In 1822, a most dangerous and extensive conspiracy of the black population in and about Charleston, was discovered. It had been chiefly planned and devised by foreign free persons of color, who had seduced and corrupted the native free blacks and slaves.... The trial of the culprits elicited the most irrefragable evidence of their active agency, and of the dangers arising from the intermingling of foreign blacks with our slaves, and humanity demanded, both for the slave and the master, that they should be protected from these seductions.[65]

In studied contrast to the apocryphal warning that *Charleston Times* editor Edwin Holland sounded in the wake of the Vesey conspiracy—"Let it never be forgotten that, the 'our NEGROES are truly the *Jacobins* of the country; that they are the *anarchists* and the *domestic enemy*"—Aiken's revisionist history transferred this danger posed by "*our* slaves" to the spectral figures of "foreign free persons of color."[66] Foreignness defined the racial boundaries of a kind of liminal inclusion for those "native free blacks and slaves" who existed within the imagined social order of the slave state. Aiken's "appeal to history," as the *New Englander* observed, sought, among other things, to locate insurrectionary desire for freedom in an external "foreign" population, even though the trial testimony of suspects named in the Vesey conspiracy tended to "prove that this, like all other attempts of this kind, sprung from internal causes."[67] Rather than acknowledge the "domestic" origins of slave unrest, southern legislators and officials had begun to represent "the rank and file of the conspiracy as the victims of *foreign* seduction" in the concerted effort to redirect the source of revolutionary black agency elsewhere beyond the boundaries of the state. This discourse of seduction paralleled the fantasies of individual slaveholders such as Samuel Tredwell Sawyer, who remained convinced that John S. Jacobs would return to him, reimagining the escape of their slaves as the work of meddlesome white abolitionists who had "decoyed" them away. "Southern imagination, unrestrained by the literal record," proclaimed the *New Englander*, had become the unlikely rationale for the enactment of those "obnoxious laws" under which free black northern citizens suffered without access to any legal means of redress.[68]

The South Carolina law quickly became, in the words of the *Southern Quarterly Review*, the gravest question to agitate the Union "since the formation of the government," hastening sectional divisions and plunging the nation into international conflicts with Great Britain and France.[69] Police officials began to seize and incarcerate all free black seamen found aboard vessels arriving into Charleston Harbor once the law went into effect in 1823. Not a single crewmember was left aboard a British vessel in one "remarkable" case.[70] These actions immediately ignited protests from affected French, British, and American sailors and shipmasters, who appealed to their national and state governments for relief. France first petitioned the U.S. government in 1837, and the minister of marine on numerous occasions issued circulars to French shipmasters warning them of these Negro Seamen Acts.[71]

The case of Jamaica-born free black Henry Elkison was the first of many unsuccessful British lawsuits to test the South Carolina Negro Seamen Act. Stratford Canning, the British minister in Washington, secured an early pledge from Secretary of State John Quincy Adams that British seamen would not be seized in Charleston Harbor. The British consul brought charges against the Charleston sheriff, Francis Deliesseline, and petitioned U.S. Supreme Court Justice William Johnson, a Charleston native, for a writ of habeas corpus to release Elkison after authorities, at the urging of the South Carolina Association—an extralegal organization of private citizens (many of whom were Charleston public officials)—arrested him off the Liverpool merchant vessel *Homer*.[72] Johnson heard *Ex parte Henry Elkison v. Francis G. Deliesseline* (1823) while riding circuit, and his ruling, which dismissed the habeas request on procedural grounds, proffered perhaps one of the more controversial instances of judicial dictum until Taney's *Dred Scott* opinion.[73]

Before a crowded summer courtroom, Justice Johnson ceded authority to the slave state in the case, even though he admitted, in what was tantamount to a declaration of the law's inherent law*less*ness, that Elkison's "right to his liberty" without "remedy to obtain it" was an "obvious mockery" of law.[74] Habeas corpus jurisdiction only extended to persons held under U.S. authority, and Elkison, as Johnson acknowledged, was confined "arbitrarily and without authority by a *state* officer, a case to which our power to issue this writ does not extend."[75] Indeed, these sailors, in F.C. Adams's evocative imagery, were thus "held by the thumb-screws of law."[76] Johnson denounced the Seamen Act as a violation of both the enumerated congressional power to regulate commerce with foreign nations and the 1815 treaty with Great Britain establishing "reciprocal liberty of commerce" and the "right of navigating their ships in their own way."[77] Even though such criticisms were mere dicta without binding legal power once Johnson professed his lack of jurisdiction, some antislavery newspapers misreported them as cause for celebration.[78] In response, the *Charleston Mercury* rather smugly announced "that the act of the South Carolina Legislature, so far from being suspended, since the trial of Elkison, proceeds in operation more rigorously, perhaps, than before."[79] Regional papers ranging from the *Baltimore Patriot & Mercantile Advertiser* to Maine's *Eastern Argus* likewise noted "that, from the continued arrivals of free persons of color at that port, the people of the north have been led into an error by the publication of Judge Johnson's opinion."[80] Indeed, Johnson gave federal sanction (albeit grudgingly) to the legality of the South Carolina act: like later U.S. officials beleaguered by similar petitions, he possessed, in his words, "no power to issue the writ of Habeas Corpus" and referred Elkison's consul to the South Carolina government.[81]

Elkison's case, as reported in Britain, brought pressure to bear on the uncertain status of blacks in a nation still internally divided over the question of immediate or gradual abolition in the West Indies. The British *Christian Register*, for example, remarked on the striking "resemblance of the American slave logic to the similar argumentation of our West Indian Man-owners."[82] Indeed, the southern "tirade" in *Elkison*, this British periodical continued, "resembles many of the West Indian flights on the same subject," including declarations of "the rights of property, separation from Great Britain."[83] Reportage of Elkison's case in the United States also deepened the rift between the free and slave states. Johnson's pronouncements in *Elkison*, needless to say, were highly unpopular in the South, and many southerners eagerly echoed South Carolina Association solicitor Isaac E. Holmes's strident letter to the *Charleston Mercury*: "if South Carolina was deprived of the right of regulating her colored population—it required not the spirit of prophesy to foretell the result, and that, rather than submit to the destruction of the state, I would prefer the dissolution of the union."[84] Holmes's antiunionist words anticipated the tenor of the "nullification crises" that pitted South Carolina against President Andrew Jackson over the federal tariff acts of 1828 and 1832.[85] Charleston newspapers, fearing riots, deemed it "inexpedient to publish ... Judge Johnson's Opinion," but *Niles' Weekly Register* published the complete transcript of Johnson's opinion in September, and editorialized versions of the case soon began appearing in northern newspapers.[86] Johnson's opinion and the arguments of Benjamin

Faneuil Hunt, whom the South Carolina Assembly had engaged to defend Sheriff Deliesseline, were published later that year in Charleston as the pamphlet *The Argument of Benj. Faneuil Hunt, in the Case of the Arrest of the Person Claiming to Be a British Seaman*.[87]

Hunt, an ardent unionist, voiced many of the key arguments that the state used to defend its police laws against "foreign negroes," affirming the state's right to use a range of force that at first restricted and then revoked the personal liberties of black citizens and foreign nationals alike. Classic theories of state formation hold that "modernity begins when government claims a monopoly on legitimate violence within its territory," and, as John Torpey contends, modern states seized, in a parallel action, the authority to regulate movement and to identify "unambiguously who belongs and who does not—in order to 'embrace' their members more effectively and to exclude unwanted intruders."[88] In this vein, Hunt drew largely from Swiss legal philosopher Emmerich de Vattel's *Law of Nations* (1758) to argue that South Carolina merely exercised its right as a sovereign state to "interdict altogether the entry of foreigners into his dominions."[89] This right to control entry was an essential feature of state sovereignty, which Hunt likened to the patriarchal *imperium*:

> the civilized man can secure his family against the contagion of the dissolute or depraved, by closing his doors, or selecting his visitors;—So, every sovereign state, has the perfect right of interdicting all intercourse with strangers, or of selecting those whose influence or example she may fear, and confining the exclusion to them. A master of a family receives or excludes his visitors, according to the peculiar situation and feelings of his own household. A State must be the sole judge to decide what strangers may or may not enter. The power to exclude or to admit strangers, implies the right to direct the terms upon which those who are admitted shall remain. As an individual may direct what apartment his guest shall occupy, a state may confine strangers to such limits, as its own policy may dictate.[90]

Hunt implicitly evokes a Federalist understanding of *imperium in imperio*, or "sovereignty within sovereignty" (the division of power within one jurisdiction), to argue that the state, when acting in the service of protecting its populace from harm (like the patriarch over his household), should not be subject to constitutional scrutiny.[91]

The regime of police laws that Hunt defends and likens to the patriarchal *imperium* increasingly restricted what constituted acceptable forms of social relations. The "preservation" and "defense" of such slaveholding customs required the continual reinforcement of police power against free blacks.[92] The regulation of free "foreign negroes" was vital to the so-called moral health of the slave population. "This State," as Hunt explains, "having a large slave population, conceives it prudent to guard against the moral contagion which the intercourse with foreign negroes produces, and therefore she prohibits them from remaining in any other part of the State."[93] Free blacks, by definition, were threats to a slaveholding society founded on violently enforced racial dichotomies between slave and citizen, foreigner and native, black and white. In thus "monopolizing the legitimate means of movement," to borrow Torpey's words, the slave state further established its identity in the process of excluding and thereby distinguishing foreigners and aliens from its *native* populace.[94] Hunt's strategic and repeated use of the term "foreign negroes" constructs black Americans who were citizens of sister states as outsiders to their own nation. What did it mean to be a citizen in a northern state but not have the "privileges and immunities" of citizenship once in a southern jurisdiction? Whereas antislavery periodicals like the *Liberator* distinguished "foreign seamen" from "native American seamen," advocates of the South Carolina regulation effectively redefined *all* black sailors as "foreigners."

This doctrine of self-preservation and states' rights was the cornerstone of the southern defense of its increasingly punitive Negro Seamen Acts. When the British consul in Charleston again protested the imprisonment of free black seamen, the *Charleston Mercury* argued that this law "has its foundation in the right of every organized society to protect itself,—a right which no Government can be expected to surrender."[95] The state's sovereign right to self-protection cannot be compromised for the sake of respecting the civil liberties of a few foreign nationals: "The safety of a whole State must be consulted, although it results in temporary inconvenience and annoyance to a coloured or even a white British seaman."[96] Governor John Means, facing one of the more concerted diplomatic assaults on the law in 1852, stressed with hyperbolic certainty, as did nearly every other South Carolinian before him, that "the right of self-preservation ... [is] a right which is *above all constitutions, and above all laws*, and one which never was, nor never will be, abandoned by a people who are worthy to be free" (*MP*, 356; emphasis added). In defending the necessity of the Seamen Act, Means invokes a natural right (of self-preservation) that exists outside or "above" the existing legal order. This law is paradoxically enacted precisely to deal with this "extralegal" situation. Such contradictions within South

Carolina's governmentality illustrate powerfully what Giorgio Agamben describes as the "state of exception": no system of law is fully complete unto itself but relies upon an "exception"—a suspension of the norm—that exists both within and outside the juridical order that it helps constitute.[97] The South Carolinian defense of the Negro Seamen Act, its law that becomes a "right which is . . . above all laws," thus reveals the necessary incoherence of the slave state in relation to the law.

Sectional Crisis and the Denationalization of Black Citizenship

Throughout the antebellum period, Great Britain continued to demand "redress and reparation" for the arrest and confinement of its black mariners in the United States, and it lodged eight more petitions with the U.S. government for such "violent and unjustifiable act[s]" and "outrage[s]."[98] Within a year of *Elkison*, the British minister Henry Addington brought the *Marmion* case before President James Monroe, seeking the repeal of South Carolina's "very grievous law."[99] The *Marmion*, according to its captain, Peter Petrie, "was not well moored at the wharf, before the officers, who were appointed to put this law into execution, came on board, and forcibly carried one of the four of these men to jail, where he remained during my stay in Charleston." Three other black crewmen whom Petrie had safely transferred onto a New York bound packet were, according to his testimony, "apprehended by men who seemed anxious only to get their fees, and thrown into prison, depriving them of the opportunity to comply with the law, which they would have done in a few hours."[100] Charleston police, however, continued to enforce its law against black British mariners despite the inquiries of successive U.S. secretaries of state, especially after the discovery of David Walker's incendiary *Appeal* circulating among Charleston slaves in early 1830.

South Carolina reacted violently to the discovery of Walker's *Appeal* and rejected these diplomatic appeals to suspend the operation of its police law against black British subjects. British Foreign Minister to the U.S. Charles Vaughan called on Secretary of State Martin Van Buren to intervene on behalf of yet another black Briton, a cook named Daniel Fraser, who was seized from his Liverpool merchant vessel, the *Atlantic*.[101] Vaughan's formal remonstrance sought to impress on Van Buren "how hopeless it is to expect that the magistrates of Charleston will set at liberty Daniel Fraser, or to look forward with any confidence to the repeal of the obnoxious act by the legislature of the State."[102] Indeed, the circulation of Walker's pamphlet coincided with a marked change in national policy toward these state police laws. In 1831, after recent protests against the Negro Seamen Acts, Attorney General John Berrien overruled former Attorney General William Wirt to declare, according to Fehrenbacher, that "state police powers protected in the Tenth Amendment took precedence over federal power to regulate commerce."[103]

British diplomatic protests against South Carolina again erupted in 1843 over the seizure and incarceration of a black steward from the British vessel *Higginson*. Police officers physically assaulted and committed the steward to solitary confinement after he refused to labor for them. Coerced labor was not uncommon among imprisoned sailors. "The law," as the *Charleston Courier* observed, "does not define the power of jailors over the persons confined under its provisions, and had provided no efficient means of securing to them comfortable quarters and protection from tyranny and cruelty."[104] George Tolliver, a free black American sailor who had been incarcerated on seven different occasions reported that "when thus imprisoned, he was denied a sufficiency of food, and compelled to perform various menial and disgusting offices in the prison; though ... the captain was obliged to pay a full, if not an exorbitant price for his board."[105] Undermining the distinction between the free and enslaved, the unwaged labor coerced from these incarcerated sailors anticipated the one exception to the legislated abolition of slavery reinstated in the Thirteenth Amendment, which permitted "involuntary servitude for those convicted of crimes."

The British were not alone in their demands for the repeal of "the obnoxious law." Massachusetts *Whig Journal* editor David Child's address before the New England Anti-Slavery Society noted, "Forty respectable master[s] of American vessels lying in the port of Charleston, whose men had been seized and were then in prison, petitioned Congress for redress in 1823."[106] Led by Captain Jared Bunce of the *Georgia*, a regular trader between Philadelphia and Charleston, the petitioners urged the federal government to "adopt such energetic measures as will relieve ... their free colored mariners ... [from] an unlawful imprisonment, and their vessels ... [from] an enormous and unnecessary expense and detention." Bunce had appealed "to a court of the state of South Carolina for a habeas corpus, to inquire into the cause of the arrest and detention of Andrew Fletcher, (steward), and David Ayres, (cook), both free colored persons, and native citizens of the United States."[107] The case eventually came before the South Carolina Supreme Court, where "the case was suspended, and the prisoners were deprived of the relief for which they moved; and do still remain in confinement."[108] Indeed, the South Carolina Supreme Court employed this tactic with similar results in the case of Portuguese sailor Manuel Pereira, examined at length later in this chapter. Bunce's congressional petition, like his stalled court case, "appear[s] to have been disposed of among a mass of matters," even though "[c]itizens of free states, Maine, New-Hampshire, Vermont, Massachusetts, Rhode-Island, Connecticut, New-York, and Pennsylvania" continue to be "seized and sold into bondage."[109]

In Massachusetts, a state historically identified with both maritime commerce and abolitionism, mercantile interests and antislavery "radicals" found a peculiar and uneasy alliance in their united protests against the Negro Seamen Acts. Petitions protesting the seizure and imprisonment of black mariners were repeatedly brought before the state legislature. Massachusetts lawmakers were sympathetic to the plight of shipmasters and crewmen, yet they carefully couched their protests in terms of commerce and constitutional right while avoiding arguments that might be misconstrued as endorsing abolitionism. The Massachusetts legislature revisited the issue in 1839, when it appointed a Special Joint Committee "to inquiry into the expediency of providing for the deliverance of citizens of this Commonwealth, who may be imprisoned and liable to be sold as slaves."[110] The committee's minority report catalogued the recent outrages against free black northern citizens with a number of affidavits from "colored citizens of New Bedford . . . who have suffered under the laws in question."[111] John Cory, "a free born citizen of Massachusetts, a native of the town of Westport," reported that "a couple of persons, calling themselves officers, came on board" and seized him off the trading sloop *Rodman* in 1824. "[S]even others, colored like myself, were in prison," according to Cory, even though "[n]o offence was charged upon any of us." The Charleston police dealt similarly with Richard Johnson, the wealthy black merchant who underwrote the *Rodman*'s commercial voyage south. The report concluded "that facts of this kind may be obtained from the captain of every northern vessel, that has visited Charleston with colored persons on board."[112]

In the 1840s, public protest over the imprisonment of northern seamen in Charleston crystallized into a specifically regionalized dispute between Massachusetts and South Carolina that further aggravated sectional feelings throughout the nation. South Carolina's stubborn refusal to modify its law may be explained, as Guyora Binder argues, "as a dialectical moment in its controversy with the North over slavery itself," which simultaneously forced free states such as Massachusetts to solidify their liberal ideologies.[113]

Massachusetts and South Carolina each responded to the issue of slavery through the extreme territorializing of its state power. South Carolina admitted the right of Massachusetts "to elevate the descendants of the African race to the rank or status of free white persons... within her *own* limits" but vigorously denied "that she has any right to require us to extend to such of them as may enter *our* limits."[114] Advocates of South Carolina argued that southerners often had "on board their own vessels, colored seamen who were slaves. If one of these vessels went into a port of the state of Massachusetts all those slaves were instantly emancipated."[115] Chief Justice Lemuel Shaw of the Massachusetts Supreme Court had indeed begun in 1844 to free slaves brought into the state on board ships, in *Commonwealth v. Potterfield* and *Commonwealth v. Fitzgerald*. Coastal slave states persisted in arresting black sailors who arrived on their shores, just as free states led by Massachusetts began to free, by writ of habeas corpus, those slaves who were brought within their bounds by traveling slaveholders.

These Negro Seamen Acts made it impossible for abolitionists to address the problem of slavery without attending to the condition of free blacks within the American polity. Abolitionists insisted that these "severe penal restrictions" were an outgrowth of "that cursed system of murder, robbery, adultery, and every other sin under heaven, called American slavery," even as merchants, British diplomats, and state legislators continued to couch their protests in far less politicized terms.[116] The Massachusetts legislature, for example, authorized the governor to appoint agents in Charleston and New Orleans "for the purpose of collecting and transmitting accurate information respecting the number and the names of citizens of Massachusetts, who have heretofore been or may be... imprisoned without the allegation of any crime."[117] The Charleston appointment was initially extended to Benjamin F. Hunt, the same man who passionately defended South Carolina law in *Elkison*, in the effort to distance this resolution from the divisive "question of abolition."[118] This desire to dissociate protest against South Carolina's Negro Seamen Act from abolitionist politics was not unusual. The American Colonization Society's *African Repository*, for example, protested in sympathy with "respectable" ship owners who were forced to suffer economic hardships, but it remained firmly set against "the question of abolition."[119]

Sectional feelings reached a tipping point when, in 1844, the newly elected Massachusetts governor, George N. Briggs, commissioned Samuel Hoar as his representative to Charleston and Henry Hubbard to New Orleans, directing the two to prosecute lawsuits on behalf of Massachusetts citizens at the expense of the public treasury. A lawyer specializing in maritime law, Hoar would have brought a civil suit before the U.S. Supreme Court to test the constitutionality of the Negro Seamen Act.[120] However, the South Carolina legislature, once notified of Hoar's appointment, condemned his mission and issued a nearly unanimous series of resolutions authorizing Governor William Aiken, Jr., to expel him as an "emissary of a Foreign Government, hostile to our Democratic Institutions, and with the sole purpose of subverting our internal police."[121] It furthermore declared that "free negroes and persons of color are not citizens of the United States, within the meaning of the Constitution, which confers upon the citizens of one state the privileges and immunities of citizens of the several States."[122] This denationalization of black citizenship closely echoed the statements of former Attorney General Roger B. Taney, as he tried to forestall British diplomatic efforts to redeem sailors seized under North Carolina's Negro Seamen Act, statements that Taney later developed in his *Dred Scott* opinion: "The African race in the United States even when free, are everywhere a degraded class, and exercises no political influence."[123] The South Carolina attorney general, fearing the national condemnation that would be levied on the state if Hoar should be lynched, charged the Charleston sheriff to escort him from the city.[124]

Garrison's *Liberator* seized on Hoar's banishment as an opportunity to consolidate public opinion against "slaveholding power," condemning it as tantamount to South Carolina's extraordinary rejection of a *white* citizen's constitutional right to unmolested free travel.[125] The excessive measures taken against Hoar offered the antislavery weekly a "fresh confirmation of the hideous fact, that no man who is suspected of being an abolitionist can travel in any slaveholding state, without endangering his property, his liberty, or his life!"[126] Stunned by South Carolina's excessive measures, many newspapers saw Hoar's expulsion as a "gross insult" to a sister state in defense of an "outrageous law."[127] Hoar's expulsion as an "enemy" of the state did seem to be a grave misstep in South Carolinian statecraft, diplomacy, and public relations, and a number of concerned commentators saw the escalating conflicts between the two states as further "weaken[ing] the bonds which unite the different sections of the confederacy."[128] To some northerners, these actions were all the more galling because they had been taken against a "free white citizen of Massachusetts," and the *Liberator* cautioned against this slippery slope of restrictions on interstate travel: "The insatiable appetite of the slave power is no longer satisfied with black victims," and "the jails of the South are fast filling up with victims from the ranks of the whites—the educated and refined—the old colony stock of ancient Puritan blood!"[129] Many northerners were apoplectic over this refusal to grant the venerable statesman his "privilege of locomotion, under the American Constitution!"[130] "The sovereignty and dignity of the State of Massachusetts," as other partisan papers reported, "were represented by Mr. Hoar.... Massachusetts herself appeared in his person... and it is Massachusetts, in the person of Mr. Hoar, that is EXPELLED from South Carolina."[131]

The uncivil treatment of black *and* white northern citizens angered many people, who argued that South Carolina did not offer the "same degree of protection" to American citizens as it did to "those of foreign powers" such as Britain and France.[132] Sectional rhetoric often accompanied such critiques of this preferential treatment of black Britons. Such references to the "foreign" gave a nationalistic edge to the discourse of U.S. sectionalism, especially given the fact that these claims were patently untrue. Charleston officials continued to seize and imprison black Britons, even though American antislavery activists often claimed otherwise. American antislavery print culture thus appropriated the proslavery discourse of "foreign negroes": "foreigners" became opposed to American "countrymen" in editorials deriding southern discrimination against "citizens of the free States of the Union."[133] Abolitionist campaigns for the repeal of these Negro Seamen Acts were thereby articulated with U.S. nation-building projects that sought to secure the boundaries of national identity. John Palfrey's *Papers on the Slave Power* (1846), for example, hyperbolically reported that "the British Lion... gave a growl and snap, and the Carolina people presently found out that it was perfectly safe to let British blacks come and go without hindrance or harm, even though they should be lately emancipated slaves from Barbadoes or Jamaica; while they cannot see to this day that it is at all safe to take the same course with blacks from Massachusetts."[134] Such references to the South's preferential treatment of British over American seamen sought to enlist nationalist loyalties and identifications in the antislavery campaign to repeal the Negro Seamen Acts, even as these activists eagerly sought to rally transatlantic support for their efforts. As U.S. sectional tensions flared in the 1850s, British abolitionists, in an analogous gesture, denounced American aggression against British civil liberties in their efforts to rouse public opinion against slavery and to further identify freedom with British law and cultural heritage.

The Afterlife of Manuel Pereira in the Transatlantic Antislavery Campaign

> The people of Charleston might now inquire why they have so much law and so little justice?
> —F. C. Adams, *Manuel Pereira; or, The Sovereign Rule of South Carolina*, 1853

A new spate of transatlantic disputes over the incarceration of black British seamen erupted in the early 1850s, as Great Britain, pressed by an outraged public, increased its diplomatic efforts to secure the repeal of the South Carolina Negro Seamen Act. This section charts this final decade of popular mobilizations to repeal the regulation, as three cases in quick succession captivated the British public. Abolitionists challenged Britain's commitment to protecting the rights of its newly emancipated black subjects. A number of editorials surfaced in the *London Times* expressing the public condemnation of what was viewed as an arbitrary law of racial exclusion that was a violation of British rights and an affront to the nation. One letter, addressed to Lord Palmerston, offered an eyewitness account of the routine workings of "white law" in Charleston: "I was in America in 1839 and 1840, and remember very clearly that the entire black crew of a ship from St. Domingo, captain, able hands, and all, were packed into prison during the whole time the vessel remained in the same port of Charleston, South Carolina."[135] The British and Foreign Anti-Slavery Society regularly devoted columns of its monthly publication, the *Anti-Slavery Reporter*, to the "Imprisonment of Coloured Seamen" as it informed the British public of the depredations perpetrated on its free black subjects. It offered ample coverage of the Parliamentary deliberations over the case of sailor Manuel Pereira, who had become something of a cause célèbre, alongside moving narrative accounts of British seamen seized and sold into slavery. Anglo-American abolitionists sought less to address the abstract points of law than to guide public sympathy toward the harrowing plight of black mariners in southern ports.

The *Anti-Slavery Reporter* was one of the earliest newspapers to report on the seizures of Isaac Bowers and Rueben Roberts, calling on "the British press and public to demand from Government immediate measures to prevent future outrages of this kind" and insisting that it "must receive a definitive answer, whether the colored population belonging to this country and its various dependencies are to be treated as felons and slaves in any ports of the United States."[136] Great Britain's concerted efforts in the 1850s to dispute South Carolina's Negro Seamen Act brought international scrutiny to bear on the questions both of federal powers and of institutional slavery in the United States. Britain's refusal to indemnify U.S. slaveholders for slaves set free from distressed or wrecked American vessels in the British West Indies did not contribute to amicable foreign relations. In 1841, Secretary of State Daniel Webster petitioned in vain for the extradition of the slaves who mutinied aboard the *Creole* and had become free, according to British officials, by virtue of landing in Nassau in the British Bahamas.[137] West Indian Emancipation had radically reshaped the boundaries of freedom and slavery throughout the Atlantic world. Indeed, in 1851, the French National Assembly declared slavery and the imprisonment of black sailors to be "barbarous," as Great Britain continued its fruitless negotiations with the intractable South Carolina Assembly. "Neither France nor England," France's General Lahitte reportedly declared, "have been able to persuade the government of the United States to enter into the ways of civilization and humanity, which we will persevere to march in."[138] Lahitte's disdainful words chart the Enlightenment's unfinished journey from Europe to the so-called New World as France and Great Britain began to reshape themselves as free nations in the wake of abolition and emancipation.[139]

Fresh from governorship of the Bahamas, George Buckley-Mathew, the British consul-general of the Carolinas, initiated diplomatic negotiations with South Carolina's Governor Means in "hopes that the law by which any of H.B.M.'s subjects are taken from the protection of the British flag and imprisoned, should not be extended to foreigners."[140] Charleston police officers had seized Isaac Bowers, "a coloured man, a native of Antigua, and, of course, a British subject," and incarcerated him for two months while his vessel *Mary Ann* was refitted for its transatlantic journey.[141] Bowers was the first of three highly publicized cases of British seamen who were incarcerated and, in one instance, sold into slavery by the Charleston police. Over the next few years of heightened protest, transatlantic antislavery print culture freely disseminated these stories as powerful symbols of slavery's inexorable workings, leading to the law's modification in December 1856.[142] The British and Foreign Anti-Slavery Society addressed a memorial to Palmerston, the British secretary of foreign affairs, urging the government to take more active measures to prevent the ongoing violation of "the just liberties of a large body of mariners," after it determined that Bowers was "not likely to obtain any redress for the indignity and injury he . . . suffered at the hands of the American authorities."[143] Public interest was further aroused when, after returning to Britain, Bowers brought suit against his former captain for withholding wages "on the ground that he had paid for the steward's support while in gaol."[144] The prosecuting attorney condemned Capt. William Waddington for his passive acquiescence to "the unjustifiable imprisonment of Bowers," since he had "made no representation to the British Minister at Washington City, or even sought the protection of the British Consul."[145] The combined efforts of mariners such as Bowers and Anglo-American abolitionists intensified public protests, forcing Parliament to take more-active measures to secure the repeal of those "obnoxious laws."[146] "[P]ublic indignation in [Great Britain] had been greatly excited by the statements in the newspapers," and Palmerston was asked to satisfy the "people . . . that the Government . . . [would] take any practicable steps towards remonstrating against and putting an end to the practice in question."[147]

Under this public pressure, Palmerston issued yet another appeal to the U.S. government on behalf of the "plain rights of British subjects."[148] U.S. Secretary of State John Clayton, unwilling to interfere in a "local" concern, referred British Consul Mathew to Governor Means. Newspaper accounts of Mathew's rather unprecedented private negotiations with Means outlined the long unresolved conflict between South Carolina's local laws and the federal treaties between Britain and the United States.[149] The British press denounced the violation of Bowers's rights as a free Englishman, even though it generally cautioned against extreme diplomatic measures, unlike the radical position of *Littell's Living Age*, which condemned the "gratuitous imprisonment of a whole class of British subjects" as amounting "to a diplomatic grievance of the first magnitude."[150] The editor of *Littell's* even demanded reparations for the imprisonment of all British crewmen whose "complexion falls below a recognized standard of olive" as "amends for the insult put upon our colored fellow-countrymen."[151] The vexed status of black Britons that had been raised in *Elkison* reemerged in postemancipation Britain as the British and Foreign Anti-Slavery Society urged the government to "do its duty" to protect the "personal freedom of all British subjects, without distinction of colour."[152]

The South Carolina legislature remained obstinate, even though Louisiana, pressured both by popular opinion and by its British consul later that year, "passed an act amending the colored law of the State, by abolishing the penalty of imprisonment, and permitting free persons of color to come on shore, with passports from the Mayor."[153] Failing in various appeals to the South Carolina legislature, Mathew, at the direction of the charge d'affaires in Washington, decided to challenge the "police law" through the courts. He began legal actions on behalf of two recently arrested black seamen, Manuel Pereira, a Portuguese sailor articled to service on the English brig *Janson*, and Rueben Roberts, a native of Nassau in the British West Indies and cook aboard the English schooner *Clyde*. It is likely that the two men shared the same Charleston jail cell. Although South Carolina's Negro Seamen Act, as a number of newspapers noted, was "to be tested in more forms than one," the proximity of the two cases yielded reportage that confused the specifics of their separate proceedings.[154] Pereira's case was particularly effective at sensitizing British and American publics because his vessel had been "driven into the port of Charleston *in distress*," and the wrecked condition of the *Janson*'s arrival in Charleston Harbor was key in Pereira's case against the police law.[155] Newspapers ranging from the *London Times* to the *Liberator* noted that Pereira's incarceration was particularly repugnant because of "the involuntary character of his visit to the shores of Carolina."[156] Even the *Charleston Mercury* admitted, albeit with some ambivalence, that the police law "was passed to reach only those cases in which the party subject to it, voluntarily came within the jurisdiction in defiance of its provisions."[157] Consul Mathew engaged Charleston native and former Attorney General James L. Petigru, who appealed Pereira's case to the state supreme court when the lower court refused to issue a writ of habeas corpus. The South Carolina Supreme Court postponed the hearing of the appeal to the following year, forcing Pereira to "lie in jail" for eight months.[158] The South Carolina jurists, no doubt, calculated that the case would fail once Mathew obtained Pereira's release. "If Pereira is now released by paying the charges," speculated newspapers, "the case and the prospect of obtaining from the final authority a decision upon the question will fall to the ground. And it would be hard to keep the poor fellow immured long enough for the argument to be had at Charleston, and the decision rendered, so that an appeal may be taken to the Federal Judiciary."[159]

The local media and Charleston police officials disseminated distorted versions of Pereira's arrest. These accounts neglected to note that the *Janson* had been wrecked; neither captain nor crew had a vessel to which they could return. Arrested on 24 March 1852, Pereira was thus left to face the prospect of an indefinite imprisonment and eventual enslavement. Given these unusual circumstances, Mathew, acting "under instruction from his Government, to test the Constitutionality of the act," began the legal actions on Pereira's behalf.[160] Governor Means, by his own admission, had specifically directed the Charleston sheriff "not to give up the prisoner even if a writ of habeas corpus had been granted . . . while these proceeding were pending," even though he later contradicted himself in claiming that Pereira "was at perfect liberty to depart at any moment that he could get a vessel to transport him beyond the limits of the State." As the *Anti-Slavery Reporter* noted, Means left unanswered the key question of "[h]ow the unfortunate prisoner was to 'get a vessel,' under these circumstances."[161] As Mathew took steps to appeal Pereira's case before the state supreme court, the Charleston sheriff, hoping to prevent further legal action, "made an attempt to ship Pereira off," since "his presence was essential to test his right to the *habeas corpus*" (*MP,* 355, 358).[162] Mathew, "finding that his great object would thus be defeated, intercepted the sheriff, on his way to the vessel," and paid Pereira's passage to New York once they completed "the requisite arrangements for carrying on the suit in appeal."[163] Mathew was misadvised, however, and Pereira's case was eventually struck from the docket of the state court in 1853 on the grounds that he was no longer in custody.[164]

While awaiting Pereira's delayed hearing, Mathew directed Petigru to charge Charleston sheriff Jeremiah D. Yates in the U.S. circuit court for the "assault and false imprisonment" of Rueben Roberts, asking for damages in the amount of four thousand dollars "for the indignity which he had suffered."[165] Sheriff Yates had seized Roberts from the *Clyde* upon its arrival from Cuba on 19 May 1852 and jailed him for one week until the vessel was ready for sea.[166] The U.S. circuit court judge in Charleston declared the South Carolina law valid when *Roberts v. Yates* (1853) came to trial, and the case was ready for appeal to the U.S. Supreme Court once the jury decided in the sheriff's favor.[167] The *New-York Daily Times* offered a biting commentary on South Carolina's Negro Seamen Act when Roberts's case made international headlines: "Satire could hardly select a fairer mark for mirth than the spectacle of a sovereign State, represented by a Sheriff and his posse, bearing down upon every arriving merchantman, inspecting the crew, and claiming the custody of all persons, whose complexions justified a suspicion of African descent."[168] A number of newspapers saw these two cases as the culmination of decades of thwarted efforts to test the "validity of the law," a pattern of obstruction intensified since Samuel Hoar's expulsion from Charleston.[169] Many people entertained hopes for the law's imminent repeal once either of the two cases entered the U.S. Supreme Court docket; however, Roberts's case, like Pereira's, never came before that federal tribunal.

Fear of rupturing amicable trade relations with the United States prompted the British government to adopt a more judicious course to conciliate South Carolina.[170] By June 1853, it had elected to drop both lawsuits and instructed Mathew to withdraw Roberts's appeal, which was pending trial before the U.S. Supreme Court.[171] Commercial interests and the British government's unwillingness to further aggravate U.S. sectional tensions, combined with a new and less interventionist-minded British Foreign Secretary, facilitated this diplomatic course.[172] The *National Era* reported that the U.S. federal government had advised Britain that "to insist on the repeal of those laws under which the imprisonment of colored foreigners, entering South Carolina, would raise questions between the slave States and the Federal Government which would be exceeding inconvenient, if not destructive to the Union."[173] Unwilling to foment ill will with the United States, Britain announced "that the Law officers of the Crown were satisfied that Great Britain had no ground for complaining of any infraction of treaties."[174] In a November address before the state legislature, the South Carolina governor confirmed that "the cases of MANUEL PEREIRA and REUBEN ROBERTS, colored seamen, are settled." South Carolina officials undoubtedly thought they had put to rest "the awkward case ... that has been before the British and American public in more shapes than one."[175] They could not, however, expunge Pereira and Roberts from public memory, and, in the failure of law and diplomacy, a relatively unknown British writer, F.C. Adams, brought their cases before "the bar of public opinion" for proper adjudication.[176]

Manuel Pereira; or, The Sovereign Rule of South Carolina was the first of a number of popular antislavery historical fictions written by the former Savannah *Georgian* newspaper editor F.C. (Francis Colburn) Adams.[177] From the little that can be pieced together of his biography, Adams was "an Englishman ... [who] resided many years in the Southern States" and had been, according to the *Anti-Slavery Reporter*, "[o]fficially connected with one of the principal local journals, but was finally turned against slavery by what he witnessed of its atrocities."[178] An unverified account in the *Zion Herald* claimed that Adams

> resided in Charleston, where he was treated with much consideration until he took part with the British Consul Mathew in his opposition to the law imprisoning colored seamen. It was, we understand, for this offense that Mr. Adams was thrown into prison, on his release from which he went to London, in 1852, where the publication of "Our World," a novel, and other works illustrative of southern life, have given him considerable reputation in

the department of literature which has been illustrated by the genius of Mrs. Stowe.[179]

Indeed, the New York publishers Miller, Orton & Mulligan advertised *Our World* as "A Great Anti-Slavery Romance" in the back pages of Kate Pickard's *The Kidnapped and the Ransomed* (see figure 4.2). The particular regional cadences and sectional politics of the antebellum United States fascinated Adams even after his return to Britain, and he captured them in a number of short and full-length works.[180] Advance praise from the *New-York Daily Times* for Adams's third novel was particularly descriptive of his penchant for seizing on records and documents to craft compelling histories of the present, touting *Justice in the By-Ways*, another novel set in antebellum Charleston, as "emphatically a work of our age. . . . a history in the guise of fiction, history whose accuracy is attested by public records and State documents. Each character is a living reality."[181] *Manuel Pereira*, likewise, offered readers the merits of a legal treatise in the form of a "life-like" ethnographic fiction.

Buell & Blanchard of Washington, D.C., first published *Manuel Pereira* in the spring of 1852, as the international disputes over the South Carolina regulation became more heated, and the London publishing house of Clarke, Beeton, & Co. republished the novel the following year.[182] Buell & Blanchard placed a number of advertisements for the novel in its abolitionist weekly *National Era*, which had just completed its serialization of *Uncle Tom's Cabin*.[183] The *National Era* favorably commended the novel to its readers and described the work, then in press, as

> founded upon that infamous statute of South Carolina, by which her citizens claim a right to imprison *colored seamen*, of all nations, and even those cast upon their shores in distress. We have perused the book in advance of its publication, and find that it gives a life-like picture of Pereira . . . the prison regimen, character of the Charleston police, and the mendacity of certain officials, who make the law a medium of peculation.[184]

The novel's topical subject matter, the reviewer insisted, "cannot fail to interest alike the general reader, commercial man, and philanthropist"— much like the unlikely and shifting coalitions forged among free blacks, abolitionists, diplomats, and merchants had in protest of the police law over the preceding decades. As a man "raised and educated in the spirit of her institutions," Adams's autobiographical introduction establishes his

A Great Anti-Slavery Romance.

"OUR WORLD,"
OR,
Annette, the Slaveholder's Daughter.
One Illustrated 12mo. Volume, 603 Pages. Price $1.25.

OPINIONS OF THE PRESS—BRIEF EXTRACTS.

John Wesley said the best tunes had long been in the service of the devil. He thought it well to reclaim them for better purposes. The same is true of novels and romances—they have heretofore been almost exclusively devoted either to vice, or to very questionable amusement. But the tide is turning. Fiction is beginning to serve the cause of virtue and humanity. MILLER, ORTON & MULLIGAN have just brought out a new anti-slavery story, entitled "OUR WORLD," which bids fair to equal anything that has gone before it. It argues well for anti slavery, when the first publishing houses in the nation—yes, in all nations—find it for their interest to publish such works as "Uncle Tom's Cabin" and "OUR WORLD."—*Northern Christian Advocate.*

Its style is engaging, its logic weighty, and its deductions natural. It does not content itself with abusing an evil from a distance, but grapples and wrestles with it, right manfully. "Our World" will excite, first, attention, then admiration throughout the country, and take its place at the head of all recently published books.—*Buffalo Morning Express.*

It is a work not to be read and thrown aside, but a work to be read and pondered over. The novel is a perfect melodrama for startling situations and effects, and we have never read a fictitious story which so completely engrossed one's attention from commencement to close.—*Boston Evening Gazette.*

It is enough to say, that the book will make a stir in the world. It is another battering ram thundering against the wall of oppression, and is destined to make an impression second only to "Uncle Tom's Cabin."—*Western Literary Messenger.*

It is written with great power, and evinces a thorough knowledge of the subject treated.—*Buffalo Democracy.*

It is the production of one who gleans his facts not from the narratives of others, but from personal observation and experience. The author's birth and education were in New England, but he has long resided in the South, and become intimately familiar with its people and its institutions, and can, therefore, speak accurately and dispassionately of "things as they are."—*Chicago Literary Budget.*

We have no hesitation in pronouncing it one of the most remarkable and powerful original works ever published in America.—*Philadelphia Daily News.*

This work stirs the soul like a trumpet; or, like the sounds from the home of captivity, awakens untold sensations in our heart of hearts, especially if we love freedom.—*Albany Spectator.*

Nothing on this subject, since the days of "Uncle Tom's Cabin," has at all equaled it, and it promises to have a sale almost rivaling that most popular work.—*Hillsdale Gazette.*

This book will have an immense sale. Coming at the time it does, when the slave power is rapidly encroaching on free soil, everything which shows the blackness of the stain upon our nation's flag, will be welcomed. This tale shows the deep and damning sin of slavery in its true light, but at the same time gives all the good which can possibly accrue from the "peculiar institution." The author has taken a noble stand in the cause of freedom, and while sincere, is tolerant, and while just, is charitable. Every friend of Freedom will read the work.—*Poughkeepsie Eagle.*

Such a thrilling, truthful tale, so full of interest and of manly thought, we have not read since our eyes saw the *finis* of "Uncle Tom's Cabin."—*Weekly Visitor.*

This book is a picture so true to reality, that it must make its way into the family circle. The pen of the author, under the inspiration of the patriotic fires of Liberty, has diffused the convincing spirit of *fact* throughout the text, in cubic magnitude.—*Daily Advertiser.*

The work, throughout, is one of great power and intense interest. It paints in vivid and truthful colors the long train of evils, moral, social, and political, which the monster, slavery entails upon the white population of the south, no less than the wrongs inflicted upon the slaves. The author does not write from hearsay; he has spent much time in an official capacity at the South, and his position afforded him facilities for observing the workings of the monstrous institution in all its different phases.—*Christian Freeman.*

Fig. 4.2. Advertisement for F. C. Adams's antislavery fiction *Our World; or, Annette, the Slaveholder's Daughter.* Taken from the back pages of Kate E. R. Pickard's *The Kidnapped and the Ransomed.* (From the copy in the Rare Book Collection, The University of North Carolina at Chapel Hill)

personal allegiance to the regional South only to make his subsequent critique of the Negro Seamen Act as an "effect of slavery and its wrongs" all the more damning (*MP*, vii). *Manuel Pereira* begins, deceptively, as a nineteenth-century ship narrative in the fashion of Herman Melville's *Moby-Dick* or Edgar Allan Poe's *Arthur Gordon Pym*, only to become a rather dark eyewitness exposé of the capricious workings of criminal justice in Charleston. Indeed, *Manuel Pereira* challenges the romantic radicalism of current Atlantic historiography with its perverse stress on the racialized forms of containment rather than the mobile freedoms generally associated with sailors and maritime life.

In a manner resembling the "authoritative" paratexts of fugitive slave narratives, *Manuel Pereira* includes an exhaustive appendix that reproduces Consul Mathew's various petitions, his diplomatic correspondences with Governor Means, resolutions passed in the South Carolina Assembly, and local reportage from the *Charleston Southern Standard* and *Charleston Mercury*. These materials, found under the heading of "Correspondence, Etc.," were reproduced and circulated as a free-standing pamphlet entitled "The Law of Colored Seamen." Adams may very well have been the anonymous pamphleteer, given his outspoken campaign against the Negro Seamen Act. But legal documents such as these offered little insight into the subjective experiences of people whom the law afflicted. Adams's novel, in what Ian Baucom describes as a "long, Atlantic genealogy of witness," gave dramatic voice to the countless sailors who suffered silently under South Carolina's punitive regulation.[185] "[W]e speak," in the words of the introduction, "for those ... citizens to all intents (notwithstanding their dark skins) of the countries to which they severally belong—peaceable persons pursuing their avocations to provide a maintenance for their families, and entitled to the same protective rights claimed by more fortunate citizens of such countries" (*MP*, viii). The Canadian *Provincial Freeman* lauded the novel for enabling "any politician, philanthropist, human christian, (as we have the opposite,) and loyal man, to see things *as they are* and exist, appertaining to that vilest of all trafficks and abominations, namely, the buying, holding, and selling of human beings." "In such books" as *Manuel Pereira*, it declared, "THE ARMOUR OF THE ANTI-SLAVERY ADVOCATE CONSISTS."[186]

Manuel Pereira was by no means a sentimental novel in the fashion of Stowe's *Uncle Tom's Cabin*, even though its publication, as the *Anti-Slavery Reporter* observed, "has created as great a sensation in Charleston as *Uncle Tom* has done all over the world."[187] The narrative steadfastly refuses the resolutions of sentimental fiction, even as it uses aspects of sentimentalism to "properly enlighten" the public mind (*MP*, 156). Adams was quite familiar with Stowe's popular novel, as shown by his vigorous book-length commendation of it in *Uncle Tom at Home*, published in Philadelphia the following year.[188] Unlike Stowe's fiction, however, *Manuel Pereira* sought more specifically to "discuss the... question of law" by narrating "the sufferings of those who endure the wrong and injustice" of the South Carolina Negro Seamen Act (*MP*, vii). And it was far less invested in sentimentalism's injunction to personal moral reform as a means to political reform, seeking instead a more structural critique designed to effect, in the words of the *Anti-Slavery Reporter*'s review, "the bold exposure of the whole system" of law and culture that upheld the Negro Seamen Act.[189]

Aboard the *Janson*, Pereira may have been a free subject under the protection of Great Britain, but once he touched the shores of Charleston local laws remade him into a "nigger" to be beaten, imprisoned, and starved. Like the slave, he was among those abandoned before the law.[190] Little biographical information about Pereira can be gleaned from popular print culture other than a few brief and, not surprisingly, derisive remarks. The novel, therefore, offers one of the most sustained accounts of the free black seamen unwittingly caught up by the South Carolina Negro Seamen Act, as it asks its readers to consider the historical Pereira in the context of an ensemble of local and international social relations.[191]

Adams remakes the historical Pereira into a virtual Englishman to show that British freedom was woefully incomplete as long as slavery continued in the United States. "It mattered but very little" to the beloved Pereira, explains the narrator, "where he was born, for he... sailed so long under the protection of the *union-jack* of Old England that he had formed a stronger allegiance to that country than to any other" (*MP*, 11). Pereira's allegiance, according to this narrative, was due in part to England's cultural heritage of freedom, for "the flag was sure to protect his rights, and insure from the Government to which he sailed respect and hospitality" (*MP*, 11). Adams has the fictional Pereira repeatedly descant, in what passes for Portuguese-inflected English, some variation of his comment "I'm always sail in English ship, because I can get protection from flag and consul, where I go—any part of globe" (*MP*, 17). Once in Charleston, Pereira becomes an Englishman in elocution and manner if not by birth, as Adams imbues him with a rhetorical fluency that rivals that of Frederick Douglass's Madison Washington in *A Heroic Slave*, replacing the Portuguese accent from the opening seafaring scenes with perfectly grammatical English once Pereira begins to defend himself against the depredations of the Charleston police. At the jail, the manacled Pereira protests, "It must be humanity that puts these symbols of ignominy upon my hands" and "confines me in a dungeon lest I should breathe a word of liberty to ears that know it only as a fable" (*MP,* 131–32). Indeed, Pereira's figurative transformation serves to heighten his subsequent racialization as a "foreign negro" upon arrival in Charleston. The captain is a man who "never believed in making equals of negroes," yet he too is suitably impressed by Pereira's earnest "reverence for the old jack" (*MP,* 21). His informal pledge to protect Pereira is soon tested, as the *Janson* "floated a complete wreck" into Charleston Harbor, the nearest port, for repairs. The mate, an "experienced salt" from the "north-country" reminiscent of Melville's Starbuck in his clarity of perception, offers the captain a sobering account of the reception Pereira was certain to receive in Charleston: "The *Thebis* got a coloured man; but the owners had to pay him an enormous advance, and this, too, with the knowledge of his being locked up the whole time he was in port" (*MP,* 22). The incredulous captain, representing the ethical man of commerce, soon finds himself, like the sailing master of the *Thebis,* caught in a crisis of law.[192]

Once *Manuel Pereira* breaks from the maritime universe of the sea narrative, it quickly redefines itself as an exposé of police corruption in Charleston; it offers a scathing indictment of the unscrupulous abuse of power at the hands of men who are the professed guardians of the city. Indeed, the extreme confinement of the city jail provides the setting for the remainder of the novel. "[A]ny man connected with the city police," according to the narrator, "would not, for *conscience' sake,* scruple to hang a man for five dollars. We make no exception for colour or crime" (*MP,* 25–26). Adams's indictment of police corruption in Charleston may seem at first tangential to Pereira's story, yet the novel seeks precisely to show the reader "that the complex system of official spoliation, and the misrepresentation of the police in regard to the influence of such persons upon the slave population, is a principle feature" in the "imprisonment of free citizens of a friendly nation" (*MP,* 27). The novel minces no words in its condemnation of the Negro Seamen Act as a "municipal pretense" sustained only by the "demoralization of social life in Charleston" (*MP,* 29). The "head of police," in Adams's view, stood foremost among the city's "innumerable unmarshalled men." Digressions into the hidden and scandalous personal lives of local officials and jurists repeatedly postpone the dénouement of the story once Pereira leaves the ordered maritime world of the *Janson* for the corrupt moral universe of Charleston.

Characters in the novel, circumscribed by slave law and custom, cannot be moved to identify against their interests, as the novel thwarts the sentimentalist promise of a transformative intersubjective engagement with another's suffering through individual acts of identification.[193] *Manuel Pereira* depicts characters entirely bereft of the empathy usually found in sentimental fiction.[194] "Everything," according to the novel, "is made to conserve popular favour, giving to those in influence power to do what they please with a destitute class, whether turned into despots for miserable espionage, where the most unjust schemes are practiced upon those whose voices cannot be heard in their own defence" (*MP*, 343–44). Good-hearted, civic-minded southern characters ranging from the kindhearted jailor who supplements the prisoners' meager diet with his own humble fare to the influential Charleston solicitor (based, most likely, on Benjamin Fanueil Hunt) who befriends Capt. Thompson are all powerless to assist Pereira before the supreme authority of the city sheriff. These morally sound characters and their fruitless efforts to secure Pereira's release undercut the political efficacy of sentimentalism's moral injunction to "feel right." Moral sentiment fails before the "same cold opinions about the law, and the faith and importance of South Carolina, and her peculiar institution," and even the sympathetic heart of Mrs. Bird—the paragon of virtue from *Uncle Tom's Cabin*—could not sway, one jot, the strict construction that Pereira was, in the oft-repeated phrase, "contrary to law" (*MP*, 213).

Unlike many other antebellum southern cities, Charleston had by the 1850s an established agency for law enforcement. The unredeemable and aptly named Sheriff Grimshaw stands as the representative figure for the wrongs of a city administration that stretched back to the enactment of the first seamen act in 1822. That same year, the South Carolina legislature also established a municipal guard in Charleston to "carry into effect the laws of the State and the city ordinance, for the government of negroes and free persons of colour" and levied a heavy tax of ten dollars on all black households and licensed black mechanics within its limits to defray the expenses of establishing and maintaining this force.[195] Not only was the Charleston municipal guard founded on an onerous tax on black residents; it was established to police and enforce "the laws of the State" against them. Sheriff Grimshaw's actions are continuous with this long legislative history and the city's punitive policing of its free black population. "Jail," according to the defensive sheriff, "was intended for punishment," even though these black mariners had committed no crime. They were incarcerated simply for being "contrary to law" (*MP*, 215). Adams's repetition of this key phrase reveals that the law criminalizes not actions or deeds but an entire class of raced persons.

Sheriff Grimshaw is all too happy to fall back on the "strict construction" of the police laws in Charleston: the law "was imperative, and no consideration could be given to the circumstances, for such would be virtually destroying its validity, and furnishing a precedent that would be followed by innumerable cases" (*MP,* 95). Grimshaw repeatedly appeals to the purported objective authority of law to rebuff British Consul Mathew's requests to release Pereira: "I never do anything inconsistent with my office. The law gives me power in these cases, and I exercise it. . . . I act for the State, and not for you" (*MP,* 190, 192). Mathew recognizes the law's sanction of Grimshaw's action, yet he critically observes, "You make all these legal inconsistencies a simple and most subservient life-rent to serve your own purposes, without giving them that broad view which looks to the general interests of our people" (*MP,* 194). Sheriff Grimshaw may be a morally reprehensible character, but his repeated invocations of legal sanctions for his ruthless actions reveal that Adams's critique extends well beyond the realm of individual authority.

Grimshaw and his lackeys, whose sole interest lay "in the spoils of law," shamelessly exploit the broad discretionary powers delegated to them by the state (*MP,* 202). They prey on the vulnerable and take the life of innocents such as Tommy Ward, the petted English cabin boy and bosom companion of Pereira; unlike the orchestrated deathbed scene of Stowe's angelic Evangeline, Tommy's death symbolizes neither transcendence nor sacrifice and brings forth no redemption or moral transfiguration at the novel's end. Leaving Pereira's jail cell well after hours, Tommy becomes lost in the labyrinth of downtown Charleston; policemen arrest him for vagrancy and thrust him into a dank jail cell, where the boy, innocent of crime, contracts his mortal sickness. Charleston's lawless "contagion," as Adams plies the discourse of public health so long used to defend its police law, reaches across the Atlantic to afflict and ultimately kill Tommy well after he reaches the shores of Pereira's beloved England. There, too, is no final scene of redemptive reunion for Pereira and Tommy in the masculine universe of the novel. Pereira bathes Tommy's brow with "kisses of grief," but he arrives at the hospital too late: "Life was gone" (*MP,* 352). Tommy "breathed his last as Manuel entered the sick-chamber," and the novel concludes with his somber funeral procession. Loss mars Pereira's return to his adopted nation, and the novel ends in lamentation, "with a picture at once painful and harrowing to the feelings." "We do this," the narrator explains, "that we may be sustained by records in what we have stated, rather than give one of those more popular conclusions which restore happiness and relieve the reader's feelings" (*MP,* 351). The novel stubbornly refuses to leave the reader with any sentimental resolution: it cannot imagine a redemptive universe for the likes of Pereira or Tommy, and in resisting the supposed moral edification of a sentimental closure, it insists on the need for legal and political reform. Great Britain, the novel suggests, cannot hold itself aloof from the unfinished project of Western freedom. No one may rest complacent on his rights as a British subject as long as slavery exists in the Atlantic world.

Pereira cannot turn to the law for redress in Adams's staged scenes within and without the Charleston jail. His resistance only begets more appalling forms of punishment. Sheriff Grimshaw punishes Pereira with three weeks of solitary confinement in "a dark, unhealthy cell" for the offense of defending himself against theft (*MP,* 287). The narrator walks the reader through the dehumanizing conditions that welcome those who fall prey to the law: "you ascend a narrow, crooked stairs, and reach the second storey; here are some eight or nine miserable cells—some large and some small—badly ventilated, and entirely destitute of any kind of furniture" (*MP,* 144).[196] But Adams purposively omits the most painful scenes of Pereira's suffering in solitary confinement; he derives neither moral self-satisfaction nor pleasure from these scenes of violence. Digressions and asides delay the narrator's reportage of Pereira's story once he is placed in solitary confinement, as if the roving eye of the omniscient narrator is incapable of describing the suffering that awaits him: "To describe this miserable hole would be a task too harrowing to our feelings. We pass it for those who will come after us" (*MP,* 287). Removed from the collaborative sustenance of the other black stewards, Pereira is indeed reduced to "bare life." Digressions again overtake the narration as Pereira, caught in this prolonged political interval of civil death, threatens to disappear from the story.[197] The psychic and physical privation of this extended solitary confinement renders Pereira "so pale and emaciated" that Capt. Thompson would scarcely have recognized him "had he met him in the street" (*MP,* 306).[198] The novel thus falters before this radical devaluation of Pereira in its failure to capture, in print, his prison experience.

Pereira's entrance and eventual exit from the Charleston jail are registered in the criminal calendar, and Adams typographically reproduces these records in *Manuel Pereira* as they appeared in registry. In fact, each black mariner in the novel exits the Charleston jail and the narrative through the formal mechanism of this official bill of charges:

"*Contrary to Law.*

British brig *Janson*, } For Manuel Pereira, Coloured
Capt. Thompson.   Seaman.
1852.   To Sheriff of Charleston District.

May 15th.	To Arrest, dols. 2; Register, dols. 2	4.00 dols.
„	Recog., dol. 1.31; Constable, dol. 1.	2.31 „
„	Commitment and Discharge.....	1.00 „
„	Fifty-two days' maintenance of Manuel Pereira, at 30 cents per day............................	15.60
		22.81 dols.

Received payment,

J. D——, S. C. D.
Per Charles Kanapeaux, Clerk." (*MP,* 343)

In a footnote annotating Pereira's discharge, Adams informs us, "There were no less than sixty-three cases of colored seamen imprisoned on this charge of 'contrary to law,' during the calendar year ending on the twelfth of September, 1852" (*MP,* 342). Adams, again blurring documentary fact with fiction, reports that Grimshaw, when pressed by Governor Means for a fiscal account of the jail, kept out "the number of coloured seamen" (*MP,* 342). "The real statement," he informs us, "showed a bounty to the sheriff of fourteen hundred and sixty-three dollars in the provisions alone—a sad premium on misery" (*MP,* 342). For the jailed sailors, these financial charges stand as the only documentation of their injury. In Reuben Roberts's lawsuit against Sheriff Yates, presumably the Grimshaw of Adams's novel, his lawyers likewise sought to quantify, and thereby make legally legible, the injuries he suffered while incarcerated in Charleston. Can this quantification offer an adequate formula for justice, given the untold abuse, privation, and shame that these men underwent within and without the prison walls? Indeed, Adams's accounting of Pereira's bill of costs is, perhaps tellingly, miscalculated ($22.81 instead of the correct $22.91).

Manuel Pereira thus resists individual identification, the hallmark of the sentimental narrative, and its accompanying orchestrated scenes of suffering, to emphasize the institutional and economic mechanisms of state violence. Indeed, its relentless antisentimentalism only emphasized the urgent need for some form of legal or legislative redress. As Capt. Thompson discovers, law becomes an easy rationale for men to act inhumanely despite their sympathetic words: "for while they all talked sympathy, they acted tyranny. Cold, measured words about niggers, '*contrary to law*,' constitutional rights, inviolable laws, State sovereignty and secession, the necessary police-regulations to protect a peculiar institution, and their right to enforce them, everywhere greeted his ears" (*MP,* 201). Such passages implicitly critique the limits of moral sentiment to translate into individual action, let alone a course of diplomatic action. Parliamentarian Lord Stanley, reported a pleased *Charleston Mercury,* "paid all homage to anti-slavery opinion . . . by pronouncing the laws of which he complains 'a disgrace and a scandal to civilization,'" yet this "outbreak of sentimentalism did not, however, lead him to any expression which committed his Government to any specific action."[199] Adams's frustration with the city constabulary, corrupted by avarice and political bias, suggests that there may be no legal redress or justice to be had under slave law, even as his literate endeavors betray a powerful investment in the law's ability to dispense justice in the face of its ongoing failure.

The historical Pereira was reported to have been, like Bowers and Roberts, of African descent, although Adams transforms him into "a sort of mestizo," "born in Brazil, an extract of the Indian and Spanish" (*MP,* 101, 11).[200] Adams may have elected to craft a variant of the "tragic mulatto," in the manner of Lydia Maria Child's *The Quadroons* or William Wells Brown's *Clotel,* to facilitate the (white) reader's sympathetic identification with the protagonist, yet this choice also illuminates more vividly the processes of state racialization and criminalization. "Color and not crime," the *Liberator* reported, "was the only indictment to be found" in these cases, as the newspaper denounced this identification of black personhood with punishment.[201] The uncouth pilot who boards the listing *Janson* insists on calling Pereira a "nigger" despite the equally racialist correction of the first mate: "'Nigger? Not he!' said the mate. 'He's a Portuguese mixed breed; a kind o' sun-scorched subject, like a good many of you Southerners. A nigger's mother never had him, you may bet your 'davie on that'" (*MP,* 47). But Pereira's ethnic and national difference make him "black" as the novel exposes the legal mechanisms by which foreigners become racialized. "The law," the Charleston pilot explains, "snaps 'em up once in a while, and then, if they're ever so white, it makes 'em prove it" (*MP,* 50). Ethnic, cultural, and national differences become collapsed into "blackness," which is assumed until "proven" otherwise. The novel thus illustrates, in its own terms, that blackness is, as legal scholar Devon Carbado writes, "a form of bare life" in the slave state, given the mechanisms by which it is "included in the juridical order solely in the form of its exclusion (that is, its capacity to be subordinated)."[202]

The testimony of affected seamen and antislavery fictions such as *Manuel Pereira* reveal just how difficult it was for sailors to prove themselves "white" once Charleston police deemed them to be black. "Ye can't pass him off for a white man nohow," insists the pilot, "for the thing's *contrary to law*, and pays so well that them contemptible land-sharks of officers makes all the fuss about it, and never let one pass" (*MP,* 52). Pereira *becomes* black at the moment of arrest so that the law may punish him, even as the law sets up the conditions by which he is presumed to *be* black. Black life, in other words, is given over to an absolute state of abandonment where it is "put outside the law and put under its banner and its ban."[203] The law as represented in Sheriff Grimshaw and his officers re-creates Pereira's racial identity to suit the workings of the municipal law once the *Janson* enters Charleston Harbor. This powerful discursive formation of "blackness" justifies Pereira's arrest and the violence he subsequently must endure. Blackness, as illustrated in these proceedings, becomes, as Stephen Best and Saidiya Hartman describe, "the consequence of violence, the residue of an exercise of power."[204] Once turned "black," as it were, Pereira becomes both slave and prisoner in the eyes of the Charleston police and is treated accordingly.

Manuel Pereira is deeply cynical about the possibility of redress for such injuries, even though it insists on legal reform and federal checks on what constituted the legitimate exercise of police power. The narrator derides South Carolina for its outdated "feeble majesty," saying that "[t]he day will yet come when such a majesty will blush at its reign, and disown itself among the nations of the earth. It will look back upon itself like a gloomy curtain hanging its dark folds in the horizon of nations" (*MP,* 178). But such anachronistic allusions belie the powerful modernity of the slave state. The state of exception found in the Negro Seamen Act created a "structure of abandonment" that demarcated, in Ian Baucom's words, "a zone of law within the law in which the law legally fails to operate."[205] This racial state of exception, far from what abolitionist reformers such as Adams denounced as social atavism, constituted the political modernity of the sovereign slaveholding state.[206] The thoroughgoing discourse of archaism in Adams's impassioned exhortation, like Lahitte's barely disguised disdain for America's regrettable barbarism, characterized the tenor of abolitionist arguments in the 1850s, in newspapers from the *Liberator* to *Frederick Douglass' Paper*. In the hands of a skillful writer-editor such as Douglass,

South Carolina's oft-repeated defense became another instance of the archaic: "The Governor makes the old tyrants plea for this law—i.e., *necessity*. It is necessary to prevent the dissemination of dangerous ideas among their happy population! . . . It would not be a bad idea to establish in the city of Charleston an *'inquisition'* on the model of that of Venice, only making slavery instead the church the thing for conservation."[207] The "contagion," in Douglass's biting commentary, was not of "negro liberty" but of an unfettered modern police power seemingly antagonistic to the tenets of a democratic nation based on individual rights. *Manuel Pereira*'s narrator, likewise, ends his attack on the police law with the telling query "How is it in this progressive nineteenth century?" (*MP,* 179). This mix of anguish and rage surges from an internal struggle: the impasse of reformers such as Adams and Douglass who found their investment in progress and the modern state at odds with both their moral humanism and the promised egalitarianism of liberal democracy. "We struggle," Adams insists, "between a wish to speak well of" the sovereign state "whose power it is to practice" the laws "and an imperative duty that commands us to speak for those who cannot speak for themselves" (*MP,* 156).

The novel powerfully galvanized international public attention toward the repeal and modification of these southern regulations against free blacks. "Thousands," according to the *London Daily News*, "are interested in this case MANUEL PEREIRA, and his cry for justice excites our ears to listen for what is said of such matters."[208] The novel meaningfully individuates Pereira and other black sailors from the perspectives of the police, statesmen, and diplomats. Pereira becomes a figure invested with personal history, national loyalties, and sentiments, and he offers a counterpoint to the oft-invoked specter of racial menace pervasive in South Carolina legal and legislative discourses. The Pereira fashioned in Adams's novel is a pointedly mild-mannered laborer incapable of the threat that police officials and legislators alike claimed was posed by free "foreign negroes" to the civic order and public safety of Charleston. Adams manages, through his fictional retelling of the case, to leverage public opinion in the absence of legal remedy.

Adams's campaign against the South Carolina Negro Seamen Act did not end with the publication of *Manuel Pereira*; he drew on these Charleston cases in his lectures before the British and Foreign Anti-Slavery Society to enlist British nationalism in the cause of these imprisoned sailors. Such cases, Adams insisted in an impassioned 1854 address before the London Anti-Slavery Conference, signaled the expansion of American slavery into a "free" postemancipation Britain. "Slavery," in the figure of the Charleston police, "boarded British vessels, manacled British subjects, set at naught the appeals of Consuls, and made prison cells do the work of reducing honest freemen to the same level with her slaves."[209] Embedded in these discussions was a sharp critique of Britain's failure to defend the rights of its formerly enslaved colonial subjects. The racialized subordination found in the South Carolina act, as Adams forcefully argued on page and stage, can only be understood as the perpetuation of slavery against British subjects whose self-ownership did not make them free.[210] The popularity of *Manuel Pereira* is perhaps not surprising in a decade that, according to William Andrews, saw the dramatic increase of international public interest in the "romantic racialism" of *Uncle Tom's Cabin*, and Pereira became a touchstone for the transatlantic antislavery platform.[211] The experiences of incarcerated seamen such as Pereira had a powerful discursive afterlife in the antislavery activism of the 1850s, and campaigners later attributed South Carolina's grudging amendment of its laws to the "well-directed and continued batteries of the Press."[212]

The near simultaneous lawsuits of Pereira and Roberts in South Carolina initiated a new spate of highly public and controversial international negotiations that helped further galvanize reform movements throughout coastal southern states in the 1850s.[213] South Carolina's enforcement of its "obnoxious law for imprisoning free blacks," in studied disregard of all national and international petitions, became increasingly at odds with southern popular opinion, as neighboring states such as North Carolina began to modify their regulations in response to local reform campaigns.[214] The *New York Observer* remarked in 1851, "We have known that, for some time past, there has prevailed among the best classes of Charleston, a disposition to modify the offensive law."[215] South Carolina may have been the "head-quarters of pro-slavery ultraism," but its longstanding doctrine of self-preservation did not remain uncontested as the changing public discourse on slavery and federalism began to affect lawmaking decisions within the state. The *Charleston Courier*, marking a radical shift after three decades of support for the police law, declared, "it seems to us that our law ought to be changed on the principle of the Indiana and Illinois Constitutions," which restricted black sailors to their vessels.[216] The *Charleston Mercury* likewise asked whether the "safety of the community" could be "as effectually guarded by other and less exceptional restrictions" and suggested, with uncharacteristic sharpness, that the state "persists, from the pride of consistency, or a reluctance to make an apparent concession, in maintaining severe restrictions after the reason for them may have passed away."²¹⁷ The paper went on to note "the fact that Charleston city, in mass, favors a modification of the South Carolina law; but that through fear of Abolition incendiarism, opposition to it comes from the country planters, or country residents."²¹⁸

Proposed amendments to the law, including a modification that Governor Adams vigorously endorsed, came before the South Carolina legislature on several occasions, but they were all struck down by statesmen claiming, as before, that "[a]ll nations have the right of protecting themselves by police laws and provisions excluding from their borders those who may be regarded as dangerous to their internal peace and security."²¹⁹ The "public sentiment of the State," noted one South Carolina legislator, "is against the Act, as evidenced by memorials to the legislature, presentments of grand juries, the press, and the recommendations of every Governor for the last eight or ten years."²²⁰ The *Charleston Mercury* cautioned that this "right of self-protection" should be exercised "with the *least* injury and inconvenience to others," as it echoed those sentiments long expressed north of Mason-Dixon and across the Atlantic.²²¹

The public outcry in Charleston to amend its police regulations, however, did not necessarily mean a corresponding recognition of black citizenship. Far from an admission of either antislavery or antiracist politics, this public inclination toward modification emerged out of loyalty to the Union and the desire to further stabilize slavery in the state. An 1851 antisecessionist gathering in Greenville, for example, offered an apocalyptic vision of South Carolina as a "black State, a second San Domingo," as a result not of slave insurrection but of the state's intransigent insistence on sovereignty independent from the federal compact. The antisecessionists marshaled the specter of black Haiti as the inevitable consequence of South Carolina's extreme territorial doctrine of sovereignty, since secession would create the conditions in which "[w]hite persons may leave the State, but slaves cannot."²²² In this counterfactual new South, the radical immobility of the slave, central to the theory of mastery, would become, ironically, the very means of the undoing of slaveholding society.²²³ Neither did the local press find the desire for municipal reform incompatible with the racialist advocacy of slavery. The *Charleston Mercury* dismissed the very idea of "danger" that state officials had used to defend the state's expansion of police power: "This being forever fretfully upon guard when there is no appreciable danger, this seeming admission that we are always on the tenter-hooks of expectation of some mysterious and terrible catastrophe.

Is it not a sort of justification of the everlasting fear of the enemies of Slavery, that we have no confidence in the stability of our institutions, and no [t]rust in the loyalty of our servile populations?"[224] This ever-present threat of black insurrection, as the *Charleston Mercury* admitted, plainly betrayed the fallacy of slavery as a benevolent "paternal institution"; it represented institutional slavery as under continual assault. These heightened policing measures maintained a perpetual state of emergency that only served to confirm the power of revolutionary black agency. "Why should we, then, counterfeit fears that nobody really entertains?" the *Mercury* asked.[225] These "counterfeit fears" revealed the deep-seated fissures between the ideologies of slavery and its practice as a legal institution. Police violence was necessary to the maintenance of a subjected black population, even if southern paternalism insisted on the inherent docility of the slave.

The Circulation of Law and the Rise of Black Atlantic Radicalism

Manuel Pereira was one of a number of cautionary tales of postemancipation freedom that made their way across the Atlantic and into British antislavery print culture at midcentury. Such accounts of incarcerated black sailors placed uncomfortable pressure on the lawful liberty that Britain had purportedly secured to its black subjects, forcing the island nation to make sense of its Atlantic empire even as they deflected attention away from the growing political unrest in Britain's eastern empire.[226] Abolitionists directed these stories to British audiences as they condemned the nation's inability to protect its own citizens from the depredations of U.S. slavery. This section charts the curious circulation of another cautionary tale of British freedom to examine how Anglo-American abolitionism reappropriated South Carolina's rhetoric of self-preservation to secure British popular consensus against U.S. slavery. Black and white abolitionists rallied around the figure of John Glasgow, a "free-born British subject" shorn of his freedom through the inexorable workings of South Carolina's "most barbarous and oppressive law."[227] Glasgow lived out the remainder of his life on a Georgia plantation, far from Liverpool, where he had left wife and children, and perished in slavery. His story, however, continued to live in speeches, pamphlets, newspapers, and a popular British slave narrative as a reminder of the precariousness of British freedom in a partially free world. Countless American and British abolitionists summoned Glasgow in their efforts to rally the power of British public opinion against U.S. slavery.

The British government's failure to protect the rights of its free black subjects elicited powerful outpourings of pathos and indignation. "Think, too, of poor John Glasgow," Samuel J. May admonished the crowd gathered at the 1854 Manchester Anti-Slavery Conference, "stolen from a British ship by South Carolina officers, and now, if alive, wasting away his life as a South Carolina slave. Have the government and people of Great Britain done their duty by that man?"[228] Glasgow's story offered a powerful challenge to triumphalist narratives of British freedom that had begun with *Somerset*. Unlike the establishing scenes of "natal alienation" that typically begin the fugitive slave narrative, Glasgow's story began in the familiar settings of England, as readers and auditors followed the torturous passage of a free man into chattel slavery. The story presumes the reader's identification with Glasgow from the outset; it also shares the formal emplotment found in Solomon Northrup's popular *Twelve Years a Slave* (1853) and Kate Pickard's *The Kidnapped and the Ransomed* (1856).[229] By thus depicting the unlawful *theft* of freedom, transatlantic antislavery activists more effectively insisted on the U.S. institutional processes that *made* these free British subjects into chattel slaves. These writers and orators gave powerful expression to the poetics of theft that had earlier organized Peter Still's dictated autobiography and Lucy Ann Delaney's postemancipation slave narrative.

A "native of Demerara, born of free negro parents, whose free condition he inherited," Glasgow, according to the first iterations of his personal history, was an enterprising young man who took to the sea, quickly working himself up from cabin boy to able-bodied seaman on the ship's register.[230] Various versions of the story took pains to show that Glasgow rejected the itinerancy of seafaring life to embrace full integration into British society ashore. He prospered, married a Liverpool lass, commenced farming, and returned to the sea only to "meet the expenses of a large family." Glasgow was a model of masculine providership, and he "engaged to go out to Savannah in Georgia, in an English vessel, and under a English captain" on what was to be (pathetically) his "last voyage to so distant a country."[231] This unfortunate journey parts Glasgow forever from his family and country, as the "black law of Georgia, like that of South Carolina is no respecter of freedom."[232] The "English captain" turns out to be unprincipled and, since Glasgow is "'only a nigger after all,' . . . refused to pay the jail-fees, and set sail without John," consigning him to the "auction-block."[233] Glasgow suffers a life of unremitting psychological and physical subjection enslaved to his vindictive new master, "Thomas Stevens, of Baldwin country, Georgia." Graphically orchestrated spectacles of violence chart his bloody passage from a "free-born British subject" to an abject American slave as Stevens brutally forces Glasgow, like young Peter and Levin Still, to renounce his past in order to reconstruct him into a thing without history. "Similar has been the fate," cautions the *Anti-Slavery Reporter*, "of hundreds of others, black, brown, and white, free men and women, born on British, Portuguese, or any other soil, and of whose melancholy end their relatives have never learnt."[234]

There was a witness to "tell the tale" of Glasgow's "agonizing case," unlike for the countless others that undoubtedly went unknown and unheard. An escaped slave "who was many years John Glasgow's companion in bondage" related Glasgow's story to the British and Foreign Anti-Slavery Society, which first published it on 1 July 1853 in the *Anti-Slavery Reporter*. The fugitive informant hoped that the publication of Glasgow's narrative "would lead to a discovery of the whereabouts of the poor fellow's English wife and children," since he owed Glasgow "a debt of gratitude, for he it was who taught him to love and seek liberty."[235] Glasgow's story, as mediated through this informant, bore out the inflammatory threat that South Carolina lawmakers had endeavored to prevent with its punitive antiblack police laws. Indeed, the police law created the conditions of Glasgow's radicalization as it transformed him into the very figure of the proscribed "free foreign negro" that states such as South Carolina had sought to cordon from its "domestic" slave populations. The enslaved Glasgow, in turn, "taught" this American slave "to love and seek liberty." His presence radically altered the lives of those slaves whose status the Negro Seamen Act had mandated that he share. The *Anti-Slavery Reporter* thus transformed for its own purposes the amorphous *threat* of black revolt so often exploited by slave states into its *certainty*.

The British abolitionist Wilson Armistead immediately published a more embellished version of Glasgow's story in his *Leeds Anti-Slavery Tract* series, which *Frederick Douglass' Paper* republished the following year. Armistead's version named the fugitive informant in London as one "John Brown."[236] This was the American fugitive slave Fed, who renamed himself John Brown upon his escape to England, where he remained until his death in 1876 (see figure 4.3). He dictated his experiences in slavery to Louis Alexis Chamerovzow, secretary of the British and Foreign Anti-Slavery Society, who edited and originally published the account as *Slave Life in Georgia: A Narrative of the Life, Sufferings, and Escape of John Brown, a Fugitive Slave, Now in England* (1855). Copies were available for one shilling, and it was successful enough to warrant a limited second edition, which was later translated into German.[237] *Slave Life in Georgia* was among a number of widely popular American slave narratives that were published in Britain and written for primarily British audiences, including those of Moses Roper (1837), William Wells Brown (1852), William and Ellen Craft (1860), and Jacob Green (1864). Glasgow's tragic story is embedded within Brown's *Slave Life in Georgia*. The fourth chapter, "The Story of John Glasgow," interrupts the first-person narrative in one of three chapters speculated to be primarily the work of Chamerovzow. "I must interrupt my own narrative here," Brown insists, "to relate the story of John Glasgow. I had it from his own lips; and acting on the advice of the Secretary of the *British and Foreign Anti-Slavery Society*, I have made a declaration in his presence, before a notary public, to the effect that, as given below, the narrative is substantially correct" (*SL*, 29). What follows in Brown's narrative is the verbatim text of Glasgow's story as it first appeared in the *Anti-Slavery Reporter*, and Brown's duly notarized "Declaration," dated 29 May 1854, numbers among the many paratextual supplements included at the autobiography's end.

Brown's account of political radicalization through sympathetic identification with the black Briton helped reaffirm, even while possibly unsettling, the prevailing narratives of British national culture. Brown finds himself irresistibly drawn to the black stranger: "It was reported and believed amongst the slaves on the plantation that this John Glasgow had been a free British subject, and this circumstance . . . has tended to fix the following facts strongly in my recollection" (*SL*, 188). Their shared loss cements their intimacy: "He also felt for me in my grief at parting from my former relations, and endeavoring to console me as best he could, frequently spoke to me of his own previous history, particularly of his residence and relatives in England" (*SL*, 188). Glasgow's longing for kin and country incites in Brown a sympathetic yearning that reestablishes the nationalistic contours of British freedom. "These kind words from John Glasgow," he recalls, "gave me better heart, and inspired me with a longing to get to England, which I made up my mind I would try and do some day" (*SL*, 24). Later chapters further emphasize the direct causal relation between these fugitive desires and Glasgow's stories of British freedom: "My mind had long been made up to run away," and "I was constantly dwelling on what John Glasgow had told me about freedom, and England, and becoming a man" (*SL*, 61, 64). "[G]etting off to England" became firmly fixed in Brown's mind, and he found himself in July 1850 "safely landed in the town where poor John Glasgow left his wife and children so many year before" (*SL*, 77, 141). "These are the facts," Brown announces, "I thus learnt and believe"

Fig. 4.3. Portrait of John Brown. From *Slave Life in Georgia*. (Courtesy of the Manuscripts, Archives and Rare Books Division, Schomburg Center for Research in Black Culture, The New York Public Library, Astor, Lenox and Tilden Foundations)

(*SL*, 188). Brown "returns" to Britain in Glasgow's stead, as if to emphasize further the painful fungibility of black personhood under slave law, as the historical Glasgow undergoes the transformation into an abolitionist story.

Glasgow's cautionary tale of freedom offered British abolitionists the opportunity further to define their cultural identity against a tyrannous American nation, becoming, for abolitionists such as Armistead, the groundwork for an ever more powerful national advocacy of a deterritorialized, and indeed universal, freedom. The events that befell Glasgow demanded British "interference," for, in Armistead's words, an "unscrupulous aggressive tyranny, such as the slave power has shown itself, endangers all its free neighbors; and therefore an ordinary regard for self-preservation should lead us, in our national capacity, to resist its assumptions."[238] The slaveholding United States could not exist peaceably within a community of free European nations. In these acts of aggression against black British subjects, the United States threatened a uniquely British way of life. The doctrine of self-preservation is here mobilized for entirely different ends, as Armistead reshapes it into a rallying cry for the extension of British freedom to the Americas—which he sees as a "national obligation."

The stories of Bowers, Pereira, Roberts, and Glasgow forced Britain to wrestle with its governmental responsibilities to the black Britons living in its far-flung territories.[239] Armistead openly questioned the place of black subjects within postemancipation Britain and intimated that the national project of freedom was far from complete: "has not our Government a right to insist that all its subjects should travel when they please, in the territories of our allies, as long as they keep the peace?" He denounced Great Britain for failing to live up to its own political ideologies: "As long as we suffer a million of our *countrymen* . . . to be excluded from entering the territories of our allies, simply and solely on the score of colour, we recognize the right to degrade those whom we have raised to political equality with ourselves, and show a cowardly falseness to our own convictions."[240]

The transatlantic abolitionist campaigns of the 1850s also endowed Glasgow with a long afterlife. Black American abolitionist Samuel Ringgold Ward, for example, dedicated numerous speeches to informing the public about these "obnoxious laws" against black sailors in southern ports; he took Glasgow as the text for his speech before the fifteenth annual meeting of the British and Foreign Anti-Slavery Society. He later reiterated Glasgow's story before a "very crowded" public meeting in Lincolnshire, which concluded with the formation of a permanent Anti-Slavery Committee in the city and the adoption of a legislative petition to be laid before

Parliament in protest of these police laws.[241] Ward recounted how he was obliged to meet, at different points in his transatlantic antislavery lecture tour, the "strong objections... that as there are no slaves in the British empire now, there is nothing for the British people to do on the subject."[242] He deployed the specter of British slaves, used so effectively by Thomas Pringle in the earlier campaign for West Indian emancipation, to mobilize Britons to the cause of U.S. abolition. The "odious law" against black sailors, Ward criticized, "is made for the security of slavery, by preventing free Negroes from associating with the slaves and teaching them the way to a free country."[243] Ward thus emphasized that British abolitionism could not be dismissed as "intermeddling with other people's affairs" when Great Britain had yet to address its "guilty complicity" in accommodating (and therefore, sustaining and perpetuating) these U.S. slave laws against its own free black subjects.[244] "The rights of a British subject, of whatever colour," he insisted, "ought not to be suffered thus to be jeopardized for the accommodation of our trade in slave-grown cotton."[245] Transatlantic abolitionists such as Adams, Armistead, and Ward argued that the futures of free black Britons and American slaves were necessarily intertwined: black sailors such as Pereira and Glasgow, regardless of their national allegiances, could not possess absolute freedom without the hemispheric abolition of racial slavery. Their stories roused British national sentiment against slavery in the Americas by showing that the problem of American slavery was *also* the problem of British freedom.

The sweeping racial dimensions of the South Carolina Negro Seamen Act itself helped determine this particular political appeal to black transatlanticism. When the British and Foreign Anti-Slavery Society first began to address the seizure of British sailors in U.S. ports, it strategically called on "the entire body of coloured persons in the emancipated colonies and in England, to make a special effort to obtain their rights in this particular." It advised all black British subjects "to call public meetings, to collect facts, and to memorialise the Government on this important point; not to desist, until the Foreign Minister shall do them justice, and extend an equal protection to them with that enjoyed by their white fellow-subjects."[246] Black American abolitionist William C. Nell, likewise, offered a transnational narrative of the causes behind British Consul Mathew's intervention into the "local" laws of South Carolina. In a letter to Douglass that Douglass subsequently published, Nell wrote, "It was by the representations principally of the people in the Bahamas, that the British government was indeed to direct the consul, Gov. Matthews, to agitate the subject at Charleston.

A recent number of the *Nassau Guardian*, the most influential journal in the Bahamas, recommends reprisals upon citizens of South Carolina."[247] In 1850, a memorial signed by more than four hundred colonial subjects of the Bahamas Islands protesting the treatment of free black seamen in the ports of the southern states, Cuba, and Puerto Rico was brought before Governor John Gregory.[248] Nell's revisionist account placed black colonial subjects at the center of British radicalization against American slavery. He re-presented Consul Mathew's efforts on behalf of Pereira and Roberts as a response to this unprecedented outpouring of black protest.

Four years passed after Pereira's misbegotten lawsuit before the South Carolina legislature approved a law that substituted the confinement of black seamen to their vessels rather than to city prisons.[249] Black crewmembers would not be imprisoned as long as they remained on board their vessels and "in all respects obey the laws of the State, and ordinances and regulations of the city or town."[250] According to the British consul's report, not one of the seventy-three black seamen who arrived in Charleston on British vessels that year was imprisoned.[251] That fact did not, however, mean the end of racialized measures against the mariners, renegades, and castaways of the black Atlantic. In 1856, Texas began imposing heavy fines on all ship captains who brought free blacks into the state, and Louisiana reenacted its police law against free black seamen in 1859.[252] The British Board of Trade instructed all shipping masters to "warn such seamen, and the masters who engage them, of the inconvenience and risk to which they may be exposed through the operations of the... stringent laws in force in the Southern States of America, with regard to the admission of free negroes," and advised those seamen to carry with them "full evidence of their place of birth and nationality."[253]

"The enactment" of these Negro Seamen Acts, as the *Anti-Slavery Reporter* noted, "not only failed wholly in its effect, but was actually the cause of increasing the very dangers which the law was intended to obviate."[254] The specifically racialized aspect of the South Carolina law, it appears, helped to create the conditions for the further radicalization of the black Atlantic in unexpected ways. Indeed, Pauline Hopkins returned to these events in her historical novel, *Winona: A Tale of Negro Life in the South and Southwest* (1902), to transform the law's negativity and limits into the source of further radicalization. Her white protagonist, Warren Maxwell, was a free British subject divested of rights and committed to a filthy Missouri jail. Awaiting his sentence of death—since he, as a white man, could not be converted into a slave—Maxwell witnessed the "full operation of the slave system":

> Infamous outrages were committed upon free men of color whose employment as cooks and stewards on steamers and sailing vessels had brought them within the jurisdiction of the State. Such men were usually taken ashore and sold to the highest bidder. One man who had his free papers on his person, produced them to prove the truth of his story; the official took the papers from him, burned them, and sold him next week at public auction.[255]

These scenes bear a striking resemblance to those found in *Manuel Pereira* and share that novel's condemnation of crimes committed under the sanction of law. "Experience," admits Maxwell upon his rescue, "is a stern teacher.... I understand the slavery question through and through."[256] Slave law thus provides the groundwork for Maxwell's radicalization, although Hopkins's historical fiction, written in the postemancipation United States, charts a reverse course from Brown's *Slave Life in Georgia*. The "free British subject" in Hopkins's novel no longer effects the radicalization of the American slave; rather, the combined forces of the enslaved heroine, Winona, and the charismatic Capt. John Brown work their political transformation on Maxwell. Once rescued from jail, Maxwell joins Brown's retaliatory strike against proslavery forces at Pottawatomie Creek.

In this fashion, the Negro Seamen Acts provided the means for their own undoing. By December 1856, South Carolina was the only remaining southern state that had not amended, repealed, or modified in some form its regulations against black seamen.[257] Officials from the other slave states had largely withdrawn their support of the South Carolina law, fearing that it would "involve [them] in a war on account of black sailors."[258] One South Carolina statesman finally proposed the expediency of modification, explaining, "[the] present law is injurious to our slaves ... *by attracting their attention to the coloured seamen, manacled and marched through the streets of Charleston*, thus opening to their mind the very matters we wish to protect them from by the law."[259] Antislavery activists had anticipated the radicalizing potential of these Negro Seamen Acts in transforming sailors such as John Glasgow and Manuel Pereira into the very revolutionary firebrands the laws proscribed. The "one effectual way ... to make him dangerous," John Palfrey dryly noted in *Papers on the Slave Power* (1846), is to "[g]o on board the ship; order him over the side; row him on shore to jail. There he will be shut up with some hundreds of his own color," where he will have "free, unrestricted, unwatched communication with them, night and day, such as no other place in Carolina would afford."[260] In the hands of abolitionists such as Adams, Armistead, and Ward, the stories of sailors such as Glasgow and Pereira further radicalized the Atlantic world against American slavery.

Statesmen, diplomats, abolitionists, merchants, slaves, and free blacks imagined (for various and even antagonistic ends) a revolutionary *black* Atlantic world. Insurgency, South Carolina officials insisted, was necessarily racialized as "black," and this dogged persistence helped make publicly accessible a discourse of revolutionary black agency that they could neither control nor contain. Local governments in the early Atlantic world, according to Bolster, had long legislative histories of enacting laws against black mariners whom they perceived as "*agents provocateurs*."[261] The complex discursive history of South Carolina's Negro Seamen Act, and the freedom suits and accompanying antislavery print culture that energized the struggle for its repeal, reveals the radicalizing possibilities within black Atlantic travels, broadly conceived. Indeed, southern lawmakers sought to recast revolutionary agency as the inevitable product of such black cosmopolitan travels. The unfettered mobility of these "free foreign negroes" of the Atlantic world unsettled slave law, even as antiblack police regulations lent further impetus to their radicalization. Southern lawmakers enlisted the fear of black seamen circulating revolutionary ideas to establish the political groundwork of their modern slave states, even as they created the conditions for further disseminating the revolutionary consciousness they so feared. "With a population of nearly 9000 free persons of colour, and with the constant transit of travelers from other States and countries," British Consul Mathew sardonically declared, "it cannot be imagined that any slave in this city or State is uninformed of the existence of negro freedom, or of the geographical limits of slavery" (*MP,* 384).

To understand better this "worlding" of black revolutionary discourse in its changing course around the Atlantic, this chapter ends, with travel's characteristic circuitousness, at the beginning. South Carolina's early insistence in 1822 on the threatening potential of black revolutionary agency became a self-fulfilling prophesy of sorts with the curious circulation history of David Walker's *Appeal to the Coloured Citizens of the World* (1829). Antislavery activists such as Walker, as this chapter has shown, participated in the creation and re-creation of the law's meaning in a variety of contexts and with different ideological consequences.[262] Walker was born free in Wilmington, North Carolina, and, according to Peter Hinks's research, he journeyed to Charleston sometime in the 1810s.[263] No record of this journey exists other than a tantalizingly brief reference in the *Appeal*. A number of scholars speculate that Walker was exposed to, if not a participant in, the events surrounding the Denmark Vesey "plot," which issued in part from the "social controversy swirling about" the newly established AME Church and its espousal of revolutionary Christianity in the heart of the slaveholding South.[264] The radical spirit of the Vesey conspiracy probably influenced, to a degree, the exhortatory rhetoric found in the *Appeal*, even though Walker never mentions it directly in the text.[265]

Walker's powerful manifesto of black radicalism tellingly begins and ends with the self-authorizing act of travel. The "Preamble" begins, "Having traveled over a considerable portion of these United States, and having, in the course of my travels, taken the most accurate observations of things as they exist—the result of my observations has warranted the full and unshaken conviction, that we, (coloured people of the United States,) are the most degraded, wretched, and abject set of beings that ever lived since the world began" (*AA*, 3). Hinks speculates that Walker began his wide-ranging perambulations soon after the Vesey trials in the summer of 1822 and ended them two years later in Boston, where he established himself as a dealer in used clothing.[266] These travels, as Walker forcefully relates, radicalized him into a passionate antislavery and anticolonial advocate. Walker's broad geographical knowledge of the slaveholding states may have inspired his unprecedented mode of circulating the *Appeal* widely throughout the South, an act that predated William Lloyd Garrison's likeminded efforts to distribute the *Liberator* in the slaveholding states.[267] Congress had anticipated concerns about the mail being used to coordinate slave revolt when it restricted free blacks from the postal service as early as 1802, well before the American Anti-Slavery Society's 1835 postal campaign.[268]

Although most of the slave uprisings that shook the South, including those that were stopped short of actualization, were local in character, Walker's *Appeal* embraced the global South in its expansive address to "*enslaved brethren all over the world.*" Walker confronted southern authorities not only with a plan that was orchestrated from a distant northern city but with one that was hemispheric in character.[269] Walker ends the *Appeal* with words that again stress the eyewitness testimony of his self-directed travels throughout the United States: "I do not speak from hear say—what I have written, is what I have seen and heard myself. No man may think that my book is made up of conjecture—I have traveled and observed nearly the whole of these things myself" (*AA*, 79). Walker's radicalizing travels were given yet another literary redaction in the plot of Martin Delany's serialized novel of slave conspiracy, *Blake; or, The Huts of America* (1859–61). The novel charts the extensive peregrinations throughout the South and Southwest of the eponymous hero, Henry Blake, as he widely disseminates his designs for a hemispheric slave revolution, designs that remain strategically undisclosed to the reader. Blake's southern peregrinations, like Walker's, radicalize him in unexpected ways, as this young Cuban aristocrat-turned-sailor is violently remade into a slave upon arrival on U.S. shores. Indeed, Blake, like Glasgow and Pereira, becomes the "foreign" incendiary so feared by southern legislatures.

Walker first published the *Appeal* in September 1829, and two more editions, each with different variations, appeared within a year. Copies of the *Appeal* began surfacing almost immediately in coastal southern towns including Savannah, New Orleans, Wilmington, and Charleston.[270] With the possible assistance of John Eli, Walker's close friend and political associate, Walker specifically employed as his agents mariners traveling to key southern ports such as Charleston. Police arrested Edward Smith, a white sailor from the Boston brig *Columbo*, for distributing copies among local black longshoremen in Charleston Harbor.[271] Smith disavowed knowledge of the *Appeal*'s inflammatory contents and testified that "a decent looking black man whom he believed to be a Bookseller . . . required . . . that he Should give them secretly to the Black people."[272] Found guilty of "seditious libel," Smith was fined one thousand dollars and sentenced to a one-year term in prison.

The legal documents surrounding Smith's trial and conviction yielded yet another curious facet in the discursive histories of the South Carolina Negro Seamen Act. Attorney General James Petigru, who later represented Pereira and Roberts, charged Smith with "falsely and maliciously contriving and intending to disturb the peace and security of this State" and to illustrate his accusations cited a verbatim transcript of some of the more inflammatory passages from the *Appeal*. Walker's ringing condemnation of the racial nation-state, in fact, constitutes almost the entire text of Smith's grand jury indictment. The unusual syntactic structures that characterize the *Appeal*'s passionate and breathless pace subtly disrupt the document's legal meanings through the absorption of the dashes that Petigru used to set off the text of his charge. Petigru offered four distinct examples of Walker's "false seditious and malicious Libel," excerpted methodically from the three longer articles of the *Appeal* (one, two, and four). Petigru did not and, it appears, simply *could not* summarize Walker's words, and he reproduced them at the cost of deforming his own legal language:

> a printed pamphlet entitled Walke[r]'s Appeal in Four Articles together with a Preamble to the coloured Citizens of the World but in particular and very expressly to those of the United States of America, in which said false and scandalous Libel are contained, among other things, divers false seditious scandalous and malicious matters according to the tenor following—Fear not the number and education of our enemies against whom we (meaning the coloured people and slaves in the United States) shall have to contend for our lawful right, guaranteed to us by our maker—for why should we (meaning the black people and slaves aforesaid) be afraid when God is, and will continue, (if we continue humble), to be on our side.... Remember Americans that we (meaning the black people and slaves of the United States) must and shall be free and enlightened as you are, will you wait until we (meaning the black people and slaves aforesaid) shall, under God, obtain our liberty by the crushing arm of power? Will it not be dreadful for you (meaning the whites)—I speak Americans for your good—We must and shall be free I say in spite of you—You may do your best to keep us in wretchedness and misery to enrich you and your children, but God will deliver us from under you—And wo, wo, will be to you (meaning the white people of America) if we (meaning the slaves aforesaid) have to obtain our freedom by fighting—against the form of the Act of the General Assembly in such case made and provided and against the peace and dignity of the same state aforesaid.
>
> James L. Petigru
Attorney General[273]

The final excerpted line of Walker's *Appeal*—"And wo, wo, will be to you (meaning the white people of America) if we (meaning the slaves aforesaid) have to obtain our freedom by fighting"—syntactically takes over the meaning of Petigru's legal document to sharply transform the indictment into a localized delineation of the racial struggle at hand: "to obtain our freedom by fighting—against the form of the Act of the General Assembly." Petigru's selection of this line to end the text of the indictment eerily resembles the menacing utterance of black Cuban insurrectionist Gofer Gondolier—"Woe be unto those devils of whites, I say!"—that concludes Delany's famously unfinished *Blake*.[274] Walker's characteristic deictic utterances resist recontextualization into Petigru's indictment (with its reappropriation of meaning), while offering an unexpected instance of black testimony, generally inadmissible against whites within southern courtrooms, without the mediated paraphrasing of white officers or witnesses. Although this epiphenomenal text is formally similar to the legal structure of Thomas Gray's *Confessions of Nat Turner*, in that it also offers a statement embedded within a counterstatement, the idiosyncratic rhetorical and syntactic forms that characterize Walker's *Appeal* lie beyond the proscriptions of the legal apparatus.[275] This alternative reading scenario, like the *Appeal*'s imperative to, in Elizabeth McHenry words, "bridge the gap between the literate and illiterate," enables us to see how Walker's text subverts the controlling mechanisms of the law through the introduction of meanings exorbitant to Petigru's indictment, as it reforms the legal document into a vehicle for black revolutionary thought.[276]

Did Walker's *Appeal* justify South Carolina's concerns about the inflammatory presence of "foreign negroes" and its specific targeting of free blacks, or did the punitive dimensions of the Negro Seamen Act facilitate the dissemination of the black radicalism that Walker espoused? The law, working according to its own logic, sought to purge from its boundaries the specter of black radicalism embodied in the figure of the "foreign negro," even while it inadvertently helped conjure the powerful imaginary of a revolutionary black Atlantic that writers later mobilized as a rallying call to end slavery and its racial oppressions.[277] Perhaps, as one *Liberator* editorial sharply suggested, the real "incendiary publications" so feared by slaveholding legislatures were less the work of radical antislavery activists such as Walker than of "the makers, printers and publishers of the black codes" themselves. The anonymous writer of the editorial (identified only as V.V.) notes with subtle sarcasm, "If any person were desirous of exciting an insurrection in Virginia or South Carolina, he could not, in my opinion, adopt any more effectual means than to print the slave laws of the State in a cheap form, and circulate copies among the slaves; and if he were to address them for the same purpose, he could say nothing more inflammatory, than to read extracts from these statutes, without a word of comment."[278] Indeed, when hecklers prevented Frederick Douglass from reading from his *Narrative* aboard the transatlantic steamer *Cambria* in 1845, he incited a riot with a dramatic reading of "what the southern legislators themselves have written—I mean the law."[279] Black revolutionary potential was powerful even when it did not pass into action or legislative act, and writers such as Walker pushed what Agamben describes as "the aporia of sovereignty to the limit," without necessarily freeing themselves from its paradoxes.[280] In the hands of southern lawmakers, revolutionary black agency became the groundwork for the expansion of state power that oppressed black subjects. Yet those very regulations, as many antislavery activists noted, became the conditions of possibility for the unexpected alliances across a partially free Atlantic world that sought to challenge and dismantle that state power. The lawsuits of sailors such as Isaac Bowers, Rueben Roberts, and Manuel Pereira, and the circulation of pamphlet, articles, and novels that accompanied those lawsuits, provided the foundation for these increasingly radicalized alliances. These peripatetic struggles forced lawmakers to draw and redraw the thresholds of exclusion from and containment within the slave state, as they brought increasing pressure to bear on the fictions of South Carolina's modern sovereignty.

Conclusion

Fictions of Free Travel

The geopolitics of freedom and slavery revealed in and exacerbated by the freedom suits discussed in this book helped to consolidate the profoundly American understanding of personal liberty as freedom of movement, an understanding that persists to this day. Black and white abolitionists had long couched their protests against punitive black exclusion laws such as the Negro Seamen Act in terms of a constitutional right to free travel, and the legacy of the territorialization of freedom and slavery ensured that the question of this right would remain a flashpoint in U.S. legal culture throughout the nineteenth century. The *Liberator* repeatedly referred to the "privilege of locomotion, under the American Constitution" to condemn these proliferating antiblack regulations, as it traced back the "privileges and immunities" of state citizenship to its "original comprehensiveness" in the Articles of Confederation: "The better to secure and perpetuate mutual friendship and intercourse among the people of the different States in this Union, the free inhabitants of each of these States, paupers, vagabonds, and fugitives from justice excepted, shall be entitled to all privileges and immunities of free citizens in the several States; and the people of each State shall have free ingress and regress to and from any other State" (art. 4). Abolitionists insisted that this "right of free entrance into any of the states of the Union is the very first among the privileges of citizens," regardless of race.[1]

These conflicts over the freedom of movement were explicitly about the question of black citizenship and black belonging in the United States. A self-professed "liberal minded Englishman" numbered the restrictions on the freedom of movement of free blacks among the principal "il-liberal acts" of the "white citizens" of the United States, contrasting such restrictions to the liberality that greeted white foreign travelers: "thousands of Foreigners, can land here and travel to any part of the union without molestation, [yet] your own citizens are compelled to prove that they are free."[2] What did citizenship mean if slave states continued to disregard the right of black northern citizens to travel freely throughout the nation? *Frederick Douglass' Paper* further expounded on this constitutional right to free interstate travel: "By the constitution of the United States, every free citizen has the right to traverse the whole length and breadth of the Union as freely as if every part of it was his home."[3] Douglass sought to counterbalance the pervasive racialist narratives of disaffiliation that deemed free blacks to be permanent sojourners in the nation and denied that any form of citizenship extended to them.

Given this identification of citizenship with the freedom of movement, abolitionists and reformers sprung into action when the U.S. State Department revealed its "customary" practice of denying passports to free blacks seeking to travel abroad. The State Department habitually refused to grant free blacks the documentation that legitimated movement beyond national borders, as it made U.S. citizenship intelligible through racial categorizations.[4] The first of a number of black passport disputes captured headlines in the summer of 1849, while Harriet and Dred Scott's freedom suit was making its way to the Missouri Supreme Court.[5] Secretary of State John Clayton rejected the application of Henry Hambleton, a freeborn Pennsylvania citizen, on the grounds that "passports are not granted by this Department to persons of color."[6] Copies of Clayton's letter rejecting Hambleton's application—what the *Liberator* styled as that "villainous document"—began appearing in newspapers both north and south of Mason-Dixon, as the proposed Fugitive Slave Bill before Congress further aggravated sectional hostilities.[7] Northern newspapers generally denounced this "refusal of passports to any of our citizens, whether colored or otherwise, as an infamous outrage."[8] Douglass's *North Star* declared, "The secular papers are discussing, with an earnestness which indicates the strength that the anti-slavery feeling had acquired, the refusal of Secretary Clayton to give a passport to a colored freeholder of Pennsylvania who desired to go abroad."[9] These antebellum disputes over the volatile relationship between black citizenship and the freedom of movement and choice rehearsed the struggles over black civil liberties that emerged fully in the era of emancipation, culminating in *Plessy v. Ferguson* (1896).

The right to travel abroad is tied to the ability to obtain a passport, which held out the surety that the bearer possessed a country of origin to which he or she would later return.[10] Passports were not required of U.S. travelers, except during wartime, until 1914, but these early disputes began to contest the meaning of black national belonging and citizenship well before *Dred Scott* reached the U.S. Supreme Court. For Garrison's *Liberator*, Clayton's refusal was a governmental decree against black national citizenship that outstripped even the "flagrant outrage" of South Carolina's Negro Seamen Act: South Carolina's "criminality, great as it is, is small in comparison to the outrage which the *General* Government commits when it follows her example, and repudiates those of her citizens born on the soil, and officially denies them the protection of her name or the acknowledgement of her paternity."[11] Some critics viewed Clayton's policy as an "attempt to destroy the value of American citizenship," which constituted a theft of birthright that was continuous with the theft of persons in slavery.[12] The *North Star* also offered numerous expositions on the expressed and implied consequences of "Secretary Clayton's Law of Passports." Black citizens of northern states—from "shipwrecked seamen, discharged servants, [to] outraged or insulted citizens"—were to be bereft of "the protection of the American government, not only in his own but in every foreign land."[13] The denial of passports curtailed the mobility of free blacks in a variety of ways. *Frederick Douglass' Paper*, for example, reported the difficulties of one free black man who, "finding things not as represented by . . . the Colonization Society, sought to return to the United States" shortly after arrival in Africa: "before he was permitted to leave, he, as his letter states, had to resort to gross deception in order to obtain a passport."[14]

The passport offered political documentation of citizenship, and its denial confirmed the statelessness of all free black Americans.[15] Under public pressure, the State Department began offering "protections" (not to be confused with seamen protection certificates) in place of passports, which extended to black northern citizens a national identity stripped of its substantive rights and constitutional guarantees. This policy was yet another aspect of the regime of racial regulation on the freedom of movement both within and without the nation-state.[16] The "pass system" in slave states had long rehearsed locally what Clayton's "law of passports" accomplished nationally, rendering individuals dependent on "states and the state system for the authorization" to traverse borders.[17] Travel for blacks in slave states was contingent on these passports or travel tickets that took the form of either a pass issued by a master or documents attesting to manumission.[18] Historian Stephanie Camp argues that slaveholders "laid out, in their statutes and in their plantation journals, a theory of mastery at the center of which was the restriction of slave movement."[19] The "right of locomotion" was essential to freedom, just as its denial was an aspect of enslavement.[20]

The demand that free blacks "prove their right to travel" through such documents was thus "a badge of slavery and a reminder of their status in society."[21] The slave state had a vested interest in regulating the movement of its black population (both slave and free) in its efforts to determine who was to be included and excluded from its polity.[22] Black northern citizens were thus deprived of the freedom of movement, as both slave states and the federal government seized on the power to determine who circulated within and crossed its borders in order to distinguish the citizen from the alien or foreigner.[23]

Secretary Clayton's "Law of Passports"

The public disputes over the State Department's "customary" practice reanimated a number of questions that had first emerged in the cases of traveling slaves brought before free- and slave-state courts. Secretary Clayton specifically distinguished between free blacks such as Hambleton who sought to travel for pleasure and those who traveled as servants to white officials. He resurrected the exception to the law of freedom that had been encoded in sojourner laws in northern states: "passports are not granted by this Department to persons of color, and . . . protections are only given to them when they are in the service of diplomatic agents, &c. of the United States, going abroad."[24] As discussed in chapter 2, for example, the U.S. minister to Nicaragua had intended to bring his enslaved servant Jane Johnson and her two sons to serve his wife and "hold them as slaves . . . in the free country of Nicaragua," and it was to accommodate situations such as these that Clayton crafted his customary regulation.[25]

Clayton's exception did not distinguish between free and enslaved black servants, and it introduced yet another contradiction into this supposed "law of passports." The American Anti-Slavery Society drew attention to the paradoxical distinctions that Clayton and past U.S. officials made. As U.S. minister to Britain, James Monroe had granted "a passport to a *Slave*, describing him as 'a citizen of the United States'": "The 'citizen' was ESSEX WHITE, a Slave of [John] Randolph, of Roanoke"; Randolph was a Virginia statesman who was appointed U.S. minister to Russia under Andrew Jackson.[26] A slave was thus granted the rights and protections that the federal government withheld from black citizens of northern states. The *Liberator* retorted, "[If] any . . . of the diplomatic agents abroad, wishes to take one of his negroes with him, to black his boots or brush his coat, Mr. Clayton would have no hesitation in granting a protection; but if a man with a drop of colored blood in his veins, crosses the ocean for any purpose of his own . . . that is quite another thing."[27] Black citizens may be guarded in "their persons and property . . . as *servants* . . . but not as *men*."[28] Frederick Douglass and others stressed the arbitrary distinction that Clayton sought to draw between black servants and black travelers: if passports "can be granted to the servants of a foreign minister, by what authority are they withheld from colored persons who wish to travel abroad at their own expense, for the transaction of business, or in the pursuit of information or amusement?"[29] Such exceptions had a long history in early American statute books, which often exempted black domestic servants from the ticket laws that regulated the mobility of all other slaves.[30] In other words, this "customary" practice sought to enforce a social *and* political exclusion that adhered to the legal logic of slavery and its racial proscriptions.

Clayton addressed a public letter to the *Boston Daily Atlas*—his most ardent supporter—defending his actions as consistent with the "established rule" of past secretaries of state: "The old officers of it, among whom is the chief clerk, who had been employed in it for twenty years, all assure me that this is the rule."[31] Clayton enclosed a second letter from a former passport clerk who verified that "it was the established rule not to grant passports to colored persons as Citizens of the U. States, knowingly."[32] The clerk distinguished between official passports and the informal "protections" granted to black applicants, "stating their names, that they were free persons of color, born in the U. States, and requesting for them in case of need all lawful aid and protection."[33] This "settled regulation" was not a law as such but a customary practice long adopted by the State Department. Clayton's deference to the "usages and precedents of his predecessors" rang hollow to critics, since no "act of Congress imposes such a rule on the department. It must rest on the discretion of the Secretary."[34] Abolitionists such as Douglass and William Lloyd Garrison challenged Clayton to express publicly what was implied by his selective withholding of passports according to race: "If Secretary Clayton thinks that colored persons are not citizens he ought to refuse them passports on that ground."[35]

Abolitionists challenged the State Department's authority to determine the meaning of federal citizenship, and newspapers such as the *Liberator*, *North Star*, and *National Era* denounced "this unjust assumption of power on the part of the Secretary of State" to decide "who shall, and who shall not be considered citizens and freemen."[36] Boston's *Emancipator & Republican* went so far as to declare that Clayton had "set himself above the

Constitution ... and undertaken to withhold from *a citizen*, because he is 'colored,' what his duty requires him to grant to citizens without any such distinction."[37] Indeed, Congress did not legislate on this matter until 1856, when it granted the State Department the exclusive authority to issue passports.[38] Even Clayton's defenders concurred that there was "no law of the United States regulating the issuing of passports or directing upon what evidence it may be done."[39] Hambleton had enclosed his birth certificate with his application, but Clayton had not found it acceptable as "evidence" of his citizenship. The *Boston Daily Atlas* made plain what Clayton had been unwilling to admit publicly: "Now if a person in his application for a passport states that he is black, or there is evidence of it ... a Secretary of State must necessarily refuse to grant it, for the legal reason, that a colored person is not considered a *citizen of the United States*."[40] The *Liberator* saw the denial of passports by the government as an act of disaffiliation that sought to deterritorialize free blacks from the nation. It condemned Clayton for declaring "with all the formality of a State paper, under the hand and seal of the Secretary of State, that the colored race ... are outcasts upon the face of the earth—that the Government under which they live has no care or concern for them—that in foreign lands they are not to invoke its aid, or appeal to its power for protection."[41]

Critics derided Clayton for strategically ignoring certain precedents, given that the State Department had in fact issued passports to free blacks on past occasions.[42] At the personal request of an influential Philadelphian, Secretary Louis McLane had issued passports to Robert Purvis and his wife (a daughter of celebrated sailmaker James Forten) for travel to Europe in 1834.[43] A number of antislavery publications cited these passports as evidence that the federal government recognized free blacks as "citizens of the United States" well before the Hambleton case broke newspaper headlines.[44] Purvis later offered an account of these events at a Philadelphia public meeting called to "consider the atrocious decision of the Supreme Court in the Dred Scott case, and other outrages to which the colored people are subjected under the Constitution of the United States."[45] Purvis had "applied to the Secretary of State for a passport, and an informal ticket of leave sort of paper was sent to him in return. He showed this to Mr. Robert[s] Vaux, ... who was so indignant that he wrote to Washington on the subject, and as the result, a formal passport, giving him the protection of the Government, as a citizen of the United States, was sent to him."[46] To many abolitionists, the passports granted to the Purvises in 1834 constituted a precedent that Clayton simply chose to ignore.[47] Clayton responded defensively to these charges, claiming that Purvis had been granted a passport but not "as a colored man."[48]

Clayton's defensive redefinition of Purvis's identity reveals the racial codifications underpinning national citizenship. "Colored" becomes the basis of exclusion not only from U.S. citizenship but from the social realms of respectability, gentility, and prosperity. According to Clayton's incongruous logic, the light-skinned Purvis was of such "scarcely perceptible African descent" that he was not disbarred—as was the general rule—from the rights of citizenship. Clayton sought to reshape Purvis's racial identity into an exception, in his words, to "accord . . . with the rule."[49] "What does this language mean?" asked one confounded newspaper: "Is it the prerogative of the Secretary of State, to consider persons negro or not, at his pleasure?"[50]

Clayton offered to continue granting protections "to persons of color, which would be equally efficient for all ordinary and useful purposes," but the unofficial recognition extended by these protections only served to accentuate the liminal status of free blacks in the U.S. polity. It constituted what legal scholar Devon Carbado terms the historical "inclusive exclusion" of black subjects, who were positioned "both inside and outside America's national imagination—as a matter of law, politics, and social life."[51] Critics observed that these certificates of protection "would not have the virtue of a passport, nor be any protection to them on the Continent of Europe."[52] Clayton's conciliatory gesture reveals the troubling mechanisms of inclusive exclusion at work in the redefinition of free blacks as Americans by birth but without the substantive rights and social privileges accorded to national citizens. Although the State Department acknowledged figures such as Douglass, Sarah Parker Remond, and William Wells Brown as Americans, it withheld the passports that signified their status as citizens. Free blacks found themselves ensnarled in the workings of inclusive exclusion as the State Department transformed them into "undocumented" travelers. The repeated crises found in the disputes over passports stem from this fundamental ambivalence of a black American identity forced to perform endlessly its racial liminality to the nation-state. Indeed, Orlando Patterson summarizes this mechanism of inclusive exclusion in the slave's "social death": the slave's natal alienation—the ritual processes by which he or she was incorporated within a given community as an internal outsider—threatened the community's social order, even as the slave symbolically sustained the stability of its social system.[53] Consequently, black Americans, in not belonging, emphasized the significance of belonging.[54]

Countering Clayton's "dictum," the *National Era* couched its defense of free black citizenship in the language of natural rights, citing Kent's *Commentaries on American Law*: "If a slave born in the United States be manumitted or otherwise lawfully discharged from bondage, or if a black man be born in the United States and born free, he becomes thenceforward a citizen, but under such disabilities as the laws of the States respectively may deem it expedient to prescribe to free persons of color."[55] Although the sovereign states possessed the authority to delimit the privileges of black birthright citizenship within their respective bounds, freeborn blacks were unequivocally "*Citizens* under our constitution and laws."[56] Northern critics argued that the disabilities that local laws levied on free blacks did not deprive them of the citizenship of the given state, with the right, like any state citizen, to secure a U.S. passport.[57] These critics insisted on the primacy of state citizenship, with federal citizenship deriving from it. The *Natchez Semi-Weekly Courier* summed up this position: "some of the States acknowledge the negro as a citizen, and that as such, he is entitled to the recognition of the Federal Government."[58]

Abolitionist print culture denounced Clayton's "law of passports" as a sentence of outlawry on all free black Americans who were citizens of northern states. Banished or exiled from nation, the outlaw existed outside the protection of the law.[59] The language of legal abandonment pervaded newspapers such as the *National Era*: "The colored man is not only insulted and wronged at home, and in half the Union is utterly defenceless, but if he would leave this cruel country he must go abroad as an outlaw. . . . he is abandoned by this great Government to the mercy of his outragers."[60] Black Americans were thus placed beyond the protection of the nation in which they were born. Black protests marshaled a powerful language of nativism to counter this practice of national disaffiliation. Black radical Martin Delany, for example, powerfully affirmed, "We are Americans, having a birthright citizenship—natural claims upon the country—claims common to all others of our fellow citizens—natural rights, which may . . . be obstructed, but never can be annulled."[61] The condemnation of this theft of nativity and birthright recontextualizes within a larger national frame the claims of kinship that animated the interstate controversies over traveling slaves. The *National Era* demanded, "We ask again, by what authority the Secretary of State denied to a respectable, native born American citizen the protection which he asks, to enable him to visit other nations unmolested?"[62] Black abolitionists and reformers insisted on their birth in and kinship with the nation to counter this "sentiment of alienism" directed against them.[63] These critics argued that Hambleton was "a native American"—indeed, a native son—with "a right to the protection of the American flag."[64]

Douglass sought to recast the racial coordinates of national belonging by distinguishing black "natives" from aliens and foreigners. In 1790, Congress limited naturalization to "any alien, being a white person," and Douglass reelaborated this exclusionary racial logic as an expression of the essential *nativism* of black Americans: "We believe the Government recognizes the existence of but two classes of population, natives, or citizens, and aliens."[65] For Douglass, nativity, or birth within the nation, was the grounds for citizenship according to the English common law doctrine of *jus soli*, or birthright citizenship: "Colored men, born on the soil, cannot be aliens; of course not. They cannot therefore, be *naturalized*. Who ever heard of a colored American being naturalized in the United States? This government naturalizes *foreigners* only. We must then be CITIZENS. Our white fellow citizens may withhold our right, but they cannot annihilate it."[66] According to Douglass's dissident counterlogic, blacks must be citizens since they could not be naturalized as foreigners. He sought publicly to illuminate the illogic of *neither* citizen *nor* alien that was operative in Clayton's "law of passports," which made "color an excuse for denying the protection of citizenship to men born on her soil."[67] Clayton's willingness to extend informal "protections" to black Americans indicated that the federal government did not define them as *aliens*, even as it refused them passports as *citizens*. Clayton stopped short of declaring blacks as foreign to the nation, but he made black American identity into the basis of exclusion from the political rights of national citizenship. These public disputes thus rehearsed what W.E.B. Du Bois later theorized as double-consciousness or the unresolvable twoness of being both "an American" and "a Negro."[68]

Clayton's "law of passports," like the transnational protests over the Negro Seamen Acts in coastal slave states, pried apart the modern fiction of nativity and nationality as it asked how black life was to be inscribed within the social order.[69] Disputes over Hambleton's passport application anticipated the questions about black citizenship that persisted through the following decade until the Taney Court's judgment in *Dred Scott v. Sandford*. The Fourteenth Amendment later redefined citizenship to overturn *Dred Scott* and encode the criteria of birth or naturalization in the nation, regardless of race: "All persons *born* or naturalized in the United States are citizens of the United States and of the State wherein they reside" (emphasis added). The nationalization of citizenship in the Fourteenth Amendment addressed in large part the conflicts raised in these black passport cases as it redefined the primacy of federal over state citizenship: "No State shall make or enforce any law which shall abridge the privileges or immunities of citizens of the United States."

The State Department's racial customs and precedents directly affected prominent black abolitionists in the course of their transatlantic antislavery campaigning. William Wells Brown had applied for a passport to travel to Europe the same summer as Hambleton: "I applied to the Secretary of State, the Hon. John M. Clayton, for a passport. I received no reply."[70] The appearance of Clayton's letter in antislavery newsprint served as Brown's notification of refusal: "[it] told me too plainly that I could receive no protection from the United States government."[71] The American Peace Society selected Brown as its delegate to the international conference in Paris, with hopes that this "talented man of colour" would help stem the progress of the American Colonization Society's imperialist campaign to resettle free blacks in Liberia.[72] Refused a passport, Brown was supplied with informal "traveling papers," commending him to antislavery sympathizers "wherever he may travel."[73] He was not the first black abolitionist forced to rely on his "sable complexion" as "a *prima facie* passport to the sympathy and friendship of the fr[i]ends of the slave."[74] Abolitionist Samuel Ringgold Ward also left U.S. shores for an antislavery tour of Great Britain with only his "endeared and untarnished name" as his passport.[75]

The telling distinction between black servants of white travelers and free black travelers rankled Brown as he was brought face-to-face with Clayton's "law of passports" on the transatlantic passage to Britain. Among the passengers, Brown took note of "a Louisiana slaveholder, who had been appointed by our Democratic government as Consul to Naples, and who was on his way out to occupy his post."[76] Brown recalled, "This Judge Chinn had with him a free colored man as servant, and I was somewhat anxious to know what kind of protection he was to receive in travelling in this country. . . . upon inquiring of this servant, he showed me his passport, which proved to be nothing less than a regular passport from the hand of the Secretary of State."[77] Minister Thomas Withers Chinn had elected to engage the services of a free black rather than risk his human property in Europe, where slave laws did not hold sway. Denied a similar passport, Brown saw the overlapping social and political dimensions of black disaffiliation as an outgrowth and "badge of slavery": "This proves conclusively that if a colored person wishes the protection of the U. States Government in going into any foreign country, he must not think of going in any other capacity than that of a boot-black. Wherever the colored man goes, he must carry with him the badge of slavery to receive the protection of the Americans."[78]

The *North Star* reprinted Brown's account to exemplify the paradox of this U.S. legal culture of travel: "A colored man who travels for the benefit of a white man, will have thrown over him the shield and panoply of the United States; but, if he travels for his own profit or pleasure, he forfeits all the immunities of an American citizen."[79] The State Department withheld its protection from free blacks who acted on their will to travel abroad but granted it to those who traveled as subordinates to white masters. Clayton's distinction recalls the peculiar kinds of legal logic found in the litigation over traveling slaves discussed in earlier chapters. Unlike fugitive slaves who acted on their will to escape, northern courts freed slave attendants such as Med, Anson, and Catharine Linda precisely because they had been subordinated to a white master's will to travel. The U.S. State Department thus distinguished between legitimate (will-less) and illegitimate (willful) forms of *free* black travel abroad as it sought to delimit citizenship and enforce the racial subordination found in slave law.

Brown's encounter with Minister Chinn's black servant became a part of his rhetorical repertoire on the antislavery platform he shared with William and Ellen Craft over a "sojourn of five years in Europe."[80] The passage of the 1850 Fugitive Slave Act made Brown vulnerable to reenslavement upon return to American soil and transformed his European engagement into an indefinite exile abroad.[81] His writings express this quandary of disaffiliation: geographic distance heightens his sense of American identity even as slavery's federal sanction forced him to flee as both a fugitive and "outlaw" to the nation. While abroad, he claimed the distinction of producing the first "history of travels" written by a "Fugitive Slave" with the publication of *Three Years in Europe* (1852), which was republished in the United States as *The American Fugitive in Europe* (1855). The final pages of Brown's travelogue discuss this theft of nativity and American birthright as the "legitimate offspring" of slavery and "Negrophobia."[82]

With feelings akin to—but not quite of—sorrow, Brown is unable to mourn the loss of a home that does not recognize his claims on it: "Whatever may be the fault of the government under which we live, and no matter how oppressive her laws may appear, yet we leave our native land (if such it be) with feelings akin to sorrow" (*AF*, 96). His claim to a "native land" must be conditioned by the resigned parenthetical qualification "if such it be." Rather than succumb to the dehumanizing logic of chattel slavery in self-purchase, Brown remained in British exile, far from his "dear ones left behind," including his daughters Josephine and Clarissa, who eventually joined him in London in 1851.[83] With no hope of safe return, Brown eventually rethought his decision and allowed British philanthropy to "ransom" him—as Douglass was—from American bondage. Brown returned in 1854 with the political intention of making the United States "his permanent home," but he remained ambivalent about his "native country," where birth heralded his entry into the social death of slavery.[84] In a letter to Garrison on the eve of his departure, Brown wrote, "it is with a palpitating heart that I look forward to the day when I must bid farewell to a country that seems like home."[85] Britain had finally extended to Brown the recognition denied in the United States; the U.S. minister to the Court of St. James had granted him a passport certifying him as "a citizen of the United States."[86]

With passport and manumission papers in hand, Brown compared the respectful treatment he received while a *foreigner* in "monarchical Europe" with the welcome he received in the United States: "I had enjoyed the rights allowed to all foreigners in the countries through which I passed; but on returning to my NATIVE LAND the influence of slavery meets me the first day that I am in the country" (*AF*, 226). Denied passage on a segregated "third-rate American omnibus" in Philadelphia, Brown protested, "[the] fact of my being an American by birth could not be denied; that I had read and understood the constitution and laws . . . but I was colored, and that was enough" (*AF*, 226–27). This rude reception after five years abroad plunged him back into the racial liminality of black American identity. His "colored" skin had indeed become "a *prima facie* passport" to his Americanness (as the "fact" of his "being an American by birth could not be denied"), yet it too served as the basis for his civic exclusion ("but I was colored, and that was enough"). Thus, the oppressive mechanisms of Americanization and racialization—its inclusive exclusion—welcomed Brown back to the "land of [his] nativity . . . which will welcome fugitives from other countries, and drive its own into exile" (*AF*, 226–27).

Under the administration of President Franklin Pierce, the State Department began officially to consolidate its racial policy against free blacks when it gave public expression to the denationalization of black citizens shortly after *Dred Scott v. Sandford* came to trial but before the Taney Court delivered its controversial ruling.[87] Secretary of State William Marcy rejected the passport applications of eleven black members of a minstrel troupe about to embark on a professional tour of Europe. He insisted that the State Department "could not certify that such persons are citizens of the United States," since the affidavits accompanying the passport requests identified the men as "Negroes."[88] "Whiteness" was "the normative identity for citizenship," and the State Department patrolled this racial pathway to citizenship.[89] The State Department recognized free blacks in powerfully ambivalent ways, as it upheld a "duty to protect" them "if wronged by a foreign Government" while withholding the document certifying their political inclusion. Another rejected applicant hoped "to go to some foreign country, and through the assistance of friends, claim its protection, or else, through their assistance, get permission to travel as an American outlaw!"[90] Marcy's announcement precipitated another series of black American passport cases—this time disputed on British soil—during the winter of 1859, exactly one decade after Hambleton's case.

In Secretary Marcy's final months of office, he directed all foreign ministers, particularly the legation in Britain, to discontinue issuing passports or visas to black Americans while abroad. During a tour of Great Britain as a lecturer for the American Anti-Slavery Society, Sarah Parker Remond galvanized British protest of this new international policy when the American embassy in London refused to visa her American passport for Paris. She had previously obtained the passport from the U.S. State Department by withholding direct mention of her "complexion" on the application.[91] Secretary Lewis Cass, who succeeded Marcy, further outraged transatlantic abolitionists when he publicly insisted, "a passport being a certificate of citizenship, has never since the foundation of the Government, been granted to persons of color. No change in this respect had taken place in consequence of the decision of the Dred Scott case."[92] His letter circulated widely in transatlantic print culture, and abolitionists found themselves repeating the arguments of a decade past: "Passports *have* been granted to persons of color by the Department of State and by our Ministers at the Court of St. James."[93] They took it upon themselves publicly to refresh "Mr. Cass's official memory," convinced as they were nearly a decade earlier in the Hambleton case that "[n]othing but strong public indignation has ever been able to make an impression on some of our public functionaries, where any right of colored men has been asserted, or any wrong resisted."[94]

Remond sent an account of her rude reception at the American embassy to the London papers as an example of "American colorphobia" on British soil: "Upon my asking to have my passport visaed at the American embassy, the person in the office refused to affix the visa on the ground that I am a person of color."[95] Remond had a rather heated exchange with

U.S. Minister George Dallas: "The Secretary said I was not a citizen of the United States, and he could not sign it. I informed him that I was a citizen of Salem in Massachusetts, and Massachusetts acknowledged my citizenship—and the fact of my having the passport was a proof of my citizenship. The Secretary still refused to sign it, and said I ought to be satisfied with his refusal."[96] When Remond insisted on her rights as an American citizen, the nettled functionary "threatened to have her put out of the door."[97] Remond entreated her British readers to "judge what the spirit of a country is that will allow such treatment to its citizens, the spirit which enslaves four million of men and women, and insults the free colored population of the United States?"[98] In the manner of Ottobah Cugoano, Remond stressed the inadequacy of language to give expression to "the mental suffering we are obliged to bear because we happen to have a dark complexion. No language can give one an idea of the spirit of prejudice which exists in the States."[99] Dallas's assistant secretary explained in no uncertain terms that Remond did not have "the indispensable qualifications for an American passport—that of the 'United States citizenship'" and insisted that "it is manifestly an impossibility by law that it should exist" after *Dred Scott*.[100]

This perceived affront to the winsome "free born American lady of color" outraged British newspapers, which happily played the gallant to Remond's injured womanhood.[101] The *New York Herald* reported, "A great noise has been made in England by the refusal of the American Minister in London to *visé* a passport issued to a young woman of color by Mr. Cass."[102] British abolitionists viewed Remond's uncivil treatment as the encroachment of U.S. slavery and its racial proscriptions on free British soil, with Edinburgh's *Scottish Press* saying that the American "antipathy to color is so deep-seated that even in free England it denies the ordinary courtesies of civilized life to ladies ... who are deemed no unworthy associates of the *elite* of our female nobility."[103] Such accounts of "American colorphobia"—like those stories of black British mariners seized in U.S. coastal states—served to reaffirm the cultural distinctiveness of British national identity in its "devotion to liberty and the rule of law."[104]

Dallas had held a rather lenient policy toward issuing passports to black Americans in Britain until the State Department began to make greater efforts to formalize its practice of denying free blacks the privileges of citizenship at home and abroad. He had acted under Secretary Marcy's new instructions: "Since the incoming of the Buchanan Administration, Mr. Dallas, our Minister to London, has been notified *not* to issue any more such passports to colored citizens of the United States."[105] The Passport Act of 1856 codified Secretary Marcy's redefinition of normative white citizenship, with punitive consequences for those functionaries who disobeyed its directives. It made the issuance of passports to noncitizens a penal offense if committed by a consular officer.[106]

The Passport Act of 1856 and the Taney Court ruling in *Dred Scott v. Sandford* lent the belated sanction of government and law to a "customary" practice that had profound legal, social, and political consequences for black life in the United States. Chief Justice Taney even made reference to "the conduct of the Executive Department of the Government" in refusing passports to free blacks as a precedent for his ruling in *Dred Scott*.[107] The exclusion of blacks from the national polity (if not American identity) both preceded and was secured in law. Custom existed outside the scope of law, but the denationalization of black citizenship in *Dred Scott* formalized the customary as law (just as Taney's ruling used this racial custom as a precedent for law). The elliptical temporality of this mechanism of inclusive exclusion confounded those abolitionists and critics who represented, incorrectly, the State Department's passport policy as an outgrowth of *Dred Scott*. Editorials in prominent abolitionist periodicals, including the *Liberator* and *New Era*, found it easier to reposition these passport regulations squarely within the legal framework of *Dred Scott*. Indeed, a number of critics assessed the most objectionable consequence of *Dred Scott* to be its punitive regulation of free black travel abroad: "the most disgraceful feature of the Dred Scott decision, is that which takes away from American citizens, travelling in foreign countries, the shield of natural protection which it should be our pride and glory always to extend over the humblest of our citizens, without regard to locality, condition or color."[108] This anachronism made past practice consistent with current law by eliding the State Department's long history of denationalizing black citizenship, which had existed outside legal sanction.

The much-publicized rejection of Remond's visa on the basis of her "dark complexion" was followed by Minister Dallas's rejection of a similar passport for Frederick Douglass. The "danger of arrest on the ground of complicity with" John Brown and the fear that he "might be kidnapped and taken to Virginia," given heightened passions after the raid on Harper's Ferry, compelled Douglass to break off his lecture tour in Canada and flee to Britain.[109] Douglass was forced again to seek refuge from U.S. slavery on British soil: "England had given me shelter and protection when the slave-hounds were on my track fourteen years before, and her gates were still open to me now that I was pursued in the name of Virginia justice"

(*LT*, 761). Little seemed to have changed in the intervening years between his arrival onto British soil as a fugitive slave in 1845 and his unexpected return in 1859 as a freeman, pursued yet again by slave law in another guise. Like Remond, Douglass soon discovered that even *free* British soil was not free from those racial proscriptions he had faced on U.S. soil: "While in England, wishing to visit France, I wrote to Mr. George M. Dallas, the American minister at the British court, to obtain a passport," but "true to the traditions of the Democratic party, true to the slaveholding policy of his country, true to the decision of the United States Supreme Court . . . the Democratic American minister, refused to grant me a passport, on the ground that I was not a citizen of the United States" (*LT*, 762).

Like Brown, Douglass recast the trope of free travel in his writings to interrogate the racial limits of freedom and citizenship in the United States. The withholding of the passport constituted a profound denial, both political and symbolic, that preoccupied Douglass well into his later life. He returned repeatedly to this incident, and his voluminous *Life and Times* offers two separate accounts of it. The second account occurs in his extended recollection of his long-deferred tour of the European continent with his second wife, Helen Pitts, as an enfranchised American citizen in 1886. Dallas's rejection lent further stimulus to Douglass's "strange dreams of travel": "In view of my disappointment and the repulse I met with at the hands of this American minister, my gratification was all the more intense" (*LT*, 1013–14).[110] The U.S. minister impeded but could not deny Douglass's will to travel: "He refused to give me a passport on the ground that I was not and could not be an American citizen. This man is now dead and generally forgotten, as I shall be; but I have lived to see myself everywhere recognized as an American citizen" (*LT*, 1014). Travel abroad as an "American citizen" sharpened Douglass's sense of liberty, and it figuratively marks the distance between slavery and the era of emancipation. He ends the chapter on his travels abroad with the reflection, "after my life of hardships in slavery and of conflict with race and color prejudice and proscription at home, there was left to me a space in life when I could and did walk the world unquestioned, a man among men" (*LT*, 1017). For Douglass, the freedom of travel is the bodily practice of America's egalitarian ideal.

Douglass and Remond eventually appealed to European governments to secure the political recognition that their own country refused to provide them, as the American Anti-Slavery Society noted: "Miss Remond subsequently obtained a passport from the British Foreign Secretary, who had not learned that a shade of the complexion is a forfeiture of human rights."[111] Douglass was undeterred when his passport to France was refused, and he "addressed a note to the French minister in London asking for a permit to visit France, and that paper came without delay" (*LT,* 762).[112] Other black Americans in Britain seeking a passport to the continent were also forced to apply to the French consul, who, "when the circumstances were explained [in a subsequent case], cheerfully granted a passport, and said, moreover, that he had written . . . to his own government, asking for power to deal with this special class of cases."[113] One abolitionist lawyer wryly remarked, "Thus, from French Imperialism the colored man obtains those rights which are insultingly denied him by Republican American."[114] These transatlantic disputes over the issuance of black American passports were thus enlisted in nation-building projects that sought to further secure the boundaries of European cultural identity in the wake of abolition and emancipation in the Caribbean.

"Epluribus Unum"

One final black passport case made newspaper headlines as the nation tottered on the precipice of Civil War. Numerous sectional newspapers touted Henry Highland Garnet's passport as marking the end of slavery and the beginning of a new era of egalitarian freedom (see figure 5.1). The *Christian Recorder* announced with playful dryness Garnet's 1861 departure for England to promote the African Civilization Society: "The Rev. H.H. Garnet, (colored,) left New York a few days ago, for Europe, with a regular passport of citizenship, signed by W.H. Seward, Secretary of State. This fact must fill Judge Taney with horror."[115] While some newspapers saw Garnet's application as "a good case to test the point whether a man is necessarily an outlaw on account of color," others simply lauded Seward for reversing "the infamous doctrine of Judge Taney touching the alien condition of free negroes in the United States, and the infamous refusal of the Buchanan Administration to grant to a free negro, going abroad, the protection guaranteed by the Government to its citizens in foreign countries."[116] The material and symbolic meaning of Garnet's passport was not lost on abolitionists and northern reformers as they plunged into "the war for the Union." One newspaper extolled, "Thus, under the great seal of the United States a black man, of unadulterated negro blood, is declared before the civilized world to be entitled to the protection of the Government, as a citizen."[117] After Lincoln's Emancipation Proclamation, the *New York Observer* marked the nation's progress in terms of this "right" to free black travel abroad: "The black man can now take out a passport and travel to the uttermost part of the earth protected by the broad aegis of the Government. All honor to Secretary Seward, who was the first to recognize this right."[118] The *Liberator* also celebrated the "Anti-Slavery Measures" of the Thirty-seventh and Thirty-eighth Congresses with reference to this right: "The colored man now travels the world over, bearing the passport of Secretary Seward that he is citizen of the United States."[119] As Saidiya Hartman notes, "the sheer capacity to move . . . provided the most palpable evidence of freedom" for former bondsmen and women, as the pass system of the former order gave way.[120]

James P. Thomas, one of Cyprian Clamorgan's "colored aristocrats," also marked this new epoch of freedom with the "new thing" of free black travel. With legislated freedom, he recalls in the manuscript of his unpublished autobiography, "the Ebony hued individual was allowed to go and come without disturbance. A new thing, or the first time in American history" (*FTS*, 163). Thomas penned these recollections shortly before his death in 1913, after a long life as a successful St. Louis entrepreneur.[121] The geopolitics of freedom and slavery had shaped his life in the same manner as it did for the many others examined in this book. His elder brother had turned fugitive and fled north at the promptings of their enslaved mother, Sally, who then "carefully laid away her earnings" to purchase her youngest son (*FTS*, 30). Like Polly Crocket, Sally urged her child to seek his freedom in the North even though his doing so entailed their permanent separation. Thomas and his brother John Rapier proceeded on more lawful routes to freedom, securing their manumission and living out the remainder of their lives in southern slave states.

Thomas seized on his newfound freedom to travel as the most palpable evidence of his enfranchisement in the reunified nation-state. Like Douglass's *Life and Times*, Thomas's autobiographical recollections offer an extended meditation on the changing meaning of black travel in the period immediately after legislated freedom. Thomas recalls his momentous decision to apply for a passport simply to test his rights as a U.S. citizen: "after all had been made free and citizens, it occurred to me that I would like to see a passport with my name on it and perhaps I might use it" (*FTS*, 180).[122] The passport extended to the then forty-five-year-old Thomas an American citizenship that took the form of a material object to be possessed.[123] He wanted to *own*, in a liberal sense, his passport and the individual freedom and rights it represented: "At all events, I could keep it. So I asked for it

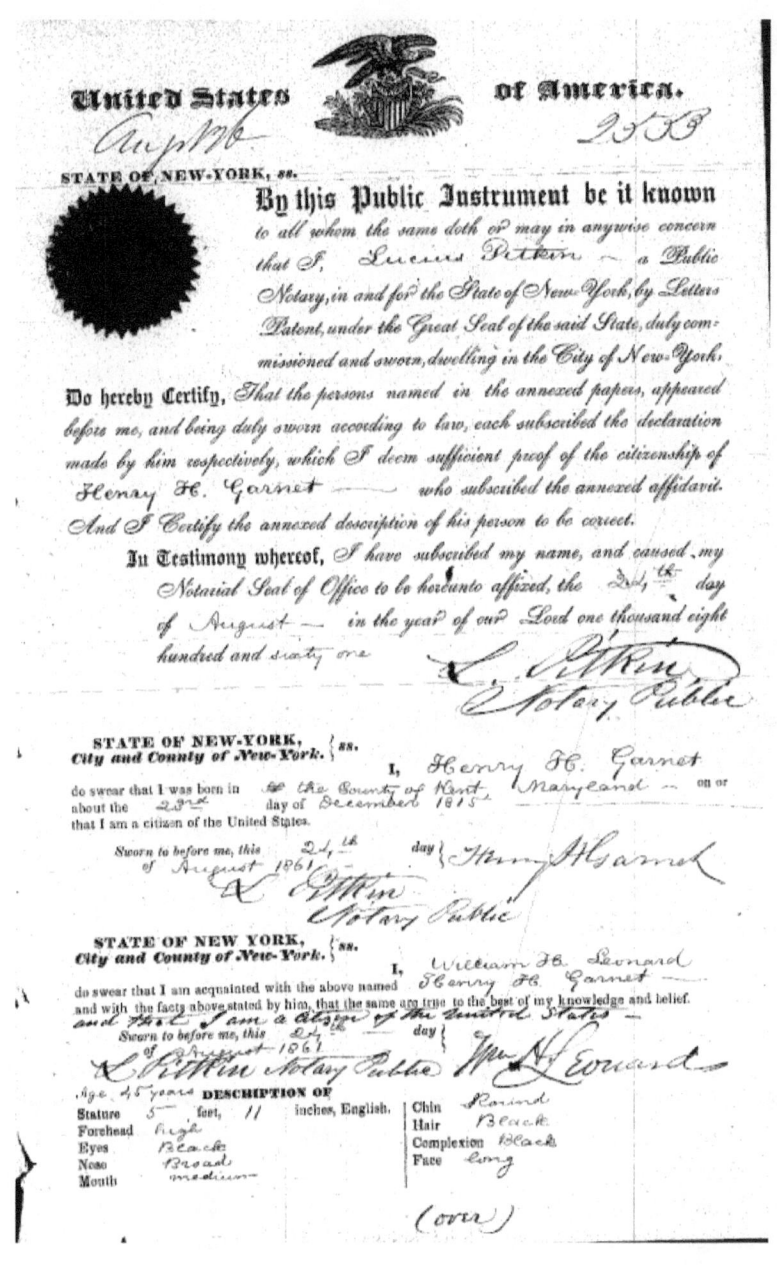

Fig. C.1. Passport application of Henry Highland Garnet, August 24, 1861, Passport Number 2553 (National Archives Microfilm Publication M1372, roll 98, Passport Applications, 1795–1905, June 1–July 20, 1861, National Archives Building, Washington, DC)

and received it. I placed it in my pocket, took it home, and there to take a look at it" (*FTS*, 180). Thomas recalls in detail the receipt of this concrete manifestation of the national citizenship that the State Department had so long denied him and others: "There was a piece of parchment about the size of a medium sized napkin. Spread over the face of it was the great American Eagle . . . a high soaring fellow, with a penetrating eye scanning the horison [*sic*], with his neck gently or gracefully curved to the left, A streamer in his beak. On it read Epluribus Unum" (*FTS*, 180). The "piece of parchment" documented black civic inclusion within the American polity and guaranteed Thomas "the right to travel where he chose and under the protection of the American flag" (*FTS*, 180). As a free black in a slave state, Thomas had faced severe restrictions on his freedom of movement: "Prior to 1861 I could not have crossed the Mississippi river from St. Louis to the Illinois shore on the ferry boat without two or three reliable citizens having made the ferry company feel they were taking no risk in carrying me into a free state" (*FTS*, 180). The passport's promise of free, self-directed travel marked the "great change that time had wrought" in the passage from slavery to freedom (*FTS*, 180).

Thomas did indeed embrace his newfound "right to travel where he choose" and embarked on an European tour that took him to thirty-two cities and six countries during the summer of 1873. Like Douglass, Thomas retraced the popular routes of the traditional "Grand Tour," although his joyful recollections of travels past were cut short by return to U.S. soil, and his manuscript ends with a caution: "Every colored man may or ought to know, although he had been eating and riding with Americans and treated as a companion, as the vessel approaches American soil, all that comes to an end. Each is supposed to take his regular place. Custom, which has a heap to say, has so ordered it" (*FTS*, 195). "Custom" too had long existed as the watchword for the State Department's decades-long refusal to issue passports to free black northern citizens.[124] Thomas uttered this warning well after the legislated end of racial slavery, yet it echoes the sentiments that Harriet Jacobs voiced on sighting the U.S. shoreline after ten months of "pure, unadulterated freedom" on British soil: "from the distance spectres seemed to rise up on the shores of the United States. It is a sad feeling to be afraid of one's native country."[125]

Thomas's circumspection provides an important counterweight to the ease with which U.S. newspapers had constructed the figure of the passport-carrying black citizen abroad as an emblem of national advancement and the triumph of egalitarian ideals over slave power. His warning brings to mind the racial "customs" that he had endured in the antebellum North as the legally emancipated servant of a southern planter. Like the freedom suits of Med and Anson, Thomas's recollections offer a far more qualified understanding of northern freedom. Thomas was eager to take in the sights and sounds of New York City, but he was advised not to go: "that I wouldn't be admitted unless I was with my boss or had one of his children. Either would pass me. I said I would like to ride up town in an Omnibus. I was told they wouldn't carry me unless I was with a white person or child" (*FTS*, 123). Such northern customs reinforced the same racial distinction that had organized Secretary Clayton's "law of passports" and the freedom suits brought by traveling slaves. Black mobility was permissible only when subordinated to white authority. Douglass's experience of segregated New England railways cars was an eerie harbinger of the regime of legalized racial segregation that emerged in the postwar South: "At the same time that they excluded a free colored man from their cars, this same company allowed slaves, in company with their masters and mistresses, to ride unmolested."[126] The law of freedom did not ensure the social equality of blacks who found their way northward. Informal racial proscriptions or "custom" governed the North as powerfully as slave law in the South.

Thomas lived out the remainder of his life in a former slave state and witnessed how quickly the "new thing" of free black movement was again curtailed. The enactment of "sweeping laws regarding labor, property rights, and the administration of criminal laws" throughout the South reinstated slavery in practice if not in name.[127] These former slave states, acting on their right to regulate their populations, sought to circumvent the congressional mandates of the Thirteenth and Fourteenth Amendments, as they further centralized the power once wielded by individual slaveholders in those states.[128] Rather than eliminating slavery outright, the Thirteenth Amendment subordinated it to legal procedure, and southern lawmakers exploited the exception of "permitting involuntary servitude for those convicted of crimes" to resist radical Reconstruction.[129] This form of resistance marked less of a shift from than a continuity with earlier racial state formations such as the prewar Negro Seamen Acts, as black codes in virtually every former slave state undermined the freedom of movement and of contract, which according to Amy Dru Stanley governed the political ideal or "worldview" of liberty in the age of slave emancipation.[130] Among these statutes, punitive vagrancy laws depriving black citizens of their right to free travel again reconstituted what Brown had referred to as the "badge of slavery or servitude."[131]

The 1875 Civil Rights Act—the last congressional effort to secure the civil liberties of African Americans until 1957—sought to ensure the social rights of equal accommodations and services that former slave states continued to withhold from black citizens. The Civil Rights Act addressed the meaning of formal citizenship without social equality: "citizens of every race and color, regardless of any previous condition of servitude . . . shall be entitled to the full and equal enjoyment of the accommodations, advantages, facilities, and privileges of inns, public conveyances on land or water, theaters, and other places of public amusement; subject only to the conditions and limitations established by law" (18 Stat. Part III, 335). Despite its egalitarian efforts to recognize the "equality of all men before the law," the bill was rarely enforced, especially after the withdrawal of federal troops from the South. Although many newspapers applauded its effort to extirpate the "discrimination of race or color in law" that existed "in defiance of the Declaration, the Constitution, and sound policy," the U.S. Supreme Court judged the law unconstitutional in 1883.[132] Douglass saw this decision as "the most flagrant example of . . . national deterioration . . . since the war for the Union" because it authorized legal segregation by race (*LT*, 966). The ensuing struggle for the legal recognition of black civil rights led to the testing of Louisiana's Separate Car Act in the landmark *Plessy v. Ferguson* (1896), which upheld the constitutionality of racial segregation in what became known as the doctrine of "separate but equal." *Plessy* was fought over equal access to the technologies of intrastate railway travel and contested the kind of racialized curtailment of mobility that the transatlantic campaign against the Negro Seamen Act had disputed from the first half of the century. And like the passport cases, the *Plessy* ruling did not insist on the exclusion of blacks from the American polity but, rather, dictated the spatial arrangements of what constituted proper or "customary" relations between the races.

The racial formations encoded in the law in the early part of the century continued to shape postbellum travel and travel culture in surprisingly similar ways.[133] Thomas offered a subtle counterpoint to the progress narratives touted in postwar political discourse, and his recollections of travel interrogate the mechanisms of inclusive exclusion that earlier black abolitionists such as Brown, Douglass, and Remond had experienced firsthand. The right of locomotion as the bodily practice of national citizenship stands out among the many lines of argumentation taken in the disputation of *Plessy*. Justice John Harlan's lone dissent in the case drew on Blackstone's *Commentaries on English Law* (1765): "Personal liberty . . . consists in the power of locomotion, of changing situation, or removing one's person to whatsoever places one's own inclination may direct, without imprisonment or restraint."[134] These racial regulations redefined the individual right to travel as normatively *white* and infringed on the "civil rights as guaranteed by the supreme law of the land" to all citizens regardless of race. The identification of personal liberty with "locomotion," and of restraint with its denial, had been forged in the largely forgotten contexts of slavery and the legal culture of travel examined in this book.[135] The sole exception to the Louisiana statute's rule of racial segregation was to be found in "nurses attending children of the other race."[136] This subordination of black movement to white authority reelaborated the longstanding exception of black servitude, outlined repeatedly in antebellum freedom suits, in a more qualified form. "Slavery, as an institution tolerated by law" may have "disappeared from our country," according to Harlan, but its racial proscriptions continued in other forms. *Plessy v. Ferguson* thus upheld the constitutionality of the state statute providing for "separate but equal accommodations," as it reinforced the racial customs that shaped and continued to unsettle the "Epluribus Unum" of the American polity.

The end of the American Civil War radically reshaped the geopolitics of freedom and slavery, as the "lines"—whether the Mason-Dixon or the parallel 36° 30'—that were once the objects of so much interstate strife and litigation faded into the realm of legal history. Ex-bondsmen and women began the long and often fruitless search for kinfolk lost in slavery, while others such as Lunsford Lane were finally free to return to the southern homes from which they had long been banished. The legislated end of slavery made these freedom suits and the legal questions they posed largely obsolete, although black citizens in the era of emancipation continued to face severe restrictions on their uniquely American "right to free travel." The "color line" policed this freedom of movement in ways that seem tragically continuous with those earlier struggles over traveling slaves, when abolitionists, jurists, slaveholders, slaves, and free blacks had endeavored to fix the volatile and shifting geographies of freedom and slavery. "We are denied the right of locomotion!" Douglass had once cried in protest of the U.S. State Department, and his words continued to serve as a rallying call in the future.[137] The right to free travel continues to be one the most enduring myths of American liberal democracy precisely because this earlier legal history of the antebellum freedom suits and the unlikely travel stories they told have been largely forgotten.

Notes

INTRODUCTION

1. *Augusta (Georgia) Sentinel*, quoted in "Outrage upon Southern Rights," *Liberator* (15 Oct. 1836): 4.
2. James Thomas, *From Tennessee Slave to St. Louis Entrepreneur* (Columbia: University of Missouri Press, 1984), 127.
3. Saidiya V. Hartman, *Scenes of Subjection: Terror, Slavery, and Self-Making in Nineteenth-Century America* (New York: Oxford University Press, 1997), 7.
4. John Hope Franklin, *A Southern Odyssey: Travelers in the Antebellum North* (Baton Rouge: Louisiana State University Press, 1976), 141.
5. Hartman, *Scenes of Subjection*, 7–8.
6. James Kent, *Commentaries on American Law*, ed. George F. Comstock, vol. 2, 11th ed. (Boston: Little, Brown, 1866), 257; emphasis removed.
7. Priscilla Wald, *Constituting Americans: Cultural Identity and Narrative Form* (Durham, NC: Duke University Press, 1995), 1–2.
8. Deak Nabers, *Victory of Law: The Fourteenth Amendment, the Civil War, and American Literature, 1852–1867* (Baltimore: John Hopkins University Press, 2006), 47.
9. For a comparative examination of North and South American freedom suits, see Keila Grinberg, "Freedom Suits and Civil Law in Brazil and the United States," *Slavery and Abolition* 22, no. 3 (2001): 66–82.
10. Ariela J. Gross, *Double Character: Slavery and Mastery in the Antebellum Courtroom* (Princeton, NJ: Princeton University Press, 2000), 3.
11. Kent, *Commentaries on American Law*, 279.
12. *Boyce v. Anderson*, 27 U.S. 150 (1829).
13. See Robert M. Cover, *Justice Accused: Antislavery and the Judicial Process* (New Haven, CT: Yale University Press, 1984).
14. Amy Kaplan, *The Anarchy of Empire in the Making of U.S. Culture* (Cambridge, MA: Harvard University Press, 2002), 212.
15. Frederick Law Olmstead, *The Cotton Kingdom: A Traveller's Observation on Cotton and Slavery in the American Slave States* (New York: Knopf, 1966), 3.
16. See Paul Finkelman, *An Imperfect Union: Slavery, Federalism, and Comity* (Chapel Hill: University of North Carolina Press, 1981).

17. Don E. Fehrenbacher, *The Dred Scott Case: Its Significance in American Law and Politics* (Oxford: Oxford University Press, 1978), 51.

18. "Selections: Seizure of Fugitive Slaves," *Liberator* (22 Feb. 1850): 29.

19. Quoted in Fehrenbacher, *Dred Scott Case*, 61.

20. Mark V. Tushnet, *American Law of Slavery, 1810–1860: Considerations of Humanity and Interest* (Princeton, NJ: Princeton University Press, 1981), 19–20.

21. Stephanie M.H. Camp, *Closer to Freedom: Enslaved Women and Everyday Resistance in the Plantation South* (Chapel Hill: University of North Carolina Press, 2004), 36.

22. Kristin Hoganson, "Garrisonian Abolitionists and the Rhetoric of Gender, 1850–1860," *American Quarterly* 45 (Dec. 1993): 559–61.

23. Intellectual historians such as David Brion Davis, Steven Mintz, and John Stauffer have queried the profound shift in moral vision that enabled the emergence of a powerful Anglo-American abolitionist movement. See, for example, David Brion Davis, *In the Image of God: Religion, Moral Values, and Our Heritage of Slavery* (New Haven, CT: Yale University Press, 2001), 8.

24. Hartman, *Scenes of Subjection*, 10.

25. For a review of the expanding field of "slavery studies" and its relevance to black politics, see Walter Johnson, "OAH State of the Field: Slavery" (paper presented at the annual meeting of the Organization of American Historians, Boston, Massachusetts, March 2004), 25–28. See also Walter Johnson, *Soul by Soul: Life inside the Antebellum Slave Market* (Cambridge, MA: Harvard University Press, 1999); Jennifer Morgan, *Laboring Women: Reproduction and Gender in New World Slavery* (Philadelphia: University of Pennsylvania Press, 2004); Dylan C. Penningroth, *The Claims of Kinfolk: African American Property and Community in the Nineteenth-Century South* (Chapel Hill: University of North Carolina Press, 2003); Gillian Brown, *The Consent of the Governed: The Lockean Legacy in Early American Culture* (Cambridge, MA: Harvard University Press, 2001); Karen Sánchez-Eppler, *Touching Liberty: Abolitionism, Feminism, and the Politics of the Body* (Berkeley: University of California Press, 1993); Hortense J. Spillers, *Black, White, and in Color: Essays on American Literature and Culture* (Chicago: University of Chicago Press, 2003); Cindy Weinstein, *Family, Kinship, and Sympathy in Nineteenth-Century American Literature* (Cambridge: Cambridge University Press, 2004); Amy Kaplan, *The Anarchy of Empire in the Making of U.S. Culture* (Cambridge, MA: Harvard University Press, 2002); David Kazanjian, *The Colonizing Trick: National Culture and Imperial Citizenship in Early America* (Minneapolis: University of Minnesota Press, 2003).

26. Natalie Zacek, "Voices and Silences: The Problem of Slave Testimony in the English West Indian Law Court," *Slavery and Abolition* 24, no. 3 (Dec. 2003): 36.

27. For the politics of legal storytelling, see Richard Delgado, "Storytelling for Oppositionists and Others: A Plea for Narrative," *Michigan Law Review* 87 (Aug. 1989): 2411–41; Richard Delgado, ed., *Critical Race Theory: The Cutting Edge* (Philadelphia: Temple University Press, 1995); Jeannine Marie DeLombard, *Slavery on Trial: Law, Abolitionism, and Print Culture* (Chapel Hill: University of North Carolina Press, 2007), 144–45.

28. Hartman, *Scenes of Subjection*, 6.

29. See Elizabeth Dillon, *The Gender of Freedom: Fictions of Liberalism and the Literary Public Sphere* (Stanford, CA: Stanford University Press, 2004).

30. Hartman, *Scenes of Subjection*, 5.

31. Patricia J. Williams, *Alchemy of Race and Rights: Diary of a Law Professor* (Cambridge, MA: Harvard University Press, 1991), 219.

32. Frances Anne Kemble, *Journal of a Residence on a Georgian Plantation in 1838–1839* (Athens: University of Georgia Press, 1984), 344.

33. Vincent Brown, "Spiritual Terror and Sacred Authority in Jamaican Slave Society," *Slavery and Abolition* 24, no. 1 (April 2003): 24; Kent, *Commentaries on American Law*, 279.

34. "The Missouri Question," *The Panoplist, and Missionary Herald* (Jan. 1820): 15.

35. Frederick Douglass, *My Bondage and My Freedom*, in *Frederick Douglass Autobiographies* (New York: Library of America, 1994), 238.

36. Ibid., 130.

37. Paul Finkelman, *Slavery in the Courtroom: An Annotated Bibliography of American Cases* (Washington, DC: Library of Congress, 1985), 6.

38. Nabers, *Victory of Law*, 51.

39. Elsa Goveia, *Slave Society in the British Leeward Island at the End of the Eighteenth Century* (New Haven, CT: Yale University Press, 1965), 155.

40. *Kauffman v. Oliver*, 10 Pa. 514, Pa. LEXIS 272 (1849).

41. For a comparative reading of the two cases, see T.K. Hunter, "Geographies of Liberty: A Brief Look at Two Cases," in *Prophets of Protest: Reconsidering the History of American Abolitionism*, ed. Timothy Patrick McCarthy and John Stauffer (New York: New Press, 2006), 41–58.

42. David Thomas Konig, "The Long Road to *Dred Scott*: Personhood and the Rule of Law in the Trial Court Records of St. Louis Slave Freedom Suits," *University of Missouri–Kansas City Law Review* 75 (Fall 2006): 61.

43. Ibid.

44. "Scott's Case," *Liberator* (26 Dec. 1856): 207.

45. DeLombard, *Slavery on Trial*, 25.

46. "Case of Kidnapping a British Subject, and His Retention in Slavery for Thirteen Years," *Friends' Review* (29 May 1852): 589.

47. "Massachusetts and South Carolina," *New Englander* (Apr. 1846): 195.

48. Camp, *Closer to Freedom*, 13, 29.

49. See Amy Dru Stanley, *From Bondage to Contract: Wage Labor, Marriage, and the Market in the Age of Slave Emancipation* (Cambridge: Cambridge University Press, 1998).

50. Douglass, *My Bondage and My Freedom*, 264–65.

CHAPTER 1

1. *Report of the Committee of the Society for the Mitigation and Gradual Abolition of Slavery throughout the British Dominions* (London: Richard Tayler, 1824), 32.

2. Charles Edward Herbert Orpen, "The Principles, Plans, and Objects, of 'The Hibernian

Negro's Friend Society," Contrasted with Those of the Previously Existing 'Anti-Slavery' Societies" (Ireland: n.p., 1831), 10.

3. Elizabeth Heyrick, *Immediate, Not Gradual Abolition; or, An Inquiry into the Shortest, Safest, and Most Effectual Means of Getting Rid of West Indian Slavery* (London: J. Hatchard, 1824), 3.

4. David Scott, *Conscripts of Modernity: The Tragedy of Colonial Enlightenment* (Durham, NC: Duke University Press, 2004), 1.

5. "Anti-Slavery Society," *Christian Observer, Conducted by Members of the Established Church* (1826): 805.

6. *Report of the Committee*, 99.

7. Orpen, "Principles, Plans, and Objects," 9.

8. The case was erroneously entitled *Somerset v. Stewart* even though Somerset was the defendant and Stewart the plaintiff according to the rules governing the return of the writ of habeas corpus. F.O. Shyllon, *Black Slaves in Britain* (London: Oxford University Press, 1974), 114.

9. Thomas Clarkson, *The History of the Rise, Progress, and Accomplishment of the Abolition of the African Slave-Trade by the British Parliament*, vol. 1 (London: R. Taylor, 1808), 67.

10. Orpen, "Principles, Plans, and Objects," 10; James Walvin, "The Public Campaign in England against Slavery, 1787–1834," in *The Abolition of the Atlantic Slave Trade: Origins and Effects in Europe, Africa, and the Americas*, ed. David Eltis and James Walvin (Madison: University of Wisconsin Press, 1981), 63.

11. Christopher Leslie Brown, *Moral Capital: Foundations of British Abolitionism* (Chapel Hill: University of North Carolina Press, 2006), 5.

12. *Report of the Committee*, 69–70.

13. Brown, *Moral Capital*, 8.

14. *Report of the Committee*, 78.

15. Ibid., 29.

16. Martin R. Delany, *Blake; or, The Huts of America* (Boston: Beacon, 1970), 263.

17. James Walvin, *Black Ivory: A History of British Slavery* (Washington, DC: Howard University Press, 1994), 11–12.

18. Brown, *Moral Capital*, 92.

19. Edward Long, *Candid Reflections upon the Judgement Lately Awarded by the Court of King's Bench in Westminster-Hall on What Is Commonly Called the Negro-Cause* (London: T. Lowndes, 1772), 46.

20. Elsa Goveia, *Slave Society in the British Leeward Island at the End of the Eighteenth Century* (New Haven, CT: Yale University Press, 1965), 155.

21. Seymour Drescher, *Capitalism and Antislavery: British Mobilization in Comparative Perspective* (New York: Oxford University Press, 1987), 31.

22. Ibid., 25.

23. Orpen, "Principles, Plans, and Objects," 9.

24. James Williams, *A Narrative of Events, Since the First of August, 1834, by James Williams, an Apprenticed Labourer in Jamaica*, ed. Diana Paton (Durham, NC: Duke University

Press, 2001), 19; further references to *Narrative of Events* are to this edition and are cited parenthetically in the text as *NE*.

25. Frederick Cooper, Thomas C. Holt, and Rebecca J. Scott, introduction to *Beyond Slavery: Explorations of Race, Labor, and Citizenship in Postemancipation Societies*, ed. Frederick Cooper, Thomas C. Holt, and Rebecca J. Scott (Chapel Hill: University of North Carolina Press, 2000), 3.

26. Srividhya Swaminathan, "Developing the West Indian Proslavery Position after the *Somerset* Decision," *Slavery and Abolition* 24, no. 3 (Dec. 2003): 48.

27. John Fielding, *Extracts from Such of the Penal Laws, as Particularly Relate to the Good Order of This Metropolis* (London: A. Millar, 1762), 144–45.

28. James Oldham, "New Light on Mansfield and Slavery," *Journal of British Studies* 27 (Jan. 1988): 50.

29. Prince Hoare, *Memoirs of Granville Sharp, Esq. Composed from His Own Manuscripts, and Other Authentic Documents in the Possession of His Family and of the African Institution*, vol. 1 (London: Henry Colburn, 1828), 79. Stapylton made a second attempt to kidnap Lewis the day before the trial, and only the presence of counsel Dunning prevented it (Shyllon, *Black Slaves in Britain*, 51).

30. Oldham, "New Light on Mansfield and Slavery," 51.

31. Hoare, *Memoirs of Granville Sharp*, 91–92; George Van Cleve, "*Somerset's Case* and Its Antecedents in Imperial Perspective," *Law and History Review* 24 (Fall 2006): 622.

32. The men seized Lewis on 2 July 1770 near the garden of Sarah Banks, whose husband, William, was a member of the House of Commons. Servants reported Lewis's cries to their mistress, who contacted Sharp. Banks later underwrote the costs of Lewis's trial.

33. Clarkson, *History of the Rise, Progress, and Accomplishment*, 75.

34. Ibid., 81.

35. The poem's "Advertisement" professed that it was inspired by the account of a "Negro, belonging to the Captain of a West-Indiaman . . . [who] had left his master's house, and procured himself to be baptized" in anticipation of marriage, "but being detected and taken, he was sent on board the Captain's vessel then lying in the River." John Bicknell and Thomas Day, *The Dying Negro: A Poem*, 3rd ed. (London: W. Flexney, 1775), ii.

36. Ibid., 1.

37. James Boswell, *Life of Johnson* (Oxford: Oxford University Press, 1998), 885, 789.

38. For a discussion of Strong's case, see "Case of Jonathan Strong," *Freedom's Journal* (30 Nov. 1827): 1–2.

39. Shyllon, *Black Slaves in Britain*, 53; Hoare, *Memoirs of Granville Sharp*, 109; Oldham, "New Light on Mansfield and Slavery," 53; Helen Tunnicliff Catterall, ed., *Judicial Cases Concerning American Slavery and the Negro*, vol. 1 (Washington, DC: Carnegie Institution of Washington, 1926), 14.

40. Catterall, *Judicial Cases*, 4.

41. Peter Fryer, *Staying Power: The History of Black People in Britain* (London: Pluto, 1984), 121; Shyllon, *Black Slaves in Britain*, 82; Catterall, *Judicial Cases*, 15.

42. For an overview of the main debates over what Mansfield actually said in reaching

his narrow decision, see Oldham, "New Light on Mansfield and Slavery." Four main reports of Mansfield's decision exist: (1) the published report of Capel Lofft (which some scholars argue was augmented by Lofft's own language, (2) a report appearing in *Scot's Magazine,* (3) a report taken from the *Gentleman's Magazine,* and (4) an unsigned handwritten document in the Granville Sharp transcripts (on which F.O. Shyllon based his examination). Oldham locates two additional versions of Mansfield's decision in the manuscripts of Serjeant Hill and Dampier (Oldham, "New Light on Mansfield and Slavery," 54–55). See also Steven M. Wise, *Though the Heavens May Fall: The Landmark Trial That Led to the End of Human Slavery* (Cambridge, MA: Da Capo Press, 2005).

43. Swaminathan, "Developing the West Indian Proslavery Position," 41.

44. Shyllon, *Black Slaves in Britain,* 25–26.

45. Drescher, *Capitalism and Antislavery,* 34.

46. Deak Nabers, *Victory of Law: The Fourteenth Amendment, the Civil War, and American Literature, 1852–1867* (Baltimore: Johns Hopkins University Press, 2006), 50.

47. "London, May 25," *Essex Gazette* (25 Aug. to 1 Sept. 1772): 20.

48. Paul Finkelman, *Slavery in the Courtroom: An Annotated Bibliography of American Cases* (Washington, DC: Library of Congress, 1985), 6.

49. Don E. Fehrenbacher, *The Dred Scott Case: Its Significance in American Law and Politics* (Oxford: Oxford University Press, 1978), 54.

50. David Thomas Konig, "The Long Road to *Dred Scott*: Personhood and the Rule of Law in the Trial Court Records of St. Louis Slave Freedom Suits," *University of Missouri–Kansas City Law Review* 75 (Fall 2006): 62.

51. Eric J. Sundquist, *To Wake the Nations: Race in the Making of American Literature* (Cambridge, MA: Belknap Press of Harvard University Press, 1993), 178.

52. Francis Hargrave, *An Argument in the Case of James Sommersett, a Negro, Lately Determined by the Court of King's Bench* (London: F. Hargrave, 1772), 45.

53. Ibid., 50.

54. Clarkson, *History of the Rise, Progress, and Accomplishment,* 109. William Lloyd Garrison cited this poem in 1832 as a "beautiful panegyric upon England" while invoking the "guilt" of New England and Britain in the perpetuation of slavery in the West Indies and the United States. "The Liberator and Slavery—Guilt of New-England," *Liberator* (7 Jan. 1832): 1D–E.

55. Catterall, *Judicial Cases,* 16.

56. William Andrews, *To Tell a Free Story: The First Century of Afro-American Autobiography, 1760–1865* (Urbana: University of Illinois Press, 1986), 11.

57. Catterall, *Judicial Cases,* 1.

58. Long, *Candid Reflections,* 44.

59. Ibid., 41.

60. Ibid., 39, 44, 52.

61. Shyllon, *Black Slaves in Britain,* 107.

62. Catterall, *Judicial Cases,* 5.

63. Shyllon, *Black Slaves in Britain,* 109.

64. Mansfield reportedly proclaimed, "So high an act of dominion must derive its authority, if any such it has, from the law of the kingdom *where* executed. A foreigner cannot be imprisoned *here* on the authority of any law existing in his own country. The power of a master over his servant is different in all countries, more or less limited or extensive, the exercise of it therefore must always be regulated by the laws of the place where exercised" (Shyllon, *Black Slaves in Britain*, 108; Fryer, *Staying Power*, 125).

65. A similar case in Scotland's High Court yielded a more expansive ruling that, unlike Mansfield's, declared slavery illegal within the territorial bounds of Scotland. *Knight v. Wedderburn*, as James Boswell recalled, "went upon a much broader ground than the case of *Somerset*, which was decided in England; being truly the general question, whether a perpetual obligation of service to one master in any mode should be sanctified by the law of a free country" (Shyllon, *Black Slaves in Britain*, 178; Boswell, *Life of Johnson*, 885, 789).

66. Drescher, *Capitalism and Antislavery*, 40.

67. Ibid., 42.

68. Shyllon, *Black Slaves in Britain*, 105, 116; Drescher, *Capitalism and Antislavery*, 28.

69. Catterall, *Judicial Cases*, 35.

70. Ibid., 18. Representatives of West India interests reported that they had "obtained a promise from Mr. Stewart not to accommodate the Negro cause, but to have the point solemnly determined; since, if the laws of England do not confirm the colony laws with respect to property in slaves, no man of common sense will, for the future, lay out his money in so precarious a commodity" (Oldham, "New Light on Mansfield and Slavery," 53–54).

71. Long, *Candid Reflections*, 3, 60.

72. Ibid., 43. Long also insisted that planters as "free-born Englishman . . . had a greater right to the protection of English law" than the "'foreign' African slave." Such comments confirmed Johnson's sardonic observation on American independence: "How is it that we hear the loudest yelps for liberty among the drivers of negroes?" (Swaminathan, "Developing the West Indian Proslavery Position," 48).

73. Keith A. Sandiford, *Measuring the Moment: Strategies of Protest in Eighteenth-Century Afro-English Writing* (London: Associated University Presses, 1988), 27; *London Chronicle* 31 (23 June 1772): 598c.

74. Fryer, *Staying Power*, 68, 125; James Walvin, *England, Slaves and Freedom, 1776–1838* (Jackson: University Press of Mississippi, 1987), 41–42.

75. Shyllon, *Black Slaves in Britain*, ix, 165.

76. Brown notes that the *Somerset* case may "have sparked the first anti-slavery petition in 1773" in colonial Massachusetts. The author of the petition alluded vaguely to the "hopes raised among blacks in New England who had learned of Mansfield's decision" (Brown, *Moral Capital*, 289–90).

77. "Case of Somerset," *Freedom's Journal* (30 Nov. 1827): 2.

78. The legal attempts to protect the slave's "rights" were easily circumvented by West Indian slaveholders, who merely forced their slaves to sign or mark an indenture before leaving the colonies. The terms of indenture transformed the slave, "for the purposes of English law, into an indentured servant on arrival to England and [he or she] was thereby obliged

to accompany the planter back to the colonies, where naturally, the 'indentured' worker reverted back to his former bondage" (Walvin, *England, Slaves and Freedom*, 42).

79. Shyllon cites numerous instances of kidnapping and slave sales that occurred in England after *Somerset*; there was virtually no enforcement of Mansfield's ruling (Shyllon, *Black Slaves in Britain*, 168, 176).

80. Cugoano and Equiano number among a small group of ex-slaves who referred to themselves as the "Sons of Africa" in a number of correspondences. Quobna Ottobah Cugoano, *Thought and Sentiments on the Evil of Slavery* (New York: Penguin Classics, 1999), 187; further references to *Thought and Sentiments* are to this edition and are cited parenthetically in the text as *TS*.

81. Vincent Carretta, introduction to *Thought and Sentiments on the Evil of Slavery*, by Quobna Ottobah Cugoano (New York: Penguin Classics, 1999), xviii; Shyllon, *Black Slaves in Britain*, 40. Green informed Sharp "that when they reached the ship, the anchor was getting up, the sails set, and the captain himself at the helm; so that a single minute more of delay would have lost the opportunity of recovery. Henry confessed that he had intended to have jumped into the sea as soon as it was dark; choosing rather to die than to be carried into slavery" (Hoare, *Memoirs of Granville Sharp*, 370).

82. Olaudah Equiano, *Interesting Narrative of the Life of Olaudah Equiano, or Gustavus Vassa, the African* (New York: Penguin Books, 1995), 179–80; further references to *Interesting Narrative* are to this edition and are cited parenthetically in the text as *IN*.

83. *London Chronicle*, quoted in Equiano, *Interesting Narrative*, 181 n.505.

84. Drescher, *Capitalism and Antislavery*, 39.

85. See Stephen Best and Saidiya Hartman, "Fugitive Justice," *Representations* 92 (Fall 2005): 1–15.

86. Brown, *Moral Capital*, 296.

87. Carretta, introduction to *Thought and Sentiments*, xv.

88. Long, *Candid Reflections*, 48.

89. Marcus Wood, *Slavery, Empathy and Pornography* (Oxford: Oxford University Press, 2002), 2.

90. David Walker, *An Appeal to the Coloured Citizens of the World* (University Park: Pennsylvania State University Press, 2000), 43.

91. Sibylle Fischer, *Modernity Disavowed: Haiti and the Cultures of Slavery in the Age of Revolution* (Durham, NC: Duke University Press, 2004), 24.

92. John Haggard, *The Judgment of the Right Hon. Lord Stowell, Respecting the Slavery of the Mongrel Woman, Grace*, in *Southern Slaves in Free State Courts*, ed. Paul Finkelman (New York: Garland, 1988), 35, 26.

93. Williams entered into an agreement with his former master, Hardman, for his manumission upon payment of "30 joes," which Captain Brown of the *Holderness* advanced to him. In return, Williams indentured himself to Brown for three years at wages lower than the average rate for ordinary seamen. Catterall, *Judicial Cases*, 5.

94. Ibid., 36.

95. Frederick Douglass, *My Bondage and My Freedom*, in *Frederick Douglass Autobiographies*, ed. Henry Louis Gates, Jr. (New York: Library of America, 2004), 248.

96. "London, May 25," 20.
97. Catterall, *Judicial Cases*, 1.
98. Hargrave, *Argument in the Case of James Sommersett*, 19–20.
99. The *Essex Gazette* reported that Lord Mansfield interrogated Wallace closely when he finished his argument, "on certain positions he had advanced, particularly on that of contending, that the relation between a negro and his owner might be well maintained, on the ground of a contract between master and servant, which was incontrovertibly known to be binding, by the established usages and statute-laws of the land; his Lordship remarking, at the same time, that the nature of the proceedings contradicted this assertion in the strongest terms, and was utterly repugnant to, and destructive of every idea of contract between the parties" ("London, May 25," 20).
100. Thomas C. Holt, *The Problem of Freedom: Race, Labor, and Politics in Jamaica and Britain, 1832–1938* (Baltimore: Johns Hopkins University Press, 1991), 5.
101. Granville Sharp, *Extract from a Representation of the Injustice and Dangerous Tendency of Tolerating Slavery, or Admitting the Least Claim of Private Property in the Persons of Men* (London: n.p., n.d.), 34.
102. Ibid., 6.
103. Shyllon, *Black Slaves in Britain*, 30–31.
104. Kent does distinguish between slaves and "hired servants," in which the "relation between master and servant rests altogether upon contract," as two entirely different categories of servants (Kent, *Commentaries on American Law*, 286–87).
105. Finkelman, *Slavery in the Courtroom*, 6.
106. Mansfield may have encouraged Blackstone to alter this statement, and Blackstone later requested that Sharp cease citing "from my *first* Edition as decisive in favour" of freedom in *Injustice of Tolerating Slavery* (quoted in Shyllon, *Black Slaves in Britain*, 59, 65–66, 76).
107. William Blackstone, *Commentaries on the Laws of England: A Facsimile of the First Edition of 1765–1769*, vol. 1 (Chicago: University of Chicago Press, 1979), 412–13; Shyllon, *Black Slaves in Britain*, 60.
108. Paul Gilroy, *The Black Atlantic: Modernity and Double Consciousness* (Cambridge, MA: Harvard University Press, 1993), 39.
109. Long, *Candid Reflections*, 34.
110. Blackstone, *Commentaries*, 413.
111. Shyllon, *Black Slaves in Britain*, 64.
112. Moses Roper, *Narrative of the Adventures and Escape of Moses Roper, from American Slavery* (Berwick-Upton-Tweed, UK: Published for the Author, 1848), 53.
113. "The Slave Grace," *Anti-Slavery Monthly Reporter* 31 (Dec. 1827): 143–44.
114. Ibid.
115. Jenny Sharpe, "'Something Akin to Freedom': The Case of Mary Prince," *differences* 8, no. 1 (1996): 37.
116. Haggard, *Judgment of the Right Hon. Lord Stowell*, 6.
117. Goveia, *Slave Society*, 155n. 1.
118. Haggard, *Judgment of the Right Hon. Lord Stowell*, 14, 15.

119. Ibid.

120. Catterall, *Judicial Cases*, 35; T. B. Howells, *A Complete Collection of State Trials and Proceedings for High Treason and Other Crimes and Misdemeanors From the Earliest Period to the Year 1783*, vol. 20 (London: T. C. Hansard, 1816), 56.

121. Haggard, *Judgment of the Right Hon. Lord Stowell*, 22.

122. Ibid., 28, 42.

123. Ibid., 43.

124. The Society of Planters and Merchants contributed three hundred pounds to help defray expenses connected with Stewart's case (Shyllon, *Black Slaves in Britain*, 218–19).

125. "Negro Slavery," *The Friend: A Religious and Literary Journal* (1 Mar. 1828): 159.

126. *Liverpool Mercury* (10 Nov.1827): 363; quoted in Shyllon, *Black Slaves in Britain*, 210.

127. "Consideration on Certain Remarks on the Negro Slavery and Abolition Questions, in Lord Stowell's Judgment in the Case of the Slave 'Grace.' By a Briton" (Newcastle, UK: John Marshall, 1827), 15–16.

128. Ibid., 16.

129. Ibid., 18.

130. Stephen Best, *Fugitive's Properties: Law and the Poetics of Possession* (Chicago: University of Chicago Press, 2004), 9.

131. "In the Matter of a Slave Woman Called Grace," *London Times* (20 June 1827): 3.

132. Quoted in Shyllon, *Black Slaves in Britain*, 224n. 2.

133. *Sunday Times* (11 Nov. 1827); quoted in Shyllon, *Black Slaves in Britain*, 214, 216.

134. Haggard, *Judgment of the Right Hon. Lord Stowell*, 357.

135. *London Times* (8 Nov. 1827): 2C.

136. Shyllon, *Black Slaves in Britain*, 213.

137. "In the Matter of John Smith and Rachel, Two Slaves," *London Times* (22 Nov. 1827): 3.

138. "In the Matter of John Smith and Rachel, Two Slaves," *London Times* (10 Dec. 1827): 2.

139. "In the Matter of John Smith" (22 Nov.), 3.

140. Martin had run away from Antigua and "entered on board His Majesty's ship *Cygnet*." The commander returned Martin to his owner when it was discovered that he was a fugitive slave. "In the Matter of a Slave Named Jack Martin," *London Times* (10 Dec. 1827): 2–3.

141. Ibid.

142. Ibid.

143. "In the Matter of William Otto and William Robday, Two Slaves," *London Times* (22 Nov. 1827): 3; Shyllon, *Black Slaves in Britain*, 213

144. Helen Catterall goes so far as to refer to Stowell's judgment in *Grace* as the "Dred Scott decision of England" (Catterall, *Judicial Cases*, 8).

145. "Negro Slavery," 159.

146. Upon Grace's landing Britain, it continued, she became "literally and legally speaking" a free woman and "subject of empire . . . and as such, possessing the rights and privileges of his majesty's other subjects, had the right to travel into any part of the kingdom or the territories pertaining to it, unmolested, and to return at her own time." "Lord Stowell's Decision Concerning the Slave Grace," *Freedom's Journal* (11 Jan. 1828): 167.

147. Shyllon, *Black Slaves in Britain*, 227–28.
148. Quoted in Fehrenbacher, *Dred Scott Case*, 58.
149. Ibid., 57–58.
150. Sharpe, "Something Akin to Freedom," 37.
151. Clare Midgley, *Women against Slavery: The British Campaigns, 1780–1870* (London: Routledge, 1992), 63.
152. Mary Prince, *The History of Mary Prince, a West Indian Slave, Related by Herself*, ed. Moira Ferguson, rev. ed. (Ann Arbor: University of Michigan Press, 1997), 98; further references to *History of Mary Prince* are to this edition and are cited parenthetically in the text as *HMP*.
153. Midgley, *Women against Slavery*, 88.
154. Strickland described the narrative in a letter to friends as "a pathetic little history and is now printing in the form of a pamphlet to be laid before the Houses of Parliament." Moodie to Birds, Jan. 1831, in *Susanna Moodie: Letters of a Lifetime*, ed. Carl Ballstadt, Elizabeth Hopkins, and Michael Peterman (Toronto: University of Toronto Press, 1985), 57.
155. The twenty-four-year-old Warner died while awaiting the publication of his narrative, although he had directed Strickland to "appropriate the proceeds to the benefit of his aged mother, and the enfranchisement (should the amount prove so considerable) of his enslaved wife and child." Ashton Warner, *Negro Slavery Described by a Negro: Being the Narrative of Ashton Warner, a Native of St. Vincent's* (London: Samuel Maunder, 1831), 4; further references to *Negro Slavery* are to this edition and are cited parenthetically in the text as *NS*.
156. In *History of Mary Prince*, Prince relates Wood's reaction to the efforts of the Anti-Slavery Society: they went to "Mr. Wood to try to persuade him to let me return a free woman to my husband; but though they offered him, as I have heard, a large sum for my freedom, he was sulky and obstinate, and would not consent to let me go free" (*HMP*, 91).
157. Quoted in Moira Ferguson, *Subject to Others: British Women Writers and Colonial Slavery, 1670–1834* (London: Routledge, 1992), 282.
158. Pringle's "Supplement" reveals that James corresponded with Prince while she was in Pringle's employment. Pringle makes reference to "a letter from himself [James] to Mary, dated in April 1830, couched in strong terms of conjugal affection; expressing his anxiety for her speedy return" (*HMP*, 106).
159. Long, *Candid Reflections*, 48.
160. Pringle asserts, "Whatever opinions may be held by some readers on the grave question of immediately abolishing Colonial Slavery, nothing assuredly can be more repugnant to the feelings of Englishmen than that the system should be permitted to extend its baneful influence to this country. Yet such is the case, when the slave landed in England still only possesses that qualified degree of freedom, that a change of domicile will determine it. Though born a British subject, and resident within the shores of England, he is cut off from his dearest natural rights by the sad alternative of regaining them at the expense of liberty, and the certainty of severe treatment" (*HMP*, 124).
161. Hartman, *Scenes of Subjection*, 53, 5.
162. Midgley offers the parallel case of a slave woman named Polly, who likewise had been brought to England from Trinidad by her owner. When privately interviewed by

abolitionist Mary Capper, Polly revealed that "she knew she was thought free in England, but *she* thought she was more a slave than in the West Indies, as she had none of her acquaintance to speak to" (Midgley, *Women against Slavery*, 91).

163. Sharpe, "Something Akin to Freedom," 52–53.

164. Walvin, *England, Slaves and Freedom*, 19.

165. Scott, *Conscripts of Modernity*, 12.

166. "Case of Fanny," *Anti-Slavery Reporter* (18 July 1831): 343; "Sequel to the Case of Henry Williams, of Jamaica," *Anti-Slavery Reporter* (1 Mar. 1831): 151.

167. A man by the name of Wilson purchased the Cane Grove sugar plantation after the death of Warner's former master and seized Warner as his slave. "Mr. Wilson said," according to Warner, "that though my mother was sold I was not—that the best slaves had been sold off the estate—that I was *his* property, and he would claim me wherever I was to be found." Warner based his claim to freedom on a customary rule in the Island of St. Vincent's that "the young child at the breast is sold as one with its mother, and does not become separate property till it is five or six years old" (*NS*, 21).

168. The *Anti-Slavery Reporter* offered a "prodigious volume of information about slave society" that enabled a "much more sophisticated analysis of Caribbean slavery to emerge in the political debate" (Walvin, "Public Campaign in England," 72–73).

169. Holt, *Problem of Freedom*, 18–19, 45.

170. Heyrick, *Immediate, Not Gradual Abolition*, 23.

171. "Case of Betto Douglas, a St. Kitt's Slave—United States—Slave Population of West Indies," *Anti-Slavery Monthly Reporter* 25 (June 1827): 1–7.

172. Ibid., 2.

173. Ibid., 1, 3.

174. Ibid., 4.

175. Ibid., 6.

176. Female Society for Birmingham, *Fifth Report of the Female Society for Birmingham, West Bromwich, Wednesbury, Walsall, and Their Respective Neighborhoods, for the Relief of British Negro Slaves, Established in 1825* (Birmingham, UK: B. Hudson, 1830), 19.

177. The Anti-Slavery Society freed Asa-Asa upon writ of habeas corpus in the fashion adopted in the earlier cases of Lewis and Somerset after severe weather drove the French slave ship *Pearl* into a Cornwall port.

178. Moira Ferguson, introduction to *HMP*, 24.

179. Ibid.

180. Prince's *History* consists of a short preface, postscripts, Pringle's "Supplement," attestations, and the "Narrative of Louis Asa-Asa, a Captured African." All three editions withheld mention of Strickland as Prince's amanuensis, and it is tellingly Prince who names Strickland's intermediary role. Pringle's refusal to name Strickland can be understood as part of the devaluation of women's participation in the emancipation campaign (Midgley, *Women against Slavery*, 3–4). Strickland notified her close friends James and Emma Bird that she had "been writing Mr. Pringle's black Mary's life from her own dictation. . . . Of course my name

does not appear" (Moodie to Birds, Jan. 1831, in Ballstadt, Hopkins, and Peterman, *Susanna Moodie*, 57).

181. Female Society for Birmingham, *The First Report of the Female Society for Birmingham, West-Bromwich, Wednesbury, Walsall, and Their Respective Neighbourhoods, for the Relief of British Negro Slaves* (Birmingham, UK: R. Peart, 1826), 4–5.

182. Ladies Association for Calne, Melksham, Devizes, *The Second Report of the Ladies' Association for Calne, Melksham, Devizes, and Their Respective Neighborhoods, in the Aid of the Cause of Negro Emancipation* (Calne, UK: W. Baily, 1827), 3.

183. Strickland, introduction to *NS*, 6.

184. Swaminathan, "Developing the West Indian Proslavery Position," 50–51.

185. Ibid., 56.

186. James Macqueen, "The Colonial Empire of Great Britain: Letter to Earl Grey, First Lord of the Treasury," *Blackwood's Edinburgh Magazine* (Nov. 1831): 758.

187. Sharpe, "Something Akin to Freedom," 32.

188. This omission had been the subject of a number of studies of Prince's *History*. See Sharpe, "Something Akin to Freedom"; Ferguson, *Subject to Others*; Sandra Pouchet Paquet, "The Heartbeat of a West Indian Slave: *The History of Mary Prince*," *African American Review* 26 (Spring 1992): 131–46; A.M. Rauwerda, "Naming Agency, and 'A Tissue of Falsehoods' in *The History of Mary Prince*," *Victorian Literature and Culture* 29 (2001): 397–411.

189. "Testimony of the Christian Record of Jamaica on Colonial Slavery," *Anti-Slavery Reporter* (15 Feb. 1831): 143.

190. "The Rev. G.W. Bridges and His Slave, Kitty Hylton," *Anti-Slavery Reporter* (2 Apr. 1831): 248; "The Rev. G.W. Bridges and His Slave Kitty Hilton," *Anti-Slavery Reporter* (1 Sept. 1830): 373–82.

191. The *Anti-Slavery Reporter* describes how "[d]uring the months of May and June last, the newspapers of the island were filled with discussion on the subject" ("The Rev. G.W. Bridges," 379).

192. Ibid.

193. Ibid.

194. Another enslaved woman, named Kate, died from injuries sustained in a similar case of "correction" a year earlier in the Bahamas. Pringle offered this case in the appendix to Prince's *History* as "unquestionable evidence" of the "similar barbarity" that Prince had experienced in the West Indies. "Case Illustrative of Jamaica Society and Manners," *Anti-Slavery Reporter* (1 Aug. 1830): 345–47; "Cruelties Perpetuated by Henry and Helen Moss, on a Female Negro Slave in the Bahamas," *Anti-Slavery Monthly Reporter* 47 (Apr. 1829): 462–68.

195. Barbara Bush, *Slave Women in Caribbean Society, 1650–1838* (Bloomington: Indiana University Press, 1990), 56, 60.

196. Tactics are opportunistic and fleeting by necessity, unlike the institutionalized calculations found in strategies. Michel de Certeau, *The Practice of Everyday Life*, trans. Steven Rendall (Berkeley: University of California Press, 1984), xix–xx.

197. "State of Law and Manners in Jamaica Illustrated—Case of Eleanor Mead," *Anti-Slavery Reporter* (20 Nov. 1830): 481–86.

198. Ibid., 484–85.

199. Ibid., 482.

200. Ibid.

201. Hazel Carby, *Reconstructing Womanhood: The Emergence of the Afro-American Woman Novelist* (Oxford: Oxford University Press, 1987), 34.

202. "State of Law ... Eleanor Mead," 485.

203. Ibid.

204. Ibid.

205. Wedderburn was a central figure to proletarian abolitionism. Wedderburn's transatlantic correspondence with his half-sister Elizabeth Campbell, a Jamaican maroon, which appears in his short-lived newspaper *Axe Laid to the Root*, was facilitated through a black sailor. The colonial legislature purportedly passed disciplinary measures to curtail the further dissemination of Wedderburn's inflammatory periodical after its discovery on the island. Peter Linebaugh and Marcus Rediker, *The Many-Headed Hydra: Sailors, Slaves, Commoners, and the Hidden History of the Revolutionary Atlantic* (Boston: Beacon, 2000), 289–90, 311.

206. Robert Wedderburn, *The Horrors of Slavery and Other Writings by Robert Wedderburn* (New York: Markus Wiener, 1991), 81; further references to *Horrors of Slavery* are to this edition and are cited parenthetically in the text.

207. Wedderburn's erstwhile associates George Cannon and William Dugdale were occasional pornographers. Dugdale provided the printing facilities for *Horrors of Slavery*, and Cannon revised and possibly authored some of the work attributed to Wedderburn from 1819 to 1821. Iain McCalman, introduction to *HS*, 4–5.

208. Ibid., 16–17.

209. Douglass, *My Bondage and My Freedom*, 304–5.

210. Lucy Newlyn, "Look Back on Anger," *Essays in Criticism* 56 (Oct. 2006): 400.

211. Linebaugh and Rediker, *Many-Headed Hydra*, 287.

212. Iain McCalman, *Radical Underworld: Prophets, Revolutionaries, and Pornographers in London, 1795–1840* (Oxford: Oxford University Press, 1993), 55.

213. Sharpe, "Something Akin to Freedom," 52.

214. "State of Law ... Eleanor Mead," 486.

215. Jenny Sharpe, *Ghosts of Slavery: A Literary Archaeology of Black Women's Lives* (Minneapolis: University of Minnesota Press, 2003), 149–50.

216. Sheffield Female Anti-Slavery Society, *Concluding Report of the Sheffield Female Anti-Slavery Society* (Sheffield, UK: Iris Office, 1833), 5.

217. Holt, *Problem of Freedom*, 49. This legislation also heavily compensated slaveholders, allocating £20 million of public money to compensate planters and requiring ex-slaves to labor without wages for their masters for another six years. Paton, introduction to *NE*, xvii.

218. "Report of the British and Foreign Anti-Slavery Society," *National Era* (1 July 1847): 2.

219. "Literary," *Liberator* (19 Nov. 1836): 188.

220. Paton, introduction to *NE*, xix.

221. *Narrative of Events* should not to be confused with the *Narrative* of American fugitive slave James Williams, which Isaac Knapp published in 1838.

222. Paton, introduction to *NE*, xiii.

223. Ibid., xxxvii, xiii.

224. "Business Like," *Liberator* (25 May 1838): 84.

225. Paton, introduction to *NE*, xv, xliv.

226. Dipesh Chakrabarty, *Provincializing Europe: Postcolonial Thought and Historical Difference* (Princeton, NJ: Princeton University Press, 2000), 8–9.

227. Paton, introduction to *NE*, xiii.

228. Ibid.

229. Ibid., xli.

230. When slaveholding interests attacked the integrity of an 1838 slave narrative published by the American Anti-Slavery Society, Isaac Knapp called for a governmental investigation into the matter, citing the example taken in the case of the ex-apprentice James Williams: "A young colored apprentice was bought free in Jamaica, by Joseph Sturge, and his narrative which was published in England, was denied as positively by the slaveholders as our book has been; but the British government sent out orders to have the matter examined by commissioners on the spot, who reported that it was a great deal worse than James had related. Let us have a commission, including one abolitionist, with a guaranty of security to the witnesses, or else let those who have the power, furnish satisfactory testimony instead of wary evasions and denials." "Narrative of James Williams," *Liberator* (28 Sept. 1838): 153.

231. Paton, introduction to *NE*, xvii.

232. Holt, *Problem of Freedom*, 58.

233. Ibid., 61.

234. James Williams, *A Narrative of Events Since the First of August, 1834, by James Williams, Together with the Evidence Taken under a Commission Appointed by the Colonial Office to Ascertain the Truth of the Narrative; And the Reports of the Commissioners Thereon* (London: Central Emancipation Committee, 1838), 34.

235. Many apprentices, according to Holt, became litigious over working conditions in the months after the passage of the Abolition Act (Holt, *Problem of Freedom*, 61; Paton, introduction to *NE*, xxxvii).

236. Williams, *Narrative of Events . . . Together with the Evidence*, 18.

CHAPTER 2

1. Harriet A. Jacobs, *Incidents in the Life of a Slave Girl*, ed. Jean Fagan Yellin (Cambridge, MA: Harvard University Press, 2000), 219; further references to *Incidents in the Life* are to this edition and are cited parenthetically in the text as *IL*.

2. Jean Fagan Yellin, *Harriet Jacobs: A Life* (New York: Civitas Books, 2004), 58.

3. John Jacobs's autobiographical narrative began its four-part installation on 4 February 1861 in the *Leisure Hour: A Family Journal of Instruction and Recreation*, a publication of Britain's Religious Tract Society (Yellin, *Harriet Jacobs*, 148).

4. "Refuge of Oppression—Anti-Sabbath Convention—Buffalo Convention," *Liberator* (18 Aug. 1848): 129.

5. Yellin, *Harriet Jacobs*, 70.

6. Such invitations were not uncommon among those slaveholders whose valuable human property had turned fugitive. Slaveholder Louisa White, for example, addressed the following entreaty to her former bondsman William Henry Gilliam: "If you choose to come back you could. I would do a very good part by you." William Still, *The Underground Rail Road* (New York: Arno, 1968), 56; further references to *Underground Rail Road* are to this edition and are cited parenthetically in the text as *URR*.

7. Jacobs "did not write to return thanks for this cordial invitation" and chose, instead, to remain with her brother and children in Boston. John joined the New England Freedom Association and became a rather popular antislavery lecturer. He shared the platform with prominent abolitionists such as Jonathan Walker, famously branded as a "slave stealer" in Florida, and Frederick Douglass, who had, like John, slipped through New York City to New Bedford disguised as a sailor in 1838 (Yellin, *Harriet Jacobs*, 87, 93–94). In a private communication to Sydney Howard Gay, editor of the *National Anti-Slavery Standard*, John Jacobs indicated that both he and Harriet were well aware of the menace that belied Messmore's open expressions of heartfelt affection. "[M]y sister," John writes, "received a very affectionate letter lass week from her young mistress Mrs. Messmore. . . . now reminds my sister of her former love and in that affectionat manner so peculiar to this no soul Nation she want to know if she wont COME HOME" (quoted in Yellin, *Harriet Jacobs*, 90–91).

8. Christine MacDonald, "Judging Jurisdictions: Geography and Race in Slave Law and Literature of the 1830s," *American Literature* 71 (Dec. 1999): 632.

9. Paul Finkelman, *Imperfect Union: Slavery, Federalism, and Comity* (Chapel Hill: University of North Carolina Press, 1981), 76.

10. Ibid., 101.

11. William Andrews, *To Tell a Free Story: The First Century of Afro-American Autobiography, 1760–1865* (Urbana: University of Illinois Press, 1986), xi.

12. Jenny Sharpe, *Ghosts of Slavery: A Literary Archaeology of Black Women's Lives* (Minneapolis: University of Minnesota Press, 2003), xiii.

13. See Saidiya V. Hartman, *Scenes of Subjection: Terror, Slavery, and Self-Making in Nineteenth-Century America* (New York: Oxford University Press, 1997).

14. John S. Jacobs, "A True Tale of Slavery," in *IL*, 219.

15. Elizabeth Johnston's research reveals that two-thirds of Massachusetts transit cases involved children, whereas similar cases in other states involved primarily adult litigants and petitioners. Elizabeth Johnston, "Choosing Freedom, Risking Slavery: African Americans, Anti-slavery Activists, and the Courts in Massachusetts, 1830–1860" (paper presented at the Slavery and the Constitution seminar, Institute for Constitutional Studies, George Washington University Law School, Washington, D.C., 13–24 June 2005).

16. "The Slave Case," *New Bedford Mercury* (2 Sept. 1836): 1.

17. Gillian Brown, "Child's Play," *differences* 11, no. 3 (1999/2000): 82, 88.

18. Paul Finkelman, *Slavery in the Courtroom: An Annotated Bibliography of American Cases* (Washington, DC: Library of Congress, 1985), 29; "From the *Boston Daily Advertiser*: The Slave Case," *Connecticut Courant* (5 Sept. 1836): 2.

19. "The Slave Case—Mr. Loring's Argument," *Liberator* (24 Sept. 1836): 153–54; "Loring's Argument Continued," *Liberator* (8 Oct. 1836): 161–62.

20. Jeannine Marie DeLombard, *Slavery on Trial: Law, Abolitionism, and Print Culture* (Chapel Hill: University of North Carolina Press, 2007), 11.

21. Ibid., 2.

22. *State v. Mann*, 13 N.C. 263, N.C. LEXIS 62 (1829).

23. Eugene Genovese, *Roll, Jordan, Roll: The World the Slaves Made* (New York: Pantheon Books, 1974), 35, 47.

24. "Connecticut Coming Round," *Colored American* (16 June 1838): 66.

25. Don E. Fehrenbacher, *The Dred Scott Case: Its Significance in American Law and Politics* (Oxford: Oxford University Press, 1978), 57.

26. Brown, "Child's Play," 80.

27. *Case of the Slave-Child Med, Report of the Arguments of Counsel and of the Opinion of the Court, in the Case of Commonwealth v. Aves* (Boston: Isaac Knapp, 1836), reprinted in Paul Finkelman, ed., *Southern Slaves in Free State Courts. The Pamphlet Literature Series I*, 3 vols. (New York: Garland, 1988), 1:436.

28. Stephen Best, *Fugitive's Properties: Law and the Poetics of Possession* (Chicago: University of Chicago Press, 2004), 210–13.

29. Pierre Bourdieu, "The Force of Law: Toward a Sociology of the Juridical Field," trans. Richard Terdiman, *Hastings Law Journal* 38 (July 1987): 817. The juridical field, according to Bourdieu, "is the site of a competition for monopoly of the right to determine the law." "To varying degrees," he continues, "jurists and judges have at their disposal the power to exploit the polysemy or the ambiguity of legal formulas by appealing to . . . rhetorical devices . . . and a whole series of techniques like analogy and the distinction of letter and spirit, which tend to maximize the law's elasticity, and even its contradictions, ambiguities, and lacunae" (ibid., 827). See also Teresa Zackodnik, "Fixing the Color Line: The Mulatto, Southern Courts, and Racial Identity," *American Quarterly* 53 (2001): 420–51; Martin A. Kayman, "Lawful Writing: Common Law, Statute and the Properties of Literature," *New Literary History* 27, no. 4 (1996): 762–63.

30. Brook Thomas, *American Literary Realism and the Failed Promise of Contract* (Berkeley: University of California Press, 1997), 1–3.

31. Amy Dru Stanley, *From Bondage to Contract: Wage Labor, Marriage, and the Market in the Age of Slave Emancipation* (Cambridge: Cambridge University Press, 1998), 2–3.

32. Mark V. Tushnet, *American Law of Slavery, 1810–1860: Considerations of Humanity and Interest* (Princeton, NJ: Princeton University Press, 1981), 54.

33. Patricia J. Williams, *Alchemy of Race and Rights: Diary of a Law Professor* (Cambridge, MA: Harvard University Press, 1991), 31.

34. "Case of the Slave-Child Med," 1:436.

35. Fanny Kemble observes that Sea Island slaveholders bestowed rewards of "less work and more food" to encourage slave women toward "reckless propagation" with no regard to the "parental relation." Frances Anne Kemble, *Journal of a Residence on a Georgian Plantation in 1838–1839* (Athens: University of Georgia Press, 1984), 95, 157.

36. Thomas Ruffin's infamous judgment in *State v. Mann*, for example, spoke in terms of this analogy, which had substantially limited (to the point of negation) the rights and legal authority of slaves *and* children before the antebellum courts (Genovese, *Roll, Jordan, Roll*, 35).

37. Finkelman, *Imperfect Union*, 108.

38. Quoted in Debra Gold Hansen, *Strained Sisterhood: Gender and Class in the Boston Female Anti-Slavery Society* (Amherst: University of Massachusetts Press, 1993), 17.

39. The Boston Samaritan Asylum for indigent colored children was founded in April 1834, but by the following year, the managers had placed urgent advertisements in the *Liberator* soliciting funds to help house and maintain the thirteen children under their care. "The Samaritan Asylum for Indigent Children," *Boston Recorder* (31 Mar. 1837): 51. The asylum, according to an early promotional announcement, was designed to assume protection of colored children "whose parents are unable or unqualified to educate them." Parents and relations of the children were expected to "resign all control over them" once they were placed in the asylum. Mary Grew, "Notice," *Liberator* (27 Sept. 1834): 155.

40. Finkelman, *Imperfect Union*, 112n. 40.

41. Samuel Slater, "Refuge of Oppression," *Liberator* (15 Oct. 1836): 165.

42. Ibid.

43. L. Moreau Lislet, *A General Digest of the Acts of the Legislature of Louisiana: Passed from the Year 1804, to 1827, Inclusive*, vol. 1 (New Orleans: Benjamin Levy, 1828), 101; Genovese, *Roll, Jordan, Roll*, 32. Louisiana penal law stipulated that transgressors "shall suffer a fine not less than one thousand dollars, nor more than two thousand dollars, and an imprisonment of not less than six months, nor more than one year." M.M. Robinson, *A Digest of the Penal Law of the State of Louisiana, Analytically Arranged* (New Orleans: Published for the Author, 1841), 121–22.

44. "The Boston Slave Case," *Niles Weekly Register* (24 Sept. 1836): 55; Henry J. Leovy, *The Laws and General Ordinances of City of New Orleans: Together with the Acts of the Legislature, Decisions of the Supreme Court, and Constitutional Provisions, Relating to the City Government: Revised and Digested, Pursuant to an Order of the Common Council* (New Orleans: E.C. Wharton, 1857), 269–70.

45. Slater, "Refuge of Oppression," 165.

46. Hortense J. Spillers, *Black, White, and in Color: Essays on American Literature and Culture* (Chicago: University of Chicago Press, 2003), 232.

47. Quoted in Maria Weston Chapman, *Right and Wrong in Boston, in 1836: Annual Report of the Boston Female Anti-Slavery Society* (Boston: Boston Female Anti-Slavery Society, 1836), 67.

48. Ibid.

49. "Mr. and Mrs. Robinson," *Colored American* (13 Jan. 1838): 2A.
50. Helen Tunnicliff Catterall, ed., *Judicial Cases Concerning American Slavery and the Negro*, vol. 4 (Washington, DC: Carnegie Institution of Washington, 1926), 501.
51. Catterall, *Judicial Cases*, 502; "Trial for Kidnapping in Boston," *New-Bedford Mercury* (29 Dec. 1837): 1.
52. Catterall, *Judicial Cases*, 503.
53. Ibid.
54. "The Kidnapping Case in Boston," *New-Bedford Mercury* (5 Jan. 1838): 1.
55. "Writ of Habeas Corpus," *Liberator* (20 Oct. 1837): 171.
56. Catterall, *Judicial Cases*, 501n. 2.
57. "Kidnapping Case," 1.
58. Spillers, *Black, White, and in Color*, 217–20.
59. Chapman, *Right and Wrong in Boston*, 47–48.
60. William Lloyd Garrison to Isaac Knapp, 23 Aug. 1836, letter 53 in *Letters of William Lloyd Garrison: A House Divided against Itself, 1836–1840*, ed. Louis Ruchames, vol. 2 (Cambridge, MA: Belknap Press of Harvard University Press, 1971), 169–71.
61. Chapman, *Right and Wrong in Boston*, 63.
62. BFASS unanimously resolved to prevent "a violation of the rights of the child" after several members posing as Sunday-school teachers gained entrance into the Aves household (Chapman, *Right and Wrong in Boston*, 64).
63. Ibid.
64. Only Maria Weston Chapman married and bore children of the four Weston sisters who were among the founding members; her sisters Caroline, Anne, and Deborah remained unmarried.
65. Finkelman, *Imperfect Union*, 103.
66. Cindy Weinstein, *Family, Kinship, and Sympathy in Nineteenth-Century American Literature* (Cambridge: Cambridge University Press, 2004), 4.
67. Chapman, *Right and Wrong in Boston*, 66.
68. Med may have been enrolled in one of Boston's public African American primary schools, the first of which was opened in Rev. Thomas Paul's Belknap Street Church on 7 August 1822. Paul's daughter, Susan Paul, taught at the African School Number 2 and was one of the first African American women invited to join BFASS. Paul noted in a letter published in the *Liberator* (13 August 1836), "We have several school-mates who have been slaves, and we try to make them as happy as we can. We wish you could see how they try to learn, and how much they love our teacher. We should be glad if all the little slaves were in our school." Lois Brown, introduction to *Memoir of James Jackson, the Attentive and Obedient Scholar, Who Died in Boston, October 31, 1833*, by Susan Paul (Cambridge, MA: Harvard University Press, 2000), 10, 125.
69. David Delaney, *Race, Place, and the Law, 1836–1948* (Austin: University of Texas Press, 1998), 54; Joanne Pope Melish, *Disowning Slavery: Gradual Emancipation and "Race" in New England, 1780–1860* (Ithaca, NY: Cornell University Press, 1998), 7. Med's case even found its way to Britain, where the Glasgow Ladies Auxiliary Emancipation Society republished an

account of the case in *Three Years' Female Anti-Slavery Effort, in Britain and America* (1837). Glasgow Ladies' Auxiliary Emancipation Society, *Three Years' Female Anti-Slavery Effort, in Britain and America* (Glasgow, UK: Aird & Russell, 1837), 47.

70. "From the *Boston Daily Advertiser*," 2.

71. Finkelman, *Imperfect Union*, 114–16.

72. "From the *Boston Daily Advertiser*," 2.

73. Chapman, *Right and Wrong in Boston*, 68–70. The habeas action in Med's case had indeed offered Massachusetts an opportunity to formalize its antislavery position, and the Connecticut Supreme Court cited the "doctrine . . . decided by Chief Justice Shaw, of Mass., in the case of the slave child *Med*" as it deliberated on Nancy Jackson's successful freedom suit against Georgia slaveholder James Bulloch in 1837 (Finkelman, *Imperfect Union*, 127).

74. Hansen, *Strained Sisterhood*, 22.

75. Lydia Maria Child, "The Ladies' Fair," *Liberator* (2 Jan. 1837): 3.

76. Child reports that, on the reverse side, "the Arms of Massachusetts surmount the following lines: 'Old Massachusetts yet / Retains her earlier fires! / Still on our hills are set / The altars of our sires! / Our 'fierce democracies' / Have yet their strength unborn! / And giant power shall see / Its Gaza-gates uptorn.' August 26, A.D. 1836" (ibid., 3).

77. Melish, *Disowning Slavery*, 8.

78. In April 1851, Thomas Sims was arrested as a fugitive slave in Boston. The agent for the fugitive's alleged master in Georgia claimed that he had been ordered to take Sims, according to the *National Era* report, "out of Massachusetts, to test the law." The Massachusetts Anti-Slavery Society vehemently condemned Boston's surrender of Sims when it held its twentieth annual meeting in the city the following January. "Another Fugitive Case in Boston," *National Era* (10 Apr. 1851): 59; "The Massachusetts Anti-Slavery Society," *Frederick Douglass' Paper* (19 Feb. 1852): 1F.

79. "Speech of Wendell Phillips, Esq.," *Frederick Douglass' Paper* (26 Feb. 1852): 1A.

80. "From the Boston Commonwealth: Speech of Hon. S.E. Sewall, of Middlesex, in the Senate, on the Bill to Protect Personal Liberty," *Frederick Douglass' Paper* (24 June 1852): 1A–G.

81. "Another Slave Case," *Liberator* (22 Oct. 1836): 171A.

82. "Kidnapping in Boston," *Liberator* (29 Oct. 1836): 174C–E; Finkelman, *Imperfect Union*, 137–38.

83. Nabers, *Victory of Law*, 96.

84. "Holden Slave Case," *Christian Reflector* (1 Feb. 1839): 19.

85. Board of Directors of the Holden Anti-Slavery Society, *Report of the Holden Slave Case, Tried at the January Term of the Court of Common Pleas, for the County of Worcester, A.D. 1839* (Worcester, MA: Colton & Howland, 1839), 7.

86. Ibid., 27–28.

87. Robert M. Cover, *Justice Accused: Antislavery and the Judicial Process* (New Haven, CT: Yale University Press, 1975), 198.

88. "Court Calendar," *Liberator* (13 Aug. 1841): 131.

89. This tactic was not unusual for a slaveholder to adopt in the years after *Aves*. In the

Holden slave case, for example, Eames repeatedly claimed that "Anne was *not* restrained of her liberty *at all*. Anne was there *voluntarily*" (Board of Directors of the Holden Anti-Slavery Society, *Report of the Holden Slave Case*, 6; Finkelman, *Imperfect Union*, 117).

90. "Commonwealth v. Taylor," *Law Reporter* (Nov. 1841): 274.

91. Ibid.

92. Ibid.

93. The adjudication of the slave's ability to willfully "choose" his or her freedom or enslavement did not follow any strict formal principles and varied from case to case depending on the narratives of kinship, childhood, and consent constructed during the trial. Shaw had allowed another slave boy to choose his own judgment in an earlier unreported case, *In re Francisco* (1832). Francisco expressed his personal wish to return to Cuba with his mistress after the New-England Anti-Slavery Society intervened on his behalf, and Shaw thought him old enough to know his own mind, even though he was legally a minor, at age twelve or fourteen. The debates over whether Francisco should return to Havana or remain in Boston rehearsed many of the arguments that made their way before Shaw in *Aves*. Finkelman, *Imperfect Union*, 101–2; "Slavery Record: Supreme Judicial Court—Dec. 4," *Liberator* (8 Dec. 1832): 194–95.

94. Weinstein, *Family, Kinship, and Sympathy*, 52–59.

95. *Commonwealth [of Pennsylvania] v. Holloway* (1816) was one such case in which the slave owner returned with the slave mother while leaving the infant in Pennsylvania (Finkelman, *Imperfect Union*, 65).

96. Sharpe, *Ghosts of Slavery*, 120.

97. Joan Dayan, "Paul Gilroy's Slaves, Ships, and Routes: The Middle Passage as Metaphor," *Research in African Literatures* 27, no. 4 (1996): 10.

98. Ariela J. Gross, *Double Character: Slavery and Mastery in the Antebellum Courtroom* (Princeton, NJ: Princeton University Press, 2000), 96.

99. Brook Thomas, "Citizen Hester: *The Scarlet Letter* as Civic Myth," *American Literary History* 13 (Summer 2001): 193.

100. Nell Irvin Painter, *Sojourner Truth: A Life, a Symbol* (New York: Norton, 1996), 33.

101. Dumont initially sold Peter to Eleazer Gidney, who had intended to take him back to England as his attendant. Gidney eventually decided to send Peter to his brother Solomon, who sold him to his brother-in-law, Fowler, an Alabama planter (Painter, *Sojourner Truth*, 34).

102. Olive Gilbert, *Narrative of Sojourner Truth*, ed. Margaret Washington (New York: Vintage Books, 1993), 35; further references to *Narrative of Sojourner Truth* are to this edition and are cited parenthetically in the text as *NST*.

103. William Andrews, *To Tell a Free Story: The First Century of Afro-American Autobiography, 1760–1865* (Urbana: University of Illinois Press, 1986), 179–82.

104. Such hermeneutics can be identified in a number of contemporary critical readings of Truth's text. Christina Accomando, for example, reads Truth's advocacy of legal agency as "revealing the law as both an agent of oppression and potential tool for resistance" yet attributes, as Gilbert does, Peter's unruly desires to the agency of his master: "Coached by his

Southern owner, Peter repeatedly denies that Truth is his mother." Christina Accomando, *"The Regulation of Robbers": Legal Fictions of Slavery and Resistance* (Columbus: Ohio State University Press, 2001), 51, 59.

105. Harriet Beecher Stowe, "Sojourner Truth: The Libyan Sibyl," *Atlantic Monthly* 11 (Apr. 1863): 478.

106. Erasmus D. Hudson's name was misspelled as "Erastus" in the legal file of the case.

107. There are two competing accounts of the case in the *Liberator*. Hudson's account describes an unnamed fugitive (identified in the trial simply as "one Ruggles") as the informant, and another identifies David W. Ruggles as the person who initiated contact with Linda. "Imprisonment of Dr. Hudson," *Liberator* (19 Sept. 1845): 151; "The Climax of Slaveholding," *Liberator* (12 Sept. 1845): 146; "Dr. Hudson's Case," *Liberator* (20 Nov. 1846): 187.

108. "Imprisonment of Dr. Hudson," 151.

109. "Climax of Slaveholding," 146.

110. Ibid.

111. "Another Abolition Failure," *New-Hampshire Patriot and State Gazette* (21 Aug. 1845): 1.

112. Ibid.

113. "Curious Slave Case," *Morning News* (13 Sept. 1845): 2; "Habeas Corpus—Slave Case," *Barre Patriot* (15 Aug. 1845): 3.

114. "Habeas Corpus," 3.

115. "Imprisonment of Dr. Hudson," 151.

116. "Climax of Slaveholding," 146; "Another Chapter in the Slave Case," *Pittsfield Sun* (18 Sept. 1845): 2.

117. *Barre Patriot* (12 Sept. 1845): 2; *Morning News* (25 Sept. 1845): 3.

118. "Climax of Slaveholding," 146.

119. Ibid.

120. "Imprisonment of Dr. Hudson," 151.

121. "Letter from Dr. Hudson," *Liberator* (3 Oct. 1845): 159.

122. Ibid.

123. Ibid.

124. "Slaveholding Insolence," *Liberator* (26 Sept. 1845): 153.

125. "Imprisonment of Dr. Hudson," *Liberator* (26 Sept. 1845): 154.

126. "Dr. Hudson's Case," 187. Hudson immediately returned to his antislavery labors and was reported in the winter of 1845 to have been in pursuit of another traveling slave, "Milly," whose master, Henry B. Goodwin, according to the *Liberator*, brought her "from the South" into Massachusetts, where she had "fallen into the hands of the Goodwin family in Norton, where she is now deprived of her liberty" and "destined to be sent back again to slavery." "A Case for Investigation," *Liberator* (12 Dec. 1845): 199.

127. John Woods, for example, compelled another slave woman to lodge a complaint against his slave Mary Prince before Antiguan courts to teach her lesson.

128. "Supreme Judicial Court," *Liberator* (29 May 1846): 87.

129. Finkelman, *Imperfect Union*, 121.

130. "Second Trial of Dr. Hudson," *Liberator* (14 Apr. 1848): 58; Finkelman, *Imperfect Union*, 122.

131. "Second Trial of Dr. Hudson," 58.

132. "Betty's Case," *Monthly Law Reporter* (Dec. 1857): 455–58.

133. "A Slave Case," *Pittsfield Sun* (12 Nov. 1857): 3.

134. "Betty's Case," 456.

135. "Slave Case," 3.

136. Quoted in "A Slave Case," *Pittsfield Sun* (12 Nov. 1857): 3.

137. Ibid.

138. "The Slave Betty," *Liberator* (19 Feb. 1858): 31.

139. Delaney, *Race, Place, and the Law*, 49. See also the case of Clarissa, recounted in "Court of Appeals of Kentucky, January, 1853," *American Law Register* 1 (Mar. 1853): 295–300.

140. Bourdieu, "Force of Law," 838.

141. Finkelman, *Imperfect Union*, 127.

142. "Northern Servility," *Liberator* (7 Sept. 1855): 141.

143. To contemporary witnesses, the Crafts' flight to freedom appeared no different from the journeys of wealthy southerners who flocked to northern towns. The Crafts were keenly aware of the southern travel culture they mimicked. As it was not customary for southern women to travel alone, Ellen disguised herself as a gentleman planter, with William as her valet, on the four-day rail and steamboat journey from Macon, Georgia, to Philadelphia. See William Craft, *Running a Thousand Miles for Freedom: The Escape of William and Ellen Craft from Slavery* (Baton Rouge: Louisiana State University Press, 1999).

144. John Hope Franklin and Loren Schweninger, *In Search of the Promised Land: A Slave Family in the Old South* (New York: Oxford University Press, 2006), 16.

145. James Thomas, *From Tennessee Slave to St. Louis Entrepreneur: The Autobiography of James Thomas*, ed. Loren Schweninger (Columbia: University of Missouri Press, 1984), 121; further references to *From Tennessee Slave* are to this edition and are cited parenthetically in the text as *FTS*.

146. Franklin and Schweninger, *In Search of the Promised Land*, 81.

147. Steven Mintz, introduction to *The Problem of Evil: Slavery, Freedom, and the Ambiguities of American Reform*, ed. Steven Mintz and John Stauffer (Amherst: University of Massachusetts Press, 2007), 13–14.

148. "The Wheeler Slave Case: Passmore Williamson Committed for Contempt," *Frederick Douglass' Paper* (3 Aug. 1855): 3D–E. Two plot elements lead some scholars to believe that Johnson (who was literate) was indeed "Hannah Crafts." The fictional Mrs. Wheeler purchases the novel's narrator, Hannah, after "her two waiting maids had ran off to the North," even though she had commanded her "second waiting maid, to keep a sharp eye on Jane." Johnson also professed that she had secreted away in her trunk a suit of men's clothing, which she intended to don in New York to escape from Wheeler before they boarded the Nicaragua-bound steamer, and the narrator also avails herself of the same disguise to escape the fictional Wheelers in *The Bondswoman's Narrative*. Hannah Crafts, *The Bondswoman's Narrative*, ed. Henry Louis Gates, Jr. (New York: Warner Books, 2002), 148, 150.

149. For a popular history of the events surrounding the case, see Nat Brandt and Yanna Kroyt Brandt, *In the Shadow of the Civil War: Passmore Williamson and the Rescue of Jane Johnson* (Columbia: University of South Carolina Press, 2007); and for a fictional account based on the Johnsons' escape, see Lorene Cary, *Price of a Child* (New York: Vintage Books, 1996).

150. "Judicial Usurpation," *Liberator* (3 Aug. 1855): 122.

151. Henry Louis Gates, Jr., introduction to *The Bondswoman's Narrative*, by Hannah Crafts, xliv–xlv; Katherine E. Flynn, "Jane Johnson, Found! But Is She 'Hannah Crafts'? The Search for the Author of *The Bondswoman's Narrative*," in *In Search of Hannah Crafts: Essays on "The Bondswoman's Narrative*," ed. Henry Louis Gates, Jr., and Hollis Robbins (New York: Basic Civitas, 2004), 390. Wheeler was minister to Nicaragua when the filibusterer William Walker annexed the country and reestablish slavery there in a bid to gain southern support for his military regime. Wheeler's early support of Walker vexed the State Department (Gates, introduction to *The Bondswoman's Narrative*, xlv).

152. Flynn, "Jane Johnson," 372.

153. Pennsylvania Anti-Slavery Society, *Narrative of the Facts in the Case of Passmore Williamson* (Philadelphia: Pennsylvania Anti-Slavery Society, 1855), 3, 12.

154. Sully, as Flynn notes, had deep ties to John K. Kane that stretched back many years. Kane was a major financial backer for Sully's trip to England to paint the young Queen Victoria and also his legal counsel in the 1838 case over the portrait and its copies (Flynn, "Jane Johnson," 373).

155. "The Case of Passmore Williamson: Statement by His Father," *Frederick Douglass' Paper* (28 Sept. 1855): 1C–E.

156. Any slave brought into Pennsylvania in this manner "could have the assistance of the Committee and the advice of counsel without charge, by simply availing themselves of these proffered favors" (*URR*, 87).

157. "Judicial Usurpation," *Liberator* (3 Aug. 1855): 122.

158. Still later brought a complaint against Wheeler for "assault and battery on the person of Jane Johnson ... with an attempt to kidnap," although the constable reportedly refused to serve the warrant for Wheeler's arrest. "Passmore Williamson," *Liberator* (17 Aug. 1855): 131; Brandt and Brandt, *In the Shadow of the Civil War*, 118.

159. Pennsylvania Anti-Slavery Society, *Narrative of the Facts*, 8. Kane had faced Williamson in court earlier, when Williamson testified on behalf of the abolitionists involved in Lancaster County's 1851 "Christiana Riot" (Brandt and Brandt, *In the Shadow of the Civil War*, 68–69).

160. "A Decade of the Slave Power," *National Era* (3 Apr. 1856): 53.

161. Finkelman, *Imperfect Union*, 4–5.

162. Ibid., 145.

163. "Passing Events," *Happy Home and Parlor Magazine* (1 Sept. 1855): 196.

164. Pennsylvania Anti-Slavery Society, *Narrative of the Facts*, 23.

165. *United States ex rel. Wheeler v. Williamson*, 28 F. Cas. 682, 3 Am. Law Reg. 729 (1855).

166. "Opinions in the Williamson Case," *Frederick Douglass' Paper* (28 Sept. 1855): 1F–G; "The Wheeler Slave Case," *National Era* (2 Aug. 1855): 122.

167. "The Sway of the Slave Power—Impeachment of Judge Kane," *Liberator* (9 Nov. 1855): 180.

168. "Wheeler Slave Case," *National Era* (2 Aug. 1855): 122.

169. "'Democratic' Principles," *National Era* (7 Aug. 1856): 126; "The Wheeler Slave Case," *National Era* (6 Sept. 1855): 142.

170. "Judge Kane and His Victim—No Free States in the Union—The Common Law for Slavery—Slaveholding Millenium [sic]," *Frederick Douglass' Paper* (19 Oct. 1855): 1; Brandt and Brandt, *In the Shadow of the Civil War*, 91.

171. DeLombard, *Slavery on Trial*, 7; "The Philadelphia Martyr," *Independent* (4 Oct. 1855): 316; William C. Nell, "Letters of Negroes, Largely Personal and Private," *Journal of Negro History* 11, no. 1 (Jan. 1926): 186.

172. "Letter of Sympathy," *Frederick Douglass' Paper* (24 Aug. 1855): 1F.

173. When *Passmore Williamson's Case* (1855) came before the Pennsylvania Supreme Court, Justice Jeremiah S. Black (with Judge John C. Knox dissenting) refused to grant a writ of habeas corpus to release Williamson from the custody of the federal marshal, Francis Wynkoop. Not only did Chief Justice Black argue lack of jurisdiction in the case; he fully supported Kane's decision. He saw Williamson's refusal to respond to the writ as purposeful. "There are many persons who would gladly purchase the honours of martyrdom in a popular cause at almost any given price," reasoned Black, "while others are deterred by a mere show of punishment. Each is detained until he finds himself willing to conform." He concluded that Williamson, "therefore, carries the key of his prison in his own pocket. He can come out, when he will, by making terms with the court that sent him there." *Passmore Williamson's Case*, 26 Pa. 9, Pa. LEXIS 232 (1855).

174. "The Case of Passmore Williamson," *New York Evangelist* (27 Sept. 1855): 154; "Judge Kane's Argument, as Demonstrating His Injustice," *Independent* (25 Oct. 1855): 1; Horace Dresser, "Judge Kane and His Late Prisoner," *National Era* (22 Nov. 1855): 185. Abolitionist Richard Hildreth, who authored the hugely popular fictional slave narrative *The Slave; or, Memoirs of Archy Moore* (1836), published an American edition of *Atrocious Judges: Lives of Judges Infamous as Tools of Tyrants and Instruments of Oppression* (1856), with an appendix containing the case of Passmore Williamson (DeLombard, *Slavery on Trial*, 21).

175. Williamson later brought charges against the federal judge for false imprisonment, claiming fifty thousand dollars in damages, although Kane's death from typhoid pneumonia on 21 February 1858 prevented a judgment in *Passmore Williamson v. John K. Kane* (1857). See *Williamson v. Lewis*, 39 Pa. 9, Pa. LEXIS 159 (1861); Brandt and Brandt, *In the Shadow of the Civil War*, 145, 150.

176. "Passmore Williamson Released," *National Era* (8 Nov. 1855): 178; "Escape of Judge Kane," *Independent* (8 Nov. 1855): 356.

177. Brandt and Brandt, *In the Shadow of the Civil War*, 92.

178. Kate E.R. Pickard, *The Kidnapped and the Ransomed* (Syracuse, NY: William T.

Hamilton, 1856), 247; further references to *The Kidnapped and the Ransomed* are to this edition and are cited parenthetically in the text as *KR*.

179. "The Case of Mr. Wheeler's Slaves," *New York Daily Times* (1 Aug. 1855): 6.

180. "The Case of Passmore Williamson," *National Era* (27 Sept. 1855): 154; "Wheeler Slave Case: Passmore Williamson Committed for Contempt."

181. "The Wheeler Slave Case: Passmore Williamson Committed for Contempt." The distinction drawn between Williamson's case and the second criminal trial involving Still and the five black dockhands shows, according to DeLombard, how "federal and state courts cooperated to support a narrative of white civic agency (no matter how misguided) and black criminality (no matter how dubious)." The federal court's denial of black agency meant that the actions of Still and the black dockhands could only be construed as criminal acts (DeLombard, *Slavery on Trial*, 122–23).

182. "Wheeler Slave Case," *National Era* (6 Sept. 1855): 142.

183. "The Philadelphia Slave Case—Judge Kane's Decision," *Liberator* (3 Aug. 1855): 122.

184. Brandt and Brandt, *In the Shadow of the Civil War*, 35.

185. She married Lawrence Woodfork shortly after her arrival and lived at 1 Southack Court until his death in 1861. Johnson remarried in 1864, to William Harris, a mariner, although he died a short year later. Her son Isaiah enlisted in the Massachusetts 55th Regiment, U.S. Colored Troops and fought in the Civil War. Jane Johnson (Woodfork Harris) died August 1872 from a citywide dysentery epidemic and was buried in Woodlawn Cemetery (Flynn, "Jane Johnson," 375, 379–82).

186. Brandt and Brandt, *In the Shadow of the Civil War*, 157.

187. Flynn, "Jane Johnson," 391.

188. The jury eventually convicted Ballard and Custis of assault on Wheeler, and they were each sentenced to one week in prison and fined ten dollars (Philadelphia Anti-Slavery Society, *Narrative of the Facts*, 14, 15).

189. Witnesses for Wheeler including police officer Thomas Wallace, Capt. Andrew Heath, Robert T. Tomlinson, and William Edwards all concurred that the boys "said they wanted to go with their master." Brandt and Brandt, *In the Shadow of the Civil War*, 36–37; "The Case of the Servants or Slaves Taken from the Hon. John H. Wheeler," *Philadelphia Public Ledger* (21 July 1855): 1.

190. Johnson made her affidavit before Judge Erastus Dean Culver in New York on July 31 and resubmitted it in the U.S. Court for the District of Massachusetts shortly after her arrival in Boston. "The Wheeler Slave Case: Their Own Story," *Frederick Douglass' Paper* (10 Aug. 1855): 1C; "Case of Mr. Wheeler's Slaves," 6; Flynn, "Jane Johnson," 374; "Judge Kane Maintains His Tyrannical Position," *Frederick Douglass' Paper* (19 Oct. 1855): 3F; "The Case of Passmore Williamson," *Independent* (11 Oct. 1855): 324; "Passmore Williamson," *Circular* (18 Oct. 1855): 154; "Case of Colonel Wheeler's Slaves," *Liberator* (19 Oct. 1855): 167.

191. "The Wheeler Slave Case—Testimony of Jane Johnson," *Liberator* (7 Sept. 1855): 143.

192. "The Philadelphia Slave Case-Judge Kane's Decision," *Liberator* (3 Aug. 1855): 122. A few newspaper accounts reported, possibly erroneously, that Johnson had left two children behind in Virginia. The *Liberator* reportage of the trial of Still, Williamson, and the five black

dockhands also recorded, "She said she supposed herself to be about twenty-five years old, and has four children." "The Wheeler Case at Philadelphia," *Liberator* (7 Sept. 1855): 143.

193. Pennsylvania Anti-Slavery Society, *Narrative of the Facts*, 14.

194. "Mr. Wheeler's Slave Case," *Liberator* (3 Aug. 1855): 122.

195. "First of August Celebrations," *Liberator* (15 Aug. 1856): 130.

196. Brandt and Brandt, *In the Shadow of the Civil War*, 38.

197. Maria Weston Chapman, "The Twenty-Second National Anti-Slavery Bazaar," *Liberator* (25 Jan. 1856): 13.

198. "Wheeler Slave Case," *National Era* (6 Sept. 1855): 142.

199. Priscilla Wald, "Hannah Crafts," in Gates, *In Search of Hannah Craft*s (see note 148), 213–30.

200. Pickard wrote the narrative with distribution and profit in mind. She informed Still that "the publishing firm of Miller, Orton and Mulligan, of Auburn—one of the best publishing houses in the state"—had agreed to publish *The Kidnapped and the Ransomed*. "They published Fred. Douglas' book last year and have published several other works on slavery," she further enthused, "I think the arrangement will be a great help to the circulation of the book. *You and I must begin to plan what to do with our money.*" Kate E. R. Pickard to Peter Still, Camillus, New York, 9 May 1856, Peter Still Papers, 1850–1875, Special Collections and University Archives, Rutgers University Libraries.

201. Kate E.R. Pickard to Peter Still, Camillus, New York, 30 June 1856, Peter Still Papers, 1850–1875, Special Collections and University Archives, Rutgers University Libraries.

202. Brandt and Brandt, *In the Shadow of the Civil War*, 12.

203. Samuel J. May, introduction to *KR*, xix. Pickard lived several years in Tuscumbia, Alabama, "the very town, or neighborhood, where most of the events . . . transpired," before she married and returned north to settle in Camillus, New York (May, introduction to *KR*, xix). An endorsement of *The Kidnapped and the Ransomed* in the *Boston Daily Atlas* informed readers that the "writer of this narrative was a highly esteemed teacher in the Female Seminary at Tuscumbia, Alabama, who had every opportunity to acquire a personal knowledge of all the prominent facts and circumstances which she has narrated." "New Publications," *Boston Daily Atlas* (12 June 1856): 1.

204. Sidney's first attempt to flee with her four children failed, although she succeeded in her second attempt with just her two daughters. She rejoined her husband, Levin, who had purchased his freedom and resettled in New Jersey. The family changed its surname from Steel to Still to elude recapture.

205. Kate E.R. Pickard to Peter Still, Buffalo, New York, 24 June 1855, Peter Still Papers, 1850–1875, Special Collections and University Archives, Rutgers University Libraries.

206. Brandt and Brandt, *In the Shadow of the Civil War*, 7.

207. May, introduction to *KR*, xvii–xviii.

208. The untitled engraving may have been based on Sidney's daguerreotype. Still had forwarded daguerreotypes of his family to Pickard for the engraver, who, according to Pickard, "blundered sadly." Pickard informed Still that she had removed the offensive family portrait from the edition, fearing that it "would be an insult to you and to your friends," although

she praised the engraver's portrait of Sidney: "Your mother's face, I think, is very good—that was just copied from the daguerreotype without attempting to give her figure" (Pickard to Still, 9 May 1856, Peter Still Papers).

209. May suggested another title for Still's narrative: "Memoirs of the Life of Peter Still, forty two years a slave; of his remarkable restoration to liberty, and to his aged mother and her children; together with the subsequent liberation of his family." Samuel J. May to Peter Still, 1855, Peter Still Papers, 1850–1875, Special Collections and University Archives, Rutgers University Libraries.

210. See Saidiya Hartman, *Lose Your Mother: A Journey along the Atlantic Slave Route* (New York: Farrar, Straus, and Giroux, 2007), 84–86.

211. John Jolliffe, *Belle Scott; or, Liberty Overthrown!* (Columbus, OH: D. Anderson, 1856), 202.

212. Kemble, *Journal*, 350.

213. Spillers, *Black, White, and in Color*, 220.

214. Solomon Northrup, *Twelve Years a Slave* (New York: Dover, 1970), 61.

215. "An Impressive Story of Slave Life," *American Publishers' Circular and Literary Gazette* (5 Jul. 1856): 398.

216. William Wells Brown, *Narrative of William W. Brown, a Fugitive Slave*, in *Slave Narratives*, ed. William L. Andrews and Henry Louis Gates, Jr., 369–423 (New York: Library of America, 2000), 415.

217. Orlando Patterson, *Slavery and Social Death* (Cambridge, MA: Harvard University Press, 1982).

218. Loring and Bowditch, along with a number of notable abolitionists, published a notice endorsing Still's mission in the *Liberator*, and Loring, according to Pickard's narrative, "kindly acted as his [Still's] treasurer." "Peter Still's Case," *Liberator* (21 Jan. 1853): 11; *KR*, 324–25.

219. Kate E.R. Pickard to Peter Still, Camillus, New York, 22 Jan. 1855, Peter Still Papers, 1850–1875, Special Collections and University Archives, Rutgers University Libraries. "Have you heard anything from the little boy? Do you intend to try to get it this summer? I do hope the little fellow may be rescued from a life of slavery," she asked in another letter from Buffalo (Pickard to Still, 24 June 1855, Peter Still Papers).

220. "Habeas Corpus for Release of Slaves," *Liberator* (10 Dec. 1841): 200.

221. Benjamin Drew, *The Refugee; or, The Narratives of Fugitive Slaves in Canada, Related by Themselves, with an Account of the History and Condition of the Colored Population of Upper Canada* (Toronto: Prospero Canadian Collection, 2000), 329.

222. Thomas, "Citizen Hester," 196.

223. Walter Johnson, *Soul by Soul: Life inside the Antebellum Slave Market* (Cambridge, MA: Harvard University Press, 1999), 23.

224. Drew, *Refugee*, 88–89.

225. James W.C. Pennington, *Fugitive Blacksmith; or, Events in the History of James W.C. Pennington*, 3rd ed. (Westport, CT: Negro Universities Press, 1971), 39.

CHAPTER 3

1. See Carolyn Sorisio, "Unmasking the Genteel Performer: Elizabeth Keckley's *Behind the Scenes* and the Politics of Public Wrath," *African American Review* 34 (Spring 2000): 19–38.

2. Keckley was born Elizabeth Hobbs, the property of Colonel Armistead Burwell of Dinwiddie County, Virginia, who was her biological father. Burwell's parental relation to Keckley did not prevent him from "loaning" the fourteen-year-old to his son Robert, a Presbyterian minister, upon his marriage. This temporary transfer precipitated the violent circumstances leading to the birth of her son George in North Carolina. Keckley withheld mention that George's father was Alexander McKenzie Kirkland, the brother-in-law of imminent southern jurist Thomas Ruffian. Jennifer Fleischner, *Mrs. Lincoln and Mrs. Keckley: The Remarkable Story of the Friendship between a First Lady and a Former Slave* (New York: Broadway Books, 2003), 65–66, 125, 130.

3. Ibid., 140; Don E. Fehrenbacher, *Dred Scott Case: Its Significance in American Law and Politics* (Oxford: Oxford University Press, 1978), 253. Sanford's name was misspelled as "Sandford" in the subsequent lawsuit that the Scotts' lawyers filed in federal court. The case had already gone twice before a St. Louis circuit court.

4. Elizabeth Keckley, *Behind the Scenes by Elizabeth Keckley, Formerly a Slave, but More Recently Modiste, and Friend to Mrs. Abraham Lincoln; or, Thirty Years a Slave and Four Years in the White House* (Chicago: R.R. Donnelley & Sons, 1998), 34–35; further references to *Behind the Scenes* are to this edition and are cited parenthetically in the text as *BS*.

5. Fehrenbacher, *Dred Scott Case*, 139.

6. Garland's heirs honored this promise after he died in 1854.

7. Harriet C. Frazier, *Runaway and Freed Missouri Slaves and Those Who Helped Them, 1763–1865* (Jefferson, NC: McFarland, 2004), 78.

8. Ibid., 67, 78.

9. Fleischner, *Mrs. Lincoln and Mrs. Keckley*, 148.

10. James Thomas, *From Tennessee Slave to St. Louis Entrepreneur: The Autobiography of James Thomas*, ed. Loren Schweninger (Columbia: University of Missouri Press, 1984), 157.

11. See Rebecca Scott, *Degrees of Freedom: Louisiana and Cuba after Slavery* (Cambridge, MA: Belknap, 2005).

12. Paul Finkelman, *Dred Scott v. Sandford: A Brief History with Documents* (New York: Bedford/St. Martin's, 1997), 1–2.

13. Lea S. VanderVelde and Sandhya L. Subramanian, "Mrs. Dred Scott," in *Critical Race Feminism: A Reader*, ed. Adrien Katherine Wing (New York: New York University Press, 2003), 80.

14. Ibid., 82. Keila Grinberg also notes the significance of urban milieus and "family ties" to those slaves who became involved in freedom suits in North and South America. Keila Grinberg, "Freedom Suits and Civil Law in Brazil and the United States," *Slavery & Abolition* 22:3 (2001): 68.

15. Fehrenbacher, *Dred Scott Case*, 240.
16. Ibid., 121.
17. Ibid., 253.
18. Fehrenbacher, *Dred Scott Case*, 253. VanderVelde and Subramanian first published their findings on Harriet Robinson Scott in *Yale Law Journal*: Lea VanderVelde and Sandhya Subramanian, "Mrs. Dred Scott," *Yale Law Journal* 106 (Jan. 1997): 1033–1120.
19. Fehrenbacher, *Dred Scott Case*, 247–48.
20. VanderVelde and Subramanian, "Mrs. Dred Scott," in *Critical Race Feminism*, 82–83.
21. Fehrenbacher, *Dred Scott Case*, 244.
22. Emerson sent for the Scotts to join him in Louisiana soon after his wedding. The Scotts, alarmed by the prospect of returning to slave territory, may have brought an earlier suit against Emerson for freedom. During this period, Emerson reportedly remarked, "Even one of my negroes in Saint Louis has sued me for his freedom" (Fehrenbacher, *Dred Scott Case*, 245).
23. Court documents record the birth of Eliza "on board the Steamboat *Gipsey* north of the north line of the State of Missouri & upon the River Mississippi" in free territory, and Lizzie was born at Jefferson Barracks in St. Louis (VanderVelde and Subramanian, "Mrs. Dred Scott," *Yale Law Journal*, 1043, 1059).
24. Ibid., 1044.
25. Fehrenbacher, *Dred Scott Case*, 255, 257.
26. Mark V. Tushnet, *American Law of Slavery, 1810–1860: Considerations of Humanity and Interest* (Princeton, NJ: Princeton University Press, 1981), 29.
27. Robert Moore, Jr., "A Ray of Hope, Extinguished: St. Louis Slave Suits for Freedom," *Gateway Heritage* 14, no. 3 (Winter 1993–94): 10.
28. James Kent, *Commentaries on American Law*, ed. George F. Comstock, vol. 2, 11th ed. (Boston: Little, Brown, 1866), 284.
29. David Thomas Konig, "The Long Road to *Dred Scott*: Personhood and the Rule of Law in the Trial Court Records of St. Louis Slave Freedom Suits," *University of Missouri-Kansas City Law Review* 75 (Fall 2006): 73.
30. Moore, "Ray of Hope," 4, 10. Justice George Tompkins did qualify the difference, later emphasized in *Julia v. McKinney*, between traveling slaveholders and those who introduced slavery onto free soil by residence.
31. Ibid., 9.
32. *Winny v. Whitesides, Phebe* (Apr. 1821) Case No. 190, Circuit Court Case Files, Office of the Circuit Clerk, City of St. Louis, Missouri, available online at http://stlcourtrecords.wustl.edu (accessed 13 Sept. 2005).
33. The lower court recorded these cases with slight differences as *Julia, a woman of color v. McKenney, Samuel T.*, and *Rachel, a woman of color v. Walker, William*.
34. Konig, "Long Road to *Dred Scott*," 71.
35. Carrington had hired out Julia after telling another Pike County resident that "he had a Black Girl he wanted to hire out if he could safely do it." See *Julia, a woman of color v.*

McKenney, Samuel T. (Mar. 1831), Case No. 66, Circuit Court Case Files, Office of the Circuit Clerk, City of St. Louis, Missouri, available online at http://stlcourtrecords.wustl.edu (accessed 29 Apr. 2008).

36. *Julia v. McKinney*, 3 Mo. 270, Mo. LEXIS 32 (1833).

37. *Harriet, an infant v. McKenney, Samuel T.; Walker, William; James, Thomas D.* (Jul. 1833), Case No. 17, Circuit Court Case Files, Office of the Circuit Clerk City of St. Louis, Missouri, available online at http://stlcourtrecords.wustl.edu (accessed 23 Aug. 2007).

38. VanderVelde and Subramanian, "Mrs. Dred Scott," *Yale Law Journal*, 1073–74; Konig, "Long Road to *Dred Scott*," 75. William Wells Brown's slave narrative offers many "heart-sick" recollections of the vicious St. Louis "soul-driver" James Walker, who suffered no qualms about separating slave mothers from their children in the event of a lucrative sale. He once made a "present" to a passing stranger of a "little nigger" when the slave mother failed to quiet the child on one of his regular journeys from St. Louis to New Orleans. William Wells Brown, *Narrative of William W. Brown, a Fugitive Slave*, in *Slave Narratives*, ed. William L. Andrews and Henry Louis Gates, Jr. (New York: Library of America, 2000), 389–390, 394.

39. Konig "Long Road to *Dred Scott*," 75; VanderVelde and Subramanian, "Mrs. Dred Scott," *Yale Law Journal*, 1073.

40. VanderVelde and Subramanian, "Mrs. Dred Scott," *Yale Law Journal*, 1048.

41. Ibid.

42. Ibid., 1050.

43. *Rachael, a Woman of Color, v. Walker*, 4 Mo. 350, Mo. LEXIS 22 (1836).

44. Ibid.

45. VanderVelde and Subramanian, "Mrs. Dred Scott," *Yale Law Journal*, 1057–58.

46. *Henry, James, a boy of color v. Walker, William* (Nov. 1834), Case No. 83, Circuit Court Case Files, Office of the Circuit Clerk, City of St. Louis, Missouri, available online at http://stlcourtrecords.wustl.edu (accessed 23 Aug. 2007).

47. VanderVelde and Subramanian, "Mrs. Dred Scott," *Yale Law Journal*, 1061.

48. Lindon Barrett, "Self-Knowledge, Law, and African American Autobiography: Lucy A. Delaney's 'From the Darkness Cometh the Light,'" in *The Culture of Autobiography: Constructions of Self-Representation*, ed. Robert Folkenflick, 104-24 (Stanford, CA: Stanford University Press, 1993), 104.

49. See *Wash, Polly v. Magehan, Joseph M.* (Nov. 1839), Case No. 167, Circuit Court Case Files, Office of the Circuit Clerk, City of St. Louis, Missouri, available online at http://stlcourtrecords.wustl.edu (accessed 15 Aug. 2007).

50. Ibid.

51. Ibid.

52. Ibid.

53. Ibid.

54. See James Olney, "'I Was Born': Slave Narratives, Their Status as Autobiography and as Literature," in *The Slave's Narrative*, ed. Charles T. David and Henry Louis Gates, Jr. (Oxford: Oxford University Press, 1985), 148–75.

55. Barrett, "Self-Knowledge," 120.

56. Lucy A. Delaney, *From the Darkness Cometh the Light; or, Struggles for Freedom* (St. Louis: J.T. Smith, 1891), 12; further references to *From the Darkness* are to this edition and are cited parenthetically in the text as *FD*.

57. Eric Gardner, "'You Have No Business to Whip Me': The Freedom Suits of Polly Wash and Lucy Ann Delaney," *African American Review* 41 (Spring 2007): 35.

58. Harriet A. Jacobs, *Incidents in the Life of a Slave Girl*, ed. Jean Fagan Yellin (Cambridge, MA: Harvard University Press, 2000), 78. In Delaney's trial, her lawyer called Polly's failed escape a "voluntary return to slavery" in his effort to transform the ambivalence of slave motherhood into a powerful renunciation of freedom for the sake of maternal love.

59. Gardner, "You Have No Business to Whip Me," 40.

60. Ibid.

61. *Britton, Lucy Ann v. Mitchell, David D.* (Nov. 1844), Case No. 18, Circuit Court Case Files, Office of the Circuit Clerk, City of St. Louis, Missouri, available online at http://stl-courtrecords.wustl.edu (accessed 15 Aug. 2007).

62. Gardner, "You Have No Business to Whip Me," 37.

63. Ibid., 47n; William Ehrlich, "The Origins of the Dred Scott Case," *Journal of Negro History*, 59, no. 2 (Apr. 1974): 139.

64. Moore, "Ray of Hope," 6.

65. Ibid.

66. Barrett also notes how the courtroom scene "ostensibly produces her freedom" even as it "dramatizes an enduring state of subjection" to the laws and customs that enslaved her (Barrett, "Self-Knowledge," 119).

67. This decision was not the end of the legal disputes in the case. Mitchell lodged a motion for a new trial that was eventually dismissed. In response, Polly filed a second suit on Delaney's behalf against Mitchell for false imprisonment with damages assessed at one thousand dollars, a suit that she eventually withdrew (Gardner, "You Have No Business to Whip Me," 43, 44).

68. Eric Gardner, "'Face to Face': Localizing Lucy Delaney's *From the Darkness Cometh the Light*," *Legacy* 24, no. 1 (2007): 50–51.

69. *Revised Statutes of the State of Missouri: Revised and Digested by the Eighteenth General Assembly, during the Session of One Thousand Eight Hundred and Fifty-Four and One Thousand Eight Hundred and Fifty-Five* (Jefferson, MO: J. Lusk, 1856), 1097, 1099.

70. The court postponed consideration of *Scott v. Emerson* until the October 1850 session, one month after the passage of the new Fugitive Slave Bill further antagonized sectional strife. The Missouri Supreme Court subsequently decided to overturn precedents upholding the Northwest Ordinance's exclusion of slavery from the territories. This opinion was never written, which forced Garland and Lyman to bring Emerson's case before a newly elected slate of judges the following year. A Missouri constitutional amendment had turned the Supreme Court from an appointive to an elective body, and Judge William B. Napton, who was chosen to write the opinion of the court, was swept from office before he finished it (Fleischner, *Mrs. Lincoln and Mrs. Keckley*, 140–41; Fehrenbacher, *Dred Scott Case*, 260).

71. *Scott v. Emerson*, 15 Mo. 576, Mo. LEXIS 224 (1853).

72. "A Slavery Decision Reversed," *National Era* (15 Apr. 1852): 61.

73. The nominal title of the Scotts ownership had been transferred to Sanford. Roswell Field, the attorney for the Scotts, argued that the diversity of citizenship—Scott as a Missouri citizen and Sanford as a New York citizen—granted federal jurisdiction over the case. In spring 1854, the ailing Garland appeared before the Missouri circuit court on Sanford's behalf in *Scott v. Sandford* (Fleischner, *Mrs. Lincoln and Mrs. Keckley*, 143).

74. Frances Smith Foster, "Historical Introduction," in *BS*, xxxvi.

75. "Unconstitutionality of Missouri Compromise," *Saturday Evening Post* (14 Mar. 1857): 6; *The Friend: A Religious and Literary Journal* (28 Mar. 1857): 231.

76. See Lea VanderVelde, *Mrs. Dred Scott: A Life on Slavery's Frontier* (New York: Oxford University Press, 2009) for a recently published biographical account of Harriet Robinson Scott.

77. "Visit to Dred Scott—His Family—Incidents of His Life—Decision of the Supreme Court," *Frank Leslie's Illustrated Newspaper* (27 June 1857): 49; further references to "Visit to Dred Scott" are cited parenthetically in the text as "VDS."

78. Fehrenbacher, *Dred Scott Case*, 2.

79. "Dred Scott Owned by a Republican Member of Congress," *Fort Wayne Sentinel* (28 Mar. 1857): 1E.

80. "Dred Scott and His 'Republican' Owner," *Syracuse Daily Courier* (30 May 1857): 2D.

81. Todd C. Frankel, "Finding a St. Louis Legend: The Work of Two Groups Uncovers the Resting Place of Harriet Scott, the Wife of Dred Scott," *St. Louis Post-Dispatch*, 4th ed. (5 Mar. 2006): C1.

82. William G. Hawkins, *Lunsford Lane; or, Another Helper from North Carolina* (Boston: Crosby & Nichols, 1863), 185; further references to *Lunsford Lane* are to this edition and are cited parenthetically in the text as *LL*.

83. Quoted in VanderVelde and Subramanian, "Mrs. Dred Scott," *Yale Law Journal*, 1075.

84. Ariela J. Gross, *Double Character: Slavery and Mastery in the Antebellum Courtroom* (Princeton, NJ: Princeton University Press, 2000), 37.

85. Quoted in Jeannine Marie DeLombard, *Slavery on Trial: Law, Abolitionism, and Print Culture* (Chapel Hill: University of North Carolina Press, 2007), 75.

86. "Freedom Suits Case Files, 1814–1860," St. Louis Circuit Court Historical Records Project (21 Oct. 2007), http://www.stlcourtrecords.wustl.edu/about-freedom-suits-series.php.

87. Barrett, "Self-Knowledge," 123.

88. Konig, "Long Road to *Dred Scott*," 68.

89. Ibid.

90. Moore, "Ray of Hope," 8.

91. Fehrenbacher, *Dred Scott Case*, 251.

92. The St. Louis Circuit Court Historical Project is a collaborative collection and preservation effort by the Missouri State Archives, the Circuit Clerk of the City of St. Louis, and

Washington University in St. Louis that has produced an online database of digitized images of every surviving court document in the file of freedom suits. See http://www.stlcourtrecords.wustl.edu/about-freedom-suits-series.php.

93. Gardner, "You Have No Business to Whip Me," 44n. 35.

94. Fehrenbacher, *Dred Scott Case*, 61.

95. The Thomas Amendment, proposed by Jesse B. Thomas of Illinois, "declared slavery to be 'forever prohibited' in the remainder of the Louisiana cession lying north of parallel 36° 30'." Missouri entered the Union bordered by Illinois (1818) and the free territories that became the states of Iowa (1846), Kansas (1861), and Nebraska (1867) (Fehrenbacher, *Dred Scott Case*, 107).

96. Konig, "Long Road to *Dred Scott*," 72.

97. David Delaney, *Race, Place, and the Law, 1836–1948* (Austin: University of Texas Press, 1998), 59.

98. Kemble, *Journal*, 12.

99. Konig, "Long Road to *Dred Scott*," 71.

100. Delaney, *Race, Place, and the Law*, 57.

101. "What the Dred Scott Case Decided, and What It Did Not Decide," *New Era* (30 Jul. 1857): 124.

102. Frazier, *Runaway and Freed Missouri Slaves*, 59; Paul Finkelman, *Imperfect Union: Slavery, Federalism, and Comity* (Chapel Hill: University of North Carolina Press, 1981), 227.

103. *The Case of Dred Scott in the United States Supreme Court: The Full Opinions of Chief Justice Taney and Justice Curtis, and Abstracts of the Opinions of the Other Judges; With an Analysis of the Points Ruled, and Some Concluding Observations* (New York: Greeley & McElrath, Tribune Buildings, 1857), 38.

104. Barrett, "Self-Knowledge," 116.

105. Konig, "Long Road to *Dred Scott*," 61.

106. Gross, *Double Character*, 3.

107. Kent, *Commentaries on American Law*, 278.

108. Konig, "Long Road to *Dred Scott*," 61.

109. Barrett, "Self-Knowledge," 105.

110. Fehrenbacher, *Dred Scott Case*, 332.

111. Ibid.

112. These procedural regulations also dictated that the labor of slave litigants awaiting trial was under the command of the sheriff. The Scotts, for example, were hired out while awaiting their trials, and their wages were impounded by the court. The money collected from the hire would then be paid to the party successful in the suit. In other words, slave petitioners must declare themselves "free" subjects upon instigating a petition, yet they continue to have no autonomy over their labor until the court deems them a free subject (VanderVelde and Subramanian, "Mrs. Dred Scott," in *Critical Race Feminism*, 81).

113. William Goodell, *American Slave Code in Theory and Practice: Its Distinctive Features Shown by Its Statutes, Judicial Decisions, and Illustrative Facts* (New York: American and Foreign Anti-Slavery Society, 1853), 17.

114. Ibid., 299.

115. Ibid.

116. Some three thousand manumissions were recorded for 1860 alone (Fehrenbacher, *Dred Scott Case*, 48, 50).

117. Orlando Patterson, *Slavery and Social Death: A Comparative Study* (Cambridge, MA: Harvard University Press, 1982), 101.

118. Konig, "Long Road to *Dred Scott*," 53.

119. Moore, "Ray of Hope," 6–7.

120. Konig, "Long Road to *Dred Scott*," 55.

121. Fehrenbacher, *Dred Scott Case*, 280.

122. Ibid.

123. Lawson's *American State Trials* describes the pamphlet as a "rare publication, a copy of which is in the Lawson Library of Criminology (Univ. of Mo.)." In it, the "different pleadings are set out in full, and at the end is the certificate under seal of Benjamin F. Hickman, clerk of the Circuit Court of the United States for the District of Missouri, and dated May 25, 1854, that it contains 'a full and complete transcript of the record and proceedings had in said court in the case of Dred Scott against John A. Sanford as the same remains on file in my office.'" "The Trial of the Action of Dred Scott (a Slave) against John F.A. Sanford for False Imprisonment and Assault, St. Louis, Missouri, 1854," in John D. Lawson, *American State Trials*, vol. 13 (St. Louis: F.H. Thomas, 1914–36), 243.

124. Ibid., 243–44.

125. Ibid., 246–47.

126. Ibid., 244.

127. Ibid., 245.

128. A former St. Louis slaveholder, Montgomery Blair answered Scott's appeal and agreed to represent him without a fee. The dedicated Free-Soiler enlisted the aid of editor Gamaliel Bailey of the *National Era* to raise money for the court expenses (Fehrenbacher, *Dred Scott Case*, 281).

129. Harrison Anthony Trexler, *Slavery in Missouri, 1804–1865*, Johns Hopkins University Studies in Historical and Political Science 32, no. 2 (Baltimore: Johns Hopkins University Press, 1914), 218. Illinois "rendered unusually harsh decisions in freedom suits during the 1820s and 1830s, while across the river in slave-holding Missouri, freedom was more easily obtained" until the gruesome lynching of black steward Francis McIntosh in 1836 halted, momentarily, the number of freedom suits brought before St. Louis courts (Moore, "Ray of Hope," 11, 12).

130. DeLombard, *Slavery on Trial*, 177–79.

131. "Important Deoision [sic]," *The Friend: A Religious and Literary Journal* (13 Oct. 1827): 3; "Important Decision," *Genius of Universal Emancipation* (14 Oct. 1827): 115; "Important Decision," *Freedom's Journal* (14 Dec. 1827): 3A.

132. Ibid.

133. Ibid.

134. Meachum's African Baptist Church grew to more than five hundred members, and

the Sabbath school where he taught "was the first Sabbath school ever formed west of the Mississippi river"; new regulations closed the school in 1847. Fellow Baptist minister John Mason Peck had only praise for Meachum, whom he described as "an intelligent man of color," and for his AME Church, which he described as "one of the most orderly and efficient churches of colored people we have ever known." Donnie Bellamy, "The Education of Blacks in Missouri Prior to 1861," *Journal of Negro History* 59 no. 2 (Apr. 1974): 146, 150; John Mason Peck, "Brief View of the Baptist Interest in Each of the United States," *The American* (Nov. 1841): 173.

135. John Berry Meachum, *An Address to All the Colored Citizen of the United States* (Philadelphia: Printed for the Author, 1846), 3; further references to *An Address to All the Colored Citizen* are to this edition and are cited parenthetically in the text as *AA*.

136. Dennis L. Durst, "The Reverend John Berry Meachum (1789–1854) of St. Louis: Prophet and Entrepreneurial Black Educator in Historiographical Perspective," *North Star: A Journal of African American Religious History* 7, no. 2 (Spring 2004): 5.

137. "Capacity of Negroes to Take Care of Themselves," *Colored American* (11 Mar. 1837): 4A; "Capacity of Negroes to Take Care of Themselves," *Zion Herald* (12 Apr. 1837): 58; "Capacity of Negroes to Take Care of Themselves" *Philanthropist* (28 Oct. 1836): 3.

138. "Capacity of Negroes," *Colored American*, 4A.

139. Frederick Douglass, *My Bondage and My Freedom*, in *Frederick Douglass Autobiographies* (New York: Library of America, 2004), 377.

140. Meachum's entrepreneurial spirit was well rewarded. After arriving in St. Louis in 1815, he opened a barrel-making establishment and began buying real estate. By the 1850s, Meachum owned a farm in Illinois, where his parents had settled, and two brick buildings in St. Louis, which amounted to approximately eight thousand dollars. These real estate holdings in St. Louis alone placed him, according to Loren Schweninger, among the three largest black realty owners in the state of Missouri. Loren Schweninger, "Prosperous Blacks in the South, 1790–1880, *American Historical Review* 95, no. 1 (Feb. 1990): 44.

141. Steven Mintz, introduction to part 2, "The Antislavery Impulse," in *The Problem of Evil: Slavery, Freedom, and the Ambiguities of American Reform*, ed. Steven Mintz and John Stauffer (Amherst: University of Massachusetts Press, 2007), 127.

142. Fehrenbacher, *Dred Scott Case*, 193.

143. Deak Nabers, *Victory of Law: The Fourteenth Amendment, the Civil War, and American Literature, 1852–1867* (Baltimore: Johns Hopkins University Press, 2006), 1.

144. William Wells Brown, *Clotel; or, The President's Daughter* (Boston: Bedford/St. Martin's, 2000),187–88.

145. David Scott, *Refashioning Futures: Criticism after Postcoloniality* (Princeton, NJ: Princeton University Press, 1999), 80.

146. Brown, *Clotel*, 188.

147. *Judy (also known as Julia Logan) v. Meachum, John Berry* (Mar. 1835), Case No. 11, Circuit Court Case Files, Office of the Circuit Clerk, City of St. Louis, Missouri, available online at http://stlcourtrecords.wustl.edu (accessed 22 Sept. 2007).

148. Frazier, *Runaway and Freed Missouri Slaves*, 77.

149. *Judy v. Meachum.*

150. Ibid.

151. *Logan, Green Berry, an infant of color v. Meachum, John Berry, a free man of color* (Jul. 1836), Case No. 22, Circuit Court Case Files, Office of the Circuit Clerk, City of St. Louis, Missouri, available online at http://stlcourtrecords.wustl.edu (accessed 30 Aug. 2007).

152. Moore, "Ray of Hope," 9.

153. *Judy v. Meachum.*

154. The petitions of Aspasia, Celeste, Celestine, and Andrew reiterate almost verbatim Judy's own residency history. Lewis's petition reveals that his mother, Celeste, grandmother Judy, and aunt Aspasia had "all been pronounced free by the verdict of separate and distinct juries based upon the facts above set forth and are each of them now enjoying their freedom." *Lewis, a boy of color v. Stacker, John* (Jul. 1839), Case No. 185, Circuit Court Case Files, Office of the Circuit Clerk, City of St. Louis, Missouri, available online at http://stlcourtrecords.wustl.edu (accessed 30 Aug. 2007).

155. *Barnes, Brunetta, of color v. Meachum, John Berry* (Nov. 1840), Case No. 40, Circuit Court Case Files, Office of the Circuit Clerk, City of St. Louis, Missouri, available online at http://stlcourtrecords.wustl.edu (accessed 30 Aug. 2007).

156. *Barnes, Archibald, of color v. Meachum, John Berry* (Nov. 1840), Case No. 41, Circuit Court Case Files, Office of the Circuit Clerk, City of St. Louis, Missouri, available online at http://stlcourtrecords.wustl.edu (accessed 30 Aug. 2007).

157. Ibid.

158. *Barnes, Brunetta, of color v. Meachum, John Berry* (Nov. 1840), Case No. 123, Circuit Court Case Files, Office of the Circuit Clerk, City of St. Louis, Missouri, available online at http://stlcourtrecords.wustl.edu (accessed 30 Aug. 2007).

159. Ibid., and *AA*, 31.

160. *Barnes, Brunetta, v. Meachum.*

161. See William Ransom Hogan and Edwin Adams Davis, eds., *William Johnson's Natchez: The Ante-Bellum Diary of a Free Negro* (Baton Rouge: Louisiana State University Press, 1993); Michael P. Johnson and James L. Roark, *Black Masters: A Free Family of Color in the Old South* (New York: Norton, 1984).

162. There were far fewer slaveholding black freemen in the "upper South" (Delaware, Maryland, Washington, D.C., Virginia, North Carolina, Kentucky, Tennessee, and Missouri), but its free population was far greater than that of the lower Southern states (174,357 by 1840) (Schweninger, "Prosperous Blacks in the South," 36, 42).

163. Drawing data from the 1830 census, Carter G. Woodson's Association for the Study of Negro Life and History revealed that black slaveholding existed in the antebellum South *and* North. The majority of black slaveholders were located in southern states, but they were also recorded in Connecticut, Illinois, Maine, New Hampshire, New Jersey, New York, Ohio, and Pennsylvania. Research Department of the Association for the Study of Negro Life and History, "Free Negro Owners of Slaves in the United States in 1830," *Journal of Negro History* 9, no. 1 (Jan. 1924): 41–85.

164. Ibid., 41–42.

165. *Case of Dred Scott*, 38.

166. "Slavery in Minnesota," *Missouri Liberty Weekly Tribune* (10 Jul. 1857): 4.

167. Martin R. Delany, "Political Aspects of the Colored People of the United States," *Provincial Freeman* (13 Oct. 1855): 97–98; also reprinted in *Martin R. Delany: A Documentary Reader*, ed. Robert S. Levine (Chapel Hill: University of North Carolina Press, 2003), 282; Brown, *Narrative*, 383.

168. John Jolliffe, *Belle Scott; or, Liberty Overthrown!* (Columbus, OH: D. Anderson, 1856), 377.

169. "The Rights Secured by Naturalization," *National Era* (3 Nov. 1853): 174.

170. Benjamin Drew, ed., *The Refugee; or, The Narratives of Fugitive Slaves in Canada, Related by Themselves, with an Account of the History and Condition of the Colored Population of Upper Canada* (Toronto: Prospero Canadian Collection, 2000), 374 further references to *The Refugee* are to this edition and are cited parenthetically in the text as *TR*.

171. She prevailed on lady patrons to intercede on her behalf: "[one] succeeded in making an arrangement for me to remain in Washington without paying the sum required for a license; moreover, I was not to be molested" (*BS*, 48).

172. Lunsford Lane, *The Narrative of Lunsford Lane*, in *Flight from the Devil: Six Slave Narratives*, ed. William Loren Katz, 2–36 (Trenton, NJ: Africa World Press, 1996),10; further references to *Narrative of Lunsford Lane* are to this edition and are cited parenthetically in the text as *NLL*.

173. North Carolina statutes also made emancipation contingent on removal from the state within ninety days. W. Sherman Savage, "The Influence of John Chavis and Lunsford Lane on the History of North Carolina," *Journal of Negro History* 25, no. 1 (Jan. 1940): 23.

174. Such enemies were also not averse to using Lane's yearning for lost kinfolk in plots to reenslave him. Lane received an unsigned letter from a self-professed "Friend" who offered knowledge of a lost kinswoman of his in Cincinnati. Hawkins writes, "If it was a trick to catch Lunsford in Cincinnati for the purpose of his being kidnapped, it did not succeed; as he had no desire to undertake a journey to see a family with whom he had no acquaintance" (*LL*, 101).

175. Hunter was the father of five enslaved children, and Freeman was the father of six. Hunter's petition went before Lane's and granted him an extension of twenty days to leave the state. He eventually gained the freedom of his family and settled in Philadelphia. Freeman, however, fared far worse. Judge Badger, who held his family as slaves, took Freeman with him to Washington City. Badger later entered into an arrangement with Freeman to purchase his family (*LL*, 99–100).

176. Ian Finseth, "Geographic Consciousness in the American Slave Narrative," in *American Literary Geographies: Spatial Practice and Cultural Production, 1500–1900*, ed. Martin Bruckner and Hsuan L. Hsu, 236–58 (Wilmington: University of Delaware Press, 2007), 252.

177. While enslaved in St. Louis, Brown records how he was hired to Lovejoy, who was "at that time publisher and editor of the 'St. Louis Times,'" and he attributes to his "employment in the printing office, for what little learning [he] obtained while in slavery" (Brown, *Narrative*, 383).

178. *Case of Dred Scott*, 8.
179. Fehrenbacher, *Dred Scott Case*, 337.
180. *Case of Dred Scott*, 6.
181. Ibid., 12.
182. According to Julie Winch, the only surviving copy of *Colored Aristocracy* is located in the Missouri Historical Society in St. Louis. Julie Winch, introduction to *Colored Aristocracy of St. Louis*, by Cyprian Clamorgan, 1–20 (Columbia: University of Missouri Press, 1999), 19–20; further references to *Colored Aristocracy* are to this edition and are cited parenthetically in the text as *CA*.
183. George Fitzhugh, *Cannibals All! or, Slaves without Masters* (Richmond, VA: A. Morris, 1857).
184. Fleischner, *Mrs. Lincoln and Mrs. Keckley*, 126.
185. Fehrenbacher, *Dred Scott Case*, 7.
186. Ibid., 353.
187. *Case of Dred Scott*, 10.
188. Ibid., 11; Fehrenbacher, *Dred Scott Case*, 347.
189. See Missouri Historical Society, website homepage, http://www.umsystem.edu/shs/ (accessed 3 Dec. 2005).
190. "History: Its Uses," *Western Journal and Civilian* (May 1853): 77.
191. Ibid.
192. Ibid.
193. *Case of Dred Scott*, 10.
194. Ibid., 12.
195. Mark Twain, *Pudd'nhead Wilson and Those Extraordinary Twins* (New York: Penguin, 2004), 64.
196. Teresa Zackodnik, "Fixing the Color Line: The Mulatto, Southern Courts, and Racial Identity," *American Quarterly* 53 (2001): 424.
197. Ibid., 432.
198. Another four members of Clamorgan's St. Louis elite underwent similar racial transformations in census records that reflected the ebb and flow of economic success. A colored aristocrat, according to Winch, "who had suffered financial reverses was likely to find himself categorized as 'black,' while his neighbor, who had done well financially and perhaps acquired real estate, might make the transition in the eyes of white officials from 'black' to 'mulatto,' or possibly even 'white'" (Winch, introduction to *CA*, 10).
199. Bureau of the Census, Charleville (1860), HeritageQuest Online, http://persi.heritagequestonline.com/hqoweb/library/do/census/search/basic (accessed 3 Dec. 2005).
200. In 1860, Reynolds was listed as "mulatto," and in 1870 he was redesignated as "white." By 1900, Reynolds had again undergone the transformation back to "colored." Bureau of the Census, Norton (1870, 1900), HeritageQuest Online, http://persi.heritagequestonline.com/hqoweb/library/do/census/search/basic (accessed 3 Dec. 2005).
201. Zackodnik, "Fixing the Color Line," 422.
202. Elijah Lovejoy, "To My Fellow Citizens," *St. Louis Observer* (5 Nov. 1835): 2–3.

203. Fehrenbacher, *Dred Scott Case*, 350.

204. *Case of Dred Scott*, 10, 13, 14.

205. The legal commentator Tapping Reed voiced the North's position on marriage and slavery: "If a slave married a free woman, with the consent of his master, he was emancipated; for his master had suffered him to contract a relation inconsistent with a state of slavery" (VanderVelde and Subramanian, "Mrs. Dred Scott," *Yale Law Journal*, 1041, 1105–6).

206. Ibid., 1109.

207. *Case of Dred Scott*, 7; emphasis added.

208. In the former Spanish and French colonial territories along the Gulf Coast and Louisiana, interracial unions between colonists or *voyageurs* and enslaved or native women were encouraged, although formal marriage was prohibited. Arrangements such as the one between Clamorgan's grandfather, Jacques, and his maternal and foster grandmothers, Judith Pelissier and Esther Morgan, became so common in Louisiana that a formal practice of *placage* emerged to oversee the contracting of unions between white men and "colored" women, which obligated the men, among other things, to provide their women and progeny economic support (Schweninger, "Prosperous Blacks in the South," 34–35).

209. Jessica Adams, *Wounds of Returning: Race, Memory, and Property on the Postslavery Plantation* (Chapel Hill: University of North Carolina Press, 2007), 23.

210. *Marguerite, a free woman of color v. Chouteau, Pierre, Sr.* (Jul. 1825), St. Louis Circuit Court Records, Missouri Historical Society (St. Louis), available online at http://stlcourtrecords.wustl.edu (accessed 1 Sept. 2007).

211. *Marguerite v. Chouteau*, 3 Mo. 540; Mo. LEXIS 73 (1834); see also *Marguerite v. Chouteau*, 2 Mo. 71, Mo. LEXIS 26 (1828).

212. William E. Foley, "Slave Freedom Suits before *Dred Scott*: The Case of Marie Jean Scypion's Descendants," *Missouri Historical Review* 79, no. 1 (Oct. 1984): 3–4.

213. James Thomas, *From Tennessee Slave to St. Louis Entrepreneur* (Columbia: University of Missouri Press, 1984), 158.

214. Foley, "Slave Freedom Suits," 8, 15.

215. See Foley for a detailed discussion of the long litigation histories of Marguerite and her two siblings Catiche and Celeste to secure their freedom and the freedom of thier children and grandchildren.

216. The legal titles to Marguerite and her kinfolk changed hands repeatedly, yet the women successfully coordinated their separate freeom suits and legal strategies with the assistance of their attorneys (Foley 15).

217. *Marguerite v. Chouteau*, 3 Mo. 540; Mo. LEXIS 73 (1834).

218. Julie Winch, "The Clamorgans of St. Louis," in *CA*, 22, 34–35. Jacques Clamorgan was also known as Don Yago Clamorgan, Santiago Clamorgan, and James Morgan. One of the first "settled towns of Missouri," New Madrid "was founded by Jaque Clamorgan, a Scotchman, holding office under the Spanish government, in the year 1788 or 1789." "Art IV. Missouri: Its History," *DeBow's Review of the Southern and Western States* (Sept. 1851): 268–85.

219. Winch, "Clamorgans of St. Louis," 23–25.

220. Catherine Frances Cavanagh, "Stories of Our Government Bureaus," *Bookman; A*

Review of Books and Life (Nov. 1911): 317. Apoline never married, choosing instead to take a series of white lovers. She presented her "enfants naturels," as her father did, for baptism at the Cathedral Church. Upon her death in 1830, she left her four surviving children with modest inheritances under the custodianship of a white guardian named Charles Collins (Winch, "Clamorgans of St. Louis," 26–27).

221. Winch, "Clamorgans of St. Louis," 26–27.

222. The U.S. Land Office eventually confirmed one tract of land of almost 430 acres, and Cyprian, as Jacques Clamorgan's only surviving grandchild, sold one claim for ten thousand dollars in 1894 (ibid., 35).

223. The 1880 appeal had come before the St. Louis circuit court as *Clamorgan v. The Bellefontaine Railroad Company, and The Baden and St. Louis Railroad Company*, with Henry, Cyprian, Leon, and Julius Clamorgan as the joint litigants (ibid.).

224. This information, however, was not publicly circulated until 2006, when Ruth Ann Abels Hager, a reference specialist at the St. Louis County Library, confirmed the information with the volunteer organization and publicized it (Frankel, "Finding a St. Louis Legend," C1).

CHAPTER 4

1. David Walker, *An Appeal to the Coloured Citizens of the World* (University Park: Pennsylvania State University Press, 2000), 31; further references to *An Appeal* are to this edition and are cited parenthetically in the text as *ACC*.

2. Concerns over the maritime dimensions of a possible conspiracy that involved black seamen in the smuggling of insurrectionary correspondences to President Jean Pierre Boyer in Port-au-Prince prompted South Carolina to target all black sailors with its repressive new laws. W. Jeffrey Bolster, *Black Jacks: African American in the Age of Sail* (Cambridge, MA: Harvard University Press, 1997), 193–94.

3. Charleston authorities arrested 117 enslaved and 11 free black men whom they charged with "attempting to raise an Insurrection." The state eventually executed 29 of these prisoners and banished "beyond the limits of the United States" 40 others. Vesey's intricate plan supposedly called for the capture of the arsenal, setting Charleston on fire, and escape by ship to Haiti. Edward A. Pearson, *Designs against Charleston: The Trial Record of the Denmark Vesey Slave Conspiracy of 1822* (Chapel Hill: University of North Carolina Press, 1999), 1–4.

4. Peter Linebaugh and Marcus Rediker, *The Many-Headed Hydra: Sailors, Slaves, Commoners, and the Hidden History of the Revolutionary Atlantic* (Boston: Beacon, 2000), 299.

5. Robert Westley, "The Accursed Share: Genealogy, Temporality, and the Problem of Value in Black Reparations Discourse," *Representations* 92 (Fall 2005): 97; "Debate in the Senate on the Admission of Florida and Iowa," *Cincinnati Weekly Herald and Philanthropist* (2 Apr. 1845): 1; William J. Rich, "Lessons of Charleston Harbor: The Rise, Fall, and Revival of Pro-Slavery Federalism," *McGeorge Law Review* 36 (2005): 579.

6. Francis Colburn (or F. C.) Adams, *Manuel Pereira; or, The Sovereign Rule of South Carolina, with Views of Southern Laws, Life, and Hospitality* (Washington, DC: Buell &

Blanchard, 1853), 366 further references to *Manuel Pereira* are to this edition and are cited parenthetically in the text as *MP*.

7. Giorgio Agamben, *Homo Sacer: Sovereign Power and Bare Life*, trans. Daniel Heller-Roazen (Stanford, CA: Stanford University Press, 1998), 142.

8. "Massachusetts and South Carolina," *New Englander* (Apr. 1846): 195.

9. Joan Dayan, "Legal Slaves and Civil Bodies," in *Materializing Democracy: Toward a Revitalized Cultural Politics*, ed. Russ Castronovo and Dana D. Nelson, 53–94 (Durham, NC: Duke University Press, 2002), 57. Antiblack statutes in Washington, D.C., likewise stipulated that "if any free colored person visits the capital of the United States without free papers, or in company with some white man, by whom he can prove his freedom, he is to be imprisoned a certain length of time, and then to be sold to the highest bidder, and the money to be paid into the United States treasury." William Wells Brown to Rev. Wm. Allen, in "Selections—American Slavery," *Liberator* (12 Oct. 1849): 161. See also Orlando Patterson, *Slavery and Social Death: A Comparative Study* (Cambridge, MA: Harvard University Press, 1982).

10. Bolster, *Black Jacks*, 4–6.

11. Linebaugh and Rediker, *Many-Headed Hydra*, 31.

12. Paul Gilroy, *The Black Atlantic: Modernity and Double Consciousness* (Cambridge, MA: Harvard University Press, 1993), 27. As early as 1803, free men of color constituted 18 percent of U.S. maritime labor, and the *Cincinnati Weekly Herald* informed readers in 1846 that "more than seven hundred persons engaged in the whale fishery, each vessel averaging one colored officer . . . [and] any quantity of colored men constantly employed as officers out of the different whaling ports." Bolster, *Black Jacks*, 4–6; "Seamen," *Cincinnati Weekly Herald and Philanthropist* (11 Nov. 1846): 2.

13. F.C. Adams, *Uncle Tom at Home: A Review of the Reviewers and Repudiators of Uncle Tom's Cabin by Mrs. Stowe* (New York: Books for Libraries Press, 1970), 113.

14. Eliza J. Kenny, "Salem Female Anti-Slavery Society," *Liberator* (14 Mar. 1845): 41B–C.

15. For a revisionist understanding of the Vesey plot that emphasizes the Charleston court's agency in the making of the conspiracy, see Michael P. Johnson, "Denmark Vesey and His Co-Conspirators," *William and Mary Quarterly* (Oct. 2001): 915–76.

16. Peter P. Hinks, *To Awaken My Afflicted Brethren: David Walker and the Problem of Antebellum Slave Resistance* (University Park: Pennsylvania State University Press, 1997), 22.

17. Gerald L. Neuman, "The Lost Century of American Immigration Law," *Columbia Law Review* 93 (Dec. 1993): 1834.

18. Mary L. Dudziak and Leti Volpp, "Legal Borderlands: Law and the Construction of American Borders," *American Quarterly* (Mar. 2005): 593.

19. "Art. VII.—Mr. Hoar's Mission," *Southern Quarterly Review* (Apr. 1845): 455.

20. "Legislature of South Carolina," *Niles' Weekly Register* (25 Dec. 1824): 261.

21. Daphne A. Brooks, *Bodies in Dissent: Spectacular Performances of Race and Freedom, 1850–1910* (Durham, NC: Duke University Press, 2006), 3.

22. Agamben, *Homo Sacer*, 130.

23. Ibid., 128.

24. Charles A. Battiste, "Boarding House for Colored Seamen," *Liberator* (8 June 1842): 196; and "Rights of Our Colored Citizens," *Liberator* (4 Nov. 1842): 175.

25. "Meeting of Colored Citizens," *Liberator* (7 Feb. 1845): 23.

26. Benjamin Drew, *The Refugee; or, The Narratives of Fugitive Slaves in Canada, Related by Themselves, with an Account of the History and Condition of the Colored Population of Upper Canada* (Toronto: Prospero Canadian Collection, 2000), 363.

27. Ibid.

28. "Meeting of Colored Citizens," *Liberator* (31 Jan. 1845): 19; Stephanie H.M. Camp, *Closer to Freedom: Enslaved Women and Everyday Resistance in the Plantation South* (Chapel Hill: University of North Carolina Press, 2004), 105–6.

29. "Debate in the Senate. Part 1," *Niles National Register* (29 Mar. 1845): 55.

30. "Mutiny," *Zion's Herald and Wesleyan Journal* (11 Feb. 1857): 23.

31. "The Liberty of British Subjects Invaded in the United States," *Liberator* (10 July 1846): 109–10.

32. Virtually all these accounts involve male sailors, although Philip Hamer cites one instance involving a "black stewardess" seized from her vessel in Alabama. Philip M. Hamer, "Great Britain, the United States, and the Negro Seamen Acts, 1822–1848," *Journal of Southern History* 1, no. 1 (Feb. 1935): 26).

33. D. Lee Child, John Frost, Ray Potter, Jesse Putnum, and Joseph Southwick, "Report on the Slave Trade," *Liberator* (7 June 1834): 89–91.

34. Ibid.

35. Ibid.

36. Ibid.

37. The sailors "joined this vessel at Halifax, Nova Scotia, and signed articles for a voyage thence to Europe, and thence 'to a port of discharge in the United States,' at a rate of $24 per month." Louisiana's Seamen Act required the shipmaster to give one thousand dollars in bond for these black crewmen when the vessel arrived in New Orleans. When the vessel set sail three weeks later, the shipmaster "required the crew to sign articles for the voyage from New Orleans to Boston for $15 per month," which they signed "under protest" with the alternative of being left behind to face imprisonment and enslavement. "Stratton et al. v. Babbage," *Monthly Law Reporter* (June 1855): 94.

38. "Imprisonment of Colored Seamen," *Liberator* (18 Oct. 1850): 165.

39. "Coloured Seamen," *Anti-Slavery Reporter* 1, no. 3 (1 Mar. 1853): 50. West Indian sailor William Forster was one such case: he was seized off an American schooner in 1835 and sold into slavery according to Florida law; he remained in slavery for five years, until his shipmaster redeemed him (Hamer, "Great Britain," 18).

40. "Imprisonment of Coloured Seamen," *Anti-Slavery Reporter* 5, no. 3 (2 Mar. 1857): 60–62.

41. Simon P. Newman, "Reading the Bodies of Early American Seafarers," *William and Mary Quarterly*, 3rd series, 55, no. 1 (Jan. 1998): 59–82.

42. Stephen Best and Saidiya Hartman, "Fugitive Justice," *Representations* 92 (Fall 2005): 8.

43. Maggie Montesinos Sale, *The Slumbering Volcano: American Slave Ship Revolts and the Production of Rebellious Masculinity* (Durham, NC: Duke University Press, 1997), 28.

44. Senator Davis proposed an unsuccessful amendment to the Fugitive Slave Bill that was to require the U.S. district attorney to test the lawfulness of imprisonment under the Negro Seamen Acts through a writ of habeas corpus. "Proceedings of the U.S. Senate, on the Fugitive Slave Bill,—The Abolition of the Slave-Trade in the District of Columbia,—And the Imprisonment of Free Colored Seamen in the Southern Ports: With the Speeches of Messrs. Davis, Winthrop, and Others" (Washington, DC: Press of T.R. Marvin, 1850), 2.

45. Ibid., 4.

46. *Liberator* (3 Jan. 1851): 4.

47. "Massachusetts and South Carolina," *New Englander* (Oct. 1845): 606.

48. "Massachusetts and South Carolina," *New Englander* (July 1845): 411; "Massachusetts and South Carolina," *New Englander* (Apr. 1846): 195.

49. "Imprisonment of Colored Seamen," *North Star* (13 June 1850): 3E.

50. Linebaugh and Rediker, *Many-Headed Hydra*, 71.

51. "Proceedings of the U.S. Senate," 5.

52. Dayan, "Legal Slaves and Civil Bodies," 57.

53. "Imprisonment of Colored Seamen," 3E.

54. Deak Nabers, *Victory of Law: The Fourteenth Amendment, the Civil War, and American Literature, 1852–1867* (Baltimore: Johns Hopkins University Press, 2006), 29.

55. "Massachusetts and South Carolina," *New Englander* (Apr. 1846): 195.

56. "South Carolina Law," *New York Daily-Times* (6 Dec. 1855): 4.

57. This understanding is informed by David Kazanjian's reading of flashpoint as the transformation and emergence of a constellation of racial formations. David Kazanjian, *The Colonizing Trick: National Culture and Imperial Citizenship in Early America* (Minneapolis: University of Minnesota Press, 2003).

58. Sale, *Slumbering Volcano*, 6–7.

59. The *New Orleans Picayune*, for example, drew attention to similarly constructed *northern* police laws regulating "paupers, vagrants and other idlers" that invested "overseers or directors of houses of correction" with absolute authority over arrests and imprisonment. Such northern police laws, in the manner of the Negro Seamen Acts, used punishment as a preventative for crime. Suspected individuals were arrested "not because such persons are guilty of crimes . . . but because it has been found that idleness, destitution, debauchery and disobedience of parental authority leads to the commission of crimes." "Constitutional Rights of Free Persons of Color," *Charleston Mercury* (1 July 1852): 2.

60. James Kent, *Commentaries on American Law*, ed. George F. Comstock, vol. 2, 11th ed. (Boston: Little, Brown, 1866), 279.

61. Eric J. Sundquist, *To Wake the Nations: Race in the Making of American Literature* (Cambridge, MA: Belknap Press of Harvard University Press, 1993), 37.

62. Benjamin Faneuil Hunt, *The Argument of Benj. Faneuil Hunt, in the case of the arrest of the Person claiming to be a British Seaman, under the 3d section of the State Act of Dec. 1822,*

in relation to Negroes, &c. before the Hon, Judge Johnson, Circuit Judge of the United States, for 6th Circuit (Charleston, SC: A.E. Miller, 1823), 7–8.

63. "Art. VII.—Mr. Hoar's Mission," 455.

64. "Debate in the Senate on the Admission of Florida and Iowa."

65. Quoted in "Massachusetts and South Carolina," *Liberator* (12 Dec. 1845): 197.

66. Edwin Holland, *A Refutation of the Calumnies Circulated against the Southern & Western States, Respecting the Institution and Existence of Slavery among Them to Which Is Added, a Minute and Particular Account of the Actual State and Condition of Their Negro Population* (Charleston, SC: A.E. Miller, 1822), 86.

67. "Massachusetts and South Carolina," *New Englander* (Apr. 1846): 195.

68. Ibid.

69. "Art. VII.—Mr. Hoar's Mission," 455.

70. *The Opinion of the Hon. William Johnson, Delivered on the 7th August, 1823* (1823): 3, available online at the Library of Congress, "Slaves in the Courts, 1740–1860," http://memory.loc.gov/ammem/sthtml/sthome.html.

71. Philip M. Hamer, "British Consuls and the Negro Seamen Acts, 1850–1860" *Journal of Southern History* 1, no. 2 (May 1935): 144n.

72. Irwin F. Greenberg, "Justice William Johnson: South Carolina Unionist, 1823–1830," *Pennsylvania History: A Journal of Mid-Atlantic Studies* 36, no. 3 (July 1969): 311.

73. After failing to secure a writ of habeas corpus, Elkison's attorney filed for a writ *de homine replegiando*, having as its object his "discharge from confinement absolutely, the other his discharge on bail, with a view to try the question of the validity of the law under which he is held in confinement." *De homine replegiando* (or *repigliando*) was an ancient writ that preceded the habeas corpus and "was understood to assure the presence of the accused in a trial" (Agamben, *Homo Sacer*, 123).

74. Congress amended the Habeas Corpus Act in 1867, one month after it passed the Civil Rights Act over president Andrew Johnson's veto, which expanded federal court review of state-court decisions to imprison individuals allegedly based on race. Michael P. O'Connor, "Time Out of Mind: Our Collective Amnesia about the History of the Privileges or Immunities Clause," *Kentucky Law Journal*, 93, no. 659 (2004/2005): 663, 693.

75. *Opinion of the Hon. William Johnson*, 13.

76. Adams, *Uncle Tom at Home*, 33.

77. Rich, "Lessons of Charleston Harbor," 581; Hamer, "Great Britain," 7.

78. Connecticut's *Norwich Courier*, for example, reported on the "tyranical [sic] and as it proves unconstitutional law . . . passed by the Legislature of South Carolina," and the *Salem Gazette* declared that the South Carolina act "sets the infraction of the constitution in so clear a light, that it cannot be doubted for a moment by any impartial mind." "Law of South Carolina," *Norwich Courier* (27 Aug. 1823): 3; "Judge Johnson's Opinion," *Salem Gazette* (26 Aug. 1823): 2; "Important Decision," *Genius of Universal Emancipation* (Sept. 1823): 46; "Free People of Color," *Niles' Weekly Register* (23 Aug. 1823): 392.

79. *Baltimore Patriot* (1 Oct. 1823): 1.

80. *Eastern Argus* (7 Oct. 1823): 1.

81. *Opinion of the Hon. William Johnson*, 15. The South Carolina Assembly replaced its provision for the enslavement of free black seamen who remained unredeemed in prison with another measure that required them to leave the state under penalty of a whipping upon return. This measure remained in effect until the Assembly reenacted the provision for enslavement in 1835 (Hamer, "Great Britain," 9, 15).

82. "The American Confederacy," *Christian Register* (22 Oct. 1825): 168.

83. Ibid.

84. I.E. Holmes, "South Carolina Law," *Niles' Weekly Register* (20 Sep. 1823): 47.

85. Jackson issued a proclamation in 1832 disputing the state's right to nullify federal law after a South Carolina convention, urged on by vice president John C. Calhoun, disputed the tariff acts of 1828 and 1832 and deemed them "null, void, and no law, nor binding upon this State." The following year, Congress passed the "Force Act," which authorized the use of military force against any state that resisted the tariff acts.

86. "Judge Johnson's Opinion," *New Bedford Mercury* (29 Aug. 1823): 3. Johnson's ruling provoked a month-long series of angry editorials that publicly fortified the militant principles of states'-right extremism under the signature "Caroliniensis" in the *Charleston Mercury* (Greenberg, "Justice William Johnson," 314–15).

87. "Judicial Opinion: Judge Johnson on the S Carolina Law," *Niles Weekly Register* (6 Sept. 1823): 12.

88. John Torpey, "Coming and Going: On the State Monopolization of the Legitimate 'Means of Movement,'" *Sociological Theory* 16, no. 3 (Nov. 1998): 241. This reading is informed, in part, by Bryan Wagner's work exploring the racial moorings of police power in the post-Reconstruction U.S. South. Bryan Wagner, "Disarmed and Dangerous: The Strange Career of Bras-Coupé," *Representations* 92 (Fall 2005): 118.

89. Hunt, *Argument*, 4–5.

90. Ibid.

91. Wagner, "Disarmed and Dangerous," 119; see Hunt, *Argument*, 5.

92. Wagner, "Disarmed and Dangerous," 121.

93. Hunt, *Argument*, 7.

94. Torpey, "Coming and Going," 241.

95. *Charleston Mercury* (11 Aug. 1852): 2.

96. Ibid.

97. Giorgio Agamben, *State of Exception*, trans. Kevin Attell (Chicago: University of Chicago Press, 2005), 23; Agamben is building on Carl Schmitt, *Political Theology*, trans. George Schwab (Chicago: University of Chicago Press, 2005).

98. "Legislature of South Carolina," *Niles' Weekly Register* (25 Dec. 1824): 261; Rich, "Lessons of Charleston Harbor," 581.

99. Secretary of State John Quincy Adams was delegated the task of investigating the arrest of the four British crewmen from the *Marmion*. He appealed to Attorney General William Wirt, who provoked the ire of southerners when he declared the Negro Seamen Act unconstitutional. An openly hostile Governor George Michael Troup of Georgia proposed a

constitutional amendment, declaring, "That no part of the constitution of the United States ought to be construed, or shall be construed, to authorize the importation or ingress of any person of color into any one of the United States, contrary to the laws of such state." Adams had sought to test the constitutionality of the law with the arrest of black seaman John Gardiner, but Gardiner's discharge from prison prevented the case from coming before the courts. "A Difficult Question," *Niles' Weekly Register* (18 Dec. 1824): 242; "Legislature of South Carolina," *Niles' Weekly Register* (25 Dec. 1824): 261; Hamer, "Great Britain," 10.

100. "Legislature of South Carolina."

101. "Colored Mariners in South Carolina," *Liberator* (16 Dec. 1842): 197; "Selections: J.Q. Adams's Address," *Liberator* (3 Nov. 1843): 173–74.

102. Hamer, "Great Britain," 14–15.

103. Fehrenbacher, *Dred Scott Case*, 70.

104. "The Imprisonment of Colored Seamen," *Niles' National Register* (2 Dec. 1843): 217.

105. "Mass. Legislature—Report on the Deliverance of Citizens Liable to Be Sold as Slaves," *Liberator* (29 Mar. 1839): 49.

106. David L. Child, "Mr. Child's Speech" *Liberator* (6 July 1833): 105.

107. "Free People of Color," *Niles' Weekly Register* (15 Mar. 1823): 31–32.

108. Ibid.

109. Child, "Mr. Child's Speech," 105.

110. "Mass. Legislature: Report on the Deliverance of Citizens Liable to Be Sold as Slaves," *Liberator* (29 Mar. 1839): 49–50.

111. Massachusetts native Mary Smith, who was "seized and sold as a slave" in 1836 after she was "cast upon the shores of North Carolina," featured prominently in this catalogue of outrages. With the assistance of the Massachusetts governor, "'Mary Smith' returned to Boston. But it turned out, that this was not *the* Mary Smith, whom our worthy Governor, and other excellent individuals of Boston, had taken unwearied pains to redeem from slavery. It was another woman of the same name, who was also a native of Massachusetts, and had been seized in North Carolina as a runaway slave." This report emphasized the tragic fungibility of black personhood under slavery in its efforts to mobilize northerners against the Negro Seamen Act. "*The* Mary Smith has not yet been heard of. If alive, she is now, in all probability, wearing the chains of slavery" (ibid., 1).

112. Ibid.

113. Guyora Binder, "The Slavery of Emancipation," *Cardozo Law Review* 17 (May 1996): 2075.

114. "Massachusetts a Bond-Slave," *Liberator* (13 Dec. 1844): 198.

115. Senator John M. Berrien of Georgia referred his fellow statesmen to the "case of a negro from Virginia who had been permitted by his master to go on board of an American vessel of war. The vessel entered the harbor of Boston, the colored man was taken from on board the vessel by abolitionists, and the courts of Massachusetts decided that that man came voluntarily within the bounds of the state of Massachusetts, and they emancipated him. Now if the state of Massachusetts might say to the people of the south, if you send your colored men into our ports they must be subject to our laws, might not the southern states say the

same thing to the state of Massachusetts?" "Debate in the Senate, Part 2," *Niles' National Register* (29 Mar. 1845): 59.

116. "Torrey Meeting," *Liberator* (6 Sept. 1844): 143.

117. "Legislative. Colored Seamen. Report Resolves," *Liberator* (Mar. 1843): 45.

118. Both Hunt and John A. Maybin of New Orleans declined the appointments tendered to them. "Rights of Northern Seamen," *Liberator* (17 Nov. 1843): 183; "Massachusetts," *Niles' National Register* (18 Nov. 1843): 179; "Miscellaneous: The Imprisonment of Colored Seamen," *Niles' National Register* (2 Dec. 1843): 217.

119. "Protection of Colored Seamen," *African Repository and Colonial Journal* (Mar. 1844): 93.

120. "Massachusetts and South Carolina," *New York Evangelist* (19 Dec. 1844): 202; "Our Agent to South Carolina," *Zion's Herald and Wesleyan Journal* (25 Dec. 1844): 207.

121. "Mr. Hoar's Agency," *Boston Recorder* (12 Dec. 1844): 198; "Massachusetts and South Carolina," *Cincinnati Weekly Herald and Philanthropist* (18 Dec. 1844): 3.

122. "Massachusetts and South Carolina," *Cincinnati Weekly Herald*, 3. The South Carolina legislature, according to Fehrenbacher, went so far as to empower the governor to use the militia to prevent the release by writ of habeas corpus of any imprisoned seamen and provided "for the punishment of Persons disturbing the Peace of this State, in relation to Slaves and Free Persons of Colour" (Fehrenbacher, *Dred Scott Case*, 73).

123. Fehrenbacher, *Dred Scott Case*, 70, 340.

124. Hoar's official narrative was such "a tale [of] thrilling interest" that "[i]ts appearance in some of the daily papers of the city," according to the *Christian Reflector*, "cannot answer the demands of thousands, who read our paper, in various parts of the country; and though a long article of a *secular* kind, for us to publish, it is, in our humble opinion, far more interesting and but little less important, than many an *official* Message." "Massachusetts and South Carolina," *Christian Reflector* (16 Jan. 1845): 10.

125. "Massachusetts and South Carolina," *Liberator* (17 Jan. 1845): 9. The keeper of the hotel where the "mild spoken," elderly Hoar lodged "turned him out of doors," according to one northern account, "lest the hotel should be attacked by a mob," and the *London Times* reported that only the presence of his daughter, "who was travelling with him," protected him "from personal violence." "Our Agent to South Carolina," 207; "South Carolina and Massachusetts: Governor Prigg's Message; Mr. Hoar's Statement," *New York Evangelist* (16 Jan. 1845): 10; "Massachusetts and South Carolina," *New York Evangelist*, 202; "American Affair," *London Times* (31 Dec. 1844): 5.

126. "Another Outrage upon Personal Freedom," *Liberator* (16 Mar. 1838): 43.

127. "Massachusetts and South Carolina," *Cincinnati Weekly Herald*, 3; "The Despotism of South Carolina," *Liberator* (27 Dec. 1844): 206.

128. "Art. VII.—Mr. Hoar's Mission," 455.

129. "Massachusetts and South Carolina," *Christian Watchman* (17 Jan. 1845): 11; "Massachusetts and South Carolina," *Liberator* (7 Mar. 1845): 37.

130. "Another Outrage," 43.

131. "Massachusetts and South Carolina," *Cincinnati Weekly Herald*, 3.

132. "Is It So?" *Liberator* (17 Jan. 1845): 9.

133. "Laws of Southern States in Regard to Colored Seamen," *National Era* (6 May 1852): 74.

134. John G. Palfrey, *Papers on the Slave Power: First Published in the "Boston Whig," in July, August, and September, 1846*, 2nd ed. (Boston: Merrill, Cobb, 1846), 49.

135. "Imprisoning British Colored Seamen," *North Star* (30 May 1850): 2G.

136. "The Black Laws of South Carolina," *National Era* (27 June 1850): 102.

137. In *A Heroic Slave*, Frederick Douglass fictionalized the relatively bloodless mutiny led by the slave Madison Washington aboard the *Creole* during the passage from Virginia to Louisiana. A claims commission grudgingly awarded a small indemnity to American slaveholders after repeated appeals (Fehrenbacher, *Dred Scott Case*, 39).

138. "A Serious Affair," *North Star* (17 Apr. 1851): 3D.

139. Kazanjian, *Colonizing Trick*, 103.

140. "Great Britain and South Carolina," *Semi-Weekly Eagle* (30 Jan. 1851): 2E.

141. *Anti-Slavery Reporter* 5, no. 53 (1 May 1850): 73.

142. "Slavery in the United States," *Manchester Guardian* (15 Mar. 1851): 6.

143. "Treatment of British Coloured Subjects in the United States—Fugitives in Canada," *Anti-Slavery Reporter* 6, no. 61 (1 Jan. 1851): 4–5.

144. Bowers's lawsuit reportedly "astounded the magistrate" when it "came before the Thomas Police Court, London," which "decided in favour of the seaman, on the ground that the captain took him knowing his liability to be seized." "General Intelligence," *Christian Advocate and Journal* (23 May 1850): 83.

145. "Seizure of British Subjects at Charleston," *Anti-Slavery Reporter* 5, no. 53 (1 May 1850): 80.

146. "Imprisonment of Coloured Seamen," *Anti-Slavery Reporter* 1, no. 6 (1 June 1853): 132–33.

147. "Seizure of British Subjects," 79.

148. "News from the Old World—Rights of British Subjects in America," *North Star* (10 Apr. 1851): 2B; *Anti-Slavery Reporter* 6, no. 61 (1 Jan. 1851): 8.

149. Mathew initiated a private correspondence with Governor Means after the legation in Washington cautioned him to try more informal methods to secure the law's repeal. The *New York Evangelist* warned against this "perilous kind of diplomacy" between a British consul and a state governor, and the South Carolina Assembly took measures "directing the Governor to hold no more intercourse with the Consul—a thing he never ought to have done." British newspapers also denounced this unprecedented "correspondence between a foreign Consul and a local Government . . . as a precedent of the most dangerous kind, tending to nothing less than the establishment of provincial sovereignties in derogation of the Federal Power." Hamer, "British Consuls," 149–50; "South Carolina Diplomacy," *New York Evangelist* (5 Feb. 1852): 22; "Slavery in the United States," 6.

150. "England and South Carolina," *Littell's Living Age* (5 Apr. 1851): 42.

151. Ibid.

152. *Anti-Slavery Reporter* 5, no. 53 (1 May 1850): 73.

153. *Albion: A Journal of News, Politics and Literature* (1 May 1852): 212. According to Hamer, Great Britain employed a lobbyist to steer the passage of a bill modifying Louisiana's law in 1852, and British Consul E. Molyneux successfully secured the repeal of Georgia's law in 1854 (Hamer, "British Consuls," 142–43).

154. "Imprisonment of Colored Seamen," *New York Daily Times* (21 June 1852): 2; "Imprisonment of Colored Seamen," *Farmer's Cabinet* (5 May 1853): 3; *Bangor Daily Whig and Courier* (21 Apr. 1853): 2; "Imprisonment of Colored Seamen," *Star and Banner* (29 Apr. 1853): 2.

155. *London Times* (25 Dec. 1852): 4.

156. Ibid.

157. *Charleston Mercury* (11 Aug. 1852): 2.

158. "America," *London Times* (1 June 1852): 8.

159. Ibid.

160. "Message of the Governor of South Carolina," *Frederick Douglass' Paper* (3 Dec. 1852); "South Carolina and Great Britain," *London Times* (22 Dec. 1852): 8.

161. "Coloured Seamen," *Anti-Slavery Reporter* 1, no. 3 (1 Mar. 1853): 50.

162. Ibid.

163. Ibid.

164. Hamer "British Consuls," 158–59.

165. "Imprisonment of Colored Seamen," *New-York Daily Times* (21 June 1852): 2.

166. "The Law of Colored Seamen," *National Era* (5 May 1853): 71.

167. Hamer, "British Consuls," 159.

168. "Charleston," *New-York Daily Times* (27 Apr. 1853): 4.

169. "South Carolina in Court," *New-York Daily Times* (27 Apr. 1852): 2; "Imprisonment of Colored Seamen," *Democratic State Register* (10 May 1852): 2

170. Hamer, "British Consuls," 159–60.

171. When George William Frederick Villiers, Earl of Clarendon, took over as the British secretary of foreign affairs, he transferred Mathew to another supposedly "less lucrative and inferior" post in Philadelphia. Robert Bunch, who was named as his replacement, was directed to secure the relaxation of the police law through more conciliatory measures. "Imprisonment of Colored Seamen in Southern Ports," *Monthly Law Reporter* (July 1853): 165; "Imprisonment of Colored Seamen," *Barre Patriot* (1 July 1853): 2.

172. Charleston was one of the chief southern ports in the West India trade, and Britain had come to depend on these well-worn trade routes by the mid-nineteenth century. One U.S. newspaper observed, "This odious State enactment is even more burdensome to British interests than to those of the North. Her West Indian colonies mainly depend on their imports for corn, flour, cattle, provisions, and lumber; and to their small but numerous vessels (necessarily manned by mixed and chiefly colored crews,) the ports of North and South Carolina are more especially suitable and at all seasons accessible" "The Negro Law in South Carolina," [*New Hampshire*] *Farmer's Cabinet* (30 Jan. 1851): 2E.

173. "England and South Carolina—Imprisonment of Colored Seamen," *National Era* (30 June 1853): 102.

174. *New-York Daily Times* (27 June 1853): 4; "South Carolina Laws Concerning Colored Seamen," *New-York Daily Times* (5 Dec. 1853): 4.

175. *Albion: A Journal of News, Politics and Literature* (27 Nov. 1852): 571.

176. Frederick Douglass, letter to James M'Cune Smith, editor's preface to *My Bondage and My Freedom*, in *Frederick Douglass Autobiographies* (New York: Library of America, 1994), 106.

177. On occasion, Adams chose to write, when the humor struck him, under the flamboyant pseudonym of "Pheleg Van Trusedale." "New Publications," *American Publishers' Circular and Literary Gazette* (31 Aug. 1858): 379.

178. Review of *Manuel Pereira; or, The Sovereign Rule of South Carolina*, *Anti-Slavery Reporter* 1, no. 5 (1 May 1853): 118.

179. "The Charleston Workhouse, as Seen by a South Carolinian," *Zion's Herald and Wesleyan Journal* (6 May 1857): 1.

180. Adams's works include *Uncle Tom at Home* (1853), *Our World; or, Annette, the Slaveholder's Daughter* (1855), *Justice in the By-Ways* (1856), *The Life and Adventures of Maj. Roger Sherman Potter* (1857), *An Outcast; or, Virtue and Faith* (1861), *The Story of a Trooper* (1865), *The Siege of Washington, D.C.* (1867), *The Von Toodleburgs; or, The History of a Very Distinguished Family* (1868), and *The Washers and Scrubbers* (1878).

181. "A New Reform Novel," *New-York Daily Times* (4 Oct. 1856): 3.

182. "American Writers in England," *National Era* (26 May 1853): 82.

183. Buell & Blanchard actively promoted sales of *Manuel Pereira* and offered free copies "postage paid" as incentives for other newspapers to republish the advertisement and review. Advertisement, *National Era* (2 June 1853): 87.

184. "An Interesting Work in Press," *National Era* (17 Feb. 1853): 26.

185. Ian Baucom, *Specters of the Atlantic: Finance Capital, Slavery, and the Philosophy of History* (Durham, NC: Duke University Press, 2005), 194.

186. "Review," *Provincial Freeman* (25 Apr. 1857): n.p.

187. "Imprisonment of Coloured Seamen," *Anti-Slavery Reporter* 1, no. 8 (1 Aug. 1853): 182.

188. Adams, *Uncle Tom at Home*, 10.

189. "Imprisonment of Coloured Seamen," *Anti-Slavery Reporter* 1, no. 8 (1 Aug. 1853): 182.

190. Best and Hartman, "Fugitive Justice," 2.

191. Linebaugh and Rediker, *Many-Headed Hydra*, 74.

192. To further demystify the discursive threat of free "foreign negroes," Adams self-consciously manipulates the chronological timeline of events surrounding Pereira's arrest to include an account of John Paul and John Baptiste Pamerlie, two black mariners from French vessels who were likewise incarcerated in Charleston. Chapter 24 of *Manuel Pereira* not only further outlines the international dimensions of the South Carolina "municipal law" but also illustrates the illogic of "self-preservation" that was its rationale and defense. "We must here introduce the persons whose names fill in the caption," insists the narrator, even though

"[t]he time of their imprisonment was some two months later than Manuel's release; but we introduce them here for the purpose of furnishing a clear understanding of the scenes connected with Manuel's release" (*MP,* 289). Neither John Paul nor John Baptiste Pamerlie spoke English. John Paul, "a fine-looking French negro, very dark, with well-developed features, and very intelligent... was steward on board the French bark *Senegal*... spoke excellent French and Spanish, and read Latin very well" (*MP,* 289). John Paul, who suffered thirty-five days' imprisonment "in *mute* confinement," was unable to "comprehend the meaning of the law imprisoning a peaceable man without crime, and why the authorities should fear him when he could not speak their language" (*MP,* 294, 289). The characterization of Pamerlie's incarceration was perhaps an even more damning critique of "self-preservation" because he was "a little, pert, saucy French boy, eleven years old, who spoke nothing but Creole French" (*MP,* 295). This child, in the novel's outraged sarcasm, was manacled and carried into twenty days' captivity inside the Charleston jail (*MP,* 299).

193. Lauren Berlant, "Poor Eliza," *American Literature* 70 (Sept. 1998): 649.

194. Hattia M'Keehan, *Liberty or Death; or, Heaven's Infraction of the Fugitive Slave Law* (Cincinnati: Published for and by the Author, 1858), 90.

195. David J. McCord, ed., *The Statutes at Large of South Carolina* 6 (Columbia, SC: A.S. Johnston, 1839), 177–79.

196. "Hunger," the narrator relates, "was the great grievance of which they complained; and if their stories were true—and we afterward had *strong proofs* that they were—there was a wanton disregard of common humanity, and an abuse of power the most reprehensible" (*MP,* 147). The stewards must continually assert their humanity in the face of the prison's regimen of dehumanization. "Do not treat us like beasts!" demands the eloquent Joseph Jociquei, "a young man who had been taken from a vessel just arrived from Rio" (*MP,* 187, 168).

197. Agamben, *Homo Sacer,* 131, 138–39; Colin Dayan, "Legal Terrors," *Representations* 92 (Fall 2005): 71.

198. Dayan, "Legal Terrors," 50.

199. "Foreign Negro Seamen," *Charleston Mercury* (24 July 1852): 2.

200. "Coloured Seamen," *Anti-Slavery Reporter* 1, no. 3 (1 Mar. 1853): 49–51; *Thirteenth Annual Report of the American & Foreign Ant-Slavery Society: Presented at New-York, May 11, 1853* (New York: American & Foreign Anti-Slavery Society, 1853), 64.

201. Kenny, "Salem Female Anti-Slavery Society," 41; Saidiya V. Hartman, *Scenes of Subjection: Terror, Slavery, and Self-Making in Nineteenth-Century America* (New York: Oxford University Press, 1997), 80.

202. Devon W. Carbado, "Racial Naturalization," *American Quarterly* 57 (Sept. 2005): 639.

203. Baucom, *Specters of the Atlantic,* 189.

204. Best and Hartman, "Fugitive Justice," 10.

205. Baucom, *Specters of the Atlantic,* 185.

206. Ibid., 186, 190.

207. "South Carolina," *Frederick Douglass' Paper* (3 Dec. 1852): 2E.

208. "From the London Daily News," *Frederick Douglass' Paper* (6 Aug. 1852): 1C–D.

209. F.C. Adams, "Paper Presented by C.F. Adams [sic], Esq., Late of Charleston, South Carolina, on the Imprisonment of Coloured Seamen," *Papers Read and Statements Made on the Principal Subjects Submitted to the Anti-Slavery Conference* (London: Committee of the British and Foreign Anti-Slavery Society, 1854), 34.

210. Binder, "Slavery of Emancipation," 2103.

211. William Andrews, *To Tell a Free Story: The First Century of Afro-American Autobiography, 1760–1865* (Urbana: University of Illinois Press, 1986), 179–82.

212. "Imprisonment of Coloured Seamen," *Anti-Slavery Reporter* 5, no 3 (2 Mar. 1857): 60–62.

213. One U.S. newspaper doubted whether South Carolina would be able to "resist the arms of a foreign State, and guard against a servile insurrection at home" if it ceded from the Union, and another apprehensive periodical worried that Britain's commercial interests would encourage the "dissolution of the confederacy, and afterwards turning it to the benefit of England, by controlling the cotton trade and general commerce of the south." "Methodist Press," *Zion's Herald and Wesleyan Journal* (19 Feb. 1851): 30; "Letter from America," *Manchester Guardian* (14 May 1851): 6.

214. "Imprisonment of Colored Seamen in South Carolina," *National Era* (13 Feb. 1851): 26.

215. "A Good Spirit in South-Carolina," *New York Observer and Chronicle* (13 Mar. 1851): 85.

216. "Imprisonment of Colored Seamen," *New-York Daily Times* (7 May 1852): 3; "Discrimination against the Free States," *Liberator* (14 May 1852): 77.

217. Quoted in "A Good Spirit," 85.

218. Quoted in "Colored Seamen in South Carolina," *National Era* (20 Dec. 1855): 203.

219. "Imprisonment of Coloured Seamen," *Anti-Slavery Reporter* 3, no. 2 (1 Feb. 1855): 46; Hamer, "British Consuls," 161.

220. "Imprisonment of Coloured Seamen," *Anti-Slavery Reporter* (2 Feb. 1857): 37–38.

221. Quoted in "A Good Spirit," 85.

222. Ibid.

223. Camp, *Closer to Freedom*, 13.

224. Quoted in "Colored Seamen," *National Era*, 203.

225. Ibid.

226. Christopher Leslie Brown, *Moral Capital: Foundations of British Abolitionism* (Chapel Hill: University of North Carolina Press, 2006), 27.

227. "Case of Kidnapping a British Subject, and His Retention in Slavery for Thirteen Years," *Friends' Review* (29 May 1852): 589.

228. Samuel J. May, "The Power of Public Opinion on American Slavery," *Report of the Proceedings of the Anti-Slavery Conference and Public Meeting, Held at Manchester, on the 1st August, 1854* (London: William Tweedie, 1854), 38–39.

229. Charles Hansford Adams, preface to *The Narrative of Robert Adams, a Barbary Captive* (Cambridge: Cambridge University Press, 2005), li.

230. Wilson Armistead, "Imprisonment and Enslavement of British Coloured Seamen:

Illustrated in the Case of John Glasgow," *Leeds Anti-Slavery Series* 89 (London: W. Tweedie, 1853), 7.

231. Ibid., 8.
232. Ibid., 9.
233. Ibid.
234. "John Glasgow," *Anti-Slavery Reporter* 1, no. 7 (1 July 1853): 148.
235. Ibid.
236. Armistead, "Imprisonment and Enslavement."
237. F.N. Boney, introduction to *Slave Life in Georgia: A Narrative of the Life, Sufferings, and Escape of John Brown, a Fugitive Slave* (Savannah: Library of Georgia, 1991), x; further references to *Slave Life* are to this edition and are cited parenthetically in the text as *SL*.
238. Armistead, "Imprisonment and Enslavement," 3.
239. Brown, *Moral Capital*, 26.
240. Armistead, "Imprisonment and Enslavement," 4–5
241. Expressing the "surprise and indignation" of the "inhabitants of the Borough of Boston," the petition decried these southern laws for "inflicting ... a cruel personal wrong, and a gross national insult" and demanded that officials "urge upon the Government the adoption of prompt and effectual measure for the abolition of the laws by which such cruelty and indignity are inflicted upon British subjects." "The Den of Villany [sic]—Imprisonment and Enslavement of British Colored Seamen Illustrated in the Case of John Glasgow," *Frederick Douglass' Paper* (13 Oct. 1854): 1A–E; "British and Foreign Anti-Slavery Society," *Frederick Douglass' Paper* (23 June 1854): 1A–G; "Imprisonment of Coloured Seamen," *Anti-Slavery Reporter* 3, no. 1 (1 Jan. 1855): 10–11.
242. Samuel Ringgold Ward, *Autobiography of a Fugitive Negro* (New York: Arno, 1968), 290.
243. Ibid., 297–98.
244. Ibid.
245. Ibid.
246. *Anti-Slavery Reporter* (1 May 1850): 73.
247. "Letter from Wm. C. Nell," *Frederick Douglass' Paper* (18 Mar. 1852): 1B.
248. Hamer, "British Consuls," 139.
249. "America," *London Times* (12 Jan. 1857): 10; "Colored Citizenship," *Liberator* (24 Apr. 1857): 66.
250. "Law Concerning Colored Seamen in the Ports of South Carolina," *Merchants' Magazine and Commercial Review* (Mar. 1857): 350.
251. Hamer, "British Consuls," 167.
252. Ibid.
253. "Colored Seamen in British Ships in the American Trade," *Liberator* (29 Jul. 1859): 119.
254. "Imprisonment of Coloured Seamen," *Anti-Slavery Reporter* (2 Feb. 1857): 37–38.
255. Pauline Hopkins, *Winona: A Tale of Negro Life in the South and Southwest*, in *The*

Magazine Novels of Pauline Hopkins, 287–437 (New York: Oxford University Press, 1988), 384.

256. Ibid., 395.

257. The law remained on North Carolina and Alabama statute books, although officials were persuaded to relax their enforcement of it (Hamer, "British Consuls," 142–43).

258. Edward Stanly, "Congressional: Speech of Mr. Stanly—Concluded," *Daily National Intelligencer* (3 Apr. 1850): 1C–F.

259. "Imprisonment of Coloured Seamen," *Anti-Slavery Reporter* 5, no. 2 (2 Feb. 1857): 38.

260. Palfrey, *Papers on the Slave Power*, 49.

261. Bolster, *Black Jacks*, 146.

262. Sale, *Slumbering Volcano*, 23.

263. Peter P. Hinks, introduction to *ACC*, xx.

264. Ibid., xxi; Sundquist, *To Wake the Nations*, 67.

265. Hinks, *To Awaken My Afflicted Brethren*, 40.

266. Ibid., 63, 66.

267. Ibid., 253, 249.

268. Richard R. John, *Spreading the News: The American Postal System from Franklin to Morse* (Cambridge, MA: Harvard University Press, 1998), 140–43.

269. Hinks, *To Awaken My Afflicted Brethren*, 239.

270. Ibid., 168.

271. Ibid., 145.

272. William H. Pease and Jane H. Pease, "Walker's Appeal Comes to Charleston: A Note and Documents," *Journal of Negro History* 59 (Jul. 1974): 289.

273. Grand Jury Indictment, quoted in Pease and Pease, "Walker's Appeal Comes to Charleston," 291–92.

274. Martin R. Delany, *Blake; or, The Huts of America* (Boston: Beacon, 1970), 313.

275. Sundquist, *To Wake the Nations*, 37.

276. Elizabeth McHenry, *Forgotten Readers: Recovering the Lost History of African American Literary Societies* (Durham, NC: Duke University Press, 2002), 34–37.

277. Hinks, introduction to *AAC*, xl.

278. "Incendiary Publications," *Liberator* (3 Dec. 1831): 194.

279. Jeannine Marie DeLombard, *Slavery on Trial: Law, Abolitionism, and Print Culture* (Chapel Hill: University of North Carolina Press, 2007), 146.

280. Agamben, *Homo Sacer*, 48.

CONCLUSION

1. "Massachusetts and South Carolina," *New Englander* (Oct. 1845): 606.
2. "To the Editors of the Colored American," *Colored American* (5 Aug. 1837): 2C–D, 3A.
3. "From the London Daily News," *Frederick Douglass' Paper* (6 Aug. 1852): 1C.

4. John Torpey, "Coming and Going: On the State Monopolization of the Legitimate 'Means of Movement,'" *Sociological Theory* 16 (Nov. 1998): 242.

5. In 1839, Secretary of State John Forsyth had previously rejected the passport application of a black Philadelphian on the grounds "that the newly revised Pennsylvania Constitution did not recognize Negroes as citizens," although Forsyth's decision did not elicit the pronounced disapprobation that Secretary Clayton's sweeping generalization incited in the antebellum press. Leon F. Litwack, "The Federal Government and the Free Negro, 1790–1860," *Journal of Negro History* 43, no. 4 (Oct. 1958): 271.

6. "Official Injustice—No Protection for Colored Men," *National Era* (5 July 1849): 107.

7. "Mr. Clayton Again," *Literary Union* (11 Aug. 1849): 299. Passport applications became more uniform after the State Department circulars of 1845 and 1846; they took the form of an affidavit with a certificate of naturalization if the applicant was of "alien birth." Elihu Root and Gaillard Hunt, "The History of the Department of State," *American Journal of International Law* 6 (Jan. 1912): 121.

8. "The Passport Case," *Dover Gazette & Strafford Advertiser* (1 Sept. 1849): 2A.

9. "Official Colorphobia," *North Star* (21 Aug. 1849): 2G.

10. Rosalyn Higgins, "The Right in International Law of an Individual to Enter, Stay in and Leave a Country," *International Affairs* 49, no. 3 (July 1973): 354.

11. "Secretary Clayton's Law of Passports," *North Star* (24 Aug. 1849): 1C; "The Constitution Violated," *Liberator* (10 Aug. 1849): 126.

12. "Passports to Colored Men," *Emancipator & Republican* (16 Aug. 1849): 1E.

13. "Secretary Clayton's Law of Passports," 1C.

14. "The African Colony at Liberia," *Frederick Douglass' Paper* (20 Apr. 1855): 1G.

15. Torpey, "Coming and Going," 253.

16. According to the U.S. Department of State, Secretary Forsyth had issued the first protection to a twenty-six-year-old black freedman named John Browne in 1835. U.S. Department of State, *The American Passport: Its History and a Digest of Laws, Rulings, and Regulations Governing Its Issuance by the Department of State* (Washington, DC: Government Printing Office, 1898), 15.

17. Torpey, "Coming and Going," 239.

18. The pass system, provided by statute, existed in some form throughout all the early North American colonies. Justin S. Conroy, "'Show Me Your Papers': Race and Street Encounters," *National Black Law Journal* 19, no. 149 (2006/2007): 153.

19. Stephanie M.H. Camp, *Closer to Freedom: Enslaved Women and Everyday Resistance in the Plantation South* (Chapel Hill: University of North Carolina Press, 2004), 13.

20. Ibid., 25.

21. Conroy, "Show Me Your Papers," 153–54.

22. Torpey, "Coming and Going," 241.

23. Ibid., 239–40.

24. "Constitution Violated," 126; "Official Injustice," 107; "Meanness of the 'Freest Nation on the Globe,'" *North Star* (20 July 1849): 2E.

25. "Wheeler Slave Case," *The Friend: A Religious and Literary Journal* (15 Sept. 1855): 6.

26. American Anti-Slavery Society, *The Anti-Slavery History of the John-Brown Year; Being the Twenty-Seventh Annual Report of the American Anti-Slavery Society* (New York: American Anti-Slavery Society, 1861), 221.

27. "Constitution Violated," 126.

28. "Official Injustice," 107.

29. "Secretary Clayton's Law of Passports," 1C.

30. Camp, *Closer to Freedom*, 15.

31. "Passports to People of Color," *Boston Daily Atlas* (17 Aug. 1849): 2E; "The Secretary of State," *Boston Daily Atlas* (11 Aug. 1849): 2A.

32. "Secretary of State," 2A.

33. Ibid.

34. "Passports to Colored Men," 1E.

35. "Passports," *Emancipator & Republican* (6 Sept. 1849): 4B.

36. "Meanness of the 'Freest Nation on the Globe,'" 2E; "Constitution Violated," 126.

37. "Distinction of Color—A Cabinet Doughface," *Emancipator & Republican* (26 July 1849): 2E.

38. "Coalition Lies," *Vermont Watchman and State Journal* (23 Aug. 1849): 2G. The number of passports issued by the State Department climbed steadily over the course of the early nineteenth century. Secretary Clayton issued 4,528, and that number jumped to 12,429 under Marcy and again to 21,769 under Cass (Root and Hunt, "History of the Department of State," 126).

39. "The Passport," *Boston Daily Atlas* (23 Aug. 1849): 2B.

40. Ibid.

41. "Constitution Violated," 126.

42. The State Department granted "free person of color" Rev. Peter Williams a passport in 1836 under the assumption that he was "a white person," and he later traveled to England and France on that passport ("Passports to People of Color," 2E; "Coalition Lies," 2G).

43. Purvis had received a "Special Passport" after Horace Binney wrote to Secretary McLane on his behalf. McLane later issued Purvis a passport, numbered 3373, after receiving Roberts Vaux's letter conveying Purvis's "regret and dissatisfaction, with the *special form* of a pass-port that had been furnished to him." Passport application of Robert Purvis to Secretary of State Louis McLane, May 16, 1834, Passport Number 3373 (National Archives Microfilm Publication M1372, roll 2), Passport Applications, 1795–1905, May 13, 1833–December 31, 1834, National Archives Building, Washington DC.

44. In a letter to William Goodell, Rev. A.A. Phelps records meeting Purvis the day he received his passport. He recalls taking tea at the Fortens when "in came Robert[s] Vaux, Esq. with a passport for Robert Purvis and wife, under the seal of the Secretary of State, certifying that the said Purvis and wife were *citizens of the United States*." William Yates, *Rights of Colored Men to Suffrage, Citizenship and Trial by Jury* (Philadelphia: Merrihew and Gunn, 1838), 61n.

45. "Spirited Meeting of the Colored Citizens of Philadelphia," *Liberator* (10 Apr. 1857): 59B.

46. Ibid.

47. "A Recent Tour in Ohio. No. II," *Liberator* (21 Nov. 1856): 188B.

48. "Passports to People of Color," *North Star* (7 Sept. 1849): 1D–E. Secretary of State McLane initially rejected Purvis's application for a passport in 1834, according to Clayton's letter, and granted him "a protection as a person of color" and thus "denied him the title of a citizen of the United States" ("Passports to People of Color," *Boston Daily Atlas*, 2E).

49. "Passports to People of Color," *Boston Daily Atlas*, 2E.

50. "The Passport Case," *Emancipator & Republican* (23 Aug. 1849): 3A.

51. Devon W. Carbado, "Racial Naturalization," *American Quarterly* 57 (Sept. 2005): 638–39.

52. "Refusal of American Passports to Persons of Color," *New York Herald* (24 Jan. 1860): 6D.

53. Orlando Patterson, *Slavery and Social Death* (Cambridge, MA: Harvard University Press, 1982), 38, 47.

54. Ibid., 47.

55. "Passports for Colored People," *National Era* (27 Sept. 1849): 154; "Passports," 4B; James Kent, *Commentaries on American Law*, ed. George F. Comstock, vol. 2, 11th ed. (Boston: Little, Brown, 1866), 285–88n.

56. Kent, *Commentaries on American Law*, 285–288n.

57. "The Passport Case," *Emancipator & Republican* (30 Aug. 1849): 1E. Among the disabilities levied on black northern citizenship, Kent listed the following: "the right of voting is confined to white freemen by the constitutions of Delaware, Virginia, Kentucky, Louisiana, Mississippi, Illinois, Indiana, Ohio, Missouri, South Carolina and Georgia; and by law in Connecticut, none but free white persons can be naturalized" (Kent, *Commentaries on American Law*, 286n).

58. "A Fire from the North and South," *Natchez Semi-Weekly Courier* (31 Aug. 1849): 2C.

59. *Oxford English Dictionary*, 2nd ed., s.v. "outlawry."

60. "Official Injustice," 107.

61. Quoted in Vanessa D. Dickerson, *Dark Victorians* (Urbana: University of Illinois Press, 2008), 50.

62. "Official Injustice," 107.

63. Saidiya V. Hartman, *Scenes of Subjection: Terror, Slavery, and Self-Making in Nineteenth-Century America* (New York: Oxford University Press, 1997), 164–65.

64. "Meanness of the 'Freest Nation on the Globe,'" 2E.

65. "Colored Men Citizens," *Frederick Douglass' Paper* (25 Aug. 1854): 3A. This statement is attributed to William J. Watkins in William Cooper Nell, *The Colored Patriots of the American Revolution, With Sketches of Several Distinguished Colored Persons* (Boston: Robert F. Wallcut, 1855): 341–42.

66. "Colored Men Citizens," 3A; Najia Aarim-Heriot, *Chinese Immigrants, African Americans, and Racial Anxiety in the United States, 1848–82* (Urbana: University of Illinois Press, 2003), 87.

67. "Constitution Violated," 126.

68. W.E.B. Du Bois, *The Souls of Black Folk*, in *Du Bois: Writings*, ed. Nathan Huggins, 357–548 (New York: Library of America, 1996), 364.

69. Giorgio Agamben, *Homo Sacer: Sovereign Power and Bare Life*, trans. Daniel Heller-Roazen (Stanford, CA: Stanford University Press, 1998), 128.

70. William Wells Brown to Rev. Wm. Allen in "Selections—American Slavery," *Liberator* (12 Oct. 1849): 161C.

71. Ibid.

72. The American Peace Society was formed May 1828 when the peace societies of Maine, New Hampshire, Massachusetts, New York, and Pennsylvania unified as national organization.

73. William Wells Brown, *Narrative of the Life and Escape of William Wells Brown*, in *Clotel, or The President's Daughter* (Boston: Bedford/St. Martin's, 2000), 72.

74. "J.C. Holly," *Frederick Douglass' Paper* (12 Feb. 1852): 2C.

75. "Letter from J.R. Johnson to S.R. Ward," *Frederick Douglass' Paper* (29 Apr. 1853): 3C.

76. William Wells Brown, "Letter from Wm. Wells Brown," *Liberator* (2 Nov. 1849): 175; William Wells Brown, "From a Letter of Wm. Wells Brown to Wm. L. Garrison," *North Star* (30 Nov. 1849): 1A.

77. Ibid.

78. Ibid.

79. "Government and Its Subjects," *North Star* (9 Nov. 1849): 2D.

80. Brown made reference to the encounter at a public meeting in London shortly after his arrival as a key example of "the American prejudice against color": "He had been refused a passport to come to Europe, which the American Secretary told him was never granted except to the servants of diplomatic agents, while at the same time a regular passport was granted to the boot-black of a slaveholding Judge who was going out as Consul to Naples." "Public Reception of Wm. W. Brown in the Metropolis of England," *Liberator* (19 Oct. 1849): 166.

81. "A Fugitive Slave Turned Author," *Liberator* (12 Jan. 1855): 9. Brown traveled incessantly over this period, covering more than twenty-five thousand miles and delivering over one thousand lectures while authoring numerous essays, a travelogue, and *Clotel*.

82. William Wells Brown, *American Fugitive in Europe: Sketches of Places and People Abroad*, in *The Travels of William Wells Brown*, ed. Paul Jefferson (New York: Markus Wiener, 1991), 227; further references to *American Fugitive* are to this edition and are cited parenthetically in the text as *AF*.

83. Vanessa D. Dickerson, *Dark Victorians* (Urbana: University of Illinois Press, 2008), 67. Josephine Brown later authored a biography of her celebrated father entitled simply *Biography of an American Bondman by His Daughter* (Boston: R.F. Wallcut, 1856).

84. "Return of Wm. Wells Brown," *National Anti-Slavery Standard* (7 Oct. 1854): 3E.

85. William Wells Brown, "Letter from W.W. Brown," *Liberator* (22 Sept. 1854): 151.

86. The "Foreign Minister" functioned as a proxy for the U.S. government abroad; he

"derives all his power from our Government, acts wholly under the orders and authority of the State Department, and is its representative abroad." "Who Are Citizens of the United States?" *Kansas Herald of Freedom* (8 May 1858): 1B.

87. Don E. Fehrenbacher, *Dred Scott Case: Its Significance in American Law and Politics* (Oxford: Oxford University Press, 1978), 290, 292.

88. "Colored People Not Citizens and Not to Be Allowed Passports," *National Era* (20 Nov. 1856): 188.

89. Carbado, "Racial Naturalization," 637; Hartman, *Scenes of Subjection*, 196.

90. Litwack, "Federal Government and the Free Negro," 273.

91. Secretary Cass issued Remond a passport, numbered 10350, after receiving an application letter on her behalf signed by Joseph G. Waters, notary public, and witnessed by Samuel P. Andrews. Passport application of Sarah P. Remond to Secretary of State Lewis Cass, September 8, 1858, Passport Number 10350 (National Archives Microfilm Publication M1372, roll 73), Passport Applications, 1795–1905, August 10–October 8, 1858, National Archives Building, Washington, DC.

92. "Washington Items," *National Era* (22 Apr. 1858): 62.

93. "Who Are Citizens of the United States?" 1B.

94. Ibid.; "Passports to Colored Men," 1E.

95. "Disabilities of American Persons of Color," *New York Herald* (24 Jan. 1860): 4F.

96. "Slavery Still at Its Dirty Work," *Liberator* (20 Jan. 1860): 9; "American Colorphobia," *Liberator* (20 Jan. 1860): 10.

97. F.W. Chesson, "America Disgraced Abroad," *Liberator* (6 Jan. 1860): 2.

98. "Slavery Still at Its Dirty Work," 1.

99. Ibid.

100. "Disabilities of American Persons of Color," 4F.

101. Ibid.

102. "Refusal of American Passports," 6D.

103. American Anti-Slavery Society, *Anti-Slavery History of the John-Brown Year*, 220.

104. Christopher Leslie Brown, *Moral Capital: Foundations of British Abolitionism* (Chapel Hill: University of North Carolina Press, 2006), 5.

105. "Who Are Citizens of the United States?" 1B.

106. Root and Hunt, "History of the Department of State," 119.

107. *The Case of Dred Scott in the United States Supreme Court: The Full Opinions of Chief Justice Taney and Justice Curtis, and Abstracts of the Opinions of the Other Judges; With an Analysis of the Points Ruled, and Some Concluding Observations* (New York: Greeley & McElrath, Tribune Buildings, 1857), 18; Litwack, "Federal Government and the Free Negro," 271.

108. "The Oppression of the Buchanan Administration towards Colored Citizens," *Liberator* (16 Apr. 1858): 62.

109. Frederick Douglass, *Life and Times of Frederick Douglass, Written by Himself*, in *Frederick Douglass Autobiographies*, ed. Henry Louis Gates, Jr. (New York: Library of America, 1996), 761; further references to *Life and Times* are to this edition and are cited parenthetically in the text as *LT*.

110. In this volume, Douglass finally revealed his method of escape—a borrowed seaman's protection secured him passage aboard a Philadelphia-bound train—which he had withheld from the original *Narrative*.

111. American Anti-Slavery Society, *Anti-Slavery History of the John-Brown Year*, 220.

112. "Base and Unnatural Proscription," *Liberator* (27 Apr. 1860): 66. Douglass's travels abroad were cut short by news of his daughter Annie's death, and he returned to the United States regardless of the dangers.

113. Chesson, "America Disgraced Abroad," 2.

114. Ibid.

115. "Colored Citizenship," *Christian Recorder* (14 Sept. 1861): 2F.

116. "That Passport," *Lowell Daily Citizen and News* (30 Oct. 1861): 2C; "The Manhood of the Negro," *Independent* (24 Oct. 1861): 4.

117. "Manhood of the Negro," 4.

118. "American Anti-Slavery Society," *New York Observer and Chronicle* (21 May 1863): 164A.

119. "What Has Been Done by Congress," *Liberator* (25 Nov. 1864): 189.

120. Hartman, *Scenes of Subjection*, 150.

121. In 1984, historian Loren Schweninger published Thomas's autobiographical manuscript in a reconstructed form. Loren Schweninger, introduction to *From Tennessee Slave to St. Louis Entrepreneur: The Autobiography of James Thomas*, 1–19 (Columbia: University of Missouri Press, 1984), 15; Loren Schweninger, "The Manuscript," in *FTS*, 20.

122. The Department of State issued Thomas a passport, numbered 31234, on May 17, 1873. Passport application of James Thomas to Secretary of State Hamilton Fish, May 14, 1873, Passport Number 31234 (National Archives Microfilm Publication M1372, roll 194), Passport Applications, 1795–1905, May 9–22, 1873, National Archives Building, Washington, DC.

123. Torpey, "Coming and Going," 251.

124. Hartman, *Scenes of Subjection*, 171.

125. Harriet A. Jacobs, *Incidents in the Life of a Slave Girl*, ed. Jean Fagan Yellin (Cambridge, MA: Harvard University Press, 2000), 186.

126. Frederick Douglass, *My Bondage and My Freedom*, in *Frederick Douglass Autobiographies* (New York: Library of America, 2004), 394.

127. Michael P. O'Connor, "Time Out of Mind: Our Collective Amnesia about the History of the Privileges or Immunities Clause," *Kentucky Law Journal*, 93, no. 659 (2004/2005): 687.

128. Hartman, *Scenes of Subjection*, 170.

129. O'Connor, "Time Out of Mind," 689; Deak Nabers, *Victory of Law: The Fourteenth Amendment, the Civil War, and American Literature, 1852–1867* (Baltimore: Johns Hopkins University Press, 2006), 5.

130. O'Connor, "Time Out of Mind," 688; Amy Dru Stanley, *From Bondage to Contract: Wage Labor, Marriage, and the Market in the Age of Slave Emancipation* (Cambridge: Cambridge University Press, 1998), x.

131. The lone dissenter in the 1883 Civil Rights Cases, Justice John Harlan had also viewed "such discrimination is a badge of servitude." *Civil Rights Cases*, 109 U.S. 3 (1883).

132. O'Connor, "Time Out of Mind," 688–89.

133. Hartman, *Scenes of Subjection*, 172.

134. *Plessy v. Ferguson*, 163 U.S. 537 (1896); Blackstone's *Commentaries* reads, "This personal liberty consists in the power of loco-motion, of changing situation, or removing one's person to whatsoever place one's own inclination may direct; without imprisonment or restraint, unless by due course of law." William Blackstone, *Commentaries on the Laws of England: A Facsimile of the First Edition of 1765–1769*, vol. 1, *Of the Rights of Persons* (1765) (Chicago: University of Chicago Press, 1979), 130.

135. Camp, *Closer to Freedom*, 141.

136. *Plessy v. Ferguson*, 163 U.S. 537 (1896).

137. "The Glorious Fourth," *North Star* (3 Aug. 1849): 1E; "Secretary Clayton's Law of Passports," 1C.

Index

Abolition Act, 68–69, 276n217, 277n235
abolitionist ideology: and *Aves*, 89–91; disregard of kinship ties, 12–13, 97–98, 100, 125–26, 130–31, 280n39; gendered rhetoric, 7–8, 56–59, 79–81, 274n180; interpretation of *Somerset*, 20–21, 27–28; north-south imaginary, 8, 129; and slave agency, 93–104, 112–14
Adams, Francis Colburn: on antiblack police laws, 16, 167; campaign against South Carolina Negro Seamen Act, 222–23; historical fictions, 210–13; on state aggression, 185; use of kidnap trope, 119. See also *Manuel Pereira* (Adams)
An Address to All the Colored Citizens of the United States (Meachum), 158, 160–61, 165, 166
Agamben, Giorgio, 199, 238
Aiken, William, Jr., 193–94, 203
Alexander, William, 149
The American Fugitive in Europe (Brown), 250
The American Slave Code (Goodell), 7, 153
Andrews, William, 80, 223
Annis, John, 32–33
Anson (slave child), 92–94, 125, 131
antiblack police laws: antisecessionist arguments against, 224–25; antislavery print culture criticism of, 167–68; in border states, 167–68; and Lunsford Lane, 169–70; paradoxical logic in, 16, 167–68; in slave states, 143–44, 166–68, 304n9. See also Negro Seamen Acts; slave law; South Carolina Negro Seamen Act
antimiscegenation laws, 178–79
Appeal to the Coloured Citizens of the World (Walker), 36–37, 183, 199–200, 234–39
apprenticeship, in West Indies, 68–76
An Argument in the Case of James Sommersett, a Negro (Francis Hargrave), 28
Armistead, Wilson, 227, 230
Articles of Confederation, 108, 150, 240
The Artist and His Wife in a Garden, with a Black Servant (Richard Cosway), 35
Axe Laid to the Root (Wedderburn), 63–66

Barrett, Lindon, 151–52
Bates, Edward, 141–43
Baucom, Ian, 213, 221
Behind the Scenes; or, Thirty Years a Slave, and Four Years in the White House (Elizabeth Keckley), 127
Belle Scott; or, Liberty Overthrown! (Jolliffe), 120, 167
Benton, Thomas Hart, 157
Best, Stephen, 34, 44, 83–84
Bicknell, John, "The Dying Negro," 26
Binder, Guyora, 201
black citizenship: denationalized by *Dred Scott*, 144–45, 155, 174–75, 177, 203, 254;

denationalized by "law of passports," 241–54; denationalized by South Carolina Negro Seamen Act, 190–91, 198, 203
black exclusion regulations. *See* antiblack police laws
black mobility. *See* free black travel
black radicalism: and *Appeal* (Walker), 235, 238; and John Glasgow, 225–28; as Negro Seamen Acts justification, 184–87, 192–94, 198, 234, 238, 303n2; as Negro Seamen Acts result, 192, 225, 231–34, 238–39
Blackstone, William: and implied contract, 39–42; and right to free travel, 261–62, 324n134
Blake; or, The Huts of America (Delany), 21, 236
Blow, Peter, 131
Blow, Taylor, 131, 145
Bolster, Jeffrey, 184
Boston Female Anti-Slavery Society: attitude toward kinship ties, 80, 86, 88; and *Aves*, 79, 81, 85, 86, 88; and Jane Johnson, 113–14; and motherhood trope, 81, 88–90, 113–14; role in freedom suits, 7, 79, 83
Bourdieu, Pierre, 84, 102, 279n29
Bowers, Isaac, 206–7
British and Foreign Anti-Slavery Society, 69, 205–7, 231
Brown, Christopher, 20
Brown, Henry Box, 21, 144
Brown, John, 21, 227–30
Brown, William Wells: on African slave trade, 162; England as refuge for, 21; and kinship ties, 122–23, 179; on manumission, 159; passport denied, 249–51; on property principle of slavery, 129; on St. Louis, 167
Buckley-Mathew, George. *See* Mathew, George Buckley

Camp, Stephanie, 242
Candid Reflections upon the Judgement Lately Awarded by the Court of King's Bench (Edward Long), 29–30
Carbado, Devon, 220–21, 246
"The Case of Dred Scott in the Supreme Court of the United States, December Term, 1854" (Dred Scott), 154–57
Case of the Slave Grace: British antislavery print culture response to, 22–23; and "consent," 44–46; facts and ruling, 42–43; and Mary Prince, 50–51; as precedent, 11, 37, 46–47; and reattachment doctrine, 31, 37, 38, 47; response to, 43–48; and slave's double character, 38; and *Somerset*, 22–23, 37
Cass, Lewis, 252–53
Castello, John, 72–74
Catharine Linda v. Erastus D. Hudson, 96–101, 284n106
Chaffee, Calvin C., 145
Chapman, Maria Weston, 88, 113
Charity Still (in *Underground Rail Road* by William Still), 116
Charleston police power, 216–17
chattel principle. *See* property principle
Child, Lydia Maria, 85, 90
"choice": and Anson, 92–94, 125, 131; and Betty, 101–2; and Catharine Linda, 97–98; and Harriet Jacobs, 78–79; and Jane Johnson, 111–14; in *The Kidnapped and the Ransomed* (Pickard), 114–15, 117, 121–26; and Mary Prince, 50–53; as rejection of freedom, 131. *See also* "consent"
Chouteau, Pierre (Cadet), 127
citizenship: and Fourteenth Amendment, 248–49; race as condition of, 177, 241–54; and right to free travel, 189–90, 240–41, 261–62
Civil Rights Act of 1875, 260–61
Clamorgan, Cyprian, 174–81

Clarkson, Thomas: and British antislavery tradition, 20; and "free air" metaphor, 28–29; and John Lewis freedom suit, 25–26; and Society for the Abolition of the Slave Trade, 34
Clay, Henry, 6
Clayton, John, 207, 241–45
Clotel; or, The President's Daughter (Brown), 122, 162, 177, 179, 220
The Colored Aristocracy of St. Louis (Clamorgan), 174–81
color line: and citizenship, 177, 241–54; and Clamorgan's elite, 177–78, 301n198, 302n208; post-emancipation persistence of, 17, 262; Taney on, 177
comity. *See* legal reciprocity
Commentaries on American Law (James Kent): on black citizenship, 247, 320n57; on "doctrine of emancipation," 134; and implied contract, 39–40; on self-preservation, 192; on slave's double character, 4, 152
Commentaries on the Laws of England (Blackstone): and implied contract, 39–42; and right to free travel, 261–62
Commonwealth v. Aves: and antislavery print culture, 82; and Catharine Linda, 99; criticism of, 84–86; northern adoption of, 102; paradoxical logic in, 82–84, 90–92, 99; as precedent, 91–92, 104; and slave agency, 82, 99; and *Somerset* precedent, 12, 27, 78, 82; and travel rights, 1–2, 79. *See also* Massachusetts
Commonwealth v. Mary B. Taylor, 92–93
Commonwealth v. Robinson, 87–88
"consent": and *Aves*, 83–84, 91–93; and *Grace*, 44–46; and implied contract, 39, 93. *See also* "choice"
contract, implied, 28, 38–42, 50–51
contract theory: contradictions in, 125; and liberalism, 17, 84, 100

Cosway, Richard, *The Artist and His Wife in a Garden, with a Black Servant*, 35
Cover, Robert, 92
Cowper, William, 28–29
Craft, William and Ellen, 21, 102, 228, 250, 285n143
Crocket, Polly, 138, 137–42
Cugoano, Quobna Ottobah, 21, 31–32, 33–36, 270n80
Curtis, Benjamin, 84–85, 178–79
custom: freedom qualified by, 259; and "law of passports," 244–45, 259; as precedent in *Dred Scott*, 254

Dallas, George, 252–53
Dayan, Joan (Colin Dayan), 94, 184
Day, Thomas, "The Dying Negro," 26
de Certeau, Michel, 61, 275n196
Delaney, Lucy Ann: freedom suit as narrative, 137–38; later life, 182; portrait (in *From the Darkness*), 139; scholarly neglect of, 143; and theft theme, 119, 138, 140, 142–43
Delany, Martin, 21, 236, 247
Deliesseline, Francis, 195–97
DeLombard, Jeannine, 15, 82
deportation: and British freedom suits, 46–47; and *Grace*, 31, 42, 47; Sharp on, 39; and *Somerset*, 30–33; and "The Dying Negro" (Bicknell and Day), 26
doctrine of "once free, forever free": established in *Winny v. Whitesides*, 134; rejected in *Scott v. Emerson*, 151; Stowell on, 43
doctrine of reattachment. *See* reattachment doctrine
doctrine of self-preservation: as defense of Negro Seamen Acts, 187, 192–94, 198, 223–24; reappropriated by British abolitionists, 225–26, 230
Douglas, Betto, 55–56
Douglass, Frederick: on archaism of

slavery, 221–22; on freedom of choice, 38; on "law of passports," 241–42, 244, 248, 250; on losses entailed by freedom, 17; on manumission, 159; narrative as paradigm, 79–80; passport denied, 254–56; and retribution, 64–65; on right to free travel, 250, 255, 262; on segregation, 260–61; on Wheeler slave case, 108–9

Downman, John, *Thomas Williams, a Sailor*, 186

Dred Scott v. Sandford: and antislavery print culture, 154; and Benjamin Curtis, 84, 178–79; and black citizenship, 144–45, 155, 174–75, 177, 254; circular logic in, 153; Clamorgan's literary response to, 174–80; and Fourteenth Amendment, 248; and kinship ties, 131; as landmark case, 14; and miscegenation, 178–79; misspelled name, 291n3; and *partus sequitur ventrem*, 134; property principle affirmed by, 151, 166–67; and reattachment doctrine, 151; scholarship on, 130–31. *See also* freedom suits, St. Louis; "law of passports"; *Scott v. Emerson*

Drescher, Seymour, 30, 69

Drew, Benjamin, 168, 173

Du Bois, W.E.B., 248

"The Dying Negro" (Bicknell and Day), 26

Elkison, Henry, 195–97

Elkison v. Deliesseline, 15, 192–93, 195–97, 307n73

Emerson, Irene Sanford, 131, 132, 145, 291n3

Emerson, John, 131–32

English law: failures of, 32–37; slaveholders' manipulation of, 49–50; slave's double character in, 37–39

Equiano, Olaudah, 21, 31–33, 36, 270n80

Fehrenbacher, Don, 6, 131, 153, 154, 200

Ferguson, Moira, 57

Finkelman, Paul, 5–6

Fourteenth Amendment, 248–49, 260

Frank Leslie's Illustrated Newspaper, 145–49

free black travel: and *Plessy*, 261–62; in post-emancipation slave states, 260; in slave states, 14–15, 167–68, 183–84, 187, 242–44. *See also* "law of passports"; Negro Seamen Acts; South Carolina Negro Seamen Act

freedom: and British rhetoric, 20–21, 25–26, 28–31, 38, 42–44, 204; contract as metaphor for, 84, 125; and kinship loss, 17–18, 80–81, 125–26, 140, 168–72. *See also* law of freedom

freedom law. *See* law of freedom

freedom suits, American: and abolitionist ideology, 7–8, 12–13, 80–81, 94–98; *Aves* as precedent, 91–104, 108; and *Grace* precedent, 46–47; and habeas corpus, 3, 26, 191–92, 202; as narrative, 6–7, 137–38, 141, 154–57; paradoxical logic in, 3–5, 8, 82–84, 90–92, 99–102, 144, 152–54; and *Somerset* precedent, 27–28; as untold stories, 2–3; women as plaintiffs in, 7–8, 80–81. *See also* legal cases, American

freedom suits, British: and Louis Asa-Asa, 57, 274n177; and Henry Demane, 32; and Jack Martin, 46; and John and Mary Hylas, 26; and John Lewis (*Rex v. Stapylton*), 24–26; and John Smith and Rachel, 46; and Jonathan Strong, 26; legislative petitions, 21, 48–55, 57–60; and William Otto, 46; and William Robday, 46. *See also Case of the Slave Grace*; *Somerset v. Stewart*

freedom suits, Scottish, and Joseph Knight, 21, 26, 269n65

freedom suits, St. Louis: and abolitionist north-south imaginary, 8, 129; against Meachum, 163–66; antislavery print culture disregard of, 154; in Clamorgan's history, 176, 180–81; *Julia v. McKinney*, 134–36, 144; and Lucy Delaney, 141–43; paradoxical logic in, 152–54, 296n112; *partus sequitur ventrem* in, 14, 134–42, 163–64; and Polly Crocket, 139, 140–42; *Rachael v. Walker*, 135, 136–37; reattachment doctrine in, 144, 151; residence claim in, 14, 134–35, 134–37, 144, 150–51, 163–64; statistics on, 150; statutes governing, 143, 149, 151–54, 157; *Wash v. Magehan*, 138; white jury attitudes, 164; *Winny v. Whitesides*, 134–35. See also *Dred Scott v. Sandford*; *Scott v. Emerson*

"free will". See "choice"

From the Darkness Cometh the Light; or, Struggles for Freedom (Lucy Ann Delaney), 137–43

Fryer, Peter, 31

Fugitive Blacksmith (Pennington), 126

Fugitive Slave Act: and Elizabeth Keckley, 128; and Harriet Jacobs, 78–79; impact on William Wells Brown, 250; and interstate relations, 144; and Massachusetts, 90, 92; Peter Still's fear of, 115; and *Scott v. Emerson*, 294n70

fugitive slave narratives: and Dred Scott, 145; freedom suits as counternarrative to, 6–7, 79–81, 126; gendered rhetoric, 7–8

fugitive slaves vs. traveling slaves, 82–84, 250

Garland, Anne Burwell, 127
Garland, Hugh A., 127, 137, 144, 155
Garnet, Henry Highland, 256–58
Garrison, William Lloyd: on Abolition Act, 68; on black radicalism, 238; and Catharine Linda, 97, 99, 100–101; on criminalization of color, 220; and *Dred Scott*, 14; on Garnet's passport, 257; on "law of passports," 241–45; on manumission, 159; on Meachum, 159, 166; on Negro Seamen Acts, 185, 188; on right to free travel, 203–4, 257; and slave Betty, 101–2; and Wheeler slave case, 111

gendered rhetoric: and British antislavery print culture, 56–59, 79–81, 274n180; and colonialist propaganda, 56, 59, 60–61; and fugitive slave narrative, 7–8

Gilbert, Olive, 94–96
Gilroy, Paul, 40
Glasgow, John, 225–31
Goodell, William, 7, 153
Great Britain: law of freedom in, 11–12, 28–31; and slave trade, 19; and South Carolina Negro Seamen Act, 198–200, 205–10, 311n149; uncertain status of slaves in, 21–24, 40. See also West Indies

Greeley, Horace, 7
Gross, Ariela, 94

habeas corpus: dismissed in *Elkison*, 195–96, 307n73; South Carolina suspension of, 191–92, 310n122; as tool of freedom suits, 3, 26–27, 191–92, 202; as tool of proslavery jurisprudence, 105, 107, 109
Hargrave, Francis, 28–29, 38–39
Harlan, John, 261–62
Harriet v. Emerson, 131–32
Hartman, Saidiya: on black subjectivity, 80; on Cugoano, 34; on retelling slavery story, 8; on right to free travel, 257; on slaveholders' use of kinship ties, 9; on slave's double character, 4
Hawkins, William G., 77, 146, 168, 170–73

Henson, Josiah, 114, 124
Heyrick, Elizabeth, 19, 23, 55
Hilton, Kitty, 11, 49, 57, 60–61
The History of Mary Prince, a West Indian Slave (Mary Prince), 49–54, 57–60
History of the Colored Race in America (Alexander), 149
History of the Rise, Progress, and Accomplishment of the Abolition of the African Slave-Trade by the British Parliament (Thomas Clarkson), 20, 26
Hoar, Samuel, 202–4
Holmes, Isaac E., 196
Holt, Thomas, 39, 68
Hopkins, Pauline, 232–33
The Horrors of Slavery (Wedderburn), 64–67
Hudson, Erasmus D., 96–98, 284n106
Hunt, Benjamin Faneuil, 192–93, 197–98, 216

implied contract, 28, 38–42, 50–51
Incidents in the Life of a Slave Girl (Harriet A. Jacobs), 77–79, 121
"inclusive exclusion" of blacks, 246, 251, 254, 261
interstate comity. *See* legal reciprocity

Jacobs, Harriet A., 77–79, 121, 124, 129, 278n7
Jacobs, John S., 77–80, 278n7
Johnson, Jane, 97, 104–14, 125
Johnson, Walter, 126
Johnson, William (justice U.S. Supreme Court), 195–97
Jolliffe, John, 119–20, 167
Jones, Grace. *See Case of the Slave Grace*
Julia v. McKinney, 134–36, 144

Kane, John Kintzing, 107–9
Kaplan, Amy, 5
Keckley, Elizabeth, 127–29, 168, 291n2

Kemble, Fanny, 9–10, 120, 151
Kent, James, 4, 39–40, 134, 152, 192, 320n57
kidnap: and British freedom suits, 46–47; and *Grace*, 45, 47; of John Annis, 32–33; and Peter Still, 115, 119; Sharp on, 39; and *Somerset*, 27, 32; as trope, 119–20; as Wheeler slave case charge, 107, 109, 111–12
The Kidnapped and the Ransomed (Kate E.R. Pickard), 114–26; ambivalences in, 121–25; "choice" in, 114–15, 117, 121–26; and Jewish abolitionists, 114; motherhood trope in, 121; portrait of woman, *118*; theft of kinship in, 13, 114–25
kinship: as ambivalent right, 142–43; and fugitive slave narratives, 126; and motherhood trope, 87–89, 93; and property principle, 9, 119–20, 142–43, 280n35; and St. Louis freedom suits, 134–35, 142–43, 146–49
kinship loss: as freedom's price, 17–18, 80–81, 125–26, 140, 168–72; and Lunsford Lane, 171–72; and William Wells Brown, 250–51
kinship ties: abolitionist disregard of, 12–13, 97–98, 100, 125–26, 131, 280n39; and *Aves*, 84–86, 88; and Catharine Linda, 97–98; and *The Colored Aristocracy* (Clamorgan), 178–81; and *Commonwealth v. Mary B. Taylor*, 92–93; and *Commonwealth v. Robinson*, 87–88; and Dred Scott, 156–57; in *From the Darkness* (Delaney), 140; and Harriet Scott, 132–34, 146–49; in *The Kidnapped and the Ransomed* (Pickard), 114–25; and Polly Crocket, 138, 140–43; and slave Betty, 101–2; and "slave family" trope, 120; slaveholders' use of, 9–10, 49–50, 80, 87, 93, 97–98, 111; and Sojourner Truth, 94–96

Knapp, Isaac, 7, 81, 277n230
Knight, Joseph, 21, 26, 269n65
Konig, David, 28, 150, 154
Lane, Lunsford, 146, 168–73
Las Casas, Bartolomé, 161–62
law of freedom: "free air" substituted for, 29–31; and implied contract, 38–42; and kinship loss, 17–18, 80–81, 125–26, 140, 168–73; "law of passports" exceptions to, 243–44, 246–48; punitive use of, 16, 167–73, 300n173; qualified by custom, 259–62; role of habeas corpus, 3, 26, 191–92, 202, 307n73; and slave will, 81–84, 91–96, 102; and *Somerset*, 11–12, 28–31; and South Carolina Negro Seamen Act, 190–91. See also freedom
Law of Nations (de Vattel), 197
"law of passports": Clayton's defense of, 244, 245–46; codified by Passport Act of 1856, 253–54; condemnation of, 242–48; contrary precedents to, 245–46, 319nn42–43; denial of black citizenship, 243–44, 246–48; distinction between travelers and servants, 243–44, 249–50; impact on black abolitionist travelers, 249–56; policy repudiated, 256–59. See also *Dred Scott v. Sandford*
legal cases, American: *Catharine Linda v. Erastus D. Hudson*, 96–101, 284n106; *Commonwealth v. Fitzgerald*, 89, 202; *Commonwealth v. Mary B. Taylor*, 92–93; *Commonwealth v. Potterfield*, 89, 202; *Commonwealth v. Robinson*, 87–88; *Elkison v. Deliesseline*, 15, 192–93, 195–97, 307n73; *Harriet v. Emerson*, 131–32; Holden Slave Case, 92, 282n89; *Julia v. McKinney*, 134–36, 144, 292n33; *Lemmon v. The People of the State of New York*, 106–7; and Manuel Pereira, 208–9; *Marguerite v. [John Pierre] Chouteau*, 180–81; *Meechum v. Judy*, 163; *Plessy v. Ferguson*, 17, 241, 261–62; *Rachael v. Walker*, 135, 136–37, 292n33; *Roberts v. Yates*, 15, 208–9, 219; *Scott v. Emerson*, 37, 127, 128, 144, 151; *State [of North Carolina] v. Mann*, 83; *Stratton et al. v. Babbage*, 189, 305n37; *Sylvia v. Kirby*, 144; *Wash v. Magehan*, 138; Wheeler slave case (case of Passmore Williamson), 104–14; *Winny v. Whitesides*, 134–35. See also *Commonwealth v. Aves*; *Dred Scott v. Sandford*; freedom suits, American
legal cases, British: and Isaac Bowers, 206–7; *Rex v. Stapylton*, 24–26; *Williams v. Brown*, 37–38; *Wood v. Pringle*, 59. See also *Case of the Slave Grace*; freedom suits, British; *Somerset v. Stewart*
legal freedom. See law of freedom
legal reciprocity: and *Aves*, 83; and *Dred Scott*, 166; and freedom suits, 5–6; and Negro Seamen Acts, 190
Lemmon, Jonathan, 107
Lemmon v. The People of the State of New York, 6, 107
Lewis, John, 24–26
liberalism: and *Aves*, 90; and contract theory, 17, 84, 100; and freedom suits, 8, 94; and "free will," 84, 94, 100; and Missouri jurisprudence, 134, 149–50, 152–54, 157; paradox of, 162
Liberator. See Garrison, William Lloyd
Life and Times of Frederick Douglass (Douglass), 255–56
Linda, Catharine, 96–101
Linebaugh, Peter, 184
Locke, John, 38–39
Long, Edward: as advocate of colonial slaveholders, 22, 269n72, 270n79; on Blackstone, 41; criticism of "free air" metaphor, 29, 30; on kinship ties, 50
Loring, Charles G., 87

Loring, Ellis Gray: and *Commonwealth v. Aves*, 82–84; and *Commonwealth v. Mary B. Taylor*, 92; and *Commonwealth v. Robinson*, 87; in *The Kidnapped and the Ransomed* (Pickard), 124
Lovejoy, Elijah, 178
Lunsford Lane; or, Another Helper from North Carolina (Hawkins), 168, 170–73
Lushington, Stephen, 46–47, 48–49

Macaulay, Zachary, 54
Macqueen, James, 58–59
Mansfield, Lord (William Murray), 20–22, 24–25, 26–31, 39
Manuel Pereira; or, The Sovereign Rule of South Carolina (Adams): ambivalence regarding law in, 220–21; antisentimentalism, 213–14, 216, 217–18, 219–20; and archaism of slavery, 221–22; criminalization of color in, 220–21; as critique of South Carolina Negro Seamen Act, 213–15; impact of, 222–23; law as mechanism for violence in, 216–21; publication of, 211–13. See also South Carolina Negro Seamen Act
manumission, 158–59
Marcy, William, 251–52
Marguerite v. [John Pierre] Chouteau, 180–81
Marshall, John, 4
Massachusetts: and *Aves*, 89–91; and Fugitive Slave Act, 90, 92; personal liberty laws, 91–92; response to Negro Seamen Acts, 201–4
Massachusetts. See also *Commonwealth v. Aves*
Mathew, George Buckley, 149, 206, 207–8, 234, 311n149
May, Samuel J., 115, 226
McGirk, Matthias: and *Julia v. McKinney*, 135–36; and *Marguerite v. [John Pierre] Chouteau*, 180; and *Meechum v. Judy*, 163; and *Rachael v. Walker*, 137
McHenry, Elizabeth, 238
Meachum, John Berry, 158–66, 298n140
Mead, Eleanor, 57, 61–63
Means, John, 198, 206–9
Med (slave child). See *Commonwealth v. Aves*
Midgley, Clare, 48, 273n162
Mintz, Steven, 160
Minutes of Proceedings at Brown's Town, St.Ann's (Castello), 72–73
miscegenation, 178–79
Missouri Compromise, 14, 128, 136, 150, 166
Missouri law: antiblack police laws, 143–44, 166, 167; and black testimony, 163; as "liberal," 134–37, 149–50, 153–54, 157, 297n129; and Meachum, 158, 160; statutes governing freedom suits, 143–44, 149–54, 157; strategies of freedom under, 165–66
motherhood trope: and Boston Female Anti-Slavery Society, 81, 88–90, 113–14; and Jane Johnson, 111–14; in *The Kidnapped and the Ransomed* (Pickard), 121; resisted by Harriet Scott, 147–49; slaveholders' use of, 85, 86–87; and Sojourner Truth, 94–96
Murdoch, Francis B., 141

A Narrative of Events, Since the First of August, 1834, by James Williams, an Apprenticed Labourer in Jamaica, 69–76
"Narrative of Louis Asa-Asa, a Captured African" (Pringle), 56–57, 274n177
Narrative of Lunsford Lane (Lane), 168–73
Narrative of Sojourner Truth: A Northern Slave (Gilbert), 94–96, 114
Narrative of the Facts in the Case of Passmore Williamson (Pennsylvania Anti-Slavery Society), 108

Narrative of the Life of Frederick Douglass, 79–80
Negro Seamen Acts: antisecessionist arguments against, 224–25; antislavery print culture criticism of, 185, 188–92; black radicalism as justification for, 184–87, 192–94, 198, 234, 238; black radicalism as result of, 192, 225, 231–34, 238–39; black seamen's response to, 188; congressional debates regarding, 190–91; diplomatic protests against, 198–99, 312n153; incarcerations under, 189, 305n39; Massachusetts response to, 201–4; modification of, 223–24, 233; northern black response to, 187–88; provisions of, 15, 184, 305n37; as transatlantic issue, 15, 190, 193, 195, 205–7, 222–23, 231, 312n172. *See also* antiblack police laws; South Carolina Negro Seamen Act
Negro Slavery Described by a Negro: Being the Narrative of Ashton Warner, a Native of St. Vincent's (Ashton Warner), 49, 54–55, 60
North Carolina Negro Seamen Act, 203
Northrup, Solomon, 119–20, 176, 226
Northwest Ordinance, 128, 132, 134, 136, 164, 294n70
"Occasional Discourse on the Negro Question" (Thomas Carlyle), 71
Olmstead, Frederick Law, 5
Orpen, Charles, 19–20, 21
Our Nig (Harriet Wilson), 143

Palfrey, John, 204, 233
Papers on the Slave Power (Palfrey), 204, 233
partus sequitur ventrem: defined, 9; in St. Louis freedom suits, 14, 134–42, 163–64; Wedderburn's interpretation of, 66
Passport Act of 1856, 253–54
passport disputes. *See* "law of passports"

"pass system." *See* ticket laws
Paton, Diana, 70, 72
Patterson, Orlando, 123, 153, 184, 246
Pennington, James, 109, 126
Pereira, Manuel, 208–9. *See also Manuel Pereira* (Adams)
personhood: and antiblack police laws, 16, 167–68; black seamen stripped of, 187; and slave's double character, 4–5, 9–10, 37–39, 152–54; and St. Louis freedom suits, 14, 129–30, 143
"Peter Still" (in *Underground Rail Road* by William Still), 116
Petigru, James L., 208, 236–38
Phillips, Wendell, and *Aves*, 90–91
Pickard, Kate E.R., 13, 114–26, 289n200, 289n203, 290n219
Plessy v. Ferguson, 17, 241, 261–62
police laws. *See* antiblack police laws
Political Map of the United States (William C. Reynolds), 4
Polk, Andrew Jackson, 1, 102–4, 308n85
Prince, Mary, 21, 48–54, 57–60
Pringle, Thomas: and Ashton Warner, 49, 54–55; on colonial legal influence, 56, 273n160; gendered rhetoric, 57, 274n180; and *Grace*, 48; and Kitty Hilton petition, 60–61; and Mary Prince, 49, 50–51, 56–57; Orpen's letter to, 19–21
property principle: *Dred Scott* affirmation of, 151, 167; and kinship, 9, 119–20, 142–43, 280n35; and manumission, 159; and slave's double character, 4–5, 9–10, 37–39, 152–54; and St. Louis freedom suits, 14, 129–30, 143, 152–54. *See also* reattachment doctrine
protection, certificates of, 189–90, 242, 244, 246
Purvis, Robert, 245–46, 319n43

Rachael v. Walker, 135, 136–37

racialization: of "difference," 220–21; of mobility, 183–84, 187; of social status, 177–78
reattachment doctrine: and *Grace*, 31, 37, 38, 47; and *Scott v. Emerson*, 144, 151; and St. Louis freedom suits, 144, 151; and *Winny v. Whitesides*, 134. *See also* property principle
Rediker, Marcus, 184–85
The Refugee; or, The Narratives of Fugitive Slaves in Canada (Drew), 168, 173
Remond, Sarah Parker, 252–53
Report of the Arguments of Counsel, and of the Opinion of the Court, in the Case of Commonwealth v. Aves (ed. Isaac Knapp), 81
Representation of the Injustice and Dangerous Tendency of Tolerating Slavery (Granville Sharp), 39, 41
rescue narrative: in British antislavery print culture, 25, 56–59, 67; and Catharine Linda, 96–98; and Wheeler slave case, 113–14
Rescue of Jane Johnson and her Children (in *Underground Rail Road* by William Still), 106
Rex v. Stapylton, 24–26, 267n29
Reynolds, William C. (Political Map of the United States), 4
Right and Wrong in Boston (Chapman), 88
right of forced return, 27. *See also* deportation
right to free travel: as American myth, 262; Blackstone on, 261–62, 324n134; and citizenship, 189–90, 240–41, 261–62; Douglass on, 250, 255, 262; Garrison on, 203–4, 257; and Henry Highland Garnet, 256–58; and *Plessy*, 261–62; of slaveholders, 107–8; and South Carolina Negro Seamen Act, 189–91, 203–4; and state sovereignty, 197; and the U.S. Constitution, 108, 240

Roberts, Reuben, 208, 209, 219
Roberts v. Yates, 15, 209
Robinson, John and Sophia, 87
Roper, Moses, 21, 29, 41, 228
Ruggles, Charles, 96

Sale, Maggie, 192
Sanford, Irene. *See* Emerson, Irene Sanford
Sanford, John, 127, 144–45
Schweninger, Loren, 165, 298n140, 323n121
Scott, Dred: in antislavery print culture, 145; biographical details, 131–32, 145–46; as freedom suit plaintiff, 14; interview with *Frank Leslie's* reporter, 146–49; pamphlet on trial, 154–57; scholarship on, 131, 149
Scott, Eliza, 132, 147
Scott, Harriet: and antislavery print culture, 145; her story's significance, 132–34, 149; interview with *Frank Leslie's* reporter, 146–49; later life, 182; scholarship on, 131–32, 149
Scott, Lizzie, 132, 147
Scott v. Emerson: and Fugitive Slave Act, 294n70; and Garland, 127, 128; and *Grace*, 37; and reattachment doctrine, 144, 151; rejection of residence claim, 144; *See also Dred Scott v. Sandford*; freedom suits, St. Louis
Scott v. Sandford. See *Dred Scott v. Sandford*
Scott, William, 144
Second Treatise of Civil Government (John Locke), 38–39
sectionalism: and British diplomacy, 210; and *Elkison*, 196; and nationalist rhetoric, 204; and South Carolina Negro Seamen Act, 195, 196, 201–4
self-preservation doctrine. *See* doctrine of self-preservation
Sewall, Samuel, 87, 91, 92

Seward, William, 256–57
Sharpe, Jenny, 59, 67, 80
Sharp, Granville: antislavery pamphlet on, 44; and British freedom suits, 25–26, 32; on implied contract, 39, 41; and Society for the Abolition of the Slave Trade, 34; as *Somerset* victor, 20
Shaw, Lemuel: and *Commonwealth v. Aves*, 1, 12, 81; and "consent," 92, 93, 283n93; emancipation of slave seamen, 202; and *Linda v. Hudson*, 100; and reattachment doctrine, 47; and slave Betty, 101
Shyllon, Folarin, 31, 40
Slater, Mary, 81, 84
Slater, Samuel, 85–86
slave agency: and antislavery print culture, 93–104, 115, 117, 121; and Catharine Linda, 96–101; and *Commonwealth v. Aves*, 82, 99; and Eleanor Mead, 57, 61–63; and Harriet Scott, 147; and Jane Johnson, 111–14; in *The Kidnapped and the Ransomed* (Pickard), 115, 121–22, 123; and Kitty Hilton, 57, 60–61; and Mary Prince, 51–52, 57–60; and Rosanna, 63–67; sexualization of, 59–61; and Sojourner Truth, 94–96. *See also* willful/will-less dichotomy
slaveholders: blacks as, 165–66, 299n162–163; motherhood trope use, 85, 86–87; use of kinship ties, 9–10, 49–50, 80, 87, 93, 97–98, 104
slaveholders, traveling: defense tactics, 80, 93, 102–4; rights presumed by, 1–2, 107–8
slave law: and free black travel, 14–15, 167–68, 183–84, 187, 242–44; justice under, 220–22; Meachum's use of, 166; and self-preservation doctrine, 198–99; and St. Louis freedom suits, 143–44, 149–54; and ticket laws, 242–44, 318n18; as transatlantic issue, 230–31, 239; and willful/will-less dichotomy, 82–84, 92–93. *See also* antiblack police laws; Negro Seamen Acts; South Carolina Negro Seamen Act
Slave Life in Georgia (Brown), 227–30
"slave mother". *See* motherhood trope
slaves-as-persons: and antiblack police laws, 16, 167–68; and slave's double character, 4–5, 9–10, 37–39, 152–54
slaves-as-property: and kinlessness, 119–20, 171; and slave's double character, 4–5, 9–10, 37–39, 152–54; and traveling slaves, 108
slaves, traveling: double character of, 4–5, 9–10, 37–39, 152–54; and *Somerset* precedent, 27; status resolved by *Dred Scott*, 14, 166–67; uncertain status in Great Britain, 21–24, 40; uncertain status in U.S., 6, 14, 83, 108; vs. fugitive slaves, 3, 82–84, 250
slave trade, 19, 26, 161–62
Slave Trade Act, 26
slave women. *See* slave agency
sojourner laws: and Boston Female Anti-Slavery Society, 79; and "law of passports," 243; repeal of, 3, 6, 107, 127; traveling slaveholders reliance on, 2, 79
"Sojourner Truth: The Libyan Sibyl" (Stowe), 96
Somerset, James, 11, 26–27
Somerset v. Stewart: and *Aves*, 82; enforcement of, 31–38, 269n78; facts and ruling, 26–31; and implied contract, 28, 38–39; mythologized, 20–21; popular interpretations of, 31; as precedent, 11–12, 27–28, 108–9; Stowell on, 42–43
Sons of Africa, 31–32, 270n80
South Carolina: and doctrine of self-preservation, 187, 192–94, 198, 223–24; expulsion of Hoar, 202–4; reaction to *Appeal*, 199
South Carolina Negro Seamen Act: antislavery print culture criticism of,

205–7, 209, 225–30; black radicalism as result of, 232–33, 238; British court challenges to, 15, 207–9, 219; and British diplomacy, 198–200, 205–7, 209–10, 311n149; criminalization of color, 220–21; denationalization of black citizenship, 190–91, 198, 203; and *Elkison*, 15, 192–93, 195–97, 307n73; habeas corpus suspended by, 191–92, 310n122; Massachusetts protests against, 201–4; modification of, 206, 223–24, 232, 308n81, 312n153; and petitions for redress, 199–201; provisions of, 184; sectionalism exacerbated by, 195, 196, 201–4; Supreme Court review blocked, 185, 202–4, 209; as transatlantic issue, 222–23, 312n172; vs. federal powers, 206, 207, 210, 308n99; and Walker's *Appeal*, 236–38. *See also* Glasgow, John; *Manuel Pereira* (Adams); Negro Seamen Acts

Spillers, Hortense, 86, 120

Stanley, Amy Dru, 84, 260

State [of North Carolina] v. Mann, 83

state sovereignty: affirmed in *Elkison*, 195–97, 308n86; antisecessionist arguments against, 224–25; Hunt's defense of, 197–98; and police power, 200; and the right to free travel, 197; vs. federal powers, 206, 207, 210, 308n85, 308n99

Still, Peter, 114–15

Still, Sidney (aka Charity), 115–19, 289n208

Still, William: and Peter Still, 115, 122, 124; on threat of sale, 126; *Underground Rail Road*, 105–7, 125; and Wheeler slave case, 105, 107, 111

Story, Joseph, 47

Stowe, Harriet Beecher, 81, 96, 113, 124, 211. *See also Uncle Tom's Cabin*

Stowell, Lord, 22, 23, 30, 37–39, 42–43, 45–46

Stratton et al. v. Babbage, 189

Strickland, Susanna (Susanna Moodie), 49, 54–55, 59–60, 274n180

Stroud, George, 149

Sturge, Joseph, 21, 69–72

Subramanian, Sandhya, 130–31, 136–37, 147, 292n18

Sundquist, Eric, 192

Sylvia v. Kirby, 144

Taney, Roger B., 144–45, 151, 153, 166–67, 174–75, 177–79, 203, 254

"The Task" (William Cowper), 28–29

theft theme: in Glasgow's narrative, 226; and Harriet Scott, 146; in *The Kidnapped and the Ransomed* (Pickard), 13, 114–25; and "law of passports," 247–48, 250; and Lucy Delaney, 138, 140, 142–43; and Lunsford Lane, 168–69; and Samuel Slater, 85–86; in Scott's pamphlet, 155; in slave narratives, 13, 16

Thirteenth Amendment, 200, 260

Thomas Amendment to the Missouri Compromise, 14, 136, 150, 166, 296n95

Thomas, James P., 1, 102–4, 129, 180, 257–60

Thomas Williams, a Sailor (John Downman), *186*

Thoughts and Sentiments on the Evil of Slavery (Quobna Ottobah Cugoano), 33–36

Three Years in Europe (Brown), 250

ticket laws, 242–44, 318n18

To Tell a Free Story (Andrews), 80, 223

"True Tale of Slavery" (John S. Jacobs), 77

Truth, Sojourner, 94–96

Tubman, Harriet, 109, 122, 173

Tushnet, Mark, 7

Twain, Mark, 177

Twelve Years a Slave (Northrup), 119–20, 176, 226

Uncle Tom's Cabin (Stowe): characterist

of, 85, 95, 122, 156, 174; compared with *Manuel Pereira* (Adams), 213–14, 216, 217–18
Underground Rail Road (William Still), 105–7, 125
U.S. Constitution: fugitive slave clause, 3; and right to free travel, 240
U.S. State Department: black passports granted by, 256–59; certificates of protection, 242, 244, 246; consolidation of racial policy, 251–56; "law of passports," 17, 241–51, 259; Passport Act of 1856, 253–54
U.S. Supreme Court: and the Civil Rights Act of 1875, 261; and *Dred Scott*, 14, 144–45; on freedom claims, 151

VanderVelde, Lea, 130–31, 136–37, 147, 292n18
de Vattel, Emmerich, 197
Vesey, Denmark, 184, 185, 193–94, 235, 303n3
Vina (Peter Still's wife), 120–22
"voluntary return": and British freedom suits, 39, 46–47; and *Grace*, 44–45, 151; and implied contract, 39; as rejection of freedom, 130–31, 294n58; and St. Louis freedom suits, 151

Wald, Priscilla, 2, 114, 131
Walker, David: *Appeal to the Coloured Citizens of the World*, 234–39; circulation of *Appeal*, 199; on free black travel, 183; skepticism of English law, 36–37
Wallace, James, 29, 271n99
Ward, Samuel Ringgold, 230–31, 249
Warner, Ashton, 49, 54–55, 60, 273n155
Wash, Robert, 138, 140, 180
Wedderburn, Robert, 34, 63–67, 276n205

Weinstein, Cindy, 88–89, 93
West Indies: amelioration laws, 54–56, 61, 67; apprenticeship in, 68–76; emancipation campaign, 19–20, 23–24, 50, 68–69; gendered rhetoric, 56, 59, 60–61; response to *Grace*, 43. *See also* Great Britain
Westley, Robert, 184
westward expansion: and Meachum's unity doctrine, 160–61; and Missouri Compromise, 14, 128, 150; and north-south imaginary, 13, 129
Wheeler, John Hill, 80. 105–12, 285n148, 286n151, 286n158
Wheeler slave case: abolitionist response to, 108–9; "choice" in, 111–14; facts and ruling, 104–8; kidnap charge in, 107, 109, 111–12
Wilberforce, William, 20, 64, 67
willful/will-less dichotomy: in antislavery print culture, 56–57, 92–93, 98–99; in British emancipation debates, 56; in jurisprudence, 82–84, 92–93, 283n93; in "law of passports," 243–44, 249–50. *See also* slave agency
Williams, James, 69–76, 277n230
Williamson, Passmore, 104–14, 287n175
Williams, Patricia, 84
Williams v. Brown, 37–38
Wilson, Harriet, 143
Winny v. Whitesides, 134–35
Winona: A Tale of Negro Life in the South and Southwest (Hopkins), 232–33
Winthrop, Robert Charles, 190
Wood, John A., 48–53, 58–59
Woodson, Carter G., 165–66
Wood v. Pringle, 59

Yates, Jeremiah D., 209, 219
Yorke-Talbot opinion, 27

About the Author

Edlie L. Wong is an associate professor of English at Rutgers, The State University of New Jersey, New Brunswick, where she teaches nineteenth-century African American and American literature.

www.ingramcontent.com/pod-product-compliance
Lightning Source LLC
Chambersburg PA
CBHW032026290426
44110CB00012B/690